Inspired 3D Advanced Rigging and Deformations

Brad Clark, John Hood, Joe Harkins

THOMSON

™

COURSE TECHNOLOGY

Professional ■ Trade ■ Reference

Publisher and General Manager of Course Technology PTR: Stacy L. Hiquet

Associate Director of Marketing: Sarah O'Donnell

Marketing Manager: Heather Hurley

Manager of Editorial Services: Heather Talbot

Senior Acquisitions Editor: Kevin Harreld

Senior Editor: Mark Garvey

Marketing Coordinator: Jordan Casey

Project Editor and Copy Editor: Marta Justak

Technical Reviewer: Josh Carey

PTR Editorial Services Coordinator: Elizabeth Furbish

Interior Layout Tech: Bill Hartman

Cover Designer: Mike Tanamachi

Indexer: Kevin Broccoli

Proofreader: Cynthia Fields

ISBN: 1-59200-116-5

Library of Congress Catalog Card Number: 2004108019

Printed in the United States of America

05 06 07 08 09 BH 10 9 8 7 6 5 4 3 2 1

THOMSON

COURSE TECHNOLOGY

Professional ■ Trade ■ Reference

Thomson Course Technology PTR, a division of Thomson Course Technology
25 Thomson Place ■ Boston, MA 02210 ■ http://www.courseptr.com

*To the loves of my life, my wife Jennifer and our
amazing new baby Isabella: thank you for being part
of this long journey, because without you I could not
have made it through.*
—Brad Clark

*To Sandra and Russell Hodges, for their love and patience,
and to all of my friends, who never stopped believing in me.*
—John Hood

*For Bill Peet, whose stories sit quietly on my bookshelf as a
reminder of my childhood, and whose autobiography
inspired me to follow my dreams.*
—Joe Harkins

Acknowledgments

Brad Clark

Thank you for all your help Jennifer and for supporting me over the past 12 months that I was working on this book. You provided the encouragement and love that I needed to take on this challenge.

My parents and grandparents who allowed my interest in art to grow into a lifelong career—I thank you. To my grandfather Robert Cooper who left this world while I was working on this book, thank you for the unlimited amount of art supplies, animation books, and knowledge you gave me throughout my life. I am forever thankful.

To some of the best friends a guy could have, Jorma Auburn and John Hood. This book would have been only a shell without you. Thank you for your energy and patience and 4:00 A.M. instant message conversations about MEL, IK, and whatever else came to mind at that time of the morning. Jorma, your model for the book was spectacular; you finally made animal legs on a biped that did not look out of place.

To Joe Harkins who agreed to sign onto this crazy project in the final months to help us out. You did amazing work in a short time, and I cannot thank you enough. We would never have gotten this done without you.

Finally, special thanks go to Mike Ford, Kyle Clark, and Kevin Harreld, who allowed me the honor of writing this book in the first place and who trusted and pushed me when I felt as if they had picked the wrong guy.

John Hood

I would like to thank my mother and Russell, for all their love and kindness.

I would like to acknowledge Brad Clark, without whom I would never have embarked on this project. You were there for me when times were tough, and I thank you.

To Lisa, who always answered the phone when I needed to talk, even when it was late. Your patience and kindness were a great comfort to me.

Many great thanks to Dustin Clingman, Jorma Auburn, Casto Vocal and Max—you probably don't know each other, but you have all been a great source of inspiration to me. Dustin—one day we will make mechanical suits and take over the world. Jorma—You have been such an inspiration to me in animation—I would not be where I am without you. Casto—our paths always seem to cross, and it's always been interesting. Max—you always made me laugh—thank you.

Lorne Lanning, Sherry McKenna and Oddworld Inhabitants—thank you for giving me the opportunity to learn and grow.

I would like to thank Kevin Harreld, Marta Justak, and Josh Carey for their help and support with this project.

Last, but certainly not least, a very special thanks to Mike Ford and Kyle Clark, for giving me the opportunity to push my skills to the next level.

Joe Harkins

Thank you, Jenn, for your love and support, and for standing by me through everything. Your understanding and encouragement were a blessing to have during this project.

My family, who encouraged me to explore and create, fostered my inventive spirit, and whose wisdom has helped guide me through life. Your love and support is most appreciated.

To everyone at Tippett Studio, my former co-workers Paul Thuriot, David Richard Nelson, and Matthew Muntean who taught me everything. Thank you for your insight, for all the great experience, and for watching out for me.

To my best friend, Matthew Scott, for having someone to share this terrific journey of animation with, for all the crazy weekend adventures, and for being a true friend. To Raymond Swanland, Lorne Lanning, and all of the wonderful folks at Oddworld Inhabitants, for sharing with me your creative vision and wonderful characters, and for making me feel at home.

Very special thanks to Brad Clark for giving me this opportunity and for all of the help along the way. Thanks to John Hood, Mike Ford, and Josh Carey, whose input was a valuable resource. Thanks to Kevin Harreld and Marta Justak for making this project a reality.

The authors would also like to recognize the efforts of the following people:

Josh Carey, our technical editor, went above and beyond his duties and had an immense job to work through and double-check all our technical work for this book. Thank you, Josh, for all the extra help. And on top of editing, he even found time to write up the facial rigging tutorial for us.

Danielle Lamothe and the team at Alias® for providing us the software and support to create all the content for the book, all the authors thank you.

Special recognition and debt of gratitude for all the contributing artists and character TDs : Floyd Bishop and Bishop Animation, Josh Carey and The Animation Farm, Mike Comet, Ramahan Faulk, Steph Greenberg, Keith Lango, Shahar Levavi, Rick May, Chad Moore, Caleb "Cro" Owens, Steve Talkowski and Hornet Inc., Steve Theodore.

Additional thanks to Jason Schleifer, Erick Miller, Joe Harkins, and Paul Thuriot for their rigging master classes; they were inspiring and a great resource when it came to writing this book. And to everyone on the forums http://jonhandhisdog.com and http://creatureTD.com—you guys are such a great resource for old and new character TDs, thanks for the continued sharing of ideas and help.

Also: Jim Bloom, Doug Cooper, David Gallagher, Rick Grandy, Michael Isner, Sven Jensen, Steev Kelly, Robin Linn, Hamish Mackenzie (macroniKazoo), Shawn McClelland, Tim Naylor, Doug Nelson, Jason Osipa, Jason Parks, Bay Raitt, Steven T. L. Roselle, Ben Rush, William Todd Stinson, Mark Swain, Jeff Unay, Nathan Walpole, David Walden, Barry Weiss.

Main Character Creation

Character Design: John Hood
Final Model: Jorma Auburn
Texture UV Unwrapping: Chad Kendall
Texture Painting: Gregg Hargrove and Pio Ravago

About the Authors

Brad Clark

An award winning artist and animator, Brad Clark has worked on a wide range of projects over the past nine years, from modeling and rigging for television and video games to editing motion capture for Gollum in *The Lord of the Rings: The Two Towers*. His career has taken him around the globe: from Florida to the Philippines, from Texas to New Zealand. Brad has taught animation, character design, and setup at Full Sail, trained 2D animators on SOFTIMAGE in Manila, and has headed up internal training on motion capture, character rigging, and scripting for artists while with Acclaim Austin. Brad's most recent lectures and presentations have been for the Conceptart.org workshop and a Master Class for Alias on advanced game art development in 2004. Brad is currently an animator and Character TD at The Animation Farm in Austin, TX.

If you have any questions or suggestions for Brad or the other authors you can contact us at advancedrigging@gmail.com

Film Credits:

LOTR: Two Towers
Major Damage (Chris Bailey)
Robots_PSA (ReelFx)

Broadcast Credits:

Quest: Tales from the Ramayana

Interactive Entertainment Credits:

The Red Star
NBA JAM '04,
VEXX
NFL QBClub '02/'03
ASB 2002
SHOWDOWN: Legends of Wrestling
Turok: Evolution
100 Bullets
Alias
(All games produced for Acclaim Entertainment)

John Hood

John Hood was born the son of a mosquito rancher in the marshes of Central Florida. After achieving a degree in Liberal Studies, John abandoned a promising career of shoe-salesmanship to pursue a dream of being a computer animator. His journey began at Full Sail, where he was a Course Director for computer animation. He moved out to California to work in interactive entertainment and found gainful employment in many major companies in the field such as Eidos, Microsoft, and Oddworld Inhabitants. John is currently a Technical Animator at Sony Imageworks in Los Angeles, CA. He is working on SONY Pictures Animation's first feature film, *Open Season*.

If you have any questions or suggestions for John or the other authors you can contact us at advancedrigging@gmail.com

Film Credits:

Open Season

Interactive Entertainment Credits:

Soul Reaver (Eidos)
Soul Reaver II (Eidos)
Age of Mythology (Ensemble Studios/Microsoft)
Stranger (Oddworld Inhabitants)

Joe Harkins

Joe Harkins is a Character TD at Sony Imageworks in Los Angeles, CA, currently working on visual effects for the feature film, *Ghost Rider*. Most recently he worked on *Open Season*, Sony's first original feature-length animated movie.

Previously, Joe worked as a Creature TD at Tippett Studio in Berkeley, CA on *Mask 2: Son of The Mask*, and *Constantine*, a sci-fi thriller starring Keanu Reeves based on the Hellblazer comic series. While at Tippett, he also gained valuable experience working on such films as *Matrix: Revolutions* and *Hellboy*.

Joe's understanding as a technical artist has allowed him to share his knowledge with others by writing for industry magazines such as *3D World* and *Computer Graphics*, teaching a Maya Master Class at SIGGRAPH 2004, and mentoring students and professional artists. He has also been a guest speaker at 3December, the Academy of Art University, the Expression Center, and Full Sail.

You can contact him with questions or comments through this e-mail: joe@creaturetd.com or advancedrigging@gmail.com

Feature Film Credits:

The League Of Extraordinary Gentlemen
The Matrix: Revolutions
Hellboy
Mask 2: Son Of The Mask
Constantine
Open Season
Ghost Rider

Broadcast Credits:

Gatorade Commercial Campaign
GI Joe SpyTroops Commercial Campaign
GI Joe SpyTroops: The Movie

Contents at a Glance

Contents

Section 2
Rigging 45

Contents

Contents

xv

Section 4
Skinning 239

Contents

Section 5
Advanced Skinning 273

Contents

xvii

Introduction

The Next Generation Character Rigger

Production—anyone who has survived just one project in a production environment knows how hectic it can be, as well as how stressful, challenging, and fun. The Character Technical Director can end up deep in the middle of this tornado of creativity and get blown away if not careful. With this book, we hope to help you, the Character Technical Director (also known as the Character TD), learn better techniques for dealing with this potential storm.

In this book, we want to change your approach to rigging. Successful rigging is more manageable if you break down the most complex problems into smaller tasks. Instead of being an overwhelming process, we'll teach you to look at the individual components involved and understand how they come together as a whole. Breaking down rigging into smaller solutions also makes the entire process more flexible, with individual tools and solutions being more modular and reusable.

If you're not working at a larger studio, you may not have a programming department to support you or six months to create a character rig pipeline or skin system. In this case, with too many tasks already crammed into your day, you may not have time to do much more than hastily throw together another character rig. It often seems easier to just jump in and start working on a character without much forethought about the task as a whole. However, even quick tasks should be done in a structured way to avoid problems that will inevitably happen during production.

This sort of analysis and forethought is the most critical part of the rigging process. Careful planning is often what separates the individual artist who knows how to execute the steps from the professional Character TD who really "gets" rigging. Going through the motions without a deeper understanding of the process can get you by, but it does not work well when you're presented with unique rigging problems on a character. Also, once you are part of a studio with other people relying on your work, it's much more difficult to rig without a view of the bigger picture when you are rigging characters. We hope to expand your thinking to include the entire pipeline process and show you that taking the time up front to set up a character correctly will actually save you and your team time and headaches throughout the project.

Who This Book Is for

There are a lot of rigging tutorials, books, and DVD materials that are available, so why yet another book? Because to advance as a Character TD, you need to understand the underlying reasons for making a character rig a certain way. Many of the training materials just hold your hand through this process, leaving it up to you to figure out why the tutorial did it that way and how it will affect the rig later. This book will expose you to the choices, problems, and solutions that a professional Character TD will have to deal with. This will hopefully help you have a better idea of what you have done and why you did it. You will have the resources to tackle complex production problems and advance both the speed and quality of your work and also the work of the animators using your rig.

This book was written with the lone Character TD in mind. Perhaps you are the only character TD at your video game studio or one of a few TDs doing episodic TV with no time for complex rigs and simulation. You might have to figure out character setup on your own, but find that the tutorials and resources that are currently available don't provide usable solutions for what you need to do. With your current rigging skills, you can do a reverse foot rig in your sleep or a three-chain ik/fk arm without even having coffee in the morning after working an all-nighter, but your current projects and teams are beginning to demand more. You want to advance the quality and the efficiency of your work but don't know how. This book will provide the foundation and direction you need to start taking on those challenges and allowing yourself to grow as an artist and technician.

We will try to get you up-to-speed on the advancements in rigging inside of Maya and also cover in detail the underlying process of what it takes to get a rig production-ready. Also, when things go wrong, and they will, you will have the knowledge and understanding of proper workflows to get the problems fixed on time and without losing your mind.

We will take you through both concepts and examples to make sure your understanding of the fundamental principles is where it needs to be in order to build more complex systems later. And we will discuss the relationship of rigging to the rest of the animation pipeline. As we get into more advanced topics of rigging, we will go over the reusability of code, and leveraging MEL to help with task automation. In addition, some things that most Character TDs have to deal with, but can't find tutorials on, are props and the problems and tricks to interfacing them with the rest of the character.

Skinning and deformations cover the relationships between a character's rig and its geometry. Expanding on the basics covered in the first book *Inspired 3D Character Setup*, this section will discuss recurring problems in deforming a character, what really causes them, and how to devise a solution for them. Other deformation chapters cover how to mix techniques and tools to get complex skin and muscle movement without sacrificing speed and efficiency and without the need for a special plug-in. The goal is to create layered deformations with the maximum amount of control over the look of the character. All the rigging in the world does not matter if the final image of your character is a badly deformed mess with pinching, poor silhouettes and stretching textures because of bad skinning.

As a technical artist, you will likely encounter a slew of software beyond Maya. Having a deep and through knowledge of your computer's OS that is used at your studio is very important. Much of a Character TD's job will focus on the need to automate the process outside of your host 3D app, requiring you to call upon .bat, shell scripts, and the automation of things such as installing tools, updating models, mapping drives, accessing version control software (like Alien Arain), and dealing with the operating system at its level. Luckily, there are some great Web resources for learning how to make a windows .bat files and create UNIX shell scripts. The end results of these short quick scripts are a big part of the entire pipeline integration process and can do wonders for your studio's efficiency.

Before reading too far in this book, you should have a good understanding of the Maya interface and how to use the software. In addition, throughout this book, when possible, common tools and techniques will be presented for 3ds Max, so that the TD working in a mixed software environment will be able to transition better from one software to the other. It is fairly common in production to run across several software packages, and it is becoming more common in games. A solid understanding of core setup concepts lets you create good rigs, regardless of your chosen 3D application.

Our outlook on character rigging is that even the most complex-looking rigs are built on a foundation of small simple steps that layer together to form an "advanced rig." Regardless of how complex or simple the rig is, it must be animation-friendly with a good user interface and help organize where the animator has to look for his key frames. Thankfully, the node-based architecture of Maya provides a very open system for a TD to get his hands dirty and have control over every level of a character rig and deformations. Rigging in Maya can be a very rewarding process with the capability to mix and use almost all parts of the software to make an animator-friendly rig.

For the smaller studio, a lot of very useful tools and auto rig scripts can be downloaded from the Web, thanks to a very active user community. These free scripts are a great resource for the smaller studios or the animators who have to rig their own characters. The only downside with downloading scripts and blindly using them is that when something goes wrong or you need to do something that the free script does not do, you could be stuck and hold up the team or miss a deadline.

What Studios Look for in a Character Rigger

By looking at what film studios are searching for in an ideal Character TD in the ads below, you can see the current standards that are expected and required in high-end character setup. Although most studios list all the qualities that a perfect candidate should have, in reality most people's skill sets do not fit perfectly with any job. Regardless of where you work, the skills covered below are important for the creation of quality character rigs and tools in today's current production studios.

Both Tippett Studio and Sony Imageworks have about the same basic skill requirements for a Character TD.

Tippett Studio

Creates animation controls and surface deformations simulating an organic surface quality, which is influenced by an underlying skeletal and muscular system. Creates "puppets" that are accurate, detailed, and easily controlled by the animators.

Technical Animators—Sony Imageworks

Responsible for the creation of specific character setups and the technical support for character animation throughout a production. Works with a team on a production to determine various animation setup and support solutions.

The professional Character TD has many more job requirements than just a few years ago. The creation of complex muscle systems and the increased use of both simulation and motion capture have raised the bar for what most Character TDs have to know. The use of motion capture in games is nothing new, but what is new is the ability to have more complex deformations and more realistic film-quality characters. So TDs need a better understanding of how joint placement and anatomy help to create more natural-looking characters once they start moving. Half Life 2 from Valve software is one of the first games showcasing the use of a pseudo-muscle system of helper bones that are rigged so that roll and squash and stretch happen in real time to fix pinching and add realistic muscle bulges to the characters. This will be the rule soon, rather than the exception, as game hardware on both PC and consoles expands and becomes more powerful.

Introduction

Adding to the demands on the TD's time, the projects have become more complex and realistic while the time to create that content has shortened. There is an increased need for efficient and flexible rigging, facilitated by scripting and programming that automates redundant tasks.

Other necessary requirements beyond the technical requirements are the ability to work in a team, strong communication skills and attention to detail, and the ability to take direction from both the lead and teammates. Because any character has a long life ahead of it throughout the production process, understanding the entire pipeline that the rig must pass through is very important. You will quickly find yourself at the center of the production while having to work with modeling, animation, and lighting departments. The more you can understand the entire production process, the more it will help you plan ahead to minimize technical problems later.

Tomorrow's TD Today

So what does the future hold in terms of advanced skills that will be required for Character TDs? First, on a daily basis you will be asked to come up with solutions to problems that are unique to your production environment, such as automated custom rig/skeleton creation, skinning solutions, batch-exporting animations, or adding cloth, weapon, and prop rigs to a series of files.

Second, as 3D characters get more and more realistic, the audience's expectations will increase, which is why a deeper understanding of anatomy and bio-mechanical movement will be necessary. You'll need to examine in detail how major and visible muscle movements affect the joints and skin around those joints when animated. You'll also need to be acutely aware of the real pivot points of rotation for each joint and understand and visualize how your joint placement contributes to the deformations and overall quality of the final motion once animated.

Third, simulation, will also play a larger role in the lives of computer characters, whether a character is shown being blown up or shot in the arm or simply with tailored clothing that has special cloth wranglers that look just right so they can be ripped off its body like in *The Hulk*. Hair, clothing, simulated stunts, motion mapping and retargeting, shot sculpting, and facial specialists all might end up being different roles in the future. This book will touch on each discipline, but each one could easily take its own book to explain properly.

Regardless of how technical you are, what is important is your ability to understand the artistic side of what you're working on and have the people skills to interface with both temperamental artists and deeply technical people.

inspired 3D

ADVANCED RIGGING AND DEFORMATIONS

SECTION 1

The Essentials

chapter 1
Maya Architecture

To be an effective character rigger, it is important to understand the architecture of 3D animation software. To be a good rigger, it is important to understand why and how things work. In this chapter, we will take a look at Maya's architecture more closely.

When 3D software first began, it was very primitive, allowing simple manipulations of 3D data. Usually, this data was in the form of vertexes and planes. As software developed, new paradigms of controlling data evolved.

The Maya architecture is built on a system of nodes and connections. In Figure 1.1, the "polyCube1" node generates the points and polygons that define the cube shape. This data is passed on to the "pCube1Shape" node. This information is then passed on to the "initialShadingGroup" node for rendering. The connection is illustrated by the purple line that connects them. The triangle shape at the midpoint of the line indicates the direction of the data flow. In the Hypergraph, nodes are displayed such that data flows from left to right. The final configuration of a scene, all the geometry in it, all the shaders, lights, and effects are all the results of nodes and connections.

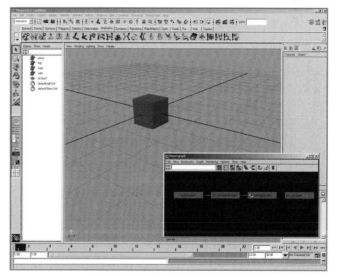

Figure 1.1
Nodes and connections for a polyCube primitive.

The Anatomy of a Node

What exactly is a node? Put simply, a node is a data object in Maya. Everything that you can select in Maya is expressed as a node—polygonal geometry, NURBS surfaces, and particles are all nodes. There are two major types of nodes—those that represent 3D objects and those that do not.

All of the nodes in Maya that represent 3D objects are called "transforms." The transform node holds all of the information Maya needs to position an object in 3D space: the translate, rotate, and scale attributes, several matrices, and bounding box information. It also holds a variety of other information,

3

such as how to draw an object, whether or not an object is visible or templated, and whether or not an object should be drawn ghosted. Transforms are built to be arranged into hierarchies to permit complex behaviors, and they serve as the anchor points for all of the renderable geometry. All the objects that are manipulated within one of Maya's modeling windows with few exceptions (such as texture placement, objects, and image planes) are transforms.

All of the transforms that contain geometry, such as polygon meshes, NURBS curves and surfaces, and subDivision surfaces, also have shape nodes. A shape node is one that holds only the data for the shape. In the case of polygon meshes, the shape node holds all of the points, edges, and faces that make up the geometry. Shape nodes must be parented under transforms—they never exist in the Maya workspace alone. To see how shape nodes work, open the Outliner from the Window→Outliner menu. Right-click in a blank area of the Outliner and select Show Shapes from the context menu. You will see that all of the transform nodes now have a [+] next to them. Click on the [+] to expand a node, and you will see the shape node. Shape nodes have the property that, when selecting, if you click on the representation of the shape node in the modeling window, Maya automatically selects the transform above it. It is important to note that, while shape nodes always have a transform parent, not all transforms have shape nodes.

The shape node is an example of a node that holds data and is visible in the modeling viewport. Maya has many other nodes that hold data, but are not visible by default. Expressions, selection sets, the IK solvers—all of these and more are represented as nodes internally. To get a feel for nodes, open the Outliner. Hold down the right mouse button to activate the context menu and toggle Show DAG Objects Only. In the Outliner, you will see all the nodes that Maya uses that aren't 3D objects. Many nodes in Maya, however, don't hold data so much as process it. A bend deformer node, for example, doesn't hold the actual positions of the vertexes it deforms. Rather, when Maya renders the geometry, the data from the mesh's shape node is passed through the deformer node, which distorts the mesh to its final state, as shown in Figure 1.2. This data flow is a common feature of 3D animation packages, and it will be covered in greater detail in a later section.

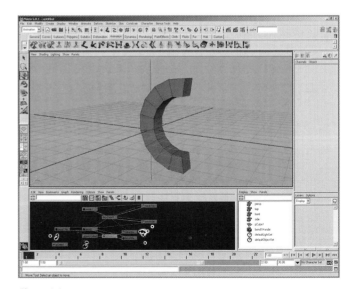

To say that the deform node doesn't hold data is not entirely true. In order to increase speed and interactivity, most nodes will hold a local copy of the data that is being processed. That way, if the user scrubs in the timeline, Maya can save time by not recalculating all of the transformations on the components. If the original mesh is changed, or the parameters of the deformer are changed, Maya will recalculate and recache. This is all done to improve speed, but from a workflow standpoint, it is safer to view deformer nodes as processors, not data storage.

It is worth noting that most nodes that process data also hold some data. Usually, this data is in the form of parameters that govern the extent or nature of the processing. When a bend deformer node is created, for example, it holds some data in the form of its curvature, high bound, and low bound attributes.

Figure 1.2
A bend deformer.

Shape Nodes

Of all the nodes in Maya, shape nodes have some interesting properties. Shape nodes contain the geometry used by a transform, whether they are NURBS curves, polygons, subdivision surfaces, or any of the other types of geometry that Maya handles. One of the most useful properties is the method of selection: whenever a geometry is clicked on in the modeling window, the transform node that is its parent is selected. This allows the creation of custom controls that ease the process of selecting nodes.

Maya provides a simplified selection tool, the selection handle, to do just that. The drawback of the selection handle is that, if you have a substantial number of them, they tend to become confusing. It becomes difficult to see easily which nodes the selection handles are related to. Another drawback of the selection handle is that it draws last in the 3D viewport. Let's say you have a character whose shoulders are selected via the handles. If you look at the character in the side view, the handles appear to overlap. If the view is rotated slightly, you see the two handles near each other, but both draw as if they were closer to the camera than the torso.

The following example illustrates how to create custom selection geometries for joints. This method can be used with any transform, but it usually applies to joints because other controls can be built off curve or polygon nodes.

1. Get the chapter01, controlCurveExample.ma file from http://www.courseptr/downloads.

2. Activate the File->Import menu Item and open the options. Make sure that the Group and Use Namespaces options are unchecked. Import the scenes/chapter_01/nurbSplineCube.mb file.

3. Select the curve cube. Use the Move, Rotate, and Scale tools to position the cube near the "left_Lshoulder" joint, as shown in Figure 1.3.

4. With the cube selected, Shift-select the "left_Lshoulder" joint. Press the "p" key to make the cube a child of the joint.

5. The cube should be selected. Leave it selected and use Modify→Freeze Transformations to zero out the cube's translation and rotation.

6. At the command line, enter the following: `parent -r -s curveShape1 left_Lshoulder`.

7. Now, select the cube. Activate the rotate gizmo and rotate it. You should see the joint rotate.

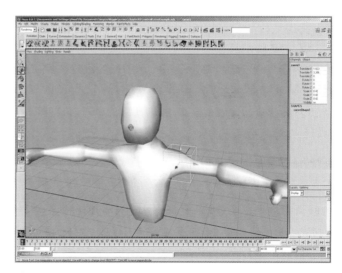

Figure 1.3
Positioning the NURBS curve.

This is an example of a custom selection shape (see Figure 1.4). Whenever the curve cube is clicked on, the joint is selected. You will notice, if you open the Outliner, that the micro-icon next to the joint will have a curve shape, but it is still a joint. It is not necessary to use a NURBS curve—any shape should be usable, from curves to polygons to NURB surfaces. Whatever shape you use will be subject to the Show menu in the 3D viewport. In this example, if you turn off Show->NURBS Curves, the selection shape will disappear. Selection shapes are editable in the same way all other shapes are.

While the selection shapes are very useful, the manipulations that must be performed are tedious. Also, there is no way of using the Outliner or the regular Maya commands to parent the shape under the joint. As a result, we have provided the parentShape MEL script. To use the script, select the transform and then Shift-select the object with the shape you want to parent under. Execute parentShape, and the parenting is done for you.

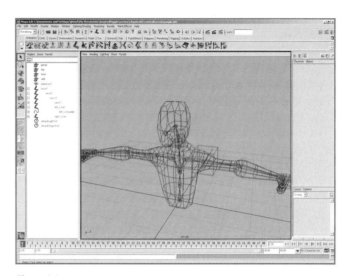

Figure 1.4
The parented curve shape.

Attributes and Plugs

In Maya, all data is communicated through attributes. Attributes have many different types. There are attributes that contain float values, string values, and so on. Attributes can also be grouped. The translate attributes ".tx," ".ty," and ".tz," for example, are children of the ".translate" attribute.

One of the most important features of attributes is that they have a "type." That is to say, an attribute holds a certain type of information. Most of the attributes are of type "float," meaning they hold real numbers out to several decimal places. A transform's translate, rotate, and scale attributes are of this type. Another type is the integer. This type of attribute can only hold whole numbers. A good example of this type is the attribute that controls the number of subdivisions when creating a sphere or a cube. A boolean type can only contain the values 0 or 1, and no other values in-between. Visibility is a good example of a boolean attribute.

All of the previous attribute types can usually be edited and keyframed, but there are many types that cannot. Attributes of type "string" cannot be keyframed or connected. Attributes of type "message" cannot be keyframed, but can be connected. Attributes such as the "inMesh" of a polygon object can be connected, but not edited. Typing is an important feature of attributes, as it helps ensure that the proper information is communicated between nodes.

Almost all the nodes in Maya also have plugs. Plugs are ports in a node where data can flow through. Almost all of the nodes in Maya have incoming and outgoing plugs. Data flows into a node via input plugs, and it can be passed on to other nodes through output plugs (see Figure 1.5).

Many plugs in Maya correspond to attributes on objects. For example, all transforms have translation, rotation, and scale attributes. Each of these attributes has an input plug and an output plug. These attributes can be seen in the channel box and can be keyframed. The same is true for many (not all) of the attributes a user can add to a node.

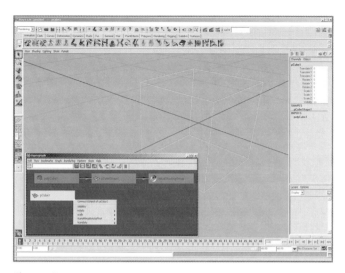

Figure 1.5
Output plugs on a node.

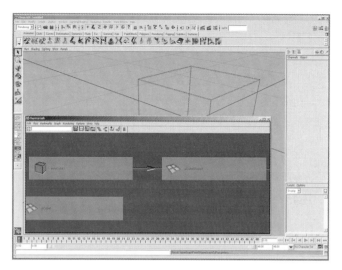

Figure 1.6
A connection between nodes in the Hypergraph.

Not all plugs have attributes, however. A shape node, for example, has an output plug for its geometry. This plug does not correspond to an attribute, but it is used to pass information to deformer nodes. It is also important to note that not all input plugs have a corresponding output plug. There can also be attributes that do not have plugs.

Connections

Connections allow data to flow from node to node in Maya's architecture. They form an internal network that is the core of all of Maya's operations. A connection is a direct link from an output plug to an input plug (see Figure 1.6). There are some rules that govern the nature of connections:

◆ Connections can only be made from output plugs to input plugs.

◆ Data can only flow in one direction through a connection, from an output to an input. If you were to connect a sphere's "translateX" to a cube's "rotateY" via a connection, you could not select the cube, type a value in the "rotateY" channel box, and have the sphere translate in X.

◆ While there can be more than one connection on a node's output plug, there can be only one connection to an input plug. Let's say you wanted the "translateX" of a cube to drive the "translateY" of five spheres. You can connect the output plug of the "cube.tx" attribute to the input plug of the sphere's ".ty" attributes. You could not have multiple spheres' .ty drive the "cube.tx."

◆ Connections can only be made between plugs of a similar type. For example, a large number of plugs are numeric values, such as "translateX." This plug can only be connected to another plug that is of a numeric type. If you were to try to connect this plug to a plug of type matrix, for example, the connection would fail.

7

Connections are the glue that holds a Maya scene together. When a scene is opened, Maya's process is to create all the nodes in a scene, set all the attributes, and then create the connections. It is important to realize how this process works when it comes to debugging rigs. Often, a change will be made in a source file that prevents a connection from being made in an interactive Maya session. When this occurs, it is often up to a TD to figure out what is going on and whether or not it affects the workflow.

Data Flow

One of the most important ideas about connections is data flow. As you create more complex rigs with networks of deformers, data flow becomes a very important issue. As mentioned in the previous section, data flows only one way through a node network, and this is called *downstream*. Data originates in a data or creation node and flows downstream. The last node in the stream represents what is seen in the Maya viewport. Whenever Maya updates, such as when the time slider is scrubbed, the entire chain is re-evaluated.

At the source of a network is a node that either holds data or generates it. For example, if you use Create→Polygon Primitives→Cube, Maya creates a cube. If you select this cube, open the Hypergraph, and Graph→Input and Output Connections, you will see several nodes appear. The first node is "pCube1." This node is a transform, and it provides the information Maya needs to position the geometry. Underneath is a network of nodes that make up the actual geometry. The "polyCube1" node is a generator—it creates geometry for a cube. This geometry is then fed into the "pCubeShape1" node. You will notice that in the Hypergraph there is no indication that the "pCubeShape1" node is a child of the "pCube1" node. While the two nodes are clearly parented in the Outliner, you must pay attention to the naming conventions in the Hypergraph to be clear which node is which. The Hypergraph will try to keep these nodes together.

Working with Nodes and Connections

There are many different ways to manipulate nodes and connections in Maya. One of the most powerful editors is the Hypergraph. In this view, it is possible to do 90 percent of your node and connection work in the Hypergraph, with some support from the Connection Editor and the Hypershade.

The Hypergraph is one of the most useful editors for the character rigger. It basically provides a map of the nodes and their connections throughout the scene file. It is a great diagnostic tool, as it allows you to see all of the incoming and outgoing connections of a node. In this book, the Hypergraph will be referenced quite a bit, so taking some time to become familiar with it is a good idea. This section will not cover all the capabilities of the Hypergraph, but only the areas that will be frequently used.

In *Inspired 3D Character Setup*, we covered the Hypergraph as it displays connections. Now we will expand upon that and use another feature of the Hypergraph—the ability to create connections. When the Hypergraph is open, you can run the mouse curser over any of the nodes. When the cursor is over the right side of the node, it changes shape. If you press and hold the right mouse button, a context menu appears with most of the output plugs of the node. If you select one from the list, you can drag a connection line to another node. Pressing and holding the right mouse button over the right side of any other node will bring up a list of the node's most used input plugs. Selecting one from the menu creates the connection.

1. In Maya, create a polyCube and a nurbSphere.
2. Use the Window→Hypergraph menu option to open the Hypergraph window.

3. Select the two nodes and activate the Input and Output Connections button. You will see the two nodes in the Hypergraph.

4. Move the mouse over the right side of the "pCube1" node. You will see the node highlight and the cursor change to the stream connections cursor (see Figure 1.7).

5. Press and hold the right mouse button, and a list of output connections appears. Select the "translateX" parameter from the translate group.

6. When the mouse button is released, the connection gizmo appears. Move the mouse pointer to the right side of the "nurbsSphere1" node.

7. When the cursor changes, press and hold the right mouse button over the node. A context menu of inputs appears. Select the rotateX attribute from the rotate group.

8. You should see the connection appear in the Hypergraph. If you select the "pCube1" node and translate it in X, "the nurbsSphere1" object will rotate.

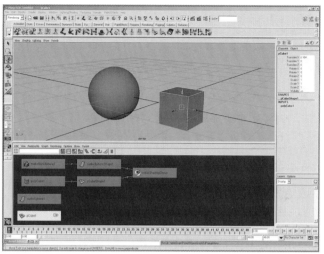

Figure 1.7
The cursor is ready to make a connection.

The Hypergraph provides a quick way to break connections as well. When you mouse-over a connection line, it highlights and the connection plugs are displayed. If you left-click on the connection, it is selected. At this point, it can be deleted like any other object by pressing the Backspace key.

There are some caveats to working with Hypergraph. As you delve into nodes and connections in Maya, there will be times when a rendering utility node is connected to a transform. When this happens, Maya uses a unitConversion connection. When creating these connections in the Hypergraph, the viewport often will not refresh properly. To see the connection, the nodes must be selected and re-graphed. When you re-graph, the connections will be visible. If you try to break the connection, Maya will not able to do so. In this case, the connection editor must be used.

In this book, the Hypershade will be used quite frequently. While most of the work is done in the Hypergraph, the Hypershade contains some useful tools for creating nodes. When you open the Hypershade, you will see the Create Bar. This panel on the left side of the window contains a list of all the render nodes Maya can create. The Hypershade functions much like the Hypergraph in terms of how nodes and connections can be manipulated—both windows use the right mouse button to connect nodes.

Non-Standard Attribute Connections

The vast majority of connection types are numeric, either floats, integers, or boolean. A boolean attribute is either "on" or "off," which translates into 0 or 1 in Maya. An integer is any whole number—1, 2, 3, 4, 5, etc., including negative whole numbers, such as -1, -2, -3, etc. Float numbers are any real number and its remainder, for example, 1.76, 3.45, -92.45. Any numeric connection can be connected to any other because the connection knows how to translate data from one to the other; for example, floats can be converted to integers, integers to booleans, etc.

There are a whole group of connection types, however, that are not numeric and not interchangeable. These connections carry specialized data from node to node. The following example illustrates how these non-numeric connections work.

1. Start with a new Maya scene.

2. Create a polygon cube.

3. Create a polygon cone.

4. Select both the cube and the cone and open the Hypergraph. Graph the input and output connections of the nodes. You should see the transform nodes, the shape nodes, and the creation nodes for each object. The creation nodes are called "polyCone1" and "polyCube1." These nodes generate points and polygons for the shape nodes. When you select the cone or the cube, you can edit the creation parameters in the Channel Box.

5. Open the Connection Editor. Select the "pCube1Shape" node and load it into the left pane. Select the "polyCone1" node and load it into the right pane.

6. Connect the "Output" attribute of the "polyCube1" node to the "inMesh" attribute of the "pConeShape1" node (see Figure 1.8).

You will see the cone becomes a cube. The creation nodes generate data that is used to create a shape, in this case, the vertexes and faces that make up a polyCube. When you direct that output into the "inMesh" of a shape node, the current shape is replaced by the new input. The same process can be used on regular shape nodes.

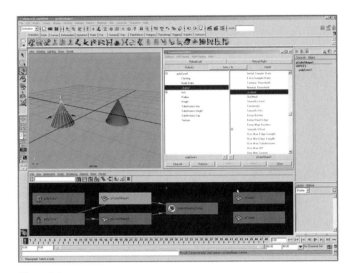

Figure 1.8
Connecting the shape generator to the shape node.

Some of the attributes on objects can only be connected through the Connection Editor. In the Hypergraph, almost any connection can be made between numeric attributes with the mouse. Other attributes generally have to be connected through the Connection Editor.

1. Start with a new Maya scene.

2. Acquire the arrow.obj file from the Web site at http://www.courseptr/downloads. Use the File->Import menu command to bring the file into the 3D workspace.

3. Create a polygon cube.

4. Select the "arrow" node and graph its input and output connections in the Hypergraph.

5. Select the "arrowShape" node. Open the Connection Editor and load the selected shape node into the left pane.

6. Select the "pCubeShape1" node and load it into the right pane.

7. Connect the "outMesh" attribute in the left pane to the "inMesh" attribute in the right pane, shown in Figure 1.9.

You will see that the shape node of the cube is now a duplicate of the arrow. If you select the "arrowShape" node, enter component mode, and begin editing the shape, you will see the duplicate shape alter to match whatever edits you make. If you select the connection between the "arrowShape" and "pCubeShape1," the relationship is removed but the geometry remains as the shape node of the polyCube.

> The functionality of this example mimics Maya's instancing feature, but it is important to note that using Duplicate with the Instance option checked creates a different relationship between the instanced node and its originator.

Anim Curves

One of the most widely used nodes is the animCurve node. When an object is animated, its animation data is held in an animation curve. The animation curve is a continuous spline curve that contains parameter/value pairs, as well as "handles" that control how the values are interpolated. Whenever Maya inputs a parameter value (usually time), the animation curve is evaluated at that point and the proper value returned. The most interesting fact of the animation curve is that the parameter input is flexible, leading to the functionality of the set driven key.

A set driven key curve's input parameter is determined by the attribute it is connected to. The input data flows from the driver's attribute into the animCurve node, which gets the value of the driven attribute. As it is one of the more useful tools in character setup, it is good to get an idea of how to control animCurve nodes. The following example shows how to solve a problem many run into when rigging—changing the driving attribute of a set driven key.

1. Get the sdk_Connection_Start.mb file from the Web site at http://www.courseptr/downloads. Open the file in Maya—you should see a simple hand setup, as shown in Figure 1.10.

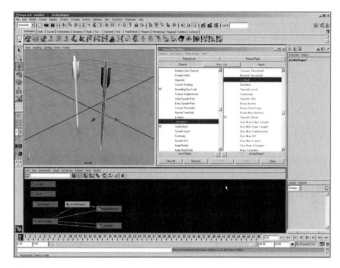

Figure 1.9
Connecting shape nodes.

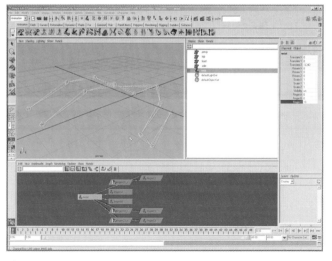

Figure 1.10
A simple hand setup.

2. Select the "wrist" node. In the Channel Box, you will see the attributes "FingerA," "FingerB," and "FingerC." If you highlight the "fingerC" attribute and drag with the middle mouse button, you will see the "fingerC" chain of joints curl.

3. Open the Hypergraph. Graph the input and output connections of the "wrist" joint. You will see connections running from the wrist node to the setDrivenKey animation curves and from those to the joints themselves.

4. In the modeling window, select the "wrist" joint and the joints that make up the middle finger: "fingerB1," "fingerB2," and "fingerB3."

5. In the Hypergraph window, graph the input and output connections. You should see the animCurves and the fingerB joints.

6. Select the "fingerC1_rotateZ," "fingerC2_rotateZ," and "fingerC3_rotateZ" nodes. Press "Ctrl+D" to duplicate them. Drag the new nodes with the left mouse button so they are arranged closer to the wrist node for convenience.

7. Click on the "fingerC1_rotateZ1" node to select it. In the Channel Box, rename the node "fingerB1_rotateZ." Rename "fingerC2_rotateZ1" to "fingerB2_rotateZ" and rename "fingerC3_rotateZ1" to "fingerB3_rotateZ."

8. In the Hypergraph, drag the mouse pointer over the right side of the "fingerB1_rotateZ" node until the pointer changes into the connection pointer. Right-click and select "output" from the context menu. Drag the connection to the "fingerB1" joint and use the right-click menu to connect it to the joint's "rotateZ" attribute (see Figure 1.11).

9. Connect the "fingerB2.output" attribute to the "fingerB2.rotateZ" and connect the "fingerB3.output" attribute to the "fingerB3.rotateZ" attribute.

10. The next step must be completed in the Connection Editor. Open it from the Window→General Editors menu item. Select the "wrist" joint and load it into the left side. Select all three of the "fingerB" animation curves and load them into the right side. Make sure the connection indicator is set to "from→to".

11. Connect the "fingerB" attribute to the "input" attribute of each of the animation curves.

12. In the modeling environment, select the wrist joint. In the Channel Box, highlight the "fingerB" channel and drag the middle mouse button. You should see the finger curl just as the other one did.

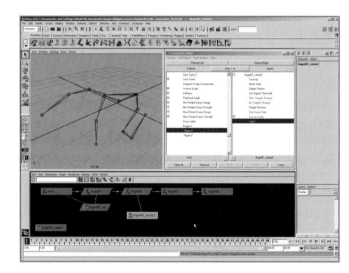

Figure 1.11
Connecting the duplicate animation curves.

The Set Driven Key mechanism is simply a mapping of a driving attribute to a curve that determines the value of the driven attribute. These curves can be duplicated, they can accept any numeric input as the parameter, and their output can be connected to anything that accepts a numeric parameter.

Automating Complex Behavior

One of the disadvantages of Maya's default Set Driven Key interface is its workflow. In order to set driven keys for complex behavior, one is required to select and deselect multiple objects multiple times and be sure that the correct channels are set when the Key button is pressed in the Set Driven Key window.

The next example will cover a simple workflow that will facilitate converting complex behaviors to set driven keys. It utilizes the nature of connections to repurpose animation curves into set driven key style behaviors.

1. Get the chapter 01 sdk_ComplexAnimStart.ma file from the Web site at http://www.courseptr/downloads.

2. In order to build the behavior, begin by keyframing the objects. Select the "door1" node. Make sure that the time slider is set to frame 0 and set a keyframe for the rotateX parameter. Do the same for the "door2" object.

3. Move the time slider to frame 27. Rotate the "door1" object to -130 on the X axis and set a keyframe. Select the "door2" object, rotate it to 130 on the X axis, and set a keyframe.

4. Select "joint1," "joint2," "joint3," "joint4," and "joint5." Move the time slider to frame 15 and set a key.

5. With those joints selected, move the time slider to frame 20. In the Channel Box, enter 70 for the rotate X value and set a keyframe.

6. Select the "joint1" node and rotate it back along the X axis so that the joint chain is oriented vertically. Set a keyframe.

7. Use the Edit→Delete By Type→Static Channels to remove any flat animCurves—leaving them around will add unnecessary work. Only the rotate Z animation curves should be left, as shown in Figure 1.12.

8. Move the time slider to 0 and press the Playback button. You should see the doors open and the joints extend out like a spring.

9. Select all of the joints and Shift-select the "door1" and "door2" nodes. Open the Hypergraph and graph the input and output connections. You should see all of the animated nodes and their associated animCurves, as in Figure 1.12. There should only be one curve per animated object.

10. Create a locator. It should appear in the Hypergraph.

11. Select the locator and open the Connection Editor window. Load the locator into the left pane. Make sure the Map button is set to "from→to."

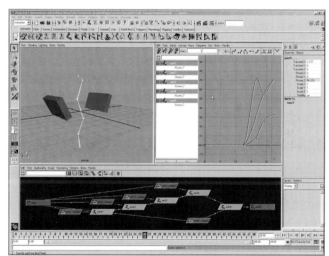

Figure 1.12
Animation on the joints.

1. Maya Architecture

13

12. In the Hypergraph, select one of the animCurve nodes. Use the Show→Show Selected Type(s) menu item to show only the animation curves connected to the objects. Select all the animation nodes and load these nodes into the right pane of the Connection Editor window.

13. In the left pane, open the locator's "Rotate" group and select the "RotateX." In the right pane, highlight the "Input" attribute of the first animCurve node. Scroll down the list and highlight all of the "Input" attributes, connecting them to the "RotateX" (see Figure 1.13).

14. In the modeling environment, select the locator. Rotate it on X, and you will see the animation play back.

This workflow allows you to edit the animation of the objects easily before converting them to Set Driven Key-like behavior. At this point, the animation can still be edited—saving keyframes on the animated channels will change the behavior. This is because the animcurves controlling the behaviors are *not* set driven key animCurves—as a result, Maya treats them exactly like regular animCurves. When an object is selected with these curves, the ticks appear in the timeline and can be edited just like regular animation curves. The only difference is that their input is not time—it is the rotation X parameter on the locator.

> After you have worked out the behavior you would like, you should lock the channels that are driven by the animation curves. While this method of working is flexible, it is also more vulnerable to being mangled by an errant setKeyframe command. Locking the channels will prevent the curves from being accidentally changed.

> Because this is the only animated object in the scene, you could select all of the animCurve nodes by entering the following command on the command line:
>
> select −r `ls −type animCurve`;

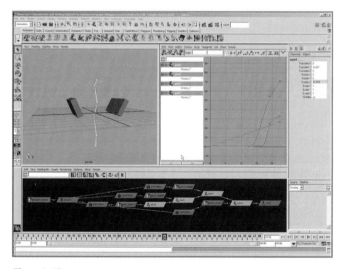

Figure 1.13
Remapping the curves to accept the locator rotation instead of the scene time.

Utility Nodes

Maya's architecture is node-based, and those nodes are related via connections. Besides being requisite information for any intrepid individual who dares to venture into the depths of a 3D package's innards, there are many new techniques that evolve from the utilization of nodes. In this section, we will look at utility nodes and how to use them.

What Are Utility Nodes?

Utility nodes are Maya nodes that perform mathematical functions on their inputs. They were originally developed to manipulate data for rendering networks. As a result, many of the nodes' input and output plugs are labeled R, G, and B as opposed to X, Y, Z. When an XYZ attribute is connected to a utility node, Maya often generates a unitConversion node to process the data. UnitConversion node connections show up as gray dotted lines in the Hypergraph.

If you open the Hypershade window in Maya, look in the Create Maya Nodes tab, and scroll down a bit, you will find a section called *General Utilities*. In this group, you will find the Utility Nodes. These are nodes that provide some simple functions that can be used to create complex object interactions in Maya.

Why Use Utility Nodes?

Utility nodes are obviously useful, but why would you go through all the trouble of setting them up and connecting them when you could just write an expression more easily?

Nodes have many advantages over expressions, including the following:

◆ Nodes are written via the Maya API and compiled into the application. As a result, they run their computations very quickly.

◆ Expressions must be interpreted on the fly by Maya, which slows down the evaluation of the scene when it needs to update.

◆ In some cases, expressions may not update fully or correctly when the time slider or an attribute changes. Nodes are always up-to-date with the current time and are fully computed when a driving attribute changes.

◆ Nodes drive attributes through connections, which are very stable and secure. Expressions must rely on naming conventions and can break if they are connected to objects that are renamed when imported into a new scene.

The last point is one of the most important. Throughout this book, one of the main recurring themes is to streamline as much as possible the workflow of the rigging process. One of the ways to do this is to create a library of components that you can import into a working scene. As you work with nodes more, you will begin to appreciate how much effort you can save.

Some Useful Node Networks

The Reverse Node

The reverse node is one of the more useful utility nodes for a rigger, as it provides an efficient way to blend between two attributes with ranges from 0 to 1. As it stands, this is a perfect way to blend between the weight attributes on multi-part constraints. This example will show how to use the reverse node to switch constraint weights on an object.

1. Create a locator and name it "locatorA".
2. Create another locator and call it "locatorB".

3. Create a polyCube.

4. Add attributes called "AtoB"" that range from 0 to 1 on the "pCube1" node.

5. Select "locatorA", "locatorB" and the polyCube and create a point constraint and an orient constraint.

6. Connect the "pCube1. AtoB" attribute to the "pCube1_pointConstraint.locatorA W0" and connect the "pCube1. AtoB" attribute to the "pCube1_orientConstraint.locatorA W0".

7. From the Hypershade window, create a Reverse node.

8. Connect the "pCube1_pointConstraint.locatorA W0" attribute to the "reverse.inputX" attribute.

9. Connect the "pCube1_orientConstraint.locatorA W0" attribute to the "reverse.inputY" attribute.

10. Connect the "reverse.outputX" attribute to the "pCube1_pointConstraint.locatorB W1" attribute.

11. Connect the "reverse.outputY" attribute to the "pCube1_orientConstraint.locatorB W1" attribute.

12. Adjust the "AtoB" attribute to see the changing weights.

When the attributes are manipulated, the weights are automatically normalized. This system works well in situations where there are two objects to constrain to, but it is not really feasible for constraints with more than two targets.

The Condition Node

The condition node allows for the creation of simple conditionals that would normally require MEL scripting. In this example, you will use a condition node and a distance node to control an object.

1. Create a locator and rename it "floor."

2. Create another locator and name it "control."

3. Create a polyCube. This cube will represent an IK end effector.

4. Open the Hypershade. From the utility nodes section, create a condition node.

5. In the Hypergraph, connect the "control.ty" attribute to the "condition1.firstTerm" attribute.

6. Connect the "floor.ty" attribute to the "condition1.secondTerm" attribute.

7. Open the "condition1" node in the Attribute Editor. Set the Operation to Less Than.

8. Connect the "floor.translate" to the "condition1.colorIfTrue" input.

9. Connect the "control.translate" to the "condition1.colorifFalse" input.

10. Connect the "conditional.outColor" to the "pCube1.translate."

11. Select the control locator. Using the Move tool, move it up and down the Y axis. You will notice that as the node reaches the Y value of the floor locator, the cube stops at the floor. If you move the controller in X or Z and then along the Y axis, you will notice it pops to the location of the floor locator.

12. Connect the "control.tx" to the "floor.tx" and connect the "control.tz" to the "floor.tz" attribute.

Now, whenever you translate the "control" object, the "floor" object will move with it. The "translateY" of the floor object can be keyframed, to facilitate characters walking up steps, for example.

The condition node provides an almost limitless array of decision networks to be created to control many aspects of a character rig. For example, in a simple rig, one can choose between FK and IK using Maya's "ikBlend" parameter. When the IK is in full effect, a controller is used to position the arm. When the animator switches to FK, however, the condition node can cause the joints' selection handles to become visible.

1. From the Web site, get the chapter 01 conditionNode_start.ma file.

2. In the Hypershade, create a condition node.

3. Plug the "ikBlend" parameter into the first term of the condition node.

4. Set the operation to "Less Than." Set the "colorIfTrueR" to 1.0. Set the "colorIfFalse" to 0. Set the second term to 1.0.

5. Connect the "outputColorR" of the condition node to the ".displayHandle" attributes of the joints.

> When connecting to the "displayHandle" attribute, sometimes Maya has trouble updating the environment initially.

Now the condition node causes the handles to display whenever the IKBlend value is less than 1, which is any time the FK joints would have influence over the limb. The condition node is better than a straight connection or a reverse node because the visibility parameter is only valid at 1 or 0. Any number less than 1, such as .83, will not be interpreted as a positive value for the visibility, because visibility is a boolean attribute. This is a simple technique that can be expanded to conform with any attribute that varies between 0 and 1.

The node and connection-based structure of the Maya architecture is one of its greatest strengths. Armed with the knowledge of how these systems work, it is possible to rewire these networks for many custom effects.

1. Maya Architecture

chapter 2
IK Solvers and Their Application

While computer animation really made its mark by creating photo-real animation, many more productions are drawing upon the legacy of 2D cartoons to make more whimsical creations. Looking at traditional animation, one of the most valued ideas in 2D animation is squash and stretch. This is the idea that, as a character deforms, his volume stays the same. As the character's leg extends, it becomes thinner. To re-create the style of 2D animation in 3D, it is important to include this capacity in a 3D character.

Building a Squash and Stretch Node

To begin, we will implement a simple squash and stretch control. This control system could be applied to all the joints in a cartoon character and would give the animator the ability to change the character's volume proportionally.

The most common way that stretching is implemented in computer animation is by manipulating the non-uniform scale of joints or objects in a rig. Maya makes this particularly easy because joint nodes in Maya are set up automatically to scale independently. This allows the animator to have local control over an object's scale without deforming the other parts of a hierarchy (see Figure 2.1).

The convention of using the non-uniform scale is a logical one, and it seems rather natural. However, it is possible that some interactive game engines will not support non-uniform scale. In such circumstances, it is possible to approximate non-unifrom scaling by driving the translate and uniform scale of the nodes in question.

One of the important things to keep in mind when using non-uniform scale is the relationships of the nodes in question. For the best result, one of the scale

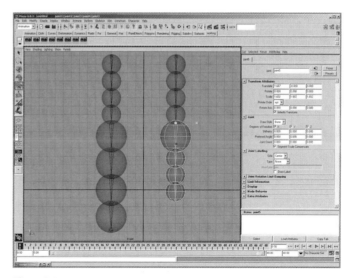

Figure 2.1
The effects of scale compensation. In the hierarchy at left, compensation is turned off. In the hierarchy on the right, scale compensation prevents the scale of one joint from affecting its children.

factors should align with the length of the bone. When using Maya's Joint tool, joints are auto-aligned so that a major axis points from a joint to its child. Care must be taken when using squash and stretch on joints with multiple children, such as wrist or ankle joints.

For this example, we are going to use Maya's default joint-orient, which means the scaleX parameter should control the length of the scaling down the length of the joint. To relate these attributes, we will adapt the formula for a volume to the scale attributes. Volume is determined by the following formula:

$$a \times b \times c = Volume$$

where a, b, and c are the length, width, and height, respectively. What we are concerned with is not the volume itself, but how the change in one of the object's scale factors would need to be offset by the other factors to maintain a consistent volume. Since the other attributes will scale by the same amount, we can simplify the formula to the following:

$$a \times b \times b = Volume$$

$$a \times b^2 = Volume$$

We will be driving a (the "scaleY" parameter), so we need to determine the value of the other two attributes. For this example, Volume = 1. For each value, we get the following:

$$b = sqrt(\ 1/x\ )$$

This formula does not represent the actual volume of the object, should this apply to geometry. What it attempts to do is to maintain a consistent scale factor. If we represent the object as a cube where all the lengths of all the sides are 1, these manipulations maintain a volume of 1.

The following exercise illustrates how to use those formulas and Maya's utility nodes to add squashing/stretching behavior to a joint.

1. In the side view, draw a leg with joints. Do not worry about adding IK at this point—we will get to this later in the chapter. Name the joints "LHip," "LKnee," "LAnkle," "Lball," and "LToe," respectively. Your leg should resemble the one in Figure 2.2.

2. Select the "LHip" joint. In the Attribute Editor, select Attributes→Add Attributes from the menu.

3. In the Add Attribute window, enter "stretch" for the Attribute Name field. Make sure the Data Type is set to Float. Enter a value of .1 in the Minimum field and a value of 1 in the Default field. It is important to realize that the

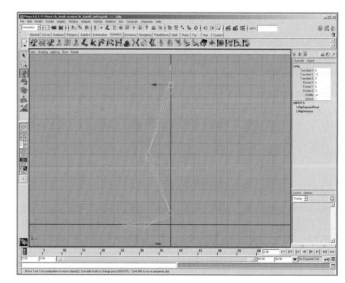

Figure 2.2
A joint hierarchy for a simple leg.

stretch control is a scale factor that will be used to divide other node values. While Maya's node system is robust, you should always avoid situations where nodes will be forced to divide by zero to prevent error.

4. Select the "LHip" joint. Use the Display→Component Display→ Local Rotation Axis to display the joint's orientation. To implement the stretch control, you will need to determine which scale factor runs down the length of the joint. If you are using the default Maya Joint tool, the joint should orient itself so that the X axis is pointing down the length of the bone.

> Maya's joint orient function orients the joint so that it is pointing at its first child joint. In situations such as the wrist, the axis may not be in alignment with the main mass of the hand. In this situation, edit the Local Rotation Axis to create a proper axis.

5. In the Hypershade, create a multiplyDivide node. Name this node "LHipInverse."

6. In the Hypergraph, connect the scaleX of the "LHip" attribute to the "inputX2" attribute of the "LHipInverse" node, as illustrated in Figure 2.3.

7. Open the multiplyDivide node in the Attribute Editor and set the "operation" to divide. In the first Input1 field, enter the value 1.0. Right-click on field and select "Lock Attribute" from the context menu.

8. In the Hypershade, create another multiplyDivide node. Rename this node "LHipSquareRoot." Connect the "outputX" attribute of the "LHipInverse" node to the input1X attribute of this node. Open the Attribute Editor and set the "operation" to power. In the first field of Input2 enter 0.5. Right-click on the field and select "Lock Attribute" from the context menu.

9. Connect the "outputX" of the node to the "scaleY" and "scaleZ" parameters of the "LHip" joint.

10. Finally, open the Connection Editor. Select the "LHip" and press the Reload Left and the Reload Right buttons. Connect the joint's stretch attribute to the "scaleX" attribute. When you are finished, what you see should resemble the node network in Figure 2.4.

Now, when you manipulate the stretch parameter, the other two scale components compensate to maintain the volume of the cube, as seen in Figure 2.5. If you repeat this process for all of the other joints, you will have a skeleton with fully implemented squash and stretch on each of the joints. Repeating this can be tedious, however, so we have provided a MEL script that allows you to do this repeatedly.

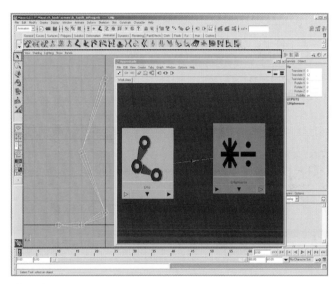

Figure 2.3
The "scaleX" attribute connected to a multiplyDivide node.

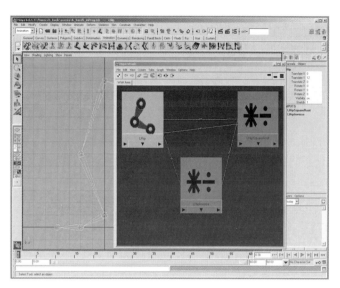

Figure 2.4
The completed stretching node network.

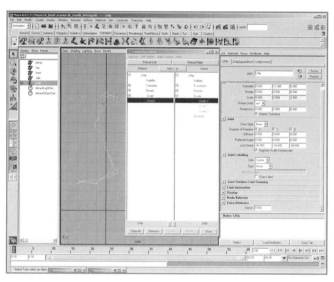

Figure 2.5
The stretch attribute on the "LHip" joint.

To use the script, download it from the Web site at http://www.courseptr.com/downloads. Now, select a node or a group of nodes. Be sure that all of the nodes have the same stretch axis. In the command line, enter the makeSandS command followed by the stretch axis in quotes. For this example, the stretch axis is X, so the command would look like this:

```
makeSandS("X");
```

If you select one of the nodes you ran this script on, you will notice that it now has a "stretch" attribute. Adjust the value of the attribute to see the node's squash and stretch. You will also notice that the scale attributes are no longer keyable. This is a little bookkeeping on the part of the script to make things more organized. Since the scale attributes are no longer directly editable by the user, it is a good idea to hide them from the Channel Box.

Another thing to keep in mind is that, in this example, the minimum value of the stretch was set to .1. This value is completely arbitrary, but you will more than likely find that as the stretch factor gets less than .1, the distortion on the model becomes extreme as it expands to maintain the volume. Feel free to adjust the minimum based on the needs of your production.

Building Stretch into an IK System

Now that we have implemented squash and stretch in a forward kinematics system, it is time to look at implementing it in an IK system. "Stretchy IK" is a term often used to describe a system where the joints that are controlled by an IK controller stretch to meet the controller when it is moved beyond the length of the joints.

One of the characteristics of good animation is the spatial relationships between successive frames of animation. In traditional animation, a character performing a jump may have his leg stretch to the ground in anticipation of his landing. This extreme stretching creates a visual continuity. In 3D, motion blur is often relied upon to spatially organize motion, but the beauty of cartoon animation is its ability to exaggerate.

To create an IK-driven stretch system, add the stretch parameter to the "Lknee" joint via the process cited previously or the makeSandS MEL script, or open the file sampleLeg.ma. You can find this file online at http://www.courseptr.com/downloads. All of the joints in the IK system will need a stretch attribute added in the following exercise.

1. Using the IKHandle tool, draw an IK handle from the "LHip" joint to the "LAnkle" joint.

2. Create a NURBS circle. This will serve as the controller for the joint. Position the circle at the ankle by using point snapping.

3. Select the IK handle and constrain it to the circle.

4. Switch to the side view. Use the Create→Measure Tools→Distance Tool to create a distance node. There should be a node called "distanceDimension1." Rename it "LLegDistance." The distance node uses the input positions of two locators and calculates the distance between them. You will use the distance locator to drive the squash and stretch on the IK system.

5. Select the "LHip" node and then Shift-select the first locator. Create a point constraint (see Figure 2.6).

6. Select the foot controller; then Shift-select the other node and create another pointConstraint.

7. Open the Hypershade Editor and create a multiplyDivide node. Rename this node "LengthRatio."

8. Connect the "distance" attribute of the "LLegDistance" node to the inputX of the "LengthRatio" node (see Figure 2.7).

9. In the modeling window, create another distance measurement tool. This will not be constrained to anything; it will be used to measure the lengths of the legs. While holding down the "v" key, point-snap the locators to the "LHip" joint and the "LKnee" joint, respectively. Write down the number of the distance dimension.

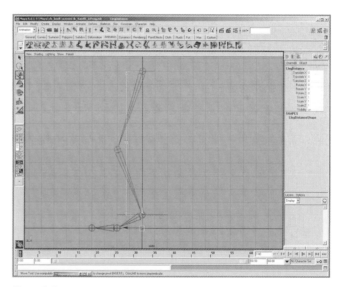

Figure 2.6
Creating the distance nodes for a stretchable IK system.

It is important that the controller be the target of the pointConstraint. It may appear that constraining to the IK handle will yield the same result. The IK handle is a bit unpredictable, as it will try to snap back to the end effector if moved beyond the length of the leg.

2. IK Solvers and Their Application

10. Snap the locators to the "LKnee" and "LAnkle" joints. Write down this number. You can delete this measurment system (the locators and their distance node) when you are done.

11. Add the numbers of the two measurements and enter the sum in the "input2X" field of the "LengthRatio" node, as in Figure 2.8. Lock this field using the right mouse-button context menu. Set the "operation" to divide.

> It is very important that your units agree when you enter the leg length in the "LengthRatio" node. If you are not running in centimeters, you could get numbers that are an order of magnitude off.

12. Open the Hypershade window. Create a condition node, and name it "LlegStretchCondition." Connect the "output1X" attribute of the "LengthRatio" node to the "firstTerm" of the "LLegStretchCondition" node. Set the "secondTerm" of the condition node to 1. Lock this attribute using the right context menu. Set the "operation" attribute to greater than.

13. Connect the "LLegStretchCondition.output1X" attribute to the "stretch" attribute of the "LHip" and "LKnee" joints.

At this point, the stretchy IK has been implemented. If you translate the circle, you will see the IK stretch to meet it. This system is a good start, and it could be enough to meet the needs of a small production. But it also has some drawbacks.

First, there is no option to turn off the stretchy IK. One of the key aspects of character rigging is the knowledge that, no matter what you add, someone will want to turn it off. Providing that flexibility whenever possible is a good idea, so now let's look at making the leg IK stretching optional.

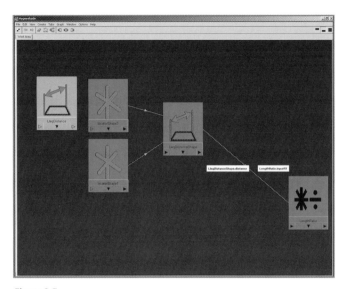

Figure 2.7
Connecting the distance node to the "lengthRatio" multiplyDivide node.

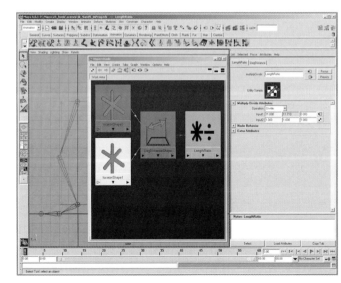

Figure 2.8
Adding the length of the bones in the leg for IK stretching.

2. IK Solvers and Their Application

Turning It Off

The first order of business is turning off the stretchy IK for the IKHandle. Let's assume that someone is animating a walk cycle for the character and wants to be able to switch the stretchyIK on and off for the foot control.

1. Select the "Control" circle.

2. In the Attribute Editor, add an attribute called "ikStretch." Set its minimum value to 0, its maximum value to 1, and the default value to 1.

3. In the Hypershade, create a blendColors node. Rename the node "LStretchyIKBlend."

4. Select the "LStretchyIKBlend" node and the "LLegStretchCondition" node and graph them in the Hypergraph. Connect the "outColorR" of the "LLegStretchCondition" node to the "color1R" attribute of the "LStretchyIKBlend" node.

5. Select the "LStretchyIKBlend" node. In the Channel Box, set the "color2R" attribute to 1. Lock this attribute with the right mouse context menu.

6. Connect the "ikStretch" attribute of the "control" object to the "blender" attribute of the "LStretchyIKBlend" node.

> In this case, stretchyIK will be on by default. Depending on the needs of your production or the desires of the animators, you may want to default stretchyIK to 0, or off.

Now, if you select the circle and move it, the leg stretches. If you manipulate the "ikStretch" attribute, however, you see that the leg will blend between its stretched position and its normal length. This not only gives the animator control of whether or not the stretch is active, but it also allows the animator to animate a smooth transition from stretch to nonstretch.

This is a good layer of flexibility, but there will surely be times when the animators want to turn off the IK system entirely and animate the joints directly. They would also like to have control of the stretch parameters as well, no doubt. Turning off the IK is easy, as Maya now has the "ikBlend" parameter on all of its IK handles. What we would like to do is turn off the IK, the IK stretch, and blend into any FK stretching on the joints.

This will require some reworking. When the IK stretching was created, we hooked into the "stretch" parameter of the affected joints. In order to have control over the joints in forward kinematics, another system will have to be implemented. Recall that when the stretch control was created for each joint, it was hooked directly to the "scaleX" parameter of the joint. It is the "scaleX" that drives the squash and stretch action. To create a blend, all that is required is to slip a blendColors node in between the "stretch" attribute and the "scaleX" parameter.

1. Select the "control" node and open the Attribute Editor. Create a new attribute called "ikBlend" with a minimum value of 0, a maximum value of 1, and a default value of 1.

2. In the Hypershade, create a blendColors node. Rename this node "LHipFKBlend."

3. Connect the "outputR" attribute of the "LStretchyIKBlend" node to the "color1R" attribute of the "LHipFKBlend" node.

4. Connect the "stretch" attribute of the "LHip" node to the "color1R" attribute of the "LHipFKBlend" node.

5. Select the "LHip" joint. In the Channel Box, break the connection coming into the "stretch" attribute. Connect the "stretch" attribute to the "color2R" attribute of the "LHipFKBlend" node.

6. Connect the "outputR" of the "LHipFKBlend" node to the "scaleX" of the "LHip" joint.

7. Repeat this process for the "LKnee" joint.

Now, when the animator adjusts the "ikBlend" parameter on the control, not only does Maya blend the IK to the FK orientations of the joints, but the stretch on the joints is blended to any forward kinematics stretching already animated.

Spline IK Squash and Stretch

The same idea that drives the stretchy IK can be used to drive squash and stretch on a spline IK system. The stretchy IK compares the linear distance of the IK target to the length of the bones that make up the leg. The resulting number is used as the scale factor that pipes into the stretch attribute of the appropriate joints. This method can be used with splineIK—all that is needed is a way to measure the length of the spline in its rest position and in its deformed position. The curveInfo node in Maya measures the linear distance of a NURBs curve. This node can be used to create a new ratio for stretching joints in a splineIK.

In the following excercise, the length of a curve will be used to control stretching on a spline IK system.

1. Start with a new Maya scene.

2. Draw a series of joints to form a spine.

3. Using the splineIK tool, create a spline IK handle from the root of "joint1" to the tip of the spine.

4. Now, add the stretch parameter to each of the joints. If you have used Maya's default Draw Joints tool, the joints should stretch along their X axis. If not, use Display→Component Display→Local Rotation Axis to determine which axis the joints should stretch along. Use the makeSandS.mel script to create stretching for each of the joints.

> To select all the joints in a chain, you can use the Select command as follows:
>
> Select -r -hi {jointName}

5. Select the NURBS curve that controls the splineIK. In the command line, enter the following command:

```
arclen -ch 1;
```

6. This command creates a curveInfo node and connects it to the curve.

7. With the curve still selected, open the Hypergraph and graph the upstream and downstream connections. You should see the curveInfo node connected to the curve.

8. Select the curveInfo node and open the Attribute Editor. There will be a field labeled Arc Length. Copy this number down—it is the length of the curve, and it will serve to create the length ratio to drive the stretch.

9. Open the Hypershade Editor. Create a multiplyDivide node and name it "curveLengthRatio." In the "input2X" field, enter the original Arc Length parameter from the previous step. Use the right mouse button context menu to lock this attribute.

10. Select the "curveLengthRatio" node and Shift-select the "curveInfo" node and graph them in the Hypergraph. Connect the "arcLength" attribute to the "input2X" attribute of the "curveLengthRatio" node.

11. Select all the joints in the splineIK system. Shift-select the NURBS curve that drives the system and graph them in the Hypergraph. Connect the "outputX" of the "curveLengthRatio" node to each of the joint's stretch attributes.

Select the NURBS curve that drives the system. Press F8 to enter component mode. Select each of the CVs and use the Deform→Create Cluster command to create a cluster for each CV on the curve.

If you select and move any of the clusters, you will see the joints scale their length to match the length of the curve. These clusters can be integrated into a control structure to drive the spine.

Once again, it is important to provide as much control as possible to the animator. While the squash and stretch capability of the spine is very powerful, it is also a good idea to be able to turn it off. The following steps will create a system to turn off stretching on the spline IK.

1. In the Hypershade, create a blendColors node. Rename this node "ikStretchScale."

2. Select the "ikStretchScale" node and Shift-select the "curveLengthRatio" node. Graph the input and output connections in the Hypergraph.

3. In the Hypergraph, connnect the "outputX" of the "curveLengthRatio" to the "input1R" attribute of the "ikStretchScale" node.

4. Select the "ikStretchScale" node and open the Attribute Editor. Set the "color2R" attribute to 1. Use the right mouse button context menu to lock the attribute.

5. Connect the "outputR" of the "ikStretchScale" node to the "stretch" attribute of each of the joints.

> If you lose the "curveLengthRatio" node, you can always add it to the selectionList with the MEL command "select –add curveLengthRatio." Another way to find the node is to select the curve that drives the IK system and graph the input and output connections in the Hypergraph. You can find the "curveLengthRatio" node by following the connections.

At this point, the blender attribute of the "ikStretchScale" node controls the stretch of the joints in the IK system. Setting the blender to 0 sets the joints' stretch to 1, disabling the stretch on the IK system. Setting the blender attribute to 1 enables the stretch.

2. IK Solvers and Their Application

chapter 3
Matrix Math

A ll 3D animation is created in an environment that is a mathematical model of reality. It is not a very precise model, but like the Matrix, it has rules. And while you can't really bend them or break them, you can definitely make use of them.

The purpose of this section is not to provide a basic primer for 3D. It is assumed that the reader has some familiarity with 3D coordinate systems and how points are located in 3D space. In this chapter, we are going to look at some of the mathematical constructs that control 3D animation and lead to the creation of CGI.

Points and Vectors

Points and vertices are similar, and yet very distinct. Both are represented in 3D space by three numbers. Points are pretty straightforward—they represent positions in space. Control vertices and polygon face vertices are examples of points.

A vector is a different beast altogether. While it is described by three numbers, it is not a position in space, but a direction and a distance. Each of the three numbers represents a displacement along the three main axes. While vectors are often represented as starting at the origin, there is no originating point. A vector can be compared to a distant light in CG—the rays of a distant light have only a direction and an intensity.

Maya uses vectors in several areas. The normals of a surface are vectors, and the normalConstraint uses these vectors to orient an object with respect to those normals. Vectors are also used with aimConstraints to determine how to orient objects (the UpVector). Maya's IK system uses pole vectors to control its behavior.

Some Vector Operations

Vectors have some interesting properties that can be used for some special operations. One of these is the dot product. The dot product is very useful for determining the oriententation of two vectors with respect to each other. The dot product of two vectors is positive when they are pointed in the same direction, negative when they are pointed opposite of each other, and zero when the two vectors are perpendicular.

1. Open the dotProduct.ma file from the Web site at http://www.courseptr.com/downloads. You should see two spline curve arrows and a cube.

2. Select "vector2" and rotate it on the Y axis (see Figure 3.1). You will notice that the cube changes size. The dot product of the two vectors has been applied to the cube's scale.

3. Set the "rotateY" attribute of vector2 to 90. The cube disappears. When two vectors are perpendicular, their dot product is 0.

4. Set the "rotateY" attribute to 180. The cube is restored. But if you select the cube and examine its scale, you will see that it is -1. When two vectors are pointing in opposite directions, their dot product is negative.

5. Feel free to rotate the vectors freely and examine the effect on the cube.

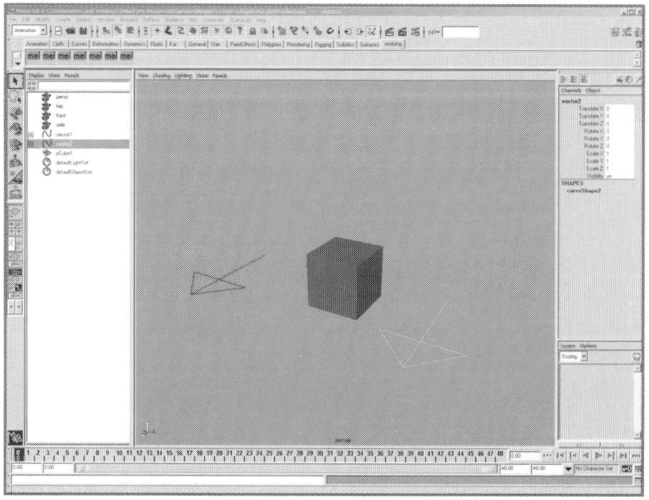

This scene uses Maya's vectorProduct node to get the dot product. If you open the Outliner, you will see that there are two locators parented under each. If you open the Hypergraph window and graph the upstream and downstream connections, you will see how this is created. The worldPosition of the locators is fed into a plusMinusAverage average node. The subtraction of one locator from the other creates the vector. The output of the subtraction is fed into a vectorProduct node. Remember that, because of the nature of vectors, it is not important what the translation of the arrows is, only their orientation.

Figure 3.1
Changing the orientation of the vectors scales the cube by the dot product.

The cross product is another operation of vectors that is the basis of the pole vector and aim-constraint up-vectors. The cross product of two vectors gives a vector that is perpendicular to the original vectors. To see an example of the cross product, open the chapter03/crossProduct.ma file. You will see the two arrows. If you rotate either arrow, you will see that the arrow in the middle flips as the two vectors move. The arrow in the middle is aim-constrained to a node that has its translate attributes connected to the vectorProduct node, which is set to cross product. The following excercise examines the property of the pole vector.

1. Open the crossProduct.ma file from http://www.courseptr.com/downloads. You should see three arrows.

2. Select the "vector2" curve under the "crossProduct" node. Rotate it on the Y axis. You should see the arrow in the middle pop between pointing straight up and straight down. The arrow is aim-constrained to a locator that is translating to the cross product.

3. Set the "rotateY" attribute of the "vector2" curve to 60.0. You should see the center arrow point straight up.

4. Select the "crossProduct" node and rotate it freely. You should see that the center arrow always points in a direction perpendicular to the other two arrows, as shown in Figure 3.2.

The cross product has the unique characteristic of always being perpendicular to the other two vectors. In this example, the cross product vector pops between two different directions, but those directions are always perpendicular to the two original vectors; however, if the two vectors are invariant, the relative position of the cross product remains constant.

Matrices

You can't investigate the nuts and bolts of 3D for long without running across matrices. The matrix is a mathematical concept that makes all 3D possible. It controls the positioning of all objects in a 3D scene for animation and rendering. While matrices are not directly edited in Maya, knowing their use is advantageous to understanding how Maya manipulates 3D objects.

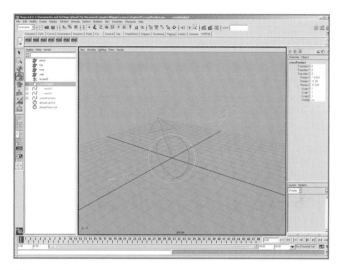

Figure 3.2
The cross product keeps the middle vector perpendicular to the other two.

The matrix is the workhorse of 3D. It is what makes sure all the appropriate points go to the appropriate places for rendering. Every vertex of geometry in Maya is processed by a matrix before being rendered to the screen. A great portion of computer animation is dedicated to manipulating the matrix over time to create motion. When objects are placed in hierarchies, it is the matrices that enable them to be manipulated in predictable ways. In fact, it is matrices that allow hierarchies to exist at all.

Matrices are composed of 16 numbers arranged in four rows and four columns. These numbers are all the information that Maya needs to translate, rotate, and scale a transform. To do this, Maya takes input from the object's attributes in the channel box and creates a series of matrices. One is created to describe the object's translation, for instance, while another is created to describe the rotation. Every transformation of the object is described as a matrix and then they are multiplied together. The result is the matrix of the object. When a transform has a shape node, all of the vertexes on the geometry are multiplied by the object's matrix to get their final position in the modeling viewport. There are a large number of smaller matrices involved in this process, but the final result is one set of 16 numbers.

Another way to look at matrices is as a coordinate system. Whenever an object is grouped under a transform, it is placed in the coordinate system of its parent. When you build hierarchies, you are creating multiple coordinate systems.

The following excercise is designed to illustrate exactly how a matrix affects points in 3D space.

1. Start with a new Maya scene file.

2. Create an empty group. Rename it "matrixGroup."

3. Create a locator and rename it "testPoint."

4. With the locator selected, open the Attribute Editor and create three float attributes: "offsetX," "offsetY," and "offsetZ."

5. Open the Hypershade. From the Utility Node bin, create a vectorProduct node. Rename the node "matrixVP."

6. When connecting matrix information, it is easier to make the connections via the Connection Editor. Matrix outputs do not show in the Hypershade or Hypergraph. Open the Connection Editor and load the "matrixGroup" into the left side and the "matrixVP" node into the right side. Make sure the window mapping is set to "from→to."

7. Connect the "matrix" attribute of the "matrixGroup" node to the "matrix" input of the "matrixVP" node.

8. Set the "operation" attribute of the "matrixVP" node to Point Matrix Product.

9. Select the "testPoint" locator and load it into the left side. Connect the "offsetX" attribute to the "input1X" attribute of the "matrixVP" node. Do the same for the "offsetY" to the "input1Y" and "offsetZ" to the "input1Z" attributes. Set the value of the "offsetZ" attribute to 5.

10. Press the Mapping button and switch it to "to←from." Connect the "output" attribute of the "matrixVP" node to the "translate" attribute of the "testPoint" locator.

11. Set the "offsetZ" parameter of the "testPoint" locator to 2.5.

12. Select the "matrixGroup" node. Rotate it freely. Notice how the locator maintains a consistent offset from the node (see Figure 3.3). Feel free to experiment with different values in the "offsetX," "offsetY," and "offsetZ" parameters.

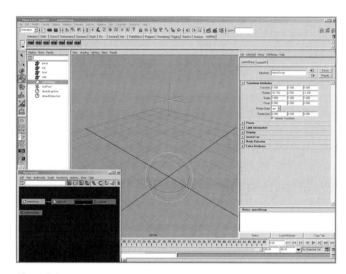

Figure 3.3
The results of matrix multiplication on the translation of a locator.

Using the offset attributes, you can move the locator around. If you select the "matrixGroup" node and rotate it, you will see that the locator's position changes so that it remains relative to the spatial location of the "matrixGroup" node. This is exactly how matrices are used to manipulate points. You will notice that the locator does not rotate or scale with the "matrixGroup" node. This is correct, as the vertices or CVs that make up geometry do not have an orientation or scale either. All of the manipulations of 3D objects are carried out via changing their worldspace positions with matrices.

Objects in Space

To illustrate the power of matrices, the following excercise utilizes them to create a custom snapping tool. One of the most necessary tools in the character rigger's toolkit is a good object snap. Many times, you will want to align two objects in the workspace. While Maya provides an Align tool, it does not take into account rotation or scale. One of the ways to deal with this is to create temporary point and orient constraints.

To access the matrix information, you can use the "xform" command.

1. Start with a new scene.

2. Open the Script Editor.

3. Enter the following commands. When entering the commands, do not press the numeric Enter key, but enter them all as a block of code.

```
global proc snap()
{
    string $sel[] = `ls -sl`;
    float $t[] = `xform -q -t $sel[0]`;
    xform -ws -t $t[0] $t[1] $t[2] $sel[1];
    float $r1[] = `xform -q -ro $sel[0]`;
    xform -ro $r1[0] $r1[1] $r1[2] $sel[1];
}
```

4. When the script is entered, use the File→Save Selected command from the Script Editor to save the script as snap.mel.

5. In the modeling environment, create a locator. Move and rotate the locator to a position away from the origin.

6. Create a polygon cube primitive.

7. Select the locator and then Shift-select the polyCube.

8. At the command line, enter the command "snap" and press Enter (see Figure 3.4).

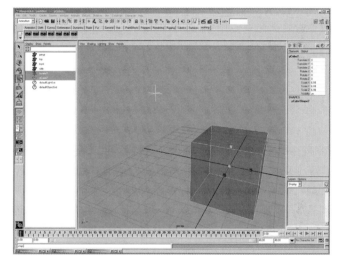

Figure 3.4
Executing the snap command.

You will see the cube position itself to the location and orientation of the locator. The cube is not constrained—it is as if the cube's attributes had been set by hand to the locator's attributes. You will notice in the script that the xform command requires 16 arguments from the $sM float array. These are the numbers that make up the matrix.

The xform command is a character riggers's best friend. An object's attributes can be an imprecise way of locating it in space. The xform command will give you dead-accurate information on an object's transformation values because it accesses the information in the object's matrix directly. Consider if the locator had been parented under another node, its attributes could be 0 for its translation, but its parent might be moved anywhere in the environment. The result would be that the cube would translate to 0 0 0, whereas the actual world position of the locator would be different.

3. Matrix Math

Pivots, Pivots

When Maya builds a transformation matrix, it multiplies a number of other matrices together. Among them are the rotate pivot and scale pivot matrices. These allow the user to control and animate different pivots for a node's rotate and scale attributes. When positioning an object in Maya, the pivot that relates to the object's translation is the rotation pivot. The scale pivot is a separate pivot that functions as the center of the scaling operation. This allows for the creation of complex behaviors in a node. When the Move tool is selected and the user presses the "Insert" key to enter pivot editing mode, it is the rotation pivot that is being repositioned.

The rotation pivot is also adjusted whenever an object has been translated from the origin and Freeze Transforms applied. The translation attributes of the object are set to zero, but the object is still able to rotate around its original pivot. This is due to the pivot's offset.

The nature of the rotation pivots has a great impact on the snap script. If you attempt to snap two objects with different rotation pivots, you will find that the objects are aligned to their rotate pivots. This is a different result than what you would get from a point constraint. Let's look at updating the snap script to account for different rotation pivots.

1. The first thing to be added to the old snap script is acquiring the rotate pivots of both of the objects. The xform command has a "-rp" flag that can be used to get the rotate pivots.
   ```
   float $rp1[] = `xform -q -rp $sel[0]`;
   float $rp2[] = `xform -q -rp $sel[1]`;
   ```

2. The rotate pivots of both nodes will need to be determined. The rotate pivot of the first object will be added to its translation and the second will be subtracted. These modifications will be seen in the command that sets the translation for the second node.
   ```
   xform -ws -t ($t[0]+$rp1[0]-$rp2[0]) ($t[1]+$rp1[1]-$rp2[1]) ($t[2]+$rp1[2]-$rp2[2]) $sel[1];
   ```

3. To see the new script work, open the snap3.mb file from the Web site http://www.courseptr.com/downloads.

   There are two cubes in the scene—if you select them, you will notice that both have a translation of 0, but are in different spaces. If you select them and create a point constraint, you will see the two cubes snap to the same location. If you run the snap.mel scrip, there will be no change—neither cube will move.

4. Select the cubes and execute the new snap function. You will see both of the cubes align properly.

This new snap works a bit more like what you want. It also doesn't rely on any connections, so it can be used to position nodes with incoming animCurve connections.

The Locator

A thorough discussion of the uses of the matrix in Maya should highlight some of the unique properties of the locator node. The locator is a transform with a shape node that creates the little cross shape. Most shape nodes in Maya inherit their worldspace orientation from their transform's matrix—you can query the location of a vertex using the xform command, but this is not a real-time, connection-driven method. The locator shape, however, has a live connection to the actual worldspace position of its shape node—that is, the point in space where the three lines that make up its shape node intersect.

This is a very useful property of the locator because it alllows the creation of rig systems where you can always directly access the worldspace position of the locator without creating a secondary node that is point-constrained to it. This can save a bit of work when building systems that use worldspace positions to get distance. In the previous examples with the vector operations, the locator's worldspace outputs are used to calculate the vectors in world space. As a matter of fact, the locator's worldspace shape node is key to the functioning of the dimension node, which measures the distance between two points in space.

dagPose

One of the most interesting and lesser known features of Maya is the dagPose. A dagPose is a node in Maya that records the matrices of a node or hierarchy of nodes and stores them for later use. The dagPose is the node that Maya uses to store the bindPose of a character when its skin is attached. The dagPose can be a really useful tool for certain modeling operations, but it has some important limitations:

◆ The dagPose cannot restore the matrix of an object with incoming connections on the translate, rotate, or scale channels.

◆ The dagPose command will not store visibility or any custom attributes. It will only store the matrices of the objects.

While these seem like some pretty hefty restrictions, the dagPose has some advantages. One is that it is fast and accurate. The other is that the dagPose is a node in the file, and does not require any external scripting or data storage. The dagPose can be especially useful for posing deformation skeletons to refine deformations.

1. Open the dagPose.ma—you can find it at http://www.courseptr.com/down-loads. You should see the medium-resolution PigGoblin character.

2. A couple of dagPoses have been saved for this character already. At the command line, enter the following:

    dagPose -restore stride;

3. You should see the character's pose change. To see another dagPose, type the following:

    dagPose -restore spreadEagle;

    The character should now resemble Figure 3.5.

4. Now let's restore the character to its bindPose. From the Skin menu, select Go to Bind Pose to return the character to its bind pose.

5. Then we will save a dagPose. Select the character's joints and position them into a jump pose (see Figure 3.6).

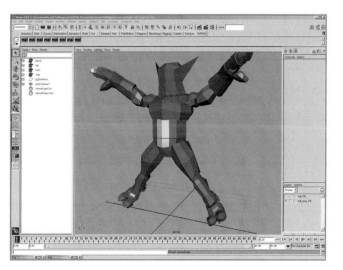

Figure 3.5
The spreadEagle dagPose restored.

3. Matrix Math

6. When you are satisfied with the pose, select the "pgDeform" node. At the command line, enter the following:

```
dagPose -s -n jumpPose;
```

You should see the figure go to a pose similar to Figure 3.6.

7. To test the pose you have saved, use the Skin→Go to Bind Pose menu item to return to the original pose. Then, at the command line, enter the following:

```
dagPose -r jumpPose;
```

You should see the character return to the pose you have created.

As mentioned before, the bindPose of a skinned character is a dagPose. This is useful to know, as many times when working with a character that has more than one skin cluster attached, the bindPose can get lost. When this occurs, the Skin→Go to Bind Pose command will not return the character to its original skinned pose. When this occurs, the dagPose command can sometimes be used to restore the skeleton. When using the dagPose command to manually restore a bindPose, it is best to use the following syntax:

```
dagPose -restore -global -bindPose;
```

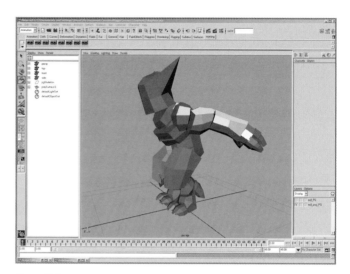

Figure 3.6
The jumpPose.

It is not necessary for anything to be selected to restore a dagPose. As you may have noticed, the dagPose command works on entire hierarchies at once. You can save a dagPose for selected objects by passing a "-sl" flag when saving a bindPose.

As you can see, the dagPose is a very useful tool for setting up deformations on a simple skeleton. This makes it easy to test deformations and store positions of objects for later reference. Since the dagPose objects are nodes, they are saved with Maya scenes for easy access.

3. Matrix Math

Mike Comet

chapter 4
Interview with Mike Comet

Mike Comet is currently the Lead Character Rigger at DNA Productions working on their second feature film titled *Ant Bully*. Mike has been a great and willing resource for both animation and technical know-how though his Web site at http://www.comet-cartoons.com and on numerous Web forums on animation. His work history covers everything from games and video productions to feature-animated films using a wide range of programs including Maya and 3DSMax. Mike is a great example of both artistic and technical abilities combining to make a whole, and we are very happy to have this interview to share some of his insight and experiences in character rigging.

How did you get started in computer graphics, Mike?

When I was younger I watched a lot of cartoons, both Warner Bros. and Disney stuff. I always loved it, but never thought I would actually get into the industry. Very early on, my father brought home an old Apple computer and then eventually PC machines. This was pretty much the days of green monochrome screens, text only and 5.25-inch disks. Anyhow, I taught myself BASIC programming and starting making text games and graphical text games using the text blocks as the graphics. I also went to computer camp and eventually when things started to handle actual graphics, I learned that.

Figure 4.1
One of Mike's personal characters.

By the time I was in high school, I had taught myself 8086/80386 assembly language and C. I wrote a basic 2D paint program that mimicked some of what Deluxe Paint did since I wanted my own proprietary format for a game I wanted to make but never completed. Around middle-school/high-school time, I learned more about animation. My aunt had procured a book by Kit Laybourne called *The Animation Book*. This book was less about the principles of animation, but instead covered the actual types of animation, like cel, stop-motion, paint on glass, and so on, and told you what type of camera to buy and how to make animation. At that point, I bought a Super8mm camera capable of doing stop-motion and started messing around in the basement.

Meanwhile, things like *Young Sherlock Holmes* and such started to appear on the big screen. I also watched some of the original minds-eye videos about computer graphics, but never thought I could ever do it. They showed an Alias workstation that was about the size of a washing machine and probably cost as much as a small house. Around 1989 or so, the Video Toaster by New Tek appeared. My dad was into videography, and we ended up at an Amiga store to check it out. I walked in and was blown away by a ray-traced looping animation being done on an Amiga. That was it; I was hooked as soon as I realized 3D computer graphics could actually be achieved on a PC. I ended up with an Amiga 3000 and Imagine 3D by Impulse and started teaching myself computer graphics.

I've worked as an animator at Volition Inc., a game company in Champaign, Illinois. I also animated, scripted, and rigged and did other work at Big Idea in Chicago. At Blue Sky Studios in New York, I did character and prop rigging for *Robots*, as well as script and tool writing for that and *Ice Age 2*. Most recently, I am now lead character rigger at DNA Productions in Dallas, Texas, for the second feature film there.

What led you to character setup?

Well, I originally was self-taught in a lot of things related to computer graphics. Since I have a programming background and a computer science degree, it flowed pretty naturally. Actually, at first I was into modeling and texturing, since that was what you kind of had to start with when working on your own projects. Once I realized there was animation, I decided to go into that and spent more time in that area. My first job was actually as an animator. However, as I learned more about rigging and scripting, more of my time was spent there, as I found I enjoyed that area more.

I was actually worried about not animating at first. While at Big Idea, a lot of my friends were telling me to go into rigging, which I think made sense since my strengths were definitely more in that area. In the end, I think it was a great move—I have to say I don't really miss animating at all. It's kind of nice not to have to deal all the time with director input and something that is subjective. Rigging tends to be pretty much a definitive goal-driven thing, where you know exactly what you have to do and have some idea of how to get there.

Can you talk about how being an animator affects the way you rig a character and vice versa?

Probably the most important thing is that it's given me an understanding of what a rig should or should not do, and why it's important to serve the animators and do things how they want. Every part of a production crew is a service to someone else. The modeling serves the rigging, the rigging serves the animation, animation serves lighting, everyone serves the audience, and so on. You can create some pretty

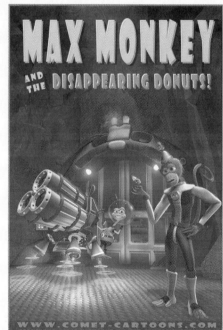

Figure 4.2
More of Mike's personal characters.

complex and cool rigs, but if animators aren't going to use them, or don't like them, it's a complete waste of effort. I remember a sign I read at the back of a retail store once—it had two rules. Rule 1: The customer is always right. Rule 2: When the customer is wrong (and they often are), refer back to Rule 1. I think that's a pretty good attitude to have in dealing with rigging, too. At the end of the day, it has to work for animation, as well as any other departments that are using it.

What was the transition like from a place like Big Idea to Blue Sky in reference to the way you worked as a Character TD?

For me personally, the biggest change was going from doing a sort of jack-of-all-trades approach to focusing on one thing. It gave me time to get back into my programming roots and pick up C++ again after about eight years of not really using it. I remember the first week or so I was there I had to keep reminding myself it wasn't a dream and that I was actually working there for real. It was quite nerve-racking at first, realizing just how much talent and experience you are surrounded by, but it was a great experience, and I learned a lot from everyone there.

What were some of the initial challenges on Robots?

I came into that production after they had already done a lot of the initial work for how the main characters were going to function. The first character rig I did there was for this small puppet-like "guard" character. He had a skirt made up of rings, and originally in the story it called for him not only to act, but also to be able to lie on the ground with them. I relied on what I had already learned about spline IK in Maya and also came up with some creative ways to give the animators control over it. Also, originally the main character's facial work was stiffer because they wanted things to look far more robotic, but I helped develop a system to allow for more organic shaping of the character's faces for the film when they decided to allow it. Probably one of the other bigger pains was cable arms. Several of the characters have a cable arm type rig. Fortunately, a lot of work on this was already done by other people, although I updated some of that work and reimplemented it on many of the characters that used them.

Can you talk about how you set up the controls on the skirt or the cable arms? For example, did you find any limitations in the spline IK that you had to create workarounds for or something along those lines?

For the most part, the splineIK rig on the guard's skirt was very straightforward. It was pretty much based on a regular spline IK type setup. The main trick was to ensure that the model would properly rotate/pivot at the right spot without intersecting. This mostly involved working with modeling and making sure that the pivots were correct. For twisting, it was simply a matter of setting up some locators that were parented properly and with the correct axis order, so that twist could be read relative to the root. It's important, I think, to understand coordinate space and rotation order and how that all relates in order to do stuff like that. To solve the animator's desired FK control but with an IK rig, the rig had the usual top, mid, and bottom IK controls that were then linked in a more FK fashion. The animators could still move/translate the lower controls, but also had the ability to pose the bottom movers more as expected. Not a ground-breaking idea, but there was a little bit of work to make sure it looked correct with Blue Sky's proprietary follow-through plug-in. The final FK hierarchy for the skirt was then linked more to a main body control, so that as the upper spine went, it was still more or less IK from the hips, but used the FK rotations, if desired. In addition, expressions to read the spline curve length allowed for handling auto-extension and retracting of the joint lengths to provide for the rings cascading inwards or extending. In the end, the character spends a lot of time behind a podium wall, so with story changes, I am not sure if the skirt is even really seen as much as was originally planned. This was a case where I was able to take the basic ideas of what I knew about rigging spline IK and extrapolated them to add extension and retraction separately, properly read the twist attributes with my own method, and linked this all together to give animators the controls they wanted. I think it's useful to learn from other people as I did here, and then to take that and figure out creative ways to implement actual rigging issues that arise.

How did you approach the R&D for the characters (animator input, film reference)?

The designs for robots are pretty much totally stylized and fantasy-based. A lot of the work on the main rigging was already put into place when I arrived, but there were always changes and requests based on animation feedback. For *Ice Age 2*, I was able to provide more groundwork in helping get more standardized auto rigging scripts in place for that film. I think the scripting approach yields a quicker turnaround time on rigging, as well as consistency, which is important when you have to go in and fix someone else's rig. A lot of times, though, the R&D was either based on some obvious problem to solve or by talking to animators about what improvements or ideas they had for what they wanted.

We definitely referred to anatomy reference books for help in placing joints and helping to figure out how things should work, but a lot of that is fairly straightforward. In addition since the show was more cartoony, trying to follow a strict real anatomy setup wasn't really a requirement.

What are the challenges of rigging robots vs. rigging organic characters?

In many ways, robots are simpler since what you see hierarchy-wise is what you get. At the same time, there's also the need for a bit of cheating, such as pistons being able to extend longer/farther than they can actually retract inside of the parent tube, or handling things like tongue-and-groove joints, and so on. I think it is great, though, because it gives you a challenge to come up with unique and strong ideas for the root structure of how the rig works. You can take that and apply the same ideas to organic models as well.

How do you approach starting a rig? What are a few things that you always do when rigging—tricks you learned or just best practices to always watch for in the rig?

Well, the number one thing I do is always check the model. Basic things like topology and proper detail are obviously critical. I usually start by figuring out the joint hierarchy and pivot locations. For the most part, at the beginning of any actual production, I figure out what basic controls the animators want. So by the time I actually have to rig an actual character, it's all known. It's just a matter of running the proper leg script or arm script, and so on, and putting it all together. But there's always a lot of back-and-forth at the start of that process to see what controls the animators like or don't like, or think are too much or not enough. The main thing to watch out for is having enough control, but not too much. You don't want a ridiculously heavy rig, but you also don't want the animators coming to you every day asking for more control. Having enough time in preproduction to evaluate and test the models is important.

I try to come up with reusable rig scripts that can be applied in various areas. For example, a basic script to rig a spine might not only do FK but also IK or spline IK, and so on, and have options when it is run for what features the rigger wants to install. Having that approach means that you can quickly and easily re-rig a character. One of the things I like to do is to parent any joints that are skin joints underneath the rig itself somewhere. Then if you need to re-rig, it's a quick matter to simply unparent them, relink them, blow away the old component of the rig, and reinstall again.

In what ways do you accommodate different animators and different shot requirements on a rig (for example, all in one rig or per shot rig)?

I think a rig should accomplish most of what it has to do in the base rig. There are usually certain things that might be required for just one specific shot, but usually a basic rig should handle most of that. In my experience, when the animators request something, it's usually something that will end up being used elsewhere anyhow.

As far as different animators, in the end, the animation director or leads really need to decide what goes in or stays out of the rigs. You can go rig-happy trying to add everything that everyone wants, but it usually just gets messy and slow. In addition, there can often be conflicting views on how to do things. The best way to handle this is to do several variations and tests and let someone with authority in animation determine how the final thing will work.

What kind of interface to a character do you find most animators like, GUI window, in-screen controls, and so on? What are the most requested fixes or changes from the animators you worked with when it comes to the rig?

I think people who have used a graphical picker prefer that. Anything small and compact but with flexibility is good. Mark Behm, who is an animator, helped develop some really cool stuff both at Big Idea and Blue Sky. I inherited a lot of that and helped to add and maintain some of his original work. The latest version (of the UI) had some pretty cool features like drag-and-drop support and customizable background images. It had the ability to float or dock inside, so everyone could be happy.

Probably some of the most usual requests or changes are small things that either get missed, or because there isn't time to fully test, get passed into a rig for animation. Blue Sky was pretty good about getting fixes done, and it was quite typical to have only an hour or so turnaround time for most animation requests to rigs.

Do you have any tips or solutions for maintaining a rig during production? How do you deal with changes or fixes to the characters, such as texture update or model changes, without adding all kinds of history to the model?

I always make sure any model geometry has its history cleaned and ready to be re-rigged. I'm a fan of referencing in the model during rigging, and then before exporting for animation, importing the model. This way the model file can be quickly and easily updated and kept clean, and the rig file when loaded will have any update to the geometry. It's also critical to have good tools to save weights for any deformation you have done, so that you are not always having to redo the entire rigging. Especially early in production when rig components can be changing often, it's important to be able to un-rig and re-rig a character in a short amount of time. Having tools to support whatever you are using is critical.

Are the character rigs done by hand or is there some kind of automation process that helps rig and skin the characters on a show like Robots?

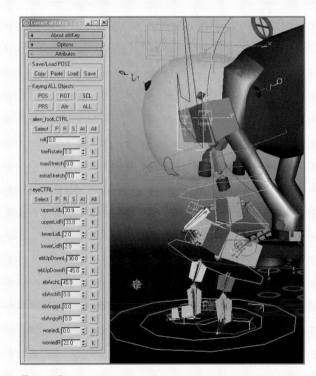

Figure 4.3
A scripted character interface inside 3ds Max. This script can be found on Mike's Web page http://comet-cartoons.com. The attribute collector script in the Maya Bonus Tools is a very close match UI-wise.

As mentioned, a lot of things are automated. Actually, for *Robots*, that wasn't always the case, but as we had time to get that done, we wrote scripts to help out. *Ice Age 2* had a lot of people able to spend time on rig setup and scripts, so that production was very nicely automated. I also did some work on going into the Maya interface for weight painting and added some features that I thought should be there but weren't, in order to help out with faster skinning.

What do you still see as major challenges for 3D characters and rigging? Is it a software or people limitation?

I think, in general, a lot of the ways rigging and skinning are done are still very close to how they were done several years ago. It will be interesting to see as technology improves how things like skin deformation and dynamics simulation change. Things like hair and cloth, which I personally always associated a lot with effects, still really also need to be animation-driven and have controls that animators can tweak. Improving these types of complex systems with faster feedback, I think will continue to be a challenge for a while. It also seems that trying to do realistic humans is still a big challenge. There's a propensity for things to look almost real, but not quite real, and thus end up looking more freaky. Personally, I prefer more cartoony type work anyhow, so I am not that keen on resolving those issues.

In fact, things like squash and stretch can also be a big issue and a lot of work. A lot of it can be done, but it takes a lot of poking and prodding to get 3D applications to give the type of a result that a hand-drawn character would have. Usually, you end up with something in-between the two.

How do you approach keeping yourself updated on new tools and rigging solutions?

I think for the most part that any good rigging team member learns for everyone on that team. As people come in and come up with solutions, there should be a lot of back and forth learning about how things are done. It's also good to try to think out of the box and keep abreast of what other studios are doing and what they explain about how they approach things.

I know you have done a lot of rigging and scripting in both Maya and Max. Can you speak about the differences in your approach to rigging in both software packages?

Actually, a lot of the work is very similar. Most of the basic tools like IK and constraints and so on can be approached in almost the same way in both packages. Probably the biggest reason why I primarily use Maya now is that it has a faster architecture for dealing with things like expressions and connections, and it allows you to do the same thing more easily and quickly.

Do you think there are tools in software like Maya that are underutilized when it comes to rigging?

I don't know that there are really parts of Maya being underused. I usually find myself augmenting software with my own tools and workflow that I prefer. One thing I would recommend to any rigger is to get into and understand basic matrix and vector math, and learn how to use the dgNode reference in Maya. Seeing what attributes Maya nodes have can be a great help and actually allow you to do things that you might not have known about.

You mention learning how to use the dgNode reference. Can you expand on this? And since we are talking about math, do you have an example of when or how understanding Matrix and Vector math helps you during rigging or helps solve a general problem? I know there are a lot of people who might want to learn about it, but don't know where to start.

The dgNode reference is useful for looking at what Maya is doing internally. This can help both with understanding how to put your own scripts or plug-ins together or also to see if something can be done. For example, if you know a little about the math behind skinning algorithms, then you might realize the basic idea is simply a current "matrix" representing a joints current transformation in space (i.e., position, rotation, scale) multiplied by the "inverse matrix" of its rest pose. The basic idea being that you get the "change" or "delta" that has occurred that way. An easy way to think about this is with translation. If a joint is at X=5 when you bind it to skin, then the change to the actual skin mesh only occurs when it changes from the default X=5. If you move the joints to X=7, then the skin reacts by moving +2 on X if it is weighted to that joint. So in effect the X=5 is the "rest pose" of the skin joint. Another way of saying this is that the X=5 is the "origin" from where the changes start. The easy way to do this is to take the current position of say 7 and subtract 5. Doing this is similar to taking a current matrix and an inverse matrix and multiplying them together. You're effectively canceling out the rest pose from the real "world origin" and now the values you have are relative to the "rest pose origin."

Anyhow, every transformation node in Maya has a "matrix" and "worldMatrix," as well as inverses. If you open up Connection Editor for a transform and list non-keyable attributes, you will see these near the top. So, with this information, if you open the Hypergraph in Maya and look at a joint and how it connected into a skinCluster you will notice that each skin joint has its "worldMatrix" attribute connected into the skinClusters "matrix" array.

With all this knowledge, you might ask if the joint is giving the "current" matrix value, how does the skinCluster know about the rest pose or "worldInverseMatrix?" The answer is found in looking in the dgNode reference Help file for the skinCluster node. If you look at the Help file, you will see the "matrix" array that is the "driving transforms array." Technically, you could plug not only a joint in here but also anything you want to act as a bone. However, the real secret is found when you read about the "bindPreMatrix" attribute array. As it lists, it is the "matrix inverse of the driving transform at the time of bind." In other words, it's the inverse of the joint matrix in its rest pose, or it's the joint's "worldInverseMatrix" attribute value when the joint is in its default location.

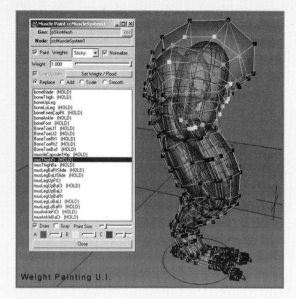

Figure 4.4
Here is an example of Mike's skin and muscle plug-in with its weights being painted—seeing advanced math concepts in action.

At this point, you can use this information to easily reset a skin joint's position without having to unskin and then re-skin. As long as the worldMatrix and the worldInverseMatrix connected into the skinCluster's matrix and bindPreMatrix, respectively are coming from an object at the same location, then the joint will have no effect. You could manually take a joint and connect its worldInverseMatrix into the proper bindPreMatrix (making sure to connect into the same array index), and at that point you could move the joint around, without any skinning effect. You could then break that connection and copy over the values with a getAttr and setAttr instead so that Maya will remember the value it had and now skin works again.

If desired, you could even make a second joint, rename it to something useful like "jointBASE," and connect its inverse matrix into the skin cluster bindPreMatrix array. Now, you have a "base" joint, in much the same way that lattices have a base. If you move both together, nothing happens but you are adjusting where the skin joint starts. If you move just the live original joint, you get deformation.

In the same way, it's also good to have a basic idea of how transforms, rotation order, and coordinate systems work together. For example, if you have an object and it gets parented to another object, then the child values are going to be "relative to the parent." In other words, they are in the space of the parent. Using this allows you to do things like group objects to zero out controls or also figure out ways to read one object's rotation or position relative to another. If the child were constrained to something else, with a point or orient constraint, then the values would be the rotation or position of whatever the constraint target was, but it will be relative to its parent—that is, the values will be in the space of the parent object. This can be useful when trying to rig automated things, like clavicles or wrist twist joints, and so on.

For someone who doesn't have a math or computer science background, there are numerous books available now that talk about math for computer graphics and explain all of these sorts of things. A good example is *Mathematics for 3D Game Programming and Computer Graphics* by Eric Lengyel. (ISBN: 1584502770). It starts with a good foundation and works all the way up to more complex items. Even just the first several parts on vectors and matrices can help people interested in rigging and give insight into what is actually going on under the hood of a commercial software package.

Do you see any major advancement in rigging for cg characters in the near future?

I expect people will work hard on trying to get more and more photorealistic work coming out. Probably a lot of things like muscle systems and hair and cloth will be improved, more readily available for commercial software.

Any last tips or advice you can give our readers who want to improve their skills.

The main thing I'd say is to study math and programming as much as you can. Having that foundation can be a big help in rigging. It's also good to delve at least a bit into animation to understand what and why things need to be done.

Thank you for your time and for the great explanation on the dgNode and matrix math, which is great stuff.

SECTION 2

Rigging

chapter 5
Planned and Organized Rigging

When you receive an asset to rig, you must make sure that the asset is ready to be used before you start doing any kind of rigging. Let's face it—it's easy to just jump in and start working on a rig because there is always a deadline looming. But this is the worst thing to do because all kinds of things can go wrong even at this stage, causing you to redo lots of hard work later. When you're rushing to get something done, you can miss even simple things, such as the model being the wrong working scale for the production or transformations that are not frozen, causing skinning or rendering problems. Stopping to evaluate the asset and making sure that you are organized and understand the rigging requirements is as important as the rigging process itself. This evaluation stage is critical—not only will it save you time later by not having to redo work needlessly, but it also will save the entire production team time down the road. The result of this whole process of preparing an asset is to make sure that you have a file that can be rigged up and handed off to the team without fear of causing problems for your team members by having it break or causing them to redo work.

Evaluation of Geometry and Starting with a Clean Plate

The pipeline in place at your studio dictates how your assets are prepared. For example, the model file might come to you in any number of file formats and geometry types, and be built in the studio or outsourced to another production company. In addition, the mesh might already be textured, or it could be handed to you at the same time it is handed to the texture artist. If this is the case, then causing changes to the mesh at this point might be more difficult since it will affect two departments and not just one. But because you know and understand the pipeline and the needs of that asset, if there is an issue with the asset, you still have to get it fixed. Early and clear communication when an issue is found is a necessity when large teams of specialists are working together. In this kind of large studio environment, the production pipeline is very wide with lots of tasks going on all at the same time, which means you are dependent on several people and several other people are dependent on you.

If you are doing all the parts of production on your own, the pipeline will probably be more linear, but you still should treat the work as separate departments. You can do this by keeping your files separated by production tasks, treating each one as if it were being done by a separate department. If you do find a problem, you can tell yourself that you have to change the mesh and quit texturing. Also because your project is organized by task, it allows for updates to one component without breaking lots of other assets. This also helps if you work later within a larger studio or remotely for a company where you work only within your 3D specialization.

In a perfect world, all software would be able to handle updating changes across the entire studio so that anyone could change files at any point in the production process. Since this is not a reality even in the best 3D software, you need to make sure that you do your best to eliminate as many chances for problems with the asset up-front before it's deep in the pipeline. Remember that the longer an asset is in the pipeline, the more dependencies build upon it, making it more costly if something is wrong.

One way to help keep these problems out of your production is to be involved with the asset from its conception. If possible, the sooner you can look over the asset's design and get fixes done before it leaves the designer, the better off you will be when you have to work with the 3D version. Fixing things early on paper is much cheaper and faster than if you wait until it's built.

Since it's not always practical or realistic that you will be involved in the concept art stage as a Character TD, you can at least start talking with the modelers as soon as they start on the mesh. Things like number of edges or vertices in deformable areas or removing detail or detaching or attaching parts of the mesh are ways that you can prevent having topology changes to the mesh once it gets to you. This is just part of the production process that you will deal with as the Character TD; the other main task will be to maintain the character throughout the life of the project.

Looking at a few excellent examples of high-quality modeling and edge-loop control from modeler Ramahan Faulk, you can get a good idea of what to look for in a ready-to-rig mesh. Proper mesh edge flow has direct impact on how the model looks during deformation. The edges should flow along the natural lines of the muscle mass on the character and provide enough detail to allow for a full range of motion (like in the shoulders). If you have too few vertices, the mesh will not hold its volume once animated; likewise, too many vertices will be slow to weight during skinning and are prone to pinching, along with overall slowing down of the file (see Figures 5.1–5.3).

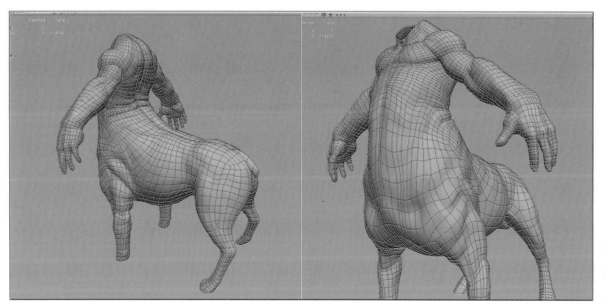

Figure 5.1
Here you can see a great example of well-structured edge loops and a blending of anatomy on a creature. Courtesy of Ramahan Faulk, fx3dartist@msn.com.

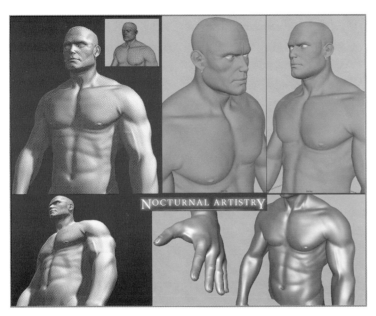

Figure 5.2
This model is a great example showing the amount of detail you can have, yet still make a clean model. Courtesy of Ramahan Faulk.

Initial Evaluation—Unit Size and Scale

Once the model gets into your control, you must keep two things in mind: working unit size and scale. Experienced modelers will do a lot of these checks for you, especially if you have worked with them before, but this is not always the case. People do make mistakes or miss things sometimes, and you must back them up and catch what they missed.

The first thing that should get checked on the mesh is that the scale and size are correct. There is nothing worse than rigging a character only to find out that your character was the wrong size or you're working in meters when the file was supposed to be in inches. Most 3D software gives you tools to measure objects in the scene. Use these tools to check the size of your character, as shown in Figure 5.4. You should have documentation somewhere that lets

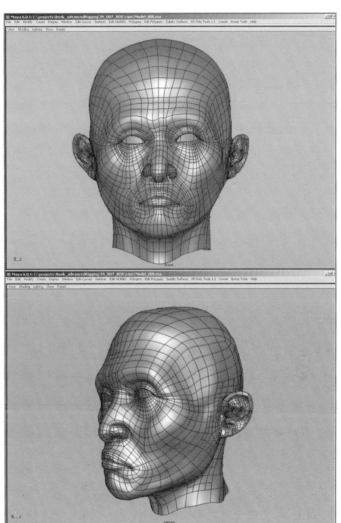

Figure 5.3
This face image shows a sub-d surface in Maya with very good edge loops following the underlying muscle structure of the face. Asymmetrical meshes like this are more realistic but more difficult to rig. Courtesy of Ramahan Faulk.

49

you know what the production is using for units, as well as a character sheet with information on the correct height in meters or feet that the character is supposed to be. Other ways to check for size consistency in your characters are to make a quick generic outline of a human at the correct project scale and add any other notes about project size and reference that go with each character. This gives you a quick visual cue as to how big the current character should be in addition to using the Distance tool.

Take time to double-check this because if you have to export your character to another software where the units are different, the export process might try to scale the character for you and can cause even more problems when trouble-shooting a complex pipeline once in production. An easy thing to miss is negative scale on objects in the model that have been mirrored over, which can even happen to the main mesh, depending on how you attach the two objects together. A fast way to check a file with lots of geometry in it is to do a quick export to .FBX, and it will catch and tell you the objects with negative scale, as shown in Figure 5.5. You can also import the file back into Maya or load this exported file into QuickTime Movie player with the .FBX for QuickTime to visually check for any strange problems with your file that are introduced at export.

> The Alias|Kaydara .FBX plug-in for Maya and QuickTime along with other tools can be found at http://www.alias.com.

Once you know the mesh is the right size, make sure that the transforms are all frozen and the mesh pivots are in the right location for your needs. Before you freeze the transforms, unparent all the geometry so that all nodes are at the top world level of your file. You will re-parent and organize the file later, but for now it will help you clear out any nodes that might not freeze correctly or are just taking up space.

The reason these steps are done first is because they are fast to do and good to get out of the way. If you find problems or need additional fixes, you can hand this new corrected mesh back to the modeler. This updates the modeler with a corrected file so that if he hands that character mesh off to someone else, it will

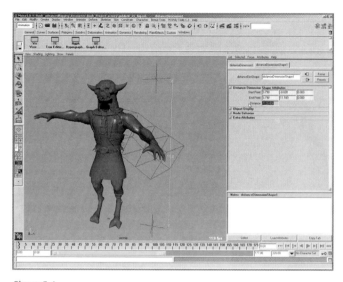

Figure 5.4
Use the Distance tool in Maya or the Measure tool in Max to check character size.

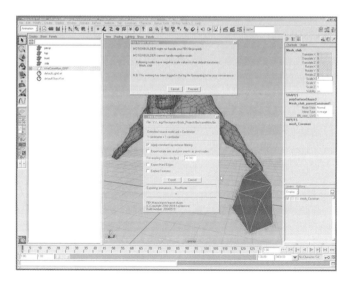

Figure 5.5
Catch scale and other errors with the .FBX exporter.

be the correct size and will not have any transform problems. After the working size of the character is checked and fixed, it is very easy to check the rest of the model because most of it is visual, like checking mesh topology and proportions.

Default Poses and Neutral Posture

Can there be more than one pose for a character? Part of the evaluation of the model file is to look at the default poses for characters. These stances or poses can vary from model to model and are really an individual Character TD's choice with the modeler as to how they would like to have the models posed to rig. Be careful because this topic can cause some fights in the workplace since everyone has an opinion on how the character should be posed for optimal texturing, rigging, and modeling.

When you rig a character for animation, you need to know the character's animation requirements, including range of movement and any special case shots that require extra rigging. If you know these details, then you can have the model built or altered to be in a neutral state for its main range of motion that is expected from that character. For example, when using game creatures that need to be optimized, the default state of the model might be built in a pose that the character will be in 90 percent of the time. If you think of this neutral state in your own body and try to visualize the difference in both the contractions of your muscles and the engagement of certain areas of your body, you will start to understand what a neutral state feels like.

Da Vinci Pose

The main example that is used frequently and found in many Web forum discussions is how the arms and shoulders should be positioned. The term "Da Vinci pose" is widely used, but most people talk about this pose as the arms straight out from the body and the legs in a spread-eagle posture. While this pose can be a valid pose for modeling the character or for making texturing easier, when it comes to deformations, it is better to take the stress and tension out of most parts of the mesh. This means that you should drop the shoulders to a relaxed posture with the arms out to the side in a 45-degree angle as shown in Figures 5.6 and 5.7. Basically, just lift your arms out from your side as far as you can without having the clavicle and shoulder start to lift. You can then adjust this posture farther forward if needed or pulled back to the side with the arms slightly bent to keep the triceps and biceps muscles neutral, with one not pulling more than the other. You will find long discussions on this in many Web forums. One of the best discussions comes from Spiraloid Digital sculpting forum titled, "*Da Vinci or Not Da Vinci?*"

> Here is the direct link to the Da Vinci or Not Da Vinci? Thread on Bay Raitt's forum:
> http://cube.phlatt.net/forums/spiraloid/viewtopic.php?TopicID=195

Legs work best when they are slightly spread shoulder-width apart and centered under the character's body with a slight bend at the knees, if needed, with the feet flat on the ground pointing straight ahead. Legs do not have a very wide range of motion compared to the shoulder area and can be less exacting in the posing. The twisting and rotation of the leg hits its limits very rapidly, and the hips and lower spine engage in order to provide the extra, added range of motion during the twisting. Also, since we are standing on our legs most of the time, it takes very little activation of the leg muscles to stay standing, again easy to build in the model detail. Putting in a slight bend in the leg at the knee to help with deformations is great. You can add more of a bend to the leg, if needed, but just remember to take into account the kneecap slide.

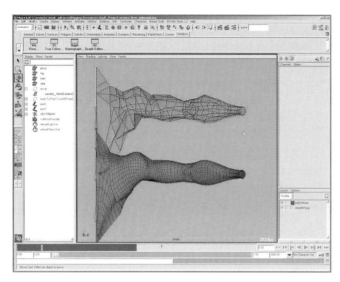

Figure 5.6
Here the arm is out from the body. You can see that the shoulder is tense, and the clavicle movement is not taken into account in the modeling.

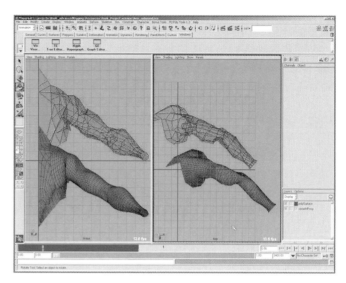

Figure 5.7
Compared to Figure 5.6, this arm is in a much more relaxed state; for example, the clavicle and the shoulder are relaxed.

Multiple Poses

The best of both worlds is to have the model built in whatever pose is the fastest to model in. Then the modeler can create a texture file, moving the model into a pose that is more open and easy to unwrap and texture. From that original modeling, both the Character TD and the modeler can adjust the pose again with rigging and skinning in mind, thus ending up with three poses: a model pose, a texture pose. and rig pose. They can be different files or a single mesh with three blend shapes/morph targets set up to get the mesh into the correct pose.

A pose that is good for skinning and deformation is not necessarily great for the default state of the rig; animation controls might end up off axis and cause extra work for the animators to mange their keyframes. With this in mind, a fourth state that comes after skinning might be required to make rigging easier, as shown in Figure 5.8. The joints can be rotated back into more of a straight alignment with the world, and the legs can be brought more inline with the body. Once in position, you can generate all your rig controls. This rig pose is also a good pose to have a character in if you are going to be applying motion capture data in some kind of retargeting operation in Maya with Trax or Motionbuilder. There are several ways to keep these poses for the mesh and the skeleton in order to update the mesh once and have all the poses update. For the mesh, you can just create a set of blend shapes in a master file that contains all the poses. Then generate the other separate mesh files from that pose by hand or automatically. In a bigger teamwork environment, you will most likely want to automate this system of pose creation for the modeling department.

Rig Pose

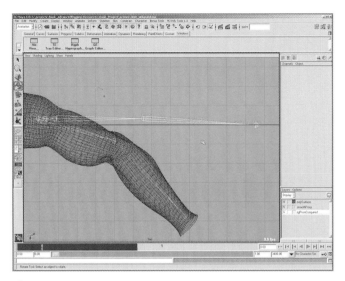

Figure 5.8
Look at the difference between the skin pose for this skeleton and the rig pose that is globally aligned.

For the skeleton and rig controls, it's a bit easier to store out the different poses and recall them when needed. Assume that you have the mesh in its skin pose for now and that the mesh is skinned to the skeleton. Maya does have the bind pose option to get the skeleton back to its skinned state, but this does not work once the character is rigged. And since this skin state is not the same as the pose you want to generate your control rig in, you will rotate the skeleton into a pose that works better for the animator and the rig. After the control rig is generated, you will want to store this rig pose, but also be able to get back to the bind pose, if needed.

Using a few different methods, you can store these poses for the rig and the skeleton. One way is to set a keyframe for your controls and save this animation with the animImportExport plug-in. Using character nodes, store your different poses as clips in Trax or one of the free Mel scripts that lets you save and apply poses to your character. You should be able to turn off the constraints and disable the IK Handles in order to get the skeleton back to the bind pose. If this does not work, it's possible, in this case, to use a copy of the skeleton that is in the correct bind pose and fit the controls of the rig back to match the bind skeleton pose and then save this pose with one of the aforementioned methods.

The other way around the problem of a rig pose being separate from the bind pose is to have a bind skeleton and a rig skeleton. Through connections and constraints, the bind skeleton is driven by the rigged skeleton and at any point you can unlink the two and get your character back to a bind pose. You should be aware of these as options in your Character TD toolkit, and it gives a foundation for why a two-skeleton system can be a good approach as demonstrated in Chapter 13.

The trick with all these methods is making sure that the pose file and the rig file do not get separated because without the poses, you might not be able to get the character back to the correct poses that are needed for skinning or games export, where it's especially important to make sure that the pose that all the animations are based on is not lost. If it is lost, then all the animations must be reanimated. For this reason, you might want to keep in mind ways to store these rig or skeleton poses in the file. Trax Clips can do this function since they can save with the file and character node or be exported to an external file. This gives you a bit of redundancy. You could also store the poses into the file with a script node that a custom attribute controls to recall the pose and get the character back to the state needed, skin or rig pose.

Bad Geometry and Other Hidden Dangers

We can now look over the visual problems and check the model for anything that can cause problems once it's skinned and animated. You can use the following checklist as a basic starting point for mesh evaluation:

◆ Is the geometry the correct type: NURBS, polygons, or subdivisional surfaces?

◆ Does the surface have enough detail or subdivisions in the areas that will be deforming?

◆ If it's for a game, is the surface triangulated?

◆ Are there stray vertices or non-merged vertices, or do the vertices have xform data on them?

◆ Are the normals correct, meaning facing out and not inverted? Freezing the transformations will make the bad normals show up as long as you're not looking at double-sided surfaces. Maya will switch on "opposite" attribute to keep the surfaces looking correct in the view and when rendered, but the normals will still be inverted and must be fixed. (Again, this is the reason that you take care of all the transformation problems first.)

◆ Is the mesh unwrapped already with the UV mapping laid out correctly, or will you have to transfer the final uv coordinates to the rig file later? It's good to keep track of what will need to be updated later on. This can be done right in the file or in an external database or asset management system. If you do keep it in the file, add it to the notes section of the object or keep a text "I" node for information that has all the scene notes in its note area.

◆ Also make sure that you check naming and grouping. The names of the mesh objects should have meaningful names and not be geometry-named, such as sphere234 or cube01. Both the transform and the shapeNode should be named properly based on the standards of your pipeline. A good example is naming the model parts with a prefix of a Character_GEO_name or MESH_Character_name—any word that lets you know what a particular object type is. The character name helps provide another level of selection filtering in a file with lots of characters.

After you're finished going through the mesh and doing any fixes that you find need to be done, you will need to create a clean file. There are lots of ways to delete history and clean up the Maya file, but it's easy to miss some extra node or break a connection that changes the mesh in a way that you were unaware of. One of the fastest ways to generate a cleaner construction history-free mesh is to export it out of Maya to an .FBX file or .OBJ file. The reason that we use the .FBX format to export to something like OBJ is because of its compatibility checks. Since the .FBX file format has become a standard among 3D software to exchange data, including mesh, animation, skeletons, materials, and so on, it's a good thing to do an export early on to .FBX, not only to create a clean file from but also to help catch anything that might not export properly later. Again, finding out there is an error now is better than finding out when you have already finished the asset, shared that asset with a different studio, or tried to take the character to Motionbuilder to have motion capture applied to it.

This cleaning process applies in 3ds Max as well. The .FBX plug-in ships with all new versions of Max. In Max you want to go through the same steps. Collapse the stack on the mesh down to the final geometry format, edit mesh, or edit poly, name your objects, make sure all the transforms are reset, and then export the model and import it back to a clean file. To use the .obj format with Max, you have to download the free plug-ins from http://www.habware.at/.

After you have exported your mesh and imported it back into Maya again, you will want to double-check that the scale is the same and that there are not any extra nodes from the import. Graphing the node in the Hypergraph window will let you see all your connections and make sure that it's a clean mesh with just a transform node and a shape node with connections to the materials. Double-check all the node names, making sure they did not get renamed by the exporter, and then you will move on to clean up the file hierarchy.

The grouping of the geometry is important to do next. At the very least, all the models that belong together should be under a group node. This lets you keep your scene graph views clean both in the Outliner and the Hypergraph. You can further break this down into deforming and ridged groups. The cleaner the file, the faster you and the animator can find parts you have to rig or skin or animate. Using selection sets is another way to help keep the geometry files linked without having them grouped if there is a restriction with using groups due to export issues in a game or other I/O issues.

> Grouping in Max is different than in Maya. While you want to keep nodes in both of them organized, in Max creating a point helper and making the mesh a child of that helper is the same thing as creating a group in Maya. The group command in Max creates an extra node but by default keeps the children from being selected or edited and adds extra work to manage without any real benefit over just parenting.

Preparing the Book Character for Rigging

For this example, we received the final model but due to time constraints, the modeler left it in an unfinished state. Most of the geometry was mirrored and instanced so we had to do a large cleanup pass on this character, which we will go through step-by-step. At this stage of the model, the basic pose of the character would have been agreed upon already and checked by the Character TD, the animation requirements should be done but might not be, and the texturing and unwrapping might or might not be done.

1. Unhide everything in the file. As you can see in Figure 5.9, we have 133 objects in the file and lots of empty nodes and default-named geometry and history on lots of objects.

2. The fast way to get started is to export this file as an .obj. This will convert any instanced geo to real geo, strip the history for the object, and quickly show you what objects need to have the normals flipped from being negative scaled.

3. Now after importing the .obj file, you get a single merged polygon object and a lot of groups from all the other parts and the black surfaces from the bad normals, which you will clean up next (see Figure 5.10).

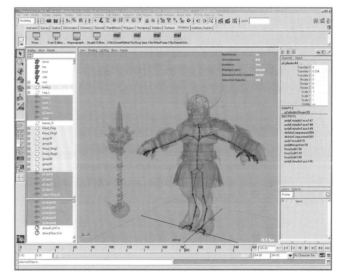

Figure 5.9
Initial file.

Figure 5.10
Cleaned file with bad normals.

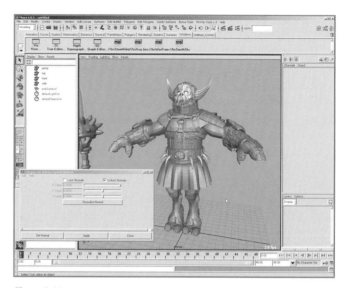

Figure 5.11
Unlocking normals with the Set Vertex Normal tool.

4. To remove the sets, select them all in the Outliner and delete them.

5. Now, you will go in and fix the normals. The side effect of exporting to the .obj file format is that after import, Maya will lock all the normals, initially making it impossible to affect them, such as when trying to reverse them.

6. Using the Set Vertex Normal tool, check on the Unlock Normals option and apply it. Do not be fooled by the fact that the surface now looks like all the normals are correct; you still have to reverse them. This happens because the object is set to double-sided, and once that is turned off, you will see the parts of the mesh that are still inverted (see Figures 5.11–12). Then just reverse the normals where needed. Also, this mesh still had objects that needed to have their verts merged or welded and then combined down into fewer object groups to clean up the scene.

Figure 5.12
Turning off double-sided setting for the model.

5. Planned and Organized Rigging

7. In Figure 5.13, we can see that we have started to separate the objects into better groups. In this case, they are grouped and named by character and then the character body parts separate from the armor and weapons. There are lots of ways to prepare the mesh and group the objects to keep your scene clean, so it's up to you.

For game meshes or film meshes, make sure always to keep the cloth objects or simulation objects separate. Depending on your engine, if it is sewn into the main mesh, the simulation might try to solve the entire mesh and not just the cloth. Keeping it as a separate object also allows you to optimize and rig the cloth objects separately without affecting the main mesh. Game exporters in general should take care of the combining of the geometry at export so that you can keep your file grouped and artist-friendly for the entire time. If you have a limitation, such as having to attach or combine all your geo into one object because of an exporter, then have the exporter fixed and changed because that should not be a limitation.

Figure 5.14 shows an example of how to go through the geometry and combine sets of objects in order to make them easier to work with and to make the number of nodes smaller when skinning and rigging.

Figure 5.13
New clean groupings of mesh pieces.

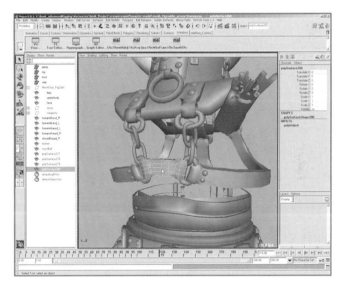

Figure 5.14
Grouping the strap with its bolts.

5. Planned and Organized Rigging

Here is the final version of the mesh with all the separated objects that would need to be rigged up. For this character, his sections of armor made sense to separate and so did any loose or dangling objects that might need to be animated or simulated (see Figure 5.15).

> In general, you want to look over the model and figure out what parts of it could be animated in addition to the main body. These objects should get named and rigged up appropriately. The other group of objects that would have special treatment are objects that would need secondary animation or tertiary animation like cloth, loose straps, or hair, and so on—things that are accessories to the character.

At this point, you will also do a final check and clean-up pass on the file.

1. Ask yourself first if it has good UV texture mapping, or does it have to be done later? If it's the latter, then you will have to update the skin mesh with the new textures and materials.

2. Double-check the object's xforms and freeze xforms again to make sure.

3. Clear all the history for the mesh. (Watch out if there are blendShapes in the file already, as you might remove those as well without knowing it.)

4. Check out the Multilister or Hypershade and clean up the shaders, if needed. This might involve naming them correctly or in Maya 6 you can create organizational bins inside the Hypershade as an additional way to group them. Create a single bin for this character and make sure the nodes are named in a way to keep them with this character. The first two initials of the character will work fine; this is a PigGoblin so the shaders will be called pg_ShaderName and placed inside of the pg_Bin (see Figure 5.16).

Figure 5.15
Final mesh groups.

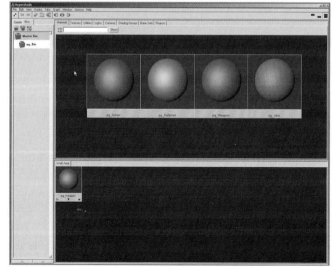

Figure 5.16
The new bin feature used to clean up the base shaders for the character.

5. An additional organizational tip is to use the new Maya 6 functionality of showing color nodes for display in the Hypergraph. This makes it easy to locate and organize the file at the node level when looking at a complex scene graph. The goal is to have a clean Outliner and a clean Hypergraph. You can do this in place of using layers for objects if you want to limit the number of layers in a file. Feel free to pick any colors you want, although we usually stick with the blue on the mesh and use this feature a lot more on our control objects later (see Figure 5.17).

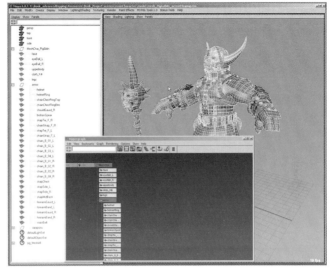

Figure 5.17
New node-based colors for helping clean up a hard-to-search Hypergraph.

From the Alias Help File...

"In the Attribute Editor for that node, go to Drawing Overrides. (You may have to expand Object Display to see this section.) Turn on Enable Overrides and set a color using the color slider. You must have Node Display Override Color turned on in the Hypergraph to display color changes. Changing the color of a layer overrides this node display setting."

Because we like to adjust these colors for lots of objects at once, we use this small script:

```
proc drawColor (int $colorID){
string $sel[] = `ls -sl`;
for ($obj in $sel) {
setAttr ($obj + ".overrideEnabled") 1;
setAttr ($obj + ".overrideColor") $colorID;
}
}
```

6. Reorder the Outliner so that the order of the objects in the Outliner is the same order that the objects appear on the character from top to bottom or just in a logical picking order for the file.

7. Also add a Quick Selection Set to this file now. In case you have to merge in other files, the selection set will stay with the file, independent of layers.

8. Lastly, the final mesh quality check is done with some surface evaluation tools that will help keep you from rigging a file only to find it had some kind of geometry bug in it. Use the Polygon Cleanup tool, set it to "Selected Geometry," and turn on the Edges with zero length, Faces with zero geometry area, Lamina Faces. If you find something the modeling artist missed after running this tool, if you can, send it back to the modeler after you have a list of fixes for him or, if appropriate, fix them yourself (see Figure 5.18).

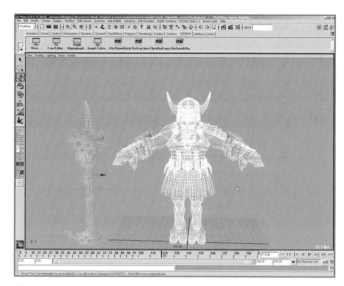

Figure 5.18
Final character mesh after all checks and cleaning.

Regardless of what software you work in or how big the project is, starting with a clean foundation for rigging your characters will benefit you throughout the life of the project. Communication and documentation are key components for making sure that you're working on the correct file and to the standards of the production. A clean foundation also helps other departments feed you files that are the way you need them, and you can do the same for them. The debate over what the best pose is for skinning and rigging a character will continue, but the important point is not to limit yourself to just one pose or think that one pose is better than another. The mesh should be in whatever poses work best for you and your pipeline.

chapter 6
The Application of Research: Establishing Your Rig's Foundation

Whether you are rigging for cartoon or photo-real characters, humans or creatures, research and development time must be appropriate for the given project. The level of R&D that goes into a project will vary based on the complexity of the character and the requirements of the production. If the character is on the level of Gollum from *Lord of the Rings*, then preproduction and R&D can take many months or even years. Several people may work to create a rig, while others write special plug-ins for skin and muscle. Still others have to figure out how to create solid, believable facial animation rigs. If, on the other hand, the animation is for a game or broadcast project, then the R&D might be the job of just one or two people. This smaller R&D team may only have a few days or weeks, if they are lucky, to figure out the best method for setting up the characters and creating or finding any scripts and tools that will help with the process. More advanced rigging requires two main kinds of research: artistic and technical. Artistic research covers anatomy and joint placement, joint movement, and biomechanics. Technical research focuses on breaking down the needs of the character, based on the artistic requirements of the project and animators and identifying any other areas that might require special tools or extra plug-ins.

Artistic Research—Finding Anatomy References for Believable Characters

In art, if you are trying to elicit a reaction or a response from people, then it is the resulting final image that really matters and not the process. The same holds true when you are building computer-generated 3D characters and their anatomy. The process is important in character rigging to the extent that good process can ensure that deadlines are met and animators aren't left to pull their hair out along the way. But ultimately, a character's believability is what matters most to viewers. If the character looks and feels right, then it is right.

Because you are aiming for believability of the deformation while in motion, you will need to combine your knowledge of anatomy and physiology with a little trial and error to determine the best placement of the joints while rigging. Keep in mind that the joints and muscles do not have to be completely anatomically correct under the mesh for them to work. However, they do have to feel, move, deform, and ultimately *look* like they are anatomically accurate in order for the audience to believe in the character. People subconsciously judge how things should move. The human eye has amazing capacity to pick up on tiny glitches and register a movement as feeling wrong or "off" somehow. As soon as they see these kinds of problems, they stop believing, and that is the last thing any production wants.

It's important to find as many surface and skeletal references as you can for the kind of character you're setting up because this will help you create a cg skeleton that, once animated, will move and subconsciously feel right to the viewer. Studying the reference material in still images is useful and finding good skeleton, muscle, and skin images is a great foundation to build from. But just as it is better to draw while looking at a live object instead of a photograph, referring to real life examples can help you understand the body makeup as a volume with mass the way an image cannot. Seeing how all the layers work together and understanding how the mechanics of the body work while tense or relaxed, while pushing or pulling, and so on, will build up the Character TD's ability to create a rig that makes believable characters. Being able to see the range of motion and how much influence on the surface of the skin that a muscle has allows for the creation of animation- and deformation-friendly rigs. Later in this chapter, we will break down the application of this reference material and show how it is directly applied to our character.

Once you have your references gathered, you can use your favorite paint software or load them in your 3-D software and draw in some joints over the reference. Sketch out ideas on movement and pay attention to troublesome areas, watching for opportunities to simplify the number of joints and still get the desired deformation. Also try and mark in your sketch areas that will need more joints or deformers in order for the character to move properly and maintain volume on the skin.

Also, look for point of contact pivots on the reference you're using; the feet are obvious examples since they touch the ground, and they will need a way to rotate from that point of contact. Mark out or quickly sketch where you might need joints at these points and remember that they might be different than joints you will skin to. Make any other little notes you have from the reference materials, such as where the skin folds or if the body part rotates or can translate/slip.

> Google image search is an amazing resource in addition to a solid reference library of anatomy books.
>
> The Amazon.com "search inside the book" lets you look at all pages in a book if the publisher allows it, just as you can at the bookstore. As Amazon scans more books, this will be an amazing resource for artists and programmers alike.
>
> The newest and biggest resource of cross-referenced images and information can be found at http://www.bbcmotiongallery.com/ where the BBC has digitized and uploaded "500 million feet of film and 400,000 hours of video." The unrivaled BBC archive spans over eight million subject categories, and it's growing by the minute.

Using Reference Material for Cartoons and Creatures

So how do you research something that can be any kind of strange shape and proportion and deformed in outrageous ways at any point in the animation? Stylized or cartoon characters also need to be researched. Luckily, most cartoons are based on some real-life counterpart like ducks, rabbits, and dogs, for example. You can use all the reference material and tips for cartoon characters that you use for a realistic character. The difference is that with a cartoon character, there can be so many different forms and stylized shapes that it becomes difficult to know where to place the joints if you're just looking at anatomy books. Realistic anatomy reference still provides a solid foundation to build your skeleton, from which you can exaggerate later to fit into the character. And, sometimes, you just have to place joints where they feel right to allow the character to hit poses that are required by the production.

You can also find other sources of reference in other cartoon characters that are similar to the ones you're trying to rig. If you have to build a 3D version of an animated 2D character, then watching that character in motion will give you a good idea of what kind of joint placement and deformers it will need in order to work in 3D. There are not any fast shortcuts for this, except perhaps to quickly place the joints and test things out as soon as you can. Keep in mind that a big part of what makes a 2D cartoon character feel the way it does is the animator's ability to control the inner surface lines of the characters and the silhouette. They also control the volume and the silhouette throughout the motion of the character.

A good deal of rigging for exaggerated characters falls more into layering the deformers and providing controls over those deformers to give animators the ability to take a character "off model" and distort it into a shape that might not be approved as a still, but is needed for the animator to get the right feel during motion. Great real-world examples of this are easy to see with recent films like *The Incredibles*, *Madagascar*, and *Chicken Little*. Each film has character rigs that allow the animators to completely warp, stretch, twist, and deform the character "off model" as much as they want in order to make the animation feel right, for comic effect or because they have a super power to stretch. Recent personal work of Jason Osipa shows some amazing deformation controls over his characters using basic Maya tools. You can find his great examples online at www.jasonosipa.com/Downloads/Movies/. Look for Squoosh examples. He also has a great thread at http://10secondclub.net/forum/index.php?showtopic=69&st=0 that goes into his techniques and is very inspiring to look at as a reference.

So far we have been talking about finding references for organic or living characters and the need for proper joint placement for deformations. We have not discussed the topic of mechanical rigging and the slight differences that you might deal with when mapping out a robotic or mechanical character. The same ideas about finding real references for the kind of mechanical joints you will be setting up apply as they do for organic characters. However, mechanical objects have engineered systems that need to work together and feel like they have a reason to exist. The gears, pistons, or cables need to feel like they work, are controlling the object, and have a purpose for being where they are on a robot or vehicle. It is up to the Character TD to work out mechanical systems that animate well, but at the same time keep the animators from having to rotate and hand keyframe all the mechanical bits in the asset. Take, for example, a robotic suit used to move heavy objects found in so many science fiction movies. If you have to rig up this kind of heavy equipment, then real construction equipment provides a great reference for how your model parts rotate and pivot, as well as how tightly they are attached or how they interact as part of the whole. And construction equipment should be easy enough to find. In a big city, you might look at cranes or fork lifts. Even in the country, a tractor would server as a good reference. Any equipment that is large enough to demonstrate the working relationship between heavy moving parts should suffice.

Breakdown of Reference for Joint Locations and Movement

One of the most common mistakes when starting a skeleton for a character is improper joint placement. The tendency may come from a lack of time, a lack of knowledge, or a rush to get to the "rigging part." People often just throw the bones into a character without much thought. But bad joint placement can be very dangerous in a production environment because it's easy to miss until the character is being animated, and if it's caught too late, it becomes very hard to fix. Trying to fix or adjust the skeleton of a rigged character without breaking animation or skinning that is already in place can be almost impossible.

When you place the joints, you want to keep in mind how the vertices once skinned will rotate around or orbit the joint location. Keeping this in mind, one trick you can use to visualize the vertex rotation is using the rotate manipulator with the joint picked. The rotation handles give you a visual set of circles that surround the joint and let you adjust your zoom to match the edge of the mesh or vertices that you want to picture on that path.

If you want a more permanent view of the bone arcs, you can use a sphere or circle to visualize quickly the vertex paths. We also use them to measure things like the arc of the arm joints to see if they are the right length when brought down the side of the body.

Studying reference materials and understanding anatomy can give you a good foundation for starting your character's joint placement. In addition, a lot can be learned about joint placement and movement just by focusing on one's own body and doing a few range-of-motion (ROM) tests. A TD can benefit from acting out motions just as an animator can from acting out his scene. We build up a mental picture over time of what we think we know about the body and joint placement, but we need to continuously challenge this image by studying reference materials and re-evaluating how our own bodies move. Studying these motions helps with character joint placement, figuring out the rotation order of your controls, and seeing how big an area is affected during movement in skin and muscle. So after you've studied up on what is anatomically accurate, get up out of your chair to observe how some of the following body parts really work.

The Foot and Ankle

Let's begin this process of movement analysis with the foot. For example, watch how your foot rolls off the ground. The reverse foot style rigging is now as much a standard as IK chains, but as people get used to doing something, the chances for new observation or enhancement become limited. Think about the movement of the foot inside of a shoe—for example, your character's foot will act differently depending on the type of shoe it's wearing and even more differently if it is barefoot. The foot bones will splay and spread out on a bare foot and roll off the blade of the foot or the inside ball of the foot, depending on the character.

The foot inside of a shoe will interact with the ground differently, is at a different height, and depending on how tight the shoe fits, will slip inside the shoe mesh at the back, lifting slightly during a walk or run. The pivot locations and distance to the bend in a shoe are going to be different than on the bare foot and when you place your joints you have to take this into consideration as well as the ankle height. A very recent example of a complex set of foot/shoe/leg rigging was the character of Puss in Boots from *SHREK 2*. Puss has articulated boots that are built around a more humanlike leg, but he can pull his leg out of the boots, at which point the leg and toes more closely follow a real cat's anatomy, with individual toes and animal-like hind legs. This kind of complex layering of pivots between the boots with two kinds of leg controls and structures is a perfect example for grasping the idea of rigging outside of the basic reverse foot rig. This is much like an IK/FK rig, but with many more options to consider.

Still looking at your reference material of your foot, ask yourself if the character is flat-footed? If it is, then the spread of the foot is even more drastic and causes the inside of the ankle to drop and roll to the inside of the foot. This motion happens with shoes on as well. The older the shoe, the less arch support it has and the more the ankle rolls in, causing the shoe to spread out. If the foot has a high arch, then the opposite action will occur. As the foot moves, it will roll off the edge or blade of the foot affecting how the motion looks all the way up the leg, just like the flat foot. All these details might all sound like overkill, but if you have ever looked at the wear patterns on your own shoes or someone else's shoes, you will see how your body distributes its weight and energy and what parts of the foot are in contact with the ground the most. Your texture artist can play to this fact—models can be adjusted, animators can tweak animation to sell this character trait, but it has to be planned from the start from character design all the way through final animation. It's these kinds of details that let you create more believable characters and rigs.

Foot Joints versus Rig Joints

A real foot has 31 joints or pivot points. The amount of joints that the foot needs to create this range of motion when rigged is not practical to animate. The basic foot rig has joints placed at the ankle, mid foot, and toe. This is usually enough for most characters, but can be augmented and should be for more complex foot interactions.

When choosing the best location to place the main joints for the foot, it is usually better to place them on the bottom of the foot mesh and down the center. The ankle joint placement works best when you split the difference between the inner and outer joint locations and have it slightly to the front of the real joint location. This can help with the skin bunching at the front and the back of the heel. Looking at the toe, the joint is placed along the ground around the center and forward of the main ball of the foot. This gives you a bit of an unrealistic foot flex since real foot joints actually run high through the foot, but it helps with ground contact, and if weighted properly, allows the foot to arch down nicely (see Figure 6.1). An alternate location for that main toe joint would be up slightly and more in the center of the ball/big toe attachment.

Keep in mind that you can still create a second layer of joints for the foot that does match the real joint locations better, which is driven by the base foot rig joints. This kind of system gives you the ground contact points needed for the rig. You can layer in additional skin joints for control over individual toes. Care must be taken with the new skin joints that during foot roll they rotate properly so as not to cause the toes to slip. However, using Set Driven Keys, you can make the new joints react and move out of the way if needed (see Figure 6.2). The Hulk's feet in *The Hulk* and Gollum in *Lord of the Rings* are great examples where you can clearly see non-shoed, fully articulated feet.

Even though we are showing an extra layer of toe joint, keep in mind that we are still just talking about joint placement for the base skeleton. Toes can really be thought of as a secondary layer of joints. If you want to apply motion capture, for example, it's easier to drive a regular two-joint foot rig that then, in turn, drives a more complex set of foot joints, rather than trying to directly map a simple mocap skeleton to a large number of joints.

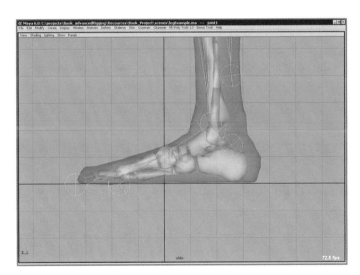

Figure 6.1
Initial joint placements for the foot.

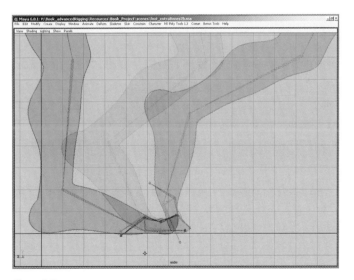

Figure 6.2
These joints have been adjusted to allow the toes to rotate properly without any need for Set Driven Key offsets for the toe joints.

Here is a quick tip about deformation. In Figures 6.3–6.5, there are a few extra joints at the heel, back ankle, and calf. These are in areas that need extra control during the smooth bind process and give a very quick initial skin that looks good. The joint affects skin areas based on where it is in the hierarchy. So keep in mind where the skin helper joints are parented in so that you get better initial skinning. Otherwise, a joint that is in the right area to skin to, but not at the same joint level as another joint in the area, will auto-skin differently depending on the tool settings. You can change the smooth skin options to bind where the joint is in relation to the vertices—fingers, legs, and toes, for example, do not skin well with this option, but other areas of the mesh skin better initially. Both ways work, and you should try both to see what gets you closer to the end result you want. These extra joints can then be used to fake muscles and skin slide.

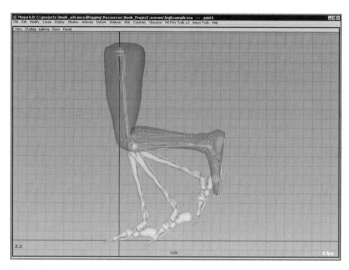

Figure 6.4
CG joints compared to real skeleton joints in motion.

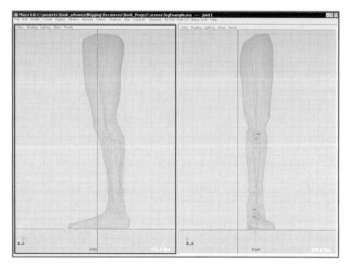

Figure 6.3
Extra-smooth skin joints in place.

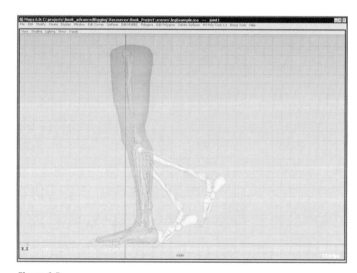

Figure 6.5
Skeleton and CG joints comparison continued. Notice the joint location is between the real bones and slightly to the front to help keep the feeling of a kneecap under the skin.

The Wrist and Elbow

We have all seen the painfully visible sings of bad wrists on 3D characters when the skin pinches flat or twists 180 degrees and the vertices pinch into a point. Also, you might notice that a lot of motion-captured characters have very overdone or exaggerated wrist movement, making a good motion look very puppet-like or fake. A real wrist does not lose volume during deformation and actually expands as tendons pull against the wrist when flexing up and down. The main motion of the wrist is easy to see, flexing up and down and side to side and twisting, but there are a few things that can be a little confusing when rigging. One thing is that the twisting that happens in the wrist is not located at the wrist at all. It happens from the elbow down. If you have your hand planted or are grasping something and try to twist your hand, it looks like your wrist is doing some twisting but what is happening is that all the bones that make up your hand are flexing, giving the appearance that your wrist is twisting separately from your hand (see Figure 6.6).

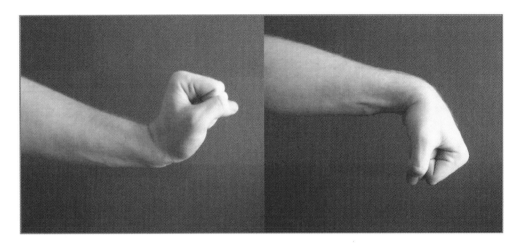

Figure 6.6
Wrist in flexion and extension. Please see **WristHandFingers.MPG** video example on the download section of the book's Web site for a moving reference of the hand and wrist in motion.

To compare the localized twisting of the forearm to the accumulated twisting (including the shoulder) of your entire arm, first straighten your arm and then twist your hand as far as it can go palm down and twist back to palm up. Notice that the upper arm and shoulder were active and generating a large amount of the twisting action, adding to what the lower arm was able to twist. Now bend your arm and do the same twisting action. This time you have localized the twist to just the lower arm bones, but notice that the bicep and triceps muscles are active during this twisting. Most skinning rigs do not take into account that when you're twisting your wrist, the muscles that cause the twist are above the joints, not below them, which is why the bicep and triceps look active during twist movement in the wrist and forearm. Look at any character rig, and you will find the same common setup: a shoulder control, a hand, and a separate arm control to IK to pose the arm, and a way to control the elbow with some kind of pole vector constraint. Grab any one of the controls and most likely they only will affect one part of the arm, not as a whole interconnected system. For animation, you want your controls to act like this, but for deformations, you want the skin to feel like its acting together across the joint boundaries.

When placing the wrist joint, it can be centered in the mesh, but if it's slightly higher in the skin, then it will help keep the feeling of bone under the skin. It should be placed inline or slightly back from the end of the ulna to allow the vertices to make a nice arching path and not just twist in on themselves. If you can use more joints, you can add a smaller joint that goes between the end of the arm and the hand joints, which lets you get a nice natural deformation across this area, emulating the large number of bones in that area of the hand.

Continuing on with our look at the lower arm and its joint locations, we discover a few things that are not easily dealt with when rigging realistic arms. First, looking at your own arm or an anatomy reference, you'll notice that the arm is not in a straight plane from the shoulder to the wrist. Once you get to the elbow, the radius and ulna angle out away from the plane of the shoulder and elbow; then they move into more of an aligned plane as you bring the wrist closer to the shoulder. Since 3D IK solutions like the joints need to be all on the same plane, we have to fudge this part of the anatomy a bit. If you just draw out the arm joints where you think they should go in the mesh, you might find that the joints are not aligned properly. If you draw them in a straight line first and then rotate them and translate the joints on x only for proper length, you will be able to properly locate the elbow and then the wrist inside the mesh, while still allowing the IK solver to work properly later on.

The elbow usually gets placed close to the arm center or offset slightly toward the top of the forearm when viewed from the front and placed just past where you think the real elbow joint is indicated in the mesh and toward the back of the arm from a side view. This helps with keeping the feeling of bone under the surface as the skin deforms.

A good deal of the joint placement in the arm and the forearm is affected by how the model was built and what pose it's in. Remember that your role is to make the character look correct during animation and deformation, so if you need to request that the model be adjusted to work, better speak up. Go talk to the modeler and work out what changes to the mesh will work best for your joints and skinning, as well as the character model/design that you're trying to stay true to graphically.

The Head and Neck

Joint placement for the head and neck can be very straightforward, but it can be more of a problem area than people think. Most of the time the problem with the neck and head joints is that they are placed down the center of the mesh and not placed where the real joints rotate from. Other common placement problems occur when the base neck joint is placed too high or too low vertically in the mesh. Also, the head joint is often found placed at the base of the character's jaw line where it attaches to the neck, or worse, it is centered between the head and body, making it very difficult for proper deformation or motion to happen (see Figure 6.7).

We find it helps out a great deal if you can place the joints into the rough mesh or lined up against the model sheets so that you can hand off the skeleton to the modeler early. It helps keep the Character TD and the modeler in better contact with each other if you are both referencing one another's work like this, and you can catch problems in the design at an earlier stage.

Have the modeler create a template file that has the model sheets in it that he will build the character from. Save it in the model directory.

Then the Character TD can reference (xRef in 3ds Max) this file into the 3D software and create a joint template file. Save this into the rig directory.

At this point, the modeler can reference your jointTempate file into his model file where he can check the joint placement compared to the mesh and use the joints as guides during the final modeling.

If it looks like there is something placed incorrectly, you now have two people looking at the locations of the joints, which should help catch potential problems. The modeler can also do quick skinning on the joints to test how the mesh is holding up or use them as modeling aids to deform the mesh.

For people using Max and Character Studio, this head and neck joint placement problem is even more evident because of the default way that the Biped (skeleton) files are created. See the red dots in Figure 6.8 for an example of where the biped skeleton defaults its joint pivots, compared to where they should be placed.

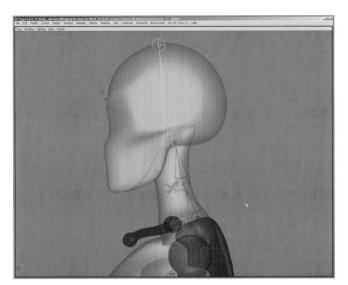

Figure 6.7
Poor neck placement showing both a centered skeleton and a head joint that is placed mid-neck and not at the skull pivot point.

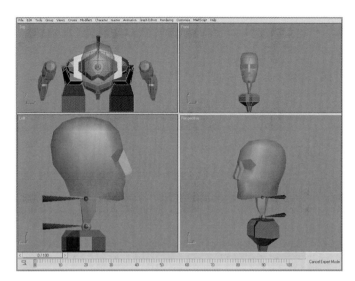

Figure 6.8
Locations of the default biped skeleton cause problems unless adjusted.

Because we watch the head and face of a character more than any other parts of the body, we need to make sure the joint placement allows the head to pivot and move in a way that looks natural on the character. Even if the joint is placed in the wrong location, the head movement might initially look fine, depending on what the motions are on that bone.

To understand where your skull pivots, you can try this example. While keeping your neck still, tilt your head up and down; you can feel where the skull connects and pivots on the tip of the neck column. Placing your fingers on the back of your neck now, do it again. You should feel the rotation of the skull, and at the same time, the tensing and outward and downward pull from the muscles that tilt your head. Now, if you grab and rotate the head bone of your character and it is rotating from the middle of the neck, you know that you have placed it in the wrong location. Basically, if you rotate the head joint, it should rotate almost in place and not move back and forth (see Figure 6.9).

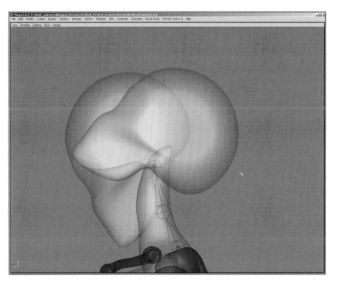

Figure 6.9
Proper head pivot location at base of skull.

69

The same process can be done for the neck to let you get a feel for how the joints contribute to each motion of tilt, roll, and twist. This time keep your head still and just let your neck and head fall forward. You will feel the pull down into your back and shoulder blades. Feeling at the back of your neck, you will find a bump—it's a vertebra, the 7th cervical vertebra, and that is where the neck starts its main rotation (see Figure 6.10).

To insure proper joint placement, you can place that one joint at the neck base just a little bit underneath the surface, still following any anatomical guide reference that you have. Basically, where that 7th vertebra that you felt on the back of your neck is located is where you want to place it. On more stylized characters or strange creatures, you should still watch and make sure that the head and neck transform in a natural way, but the position is less critical as long as it deforms well and does not cause any animation problems.

When drawing the joints for the neck, you can jump out of order in the placement, starting with the head and then doing the neck. You can lay out your joints in any order you like. We will usually draw all the joints for the root to the head in one pass, but we adjust them out of order to help make sure we get the important pivot point setup first, like the base of the neck and the base of the skull in Figure 6.11. Once those are right, we can add in extra joints or adjust any other neck joints that we might have (see Figure 6.12).

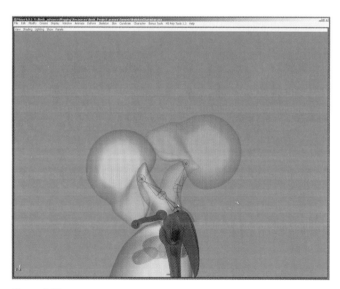

Figure 6.10
Movement of the neck and head.

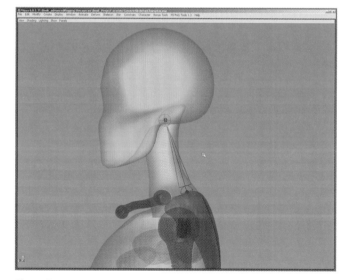

Figure 6.11
Initial placement of main neck and head joint.

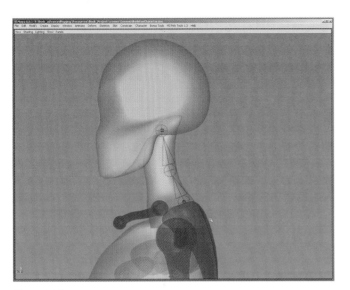

Figure 6.12
Neck bone split and center neck joint adjusted to correct location.

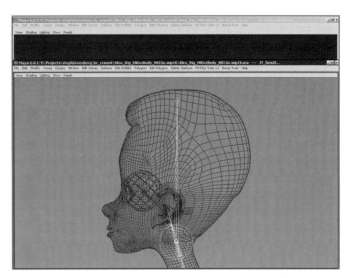

Figure 6.13
Stylized joint placement breaks our rules of proper positioning. (Model and rig courtesy of Steph Greenberg.)

In Figure 6.13, the joint placement is not accurate for human anatomy, but the style of the model is more exaggerated, so the skeleton position is adjusted to work within the constraints and requirements of both the character and animation. It happened that having the joint at the base of the head worked better for the deformation of the overall head-neck attachment.

The Waist and Lower Back

Hips, pelvis, waist, root, and center of gravity are all names for the center of your character. It's a power center for motion, reacting and initiating changes in the entire body and receiving them back from the legs and spine. It translates, rotates, and flexes, shifting weight from one leg to the other, acting as the source for posture or attitude for animators, and allowing us to walk. It is the anchor point for large amounts of intertwining muscles that all are constantly pulling on each other with large amounts of force. The pelvic triangle is another area that is often built incorrectly and the cause of bad deformation and unnatural movement.

When it comes to setting up the points of rotation for this part of the body, it is a bit tricky because the quality of the pelvic movement and deformations is determined by the combination of three joints. Where you place the upper leg joints and starting spine joint are what make your character's pelvis independent from the true root of the character (see Figure 6.14).

Sometimes people try to place the root of the character in the same location as the top of the legs, ending up with the spine and leg joints all in a row. Doing it this way means that the spine joint and the leg joints are in the wrong locations. People may do this for the ability to have the legs in a fixed position with the pelvis rotating around the legs, such as when you're sitting down or leaning over. However, this movement is better left to the separate pelvis controls on the rig, leaving the joints in a more correct anatomical triangle formation.

The Upper Back, Chest, and Shoulder

The upper torso has a very wide range of potential movement when you combine it with the complex action of the upper arm, shoulder blade, and clavicle.

Let's start with the upper chest and work our way down. Most of the main spine motion is limited to the lower back, but we do get some flexing and twist motion from the upper back. Our ribs attach in three sections. Starting from the top down, the first rib clump is attached together at the sternum and to the spine, creating a semiridged structure. These ribs also provide the major stable area that the scapula slides over and interacts with, and they provide a large area for muscle to attach to. The next section of ribs down is a smaller set of three bones, which are more loosely connected to the sternum and therefore flex and move more than the main ribcage. The last two ribs are floating ribs, and they are only attached to the spine joints. Extra joints for the rib cage can be created for help during skinning, but are not necessary. Remember for your base skeleton to keep it as light and fast as possible. You can add all kinds of deformers to your final skin rig later.

In Figure 6.15, you see two back skeletons. The first has a good number of joints for a back rig with each joint sitting at a major point of movement for the spine. The second skeleton is a reduced version of the spine, with the minimum number of joints that you can have for lower/upper back movement, good for background game characters (see Figure 6.16).

Next to it, you can see a reduced or low-resolution back skeleton. This extreme low number of back joints can be used for a background character and also works well for enemy game characters. The joints line up with the main joints on the high-resolution skeleton so that you can map motion from one to the other more easily if you have to. This capability becomes more important when working with mocap and game rigging.

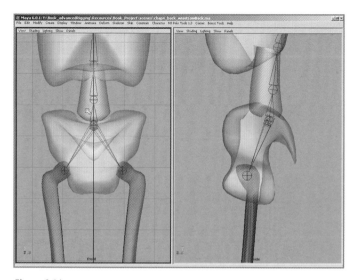

Figure 6.14
Notice the space between the upper legs and the base of the spine—this is the proper configuration of the pelvis. The root joint is the separator between the hips and the spine joints.

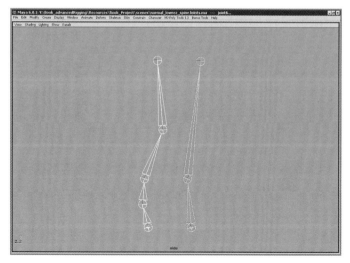

Figure 6.15
Medium- and low-resolution back skeletons.

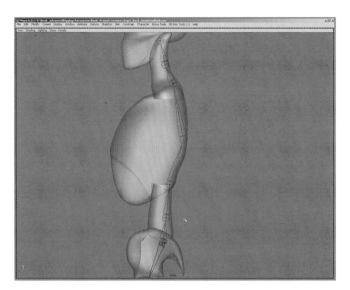

Figure 6.16
Medium-resolution spine skeleton placed in mesh.

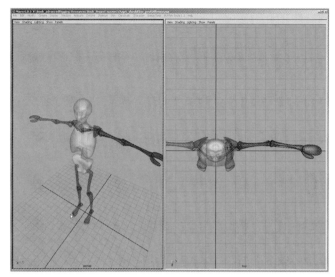

Figure 6.17
The proper clavicle location vs. a centered, improperly positioned clavicle.

The shoulder, the nemesis of many Character TDs, requires a good amount of work to look right during animation. The shoulder area is one of the more complex sets of connections on the body because of its large range of motion and the number of bones and muscles that contribute to that motion. When placing your joints for this section of a character, as always check your anatomy books and feel your own shoulder area. You will quickly see that your clavicle bone is right under the surface of your skin. You'll also notice that it pivots from the front of your chest and not the middle of your shoulder or from your spine. Again, it's common to find examples of rigs that have this joint placed in the center of the body. If the clavicle joint is in the center of the body, then when it rotates from there, you end up with the chest imploding into the body, making for some strange-looking motion. It also gives animators more trouble in posing the character. This small fact has a huge impact on how the shoulder works and looks when animated (see Figure 6.17).

When you reach forward, the entire shoulder structure rotates and translates forward and in, pulling the chest into a V-like wedge (see Figures 6.18–20). The shoulder blades slip over the rib cage, and the muscles and connecting tissue keep your shoulder in its socket as the shoulder region moves forward. Try reaching for something without letting your clavicles rotate and see the effect it has on your ability to reach for an object. Characters that have to use two-handed weapons can be very difficult to make look right if the shoulders of the characters do not work correctly in your rig.

The shoulder blade (scapula) pivots from its top corner where it joins with the clavicle. Your rig can be as simple as a single joint that transforms, or it can be an object that is influencing the skin and slides along a surface, emulating the movement of bone over the rib cage. It can rotate and translate independently of the clavicle and arm since it's an attachment point for many muscles that all can pull in different directions. Depending on the motion of the arm, the scapula can undergo a wide range of automatic movement. There are a few quick ways to emulate this motion, and depending on how detailed or how

73

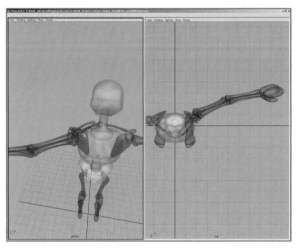

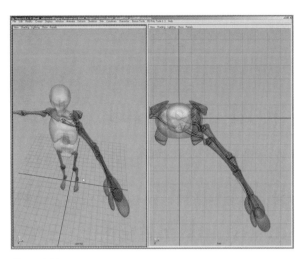

Figure 6.18
This shows the difference in motion between the clavicles in both the proper and improper locations. Take notice of the differences in reach distance along with where the mesh bone ends up—one pivots forward while the other rotates inside of the body.

Figure 6.20
And we see the problem again with rotation of the arm back. This shows clearly how one joint placed in the wrong location can cause problems for deformation later, no matter which direction it's rotating in.

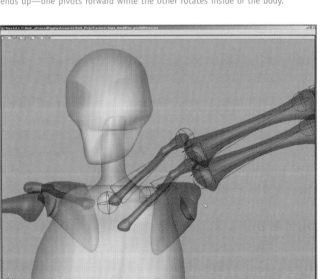

Figure 6.19
Notice the same problem happens during the arm raise as well.

accurate you want to be, there are two main pivot locations that are used. The first one is to have the scapula pivot from around the same location where the shoulder socket and clavicle meet. Starting the joint from here gives you a quick and controllable way to have the scapula behave somewhat realistically and help with skinning. This is not very accurate, but it works well enough.

A more accurate variation on this is to place the pivot in and down on the surface of the scapula as this is closer to where the bone actually rotates and slides from. It requires a bit more setup, but once skinned, you get a great feeling of the bone sliding under the surface of a mesh. See Figure 6.21 for pivot location and also the angle that the joint should spin on. The range of movement and the area that the scapula can slide is shown in Figure 6.22.

Let's look at the head of the upper arm bone. This joint location is a bit more complex than people account for when first looking at a character. At first glance, when you lift your arm it looks like it just rotates a little until the rest of the shoulder takes over and finishes lifting the arm up. This is a very simplistic view of this joint's motion. In reality, during the movement of most joints, like the shoulder, the center of rotation is actually constantly changing as the bones slip against one another, adding translation to the rotating joint. It is not practical in current 3D software to accommodate for what we will call *rotational offsetting* when using default IK solvers. The best thing to do with current 3D joint and bone systems is to find the best average for the rotation pivot and then using deformers, account for the effect of rotational offsets on the skin, rather than trying to write a new solver.

One approach is to offset the shoulder joint down slightly from the end of the clavicle joint, as shown in Figure 6.23. This has an added benefit of effectively adding an extra layer of separation onto the skinning, so that upper arm twisting is limited to the shoulder socket and not having to rotate or twist up into the chest mesh area. If you do not have this option due to mocap or game platform limits, it is better to run the shoulder joint higher in the skin than normal in order to help keep the deformations from flattening out the shoulder mesh, and it helps in keeping the volume of the shoulder area.

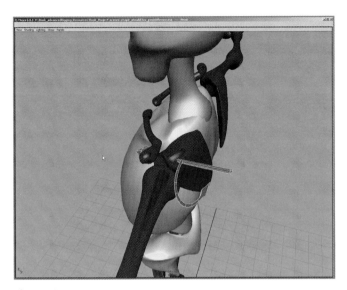

Figure 6.21
Point of rotation for the shoulder blade.

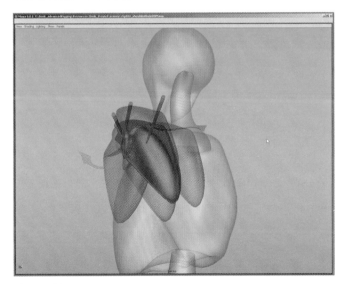

Figure 6.22
General range of motion for the scapula.

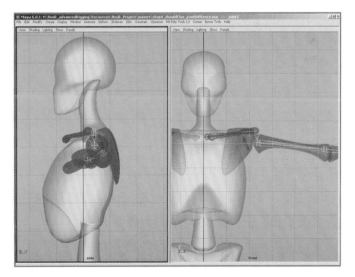

Figure 6.23
Joint offset of the upper arm from the clavicle/shoulder blade attachment.

Once you have the clavicle, shoulder joint, and scapula joints in place, the majority of the work happens in controlling the deformations with skin weights and other deformers. This comes down to understanding where each bone takes over throughout the range of motion, as well as what muscles are active during that motion along with their effect on the skin surface.

Hands and Fingers

The hands and fingers can be as complex to build and skin as any part on the body—it's comparable to rigging up five tiny arms. Each joint can curl on its own, but can flex back when doing things such as pushing down on a table. Most character finger rigs have one joint for the palm of the hand and then the fingers start at the knuckles. While this works fine, it can be very limiting to your animators. (Yes, this theme repeats itself a lot in this chapter.)

The metacarpal joints for each finger start just after the carpals in the wrist area and allow the hand to cup, flex, and spread out when weight is applied. These extra joints should be added to your character's hands to give the animators extra control to reach all of the very expressive sets of poses that can be formed by our hands. One reason for a cg character's hands to appear stiff or unnatural is because of the lack of joints and oversimplification in this area, along with poor placement.

After you have one set of joints created and oriented properly, duplicate that chain and then adjust it to fit into each finger. As you adjust the joints, make sure that the hand mesh and fingers are modeled in an arch formation because the knuckles are not in a straight line, and the mesh should not be either. Even on a nonrealistic character or creature, you will not want all the joints in a straight line.

For the fingers and the joints to work better for skinning, place them high and forward from where the joint is indicated on the mesh. This causes the skin vertices to push out slightly at the knuckle and compress up into the crease on the belly of the finger. In this case, we want to reference real anatomy, but then adjust the pivot locations until we get a proper feel from the skin that we are deforming. Keep in mind that we want to maintain mesh volume and silhouette at all times unless adjusted by the animators (see Figure 6.24).

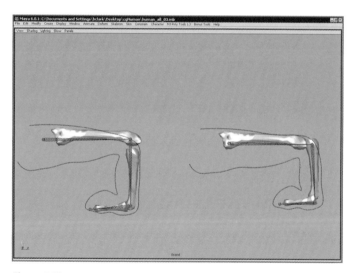

Figure 6.24
You can see the joint placement's effects on skinning on the fingers. Also notice the difference in the bones—one rotates around the tip of the parent bone and the other pivots in place.

Dependencies in the Pipeline: Research Beyond Anatomy

Beyond all the anatomy research, there is a whole different kind of research that the Character TD must do. This falls into the areas of animation requirements, user interface, and tools for the rig. Also things like internal and external pipeline requirements should be double-checked before starting the rig process.

The Animator: Friend or Foe?

Getting animators to sign off on the rig is an important aspect of the early rig design. This means that you have to talk with the animators and get to know how they like to work. If there is time available, it's good to sit with the animators and watch them animate because seeing how they use their current rig will help you understand quickly how they like to work. This also has an added benefit of just getting face time with people whom you will be making tools for and having to support, train, and work with throughout the production. During this process, you can and should be talking over with the animation leads any shots that might require special case rigs or an enhancement to the base rig.

Getting animators to accept a new rig that is different from what they were used to before can take a much longer time than people first plan for. The Character TD can ease this by keeping the animation team involved in the design of the rig early, allowing for input at any time. Setting up a Web site or a plain whiteboard for people to post ideas on and request features also helps the animators feel as though they have a say in their tools. They will be more receptive to the new tools, rigs, or workflow changes that happen if they have contributed to them. Training time and properly updated documentation of all tools using short screen-capture movies will also help prepare the animators before they get the rig.

Pipeline Planning and Questions

Another important area that the Character TD must be aware of is the pipeline requirements for the rig. There are few things worse than getting deep into production and then realizing that all the characters need to be adjusted or changed or exported to different software because of a simple oversight. This is not always avoidable, but every effort should be made to make sure you, the Character TD, know the production path for the character assets. Here are some guidelines for your current or new pipeline.

◆ Is the character staying in one software package for a show? Must it be able to be exported to another 3D application, and if so, what application and what format will be used to transfer it? What needs to transfer? Animation only, bones and skin, the whole shot with rigs? Baked mesh objects?

◆ Does the rig need to be used with mocap or just hand animation? This can mean that you need to add extra controls to your rig to allow the import and offsetting of mocap data. You might have to export the character to Motionbuilder for the motion-capture editing.

◆ What format will the mocap be in if it is brought into Maya or other 3D software? What effect does this have on your skeleton's joint orients and number and name of joints?

◆ Is there going to be cloth, and, if yes, will that cloth be rigged by hand or done with simulation or both?

◆ What will be the standard way to update a change on a character throughout the production? Animation transferring with Trax or custom script, file referencing, importing of skin rig and hooking it up to the animation rig?

◆ How will you track changes and fixes on the rig and in the files? Adding hidden attributes into the Maya file that keeps track of the date rigged and what scripts were run on it with version numbers and by whom are all great things to stick in the file. Maya has a Notes area on all nodes that can be updated with this information. Max has several places to store this as well, at the scene level or on the object as user properties.

The better the Character TD understands the entire path for the character, the better his work will be.

Applied Anatomy Using Animal and Human Anatomy as Reference for a Fantasy Creature: The pigGoblin

To start the rigging process for the character in this book, you need to build the skeleton that you will rig in Chapter 7. You can start from scratch or follow along by just downloading the model file, mesh_PigGoblin from the Web site (www.courseptr/downloads).

1. To start the rig for this character, you will set up a quick reference file system to make sure that the mesh is always the most current in the rig file. This will also keep the rig files smaller since we are not saving a new copy of the mesh in every file. For this system, create a file structure that starts with the type of asset; in this case, it's a character asset.

2. Create a folder called *Characters*. Inside of Characters, create a folder with the initials of the character name, PG for pigGoblin. Once in the PG folder, create a model folder and a rig folder. The final version of the mesh file will be saved in the models folder named mesh_"name" and then referenced into a new file that is going to be saved in the rig folder.

3. Create a new file in Maya and reference the mesh_PigGoblin file, but use the namespace option and under "this string" type in mdl (short for model), as in Figure 6.25. Then pick the mesh_File. Save this file in the rig folder as template_pigGoblin. This will become the working template file from which the rest of the rig will be built.

> The final directory structure can be adjusted as to how you like to work or how the current pipeline works at your company. This is just one recommended way of working. More pipeline issues will be covered in later chapters.

4. Before you start placing joints for this character, create a layer for the referenced character mesh and set it to reference so that it does not interfere with your joint placement. New in Maya 6 is the capability to automatically assign the objects you have selected to the layer, again saving you a few clicks. Go to Layers→Create New Layer→options and set the check box to "Selected and Children" (see Figure 6.26).

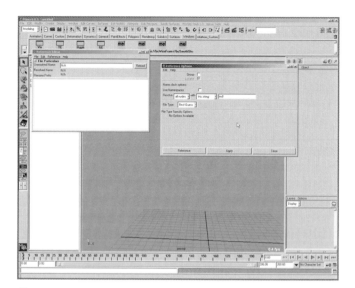

Figure 6.25
Set up the initial file reference from which to build the skeleton.

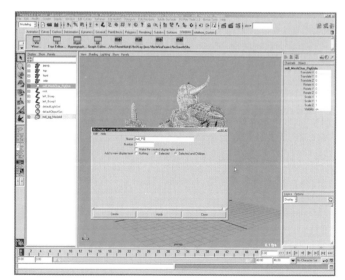

Figure 6.26
The new Maya 6 layer options.

Template Joint Placement

The concept of the template file is that it allows you to quickly place and test out the joints for the character. At this point, you're not concerned with joint angles or making sure the joint rotations are zero or that the joint orients are correct. Those things are a technical concern and will be fixed later. Right now, you just want the locations to be correct and make sure that all the joints of your base skeleton are there.

Looking over our character, we can tell right away that there are going to be some joint areas that we need to know about and understand. Since this character looks to be a mix of a pig and a biped, we will search for some pig anatomy and do some quick sketches of where our joints should go and of the general arcs that the character's skin will follow. These early drawings and studies help to let the Character TD explore placement ideas without having to be in the software. In Figure 6.27, there is a quick sketch of a real pig's leg. On the left, these joints are placed to help with overall deformation and rigging taking into account the skin. The joint locations on the right show where the joints need to be in order to have the skeleton animate correctly, but without accounting for the skin. Also, note the pivot location is not at the space between the joints, but actually before the next joint in the chain, allowing the bone to rotate around its parent joint like the real bone does. In Figure 6.28's image, there is a screen grab from Maya with our sketch for the rough joint locations, other deformers needed, possibly for clothes, and notes on the other rigging needs for the character. From quick sketches like this and close study of our reference materials, we can start on the 3D scene placing joints.

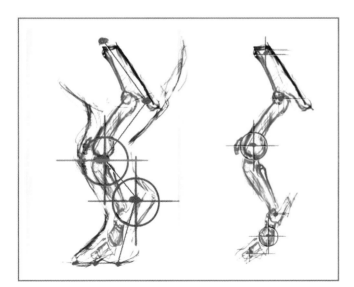

Figure 6.27
An example of how the joint placements differ on a realistic pig skeleton, one accounting for the skin and the other accounting for proper bone movement.

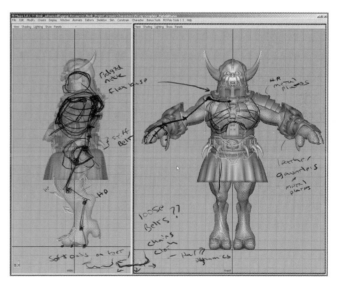

Figure 6.28
Rough joint layout sketch for our main character.

Joint Placement

Now that the folders and files are set up, you can start placing the joints for the character.

1. Start out the skeleton with the root and run up the joints for the back. From our other reference of the spine, you know where the real spine separates into its areas of flexibility. The limited number of joints is really the least you can have and still have a full range of motion (see Figure 6.29). The more nuances and subtle movements needed in the character, the more joints you will need to spread the motion across. The more joints you add, though, the more work it is to rig and skin. In most cases, you can and want to use the smaller amount of joints. Make sure that the back joints are where you need them since all the other joints are based off these joints. Because this character is covered in armor and has thick belts, you should experiment on how close to the center of the character you want to run the spine bones. Sometimes, tiny adjustments can have a large impact on how the mesh reacts once skinned. Still try to keep the joints off-centered to the back in the character mesh since having them centered leads to more work for the animators trying to make the character move naturally.

2. Next, create the leg joints, starting in the side view and placing the starting joint forward and down from the root based on where the hip joint would be. The knee and what would be the ankle on this character are placed a bit offset from where the real bone and joints would be to aid in the deformations. In the front view, you can see that we have shifted the leg joints toward the outside of the leg and not right down the center. Because of this character's wide hips and thick legs, this placement handles the deformation better here. Figure 6.30 shows the finished leg joints for the character.

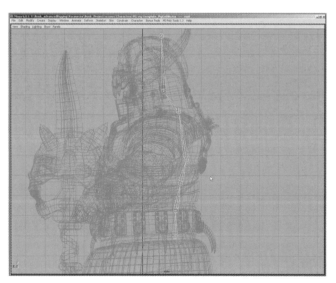

Figure 6.29
Initial joint layout for our main character.

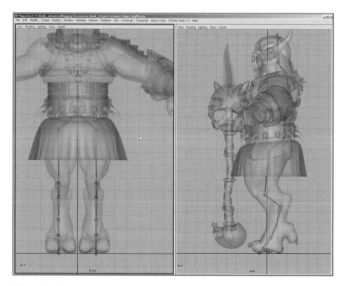

Figure 6.30
Final leg joints for the character. Compare these to our pig leg sketch and see what we used from the sketch and what we did not. The toes are a little different because some of those pivot locations will come from the rig and not the skeletons.

3. Before you parent your legs to the root, there are a few ways to hook up the legs and spine to the root of the character. Each one has a different effect, but the end result is the same: separation of the upper body from the lower body.

◆ The first way is to just parent the spine and legs directly to the root. By default, this does not let you rotate the pelvis separate from the spine; you have to counter-animate the spine against the root for this to work. For a game character when bone count is limited, then this is fine and can be worked around once rigged.

◆ The second way is to duplicate the root to make a "hip" joint that will be a child of the root and be the parents of the legs. This lets you rotate the hips without affecting the spine, but the root still affects the overall pose of the character and its spine.

◆ The third way is to add one more spine base joint, again duplicating the root joint and making this new joint the parent of the spine. This might be a bit of overkill, but it helps keep your spine and leg joints from having to counter-rotate and avoid gimbal lock on root node.

4. Arms can be difficult to place, but we have lots of references to go from and also our initial sketch should help with the placement. Looking at Figure 6.31, you can see how later you will want to adjust the bone rotation to match the mesh orientation. Starting with the clavicle, place it first and then draw out to the shoulder. The shoulder joint should be placed high and to the outside of the chest area, since the arm has to bend down and lay next to the character's side. Try to make sure that this joint when rotated down is next to the ribs, not inside them. That is the easy quick check to see if you have placed the shoulder joint too far in to the body (see Figure 6.32).

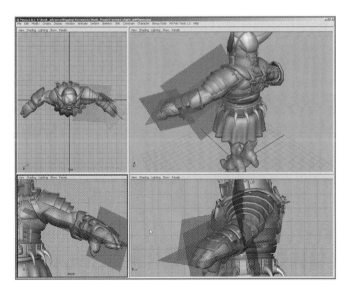

Figure 6.31
Planes that the joints will be oriented to. Notice that the upper and lower arm are not in the exact same plane.

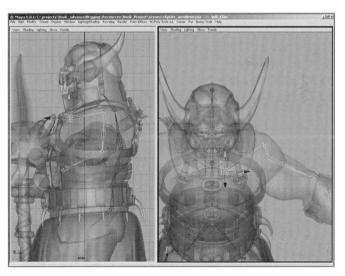

Figure 6.32
Here we have the first pass on the clavicle and arm joints.

In a game skeleton, you might not find a double-shoulder joint, but in this character you are going to offset down the real shoulder joint from the clavicle and in doing so will create an extra layer of skinning separation in an area that is always difficult to skin. This little extra joint offset lets you have a good control over the skinning for most motions (see Figure 6.33)

5. Placing the elbow next, run it just past the point of the elbow surface detail on the mesh. This placement helps when the arm bends to keep the feeling of bone under skin as the arm flexes (see Figure 6.34).

6. The wrist joint location is above center in the hand and behind the seam between the wrist and the hand. Along with the second joint right after the main wrist, that helps with up and down flexing of the hand (see Figure 6.35).

7. Parent the arm joint onto the chest joint "spine06" and then mirror this joint chain.

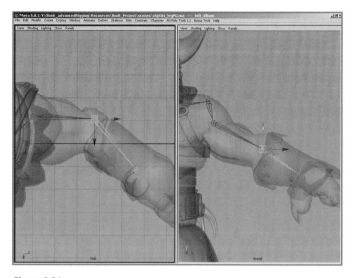

Figure 6.34
Placement for the elbow joint.

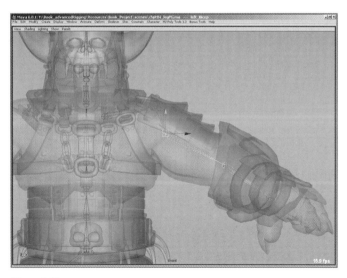

Figure 6.33
Here we have the second pass on the clavicle and arm joints.

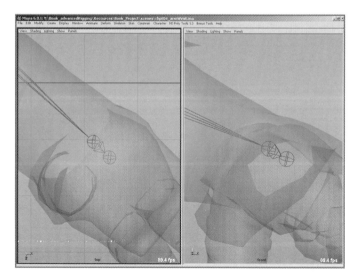

Figure 6.35
Here we have the first placement of the wrist joints.

The main template for this character is now complete. This is about the minimum amount of joints you can have and still have this character be usable. It could have a low resolution mesh assigned to it and be used in crowd software like Massive or exported to a game engine. Also, this kind of lightweight skeleton would accept motion capture data very well since it is really just a regular biped-type skeleton. Next, you will go in and add a few more joints for this character to finish out the details, such as hands and toes.

Template Joint Placement Continued—Extremities

Fingers and hands are often hard to build when they are at an angle, so we will build one hand so that it is world-aligned and then move and rotate it into place.

1. Start in the top window and create joint chains as in Figure 6.36 by snapping a new joint to the grid until you have five joints.

2. Duplicate this chain twice and move them off to the side.

3. Group them together temporarily so you can move and rotate them as a whole into place at the character's hand. Adjust the pivot of the group as needed (see Figure 6.37).

4. Fit the joints to the fingers and thumb. Because this character has large hoof-like nails on his fingers, we have used an extra joint to allow for flexing of this nail and help with the ability to pose the hands. Also, notice that the finger joints are placed high in mesh, again where the real bone is closer

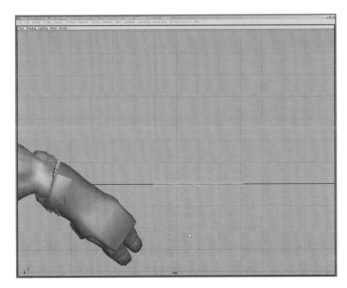

Figure 6.36
Snap out initial finger joints.

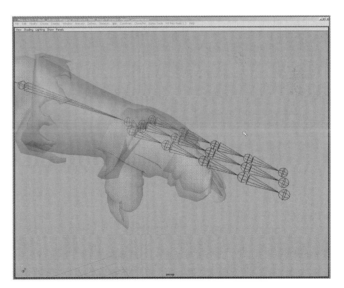

Figure 6.37
Finger joints aligned to wrist.

to the surface. This helps in making it look like there is bone under skin (see Figure 6.38).

5. Now select the tops of each finger joint and parent them to the end wrist joint. You can then just mirror over the hand joints to make sure they line up correctly on the other side.

6. The last part of creating this character is to add in the extra layer of toe joints like we did on the hand. This character has unique feet, and because he is barefoot, we have to add in individual toes. Draw out the joints in the side view for the "heelToe" and parent it in to the leg chain, as shown in Figure 6.39.

7. The toe joints will live over the top of the main toe bone in the foot and will allow us to animate each toe individually. Draw them in the side view with the Joint tool and then position them inside the foot and toe mesh (see Figure 6.40).

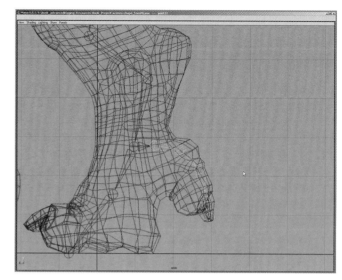

Figure 6.39
HeelToe Joint placement.

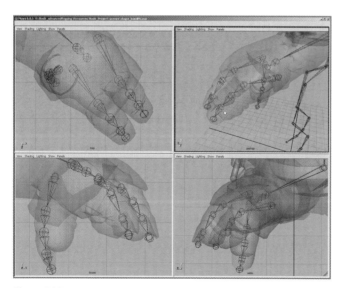

Figure 6.38
Finger joints fit inside of mesh.

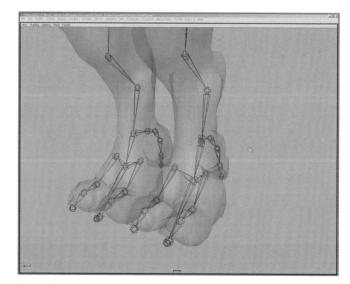

Figure 6.40
Extra smooth skin joints in place.

At this point, you have your main skeleton setup for this character, but remember that this is just a template. None of these joints will be used in our final skeleton or rig. The next stage is to create properly oriented joints that will be usable later. For now, you can do a few quick skin tests to check how the joint placement is going to work and adjust it, if needed. Remember that a small adjustment can have a huge effect on the deformations, so try out a few ideas before you commit the time for proper naming, orientation, and final passes on the skeleton (see Figure 6.41). The next chapter will cover the start of the rigging process with the conversion of the template skeleton into a final skeleton and the creation of the rig (see Figure 6.42).

All great art is based on careful study of reality. Then that reality is re-imagined by artistic interpretation, and you have a final result that is grounded in reality, giving believability to your creations, be it photo, real, or abstract. Great rigs can also be thought of in this way. The Character TD applies his vision and understanding of the research to create a solid skeleton and knows when and how to break the rules of the collected reference material when needed to fit the needs of the character.

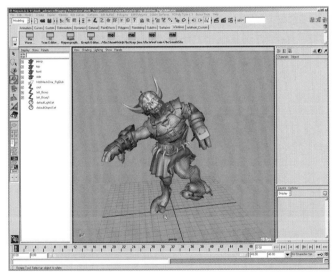

Figure 6.41
Test skin to see how the initial joints work on the mesh.

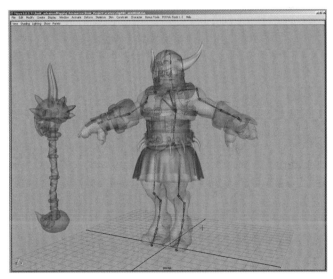

Figure 6.42
Final skeleton ready for the next part of the pipeline.

chapter 7
Stable, User-Friendly, Flexible Rigs

T he main problem with character rigs comes down to making sure the rig has all the control and power that the animator needs and at the same time is easy to understand and use, and should be fast enough to scrub and play back in the view in real time or as close to real time as possible. There are many ways to approach this task of making a rig both fast and powerful, including creating special rigs for each unique set of problems a particular shot might present or building an all-in-one rig that does one hundred percent of what the animator needs ninety percent of the time (and the rest of the time the rig can be added to or tweaked). Rig speed is even more critical once you have several characters in a single scene. For example, an extra expression you added that you thought would be fast is now being called several times over per frame and makes the animator want to pull your arms off for making the file slow. The other area that affects the speed of the rig is the layout and organization of the controls of the character and the custom attributes on those controls. We will talk about strategies for improving these areas in your rigs.

Rig Features

In general, the final control and rig options will be created out of the Character TD meetings with the lead animator. Here are some sample requests from Keith Lango for what he likes and does not like in a rig:

◆ Speed: Make it fast.

◆ Accuracy: Put as much resolution of the final mesh into the rig for checking as possible without impacting speed.

◆ Options: Don't railroad us into a single way of approaching a problem.

◆ Clear parenting constraint systems that are easy to manage (more a tool than a rig thing).

◆ Wrist that follows the arm direction like FK even when in IK mode. The ability to turn that on or off and gimbal correctors that also can be toggled on or off when needed.

◆ Silhouette manipulators for pushing the mesh off the joints for flow, line, and so on (cartoony).

◆ As much flexibility in the face as possible.

◆ No odd ghost keys on objects. (We see this a lot on arms, where the low arm control will have ghost keys for related controls like the wrist or the upper arm, and so on.)

◆ Clear, flexible, and thorough UIs. Any improvement in clearing out screen clutter will be a huge boon.

◆ New technology: On the fly real-time (not cached or sim'ed) surface collision detection that can be turned on or off per object. (This one technology alone would save studios tens of millions of dollars on a typical high-end CG animated film because it would mitigate much of the work done by finishing departments to fix intersections, pokes, penetrations, bad skinning, and so on.)

This is just a quick sample of what an animator wants. Some of the requests might be very difficult to do, but most of the animator's requests are going to be along the same lines: make it fast, easy to use, and give them as much control and detail as possible without trumping the first two issues of speed and control. The last request about the real-time collision detection might not be too far off since it has been reported that in *The Incredibles* by Pixar, they nearly had real-time skin and muscle systems set up for their animators, to the point where they were animating a character that would be what they got when rendered and not a low-res mesh that had to go through a touch-up and simulation pass.

Pixar has custom software that they use for animation. It is not possible for us to have real-time muscle systems in Maya yet, but software like Alias Motionbuilder is a real-time animation package. While this does not yet have a muscle simulation, the Motionbuilder software can play back a skinned mesh with animation exactly as it will look once rendered without having to playblast or preview to see your correct timing, and is a huge time-saver because of this.

Speeding Up Your Rig

Outside of the obvious things that can make a rig slow, such as lots of expressions or having the deforming skin in the file, there are other factors to keep in mind when creating and testing a rig for speed. Something that gets overlooked is documentation and training material for custom tools and rigs. As you might be the sole Character TD, you want to make sure you have documentation on the rig because if you are having to train and do troubleshooting while doing your normal work you can become a bottleneck in the pipeline very quickly.

For people using other software, like Max or XSI, for the most part, you should be able to do everything that we are doing in this tutorial. Be aware that we use groups a lot during this tutorial, and these are just an extra transform node, like a null/locator/point helper in other software. There are scripts for Max, for example, that emulate the grouping function in Maya by creating a point helper and parenting the selected object to it without you having to do this by hand. Figure 7.1 shows a rig in Max that has most of the features the Maya rig has.

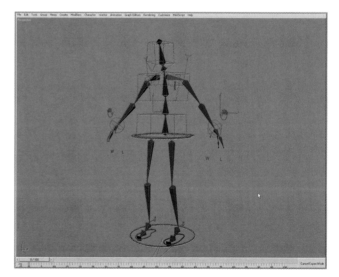

Figure 7.1
Max character rig.

7. Stable, User-Friendly, Flexible Rigs

Making short, detailed video tutorials is a fast way to have training materials for your tools that most people can learn from without you having to be at their desk showing them how to use the rig. This has an added benefit of being able to bring new people up-to-speed on the tools faster than just having them read a document or having to have someone show them how things work.

Keeping the movies updated with the latest tools can also be time-consuming. What works well is to have a few videos for the complicated tools and then small docs that are quick to update with small changes, for example, a record of email updates that are sent to the animators. Because part of your job is fixing and updating the tools during the life of a production, there needs to be a central location for submitting, tracking, and fixing bugs. You can use something simple like a shared Excel spreadsheet that is quick and easy to set up, or you can use a real bug-tracking database, such as bugzilla from http://www.bugzilla.org/, that lets you do real tracking across a large group of animators or remote workers. Another way to create a living rig document is to set up a WIKI server so that people can edit and update the information when needed without having to author the site and then upload the new contents. Check it out at http://www.openwiki.com/ for more information.

Another overlooked requirement of a rig is to be able to control the animation data export and import on the rig, as well as any custom information that is placed on the rig that may not have a keyframe on it. This is where most animation systems break down, but because we are using a two-skeleton system, we can always link the skinned skeleton to the animated skeleton without having to do complex animation transfers. Other ways to transfer animation include using the Trax to transfer animation between rig files or using custom scripts that save and load animation. This falls more into the pipeline area than the rig area, but it is something that should be thought about early in the process.

From Template to Rig

Now that the template skeleton for the character from Chapter 6 is built, we will generate the next part of the rig. This is an actual skeleton that you will skin your mesh to, as well as the base skeleton that all other parts of the rig will be created from. Any of this can be automated, but we will go through the ways to do this by hand first.

In Figure 7.2, you can see that the joint orients on the template skeleton are world aligned from having them all frozen. After we create our new skeleton, the orients will be correctly aligned to the joints.

> XSI and Maya both have very good animation transfer options. Max (without using character studio) has only one tool for loading animation, the Merge Animation script. It has its share of problems if your files are not exactly the same; luckily, it's a script so it can be edited to work better for your production.

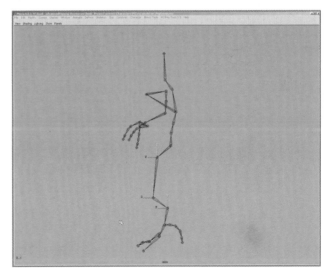

Figure 7.2
World-aligned joint orients.

1. Using the Joint tool, you will use snap-to-point to create (v is the hot key) the new joints over the template skeleton, using it as an exact guide to create the final skeleton. Snap the first new joint to the root and then down the left leg until you have a new skeleton, as shown in Figure 7.3.

   Figure 7.4 shows the same skeleton we just created with its LRA or Local Rotation Axis visible so you can see the final results of creating the new joints. Looking at the joint orients, they are now aligned with the joints, but they are not consistent. That will be fixed later once we finish the rest of the joints for the leg.

2. Continuing the process of snapping new joints over your template, you will finish the toes and parent them to the new skeleton, completing the left leg.

Fixing the LRAs for the skeleton in this case requires us to make sure that they all point in a consistent direction. For this character, we will point the Y axis forward, which makes all the Z axis animation curve data consistent once animated. This is one of the first steps toward creating a solid animation-friendly skeleton. Even plain FK systems should be built to be animated quickly and efficiently, which we would now have if we did no other rigging.

There are several ways to edit the joint orients, with lots of free scripts on the Web, but Alias did a good job updating their own Orient Joint tool (see Figure 7.4).

> To orient the end joints to match their parents, just set the Joint Orient tool orientation settings to "none," and it will set the LRA to match the parent. Or you can just set the orients to zero in the Attribute Editor, but that has to be done one at a time. You can also set the joint orients to zero using the Attribute Spreadsheet, which allows you to edit multiple values at once compared to the Attribute Editor.

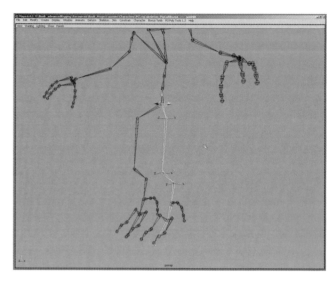

Figure 7.3
Newly created joints.

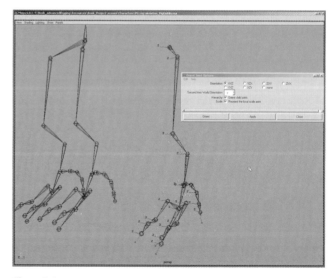

Figure 7.4
New complete leg skeleton with LRA showing and the new Joint Orient tool.

1. Use one of the Orient tools and set the joint orients so that Y is forward and Z is pointing to the right side of the character.

2. Once you have adjusted the orients on the leg to all face the same direction, you might need to rotate some by hand to help finalize the alignment of the joints.

3. Finish off the rest of the left side of the skeleton as you did the left leg and make sure all the joint's LRAs are adjusted correctly.

4. By switching the Second Axis World Orientation setting in the Orient Joint tool, the LRAs can be fixed on the arms and fingers. Fingers, hips, and the chest are harder to adjust because of the strange branching and odd angles at which they are created.

5. To get the root joint LRA to align to the first spine joint, you need to unparent the leg from the root, adjust the joint orient, and then re-parent the leg. You could also adjust it by hand, but this way is a little faster.

Figure 7.5 shows the final joint orients for the skeleton.

We will go through the naming process for the entire joint hierarchy now before we mirror over the leg and arm. Pick names that are short, easy to understand, and be consistent in how you space, capitalize, and number your joints. For this book, we try to use short hints at the start of the name like "bn_upArm_L" basically joint/bone, body part, side of body.

For now we will omit the prefix of "bn" until the end when the rig is done. At this time, while we just have the skeleton in its clean unrigged form, you will want to make a selection set for the individual joints for ease of selection and renaming later on.

1. Using the built-in Prefix tool, you can add the L and R to the start of each joint name in a hierarchy, but we prefer to have this come at the end of the name, which you cannot do with the Prefix tool. To do this, we are going to use the Rename tool from Mike Comet, who has released a very nice suite of Mel tools and plug-ins for Character TDs.

2. Once you have completed adding the suffix, mirror-over the arms and legs and delete the template skeleton.

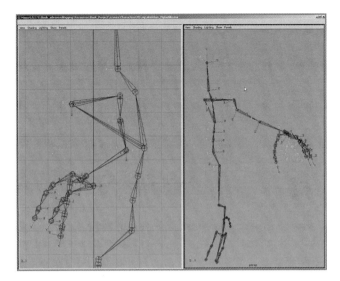

Figure 7.5
New complete left skeleton with LRA showing after tweaks are done.

For left and right naming, you do have the option in the Mirror tool to replace an L with an R, for example, but it will rename any L in the name to R; however, if you have it replace _L for _R, then it will only replace the L with the underscore before it. This is one of the reasons that we leave off the prefix of "bn" until later, after the skeleton mirroring is done, so that the Mirror tool does not rename a "bn_leg_L" to "bn_Reg_R." You could also use Comet's rename script to do search and replace on the mirrored skeleton and not use the Mirror tool rename function.

You can download the Comet scripts from http://www.comet-cartoons.com.

7. Stable, User-Friendly, Flexible Rigs

91

3. The final thing you need to do for this skeleton is to group it once and name the new group node "pgSkeleton," "pg" short for pigGoblin and "Skeleton," which is what the group contains. By doing this we keep the skeleton name non-character specific and also keep any name space problems from affecting our skeleton names if there are several characters loaded into the same file. If we prefixed the entire skeleton and rig with "pg" for the character, then it becomes more difficult to transfer animation from one character to another, adds extra name bits to the file if you have to export to a game engine, and makes it harder to sort and deal with the nodes in general in the Outliner the longer the name becomes (see Figure 7.6).

Hidden Names and Trax

The updated Trax feature in Maya 6 lets you share animation between skeletons. Trax can be used to transfer animation on the same skeleton between files, or it can remap or retarget the motion to a skeleton that is both a different size and proportion. In order to have this work and also make sure that your skeletons are at least Trax-mapping compatible, you must use the new Joint Labeling from the Skeleton-Retargeting menu. (see Figure 7.7).

In Figure 7.8, you can see the Joint Labels; they will be turned off once the labels are finished.

There are a few other things that Trax needs in order to work well, but for the basic capability of retargeting animation, this is what you need.

We are focusing on creating a solid skeleton that will flow into the rest of the setup process, giving us the best foundation we can have. Trax gives us another reason to be consistent with our joint orients on all our skeletons, because in order to have motion map from one skeleton to the next quickly, the local rotation axes need to match or be very close to the skeleton, or the skeleton could freak out and have its arms and legs rotating all different directions—not at all what we want.

Now that the skeleton file is done, we will continue with our rig file where we will build the actual controls and hook up the systems that will eventually drive this skeleton.

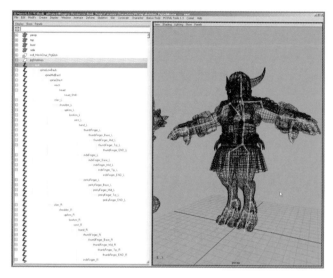

Figure 7.6
Grouped skeleton in the Outliner.

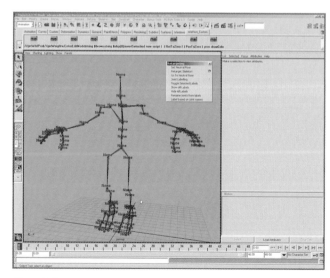

Figure 7.7
Displaying the Trax names for the joints.

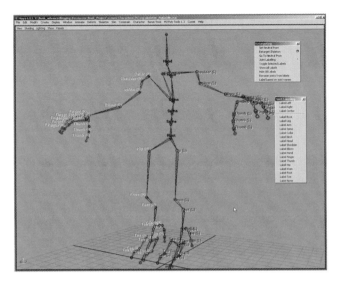

Figure 7.8
Finished joint labels.

You might look at this skeleton and think that it's not done yet, because there are all the extra straps, armor, and weapons still left to finish. And you're right, there are some things left to rig, but we consider these to be a secondary pass of skeleton joints that go on top of the base skeleton since they are not necessary for the core movement of the character. Also, you need to have a file that can be handed off to the animators to test as soon as possible. These items could also be considered a simulation element, which requires different controls than an animation rig.

The Rig File—Low-Resolution Geometry

The rig file is saved as "rig_characterName," in this case "rig_PigGoblin," and in this file we will set up our proxy geometry along with all the rig components needed for animation.

Because we want to hand this file off to the animators as fast as possible, we don't want them to wait on us to skin the mesh before they test the rig or start animating. Creating the low-res mesh can be done a few ways; it can even be automated as shown at the Maya Master Class that Paul Thuriot gave, "Hyper-Real: Body Setup." In that case, you had to have a final mesh or close to final mesh skinned to the skeleton for his script to create the proxy geometry, but it's very fast once you have it even roughly skinned.

The downside is that you need a finished mesh, and in many cases, the rig is needed before the mesh is ready. It can be faster to have the modeler build the proxy mesh. Then the Character TD can break it up and attach it to the skeleton and not wait for a final mesh. No matter how you build the proxy mesh, it should be segmented to match the volume of the character so that the animator knows if he is going to be causing intersection problems with the animation when it is applied to the final mesh. It should be very light with as few polygons as possible, but still stay true to the final model's form. And it should have one mesh object per joint normally to parent or attach in to the skeleton. Some people skin this low-res geometry, but that just causes extra slowdown that is not needed.

A quick tip about the proxy mesh is in order. To help the animators visualize the twisting and rotations on the low-res mesh, you can mark stripes across the separate mesh pieces with coloring on the polygon faces with just a simple material assigned to the faces.

Because the skeleton we skin to and the rig skeleton are separate files, we can do whatever we want to the rig file. One cool thing with the proxy geometry is to use it as the FK rig. For example, instead of having all these extra transform nodes cluttering our hierarchy, these proxy objects can just parent their shape nodes under the joints. This removes the extra nodes from the main scene graph, and it will act as a selection handle for the joints when you want to animate them in FK, if needed.

1. If you just parent the shape nodes to the joints directly, the shape will rotate out of alignment, matching the orientation of the joint.

2. To work around this, you first parent the mesh to the leg, freeze its transform to zero the mesh, and then parent the shape to the joint. There is a free script to do this process from the book's Web site at http://www.courseptr.com/downloads called (bcParentShape.mel). It uses the base Mel command parent -s -r with the joint and the mesh shape selected.

3. After they are parented, just name the shapes to match the joint they are attached to. Using *root* as an example, the shape name should be "root_prxy_Shape," so that you can find the proxy geometry quickly later. You can attach all the shape nodes into the skeleton now or wait until the rig is complete to do it.

4. The last character UI tweak you will do for the animators is to set the colors of the skeleton to match left, right, and center. Some people like to do this with layers, but we like to keep it right on the character without having to worry about whether or not the layers are in the file. Figure 7.9 shows how to use the Drawing Overrides on the top joint of the hierarchy to color the branch: blue for center, green for left, and red for right. You can do this same thing in Max, and most other 3D software has some way to do this kind of coloration.

   Notice that we picked dull-looking colors so that when we color the animation controls later we can use brighter versions of red, blue, and green. They will show up better and be easier to select.

5. For now, we will create a layer for the "prxy" geometry. Using the quick-select field, just type in *prxy* and it will select all the mesh pieces that can be added to a new layer named mdl_prxy_PG. Instead of the layer, you can use custom attributes to control the properties of the "prxy" geometry. The fewer layers you use, the better, because they are very easy to have an animator mess with and break.

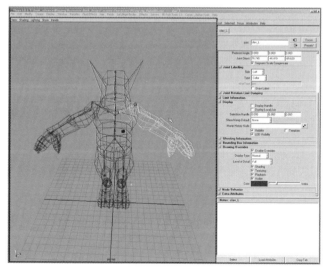

If you use a layer on the prxy geometry, the color settings of that layer will override the colors that were on the mesh. If you don't want to have this happen, you can use the user-defined colors for the mesh. You can use the MEL "color –ud # 1-8" or the gui from the Display→Wireframe Color menu to apply the colors to prxy geo that will not be affected by the layer they are assigned to. The other trick is to make sure there is something connected to the override color before it's assigned to the layer, like a keyframe.

Figure 7.9
Left and right coloration of the skeleton.

The Rig File—Rig Design and Planning

Depending on what point in production you are in when you start to rig, most of the needs for the animators should have been worked out, and now you just have to create the components to make this rig work. However, this almost never happens, so building the rig in a way that is easy to tweak and adjust or build on top of is the goal of proper planning.

Remember that this is the rig file so we can add to the hierarchy, add custom attributes, add dynamics, and add whatever else we want to because the real skeleton that will have the skin on it is in a different file. The advantage of having a plain skeleton as our base file to render is that we can take advantage of blending as many inputs as needed onto that skinned skeleton, whether it is a keyframe or motion-capture or simulation data. Keeping separate rig files from the skin file also makes it easy to update the rig either per shot or across the production and not worry about breaking something on the file that gets rendered or exported (if it's for a game). The downside is that if you need to adjust the skeleton for some reason, then keeping the skin and the rig file skeletons in sync can become a bit of work and is the main reason for having a scripted system for your rig so it only takes a few minuets to change something, and not hours.

When you sit down to begin the rig, there are going to be parts of it that are straightforward and let you rely on your old rigging tricks or styles. There are also things that require new solutions or are open to experimentation with better or easier interfaces for the animators. Because this character is mostly a normal biped, we will be using some rigging techniques that are covered very well in the first *Inspired 3-D Character Setup* book or for the most part are available in numerous forms of free files or tutorials all over the Internet. What this rig does differently is take some of those things and build upon them with advanced interface concepts tricks for speed and flexibility while keeping the complexity for the animator as low as possible. This can be a tough challenge, but it is easily accomplished once you have acquired the right concepts.

Pig Goblin Examined

Looking at this character for the book, there is an obvious and immediate challenge in rigging it, specifically its legs. We examined a huge amount of references and studied the actions of the leg and feet of a human, but this character's legs are of a pig-like creature and have very different proportions from the normal foot. Because of our understanding of anatomy, we know that there really are not any more points of articulation in an animal leg than on a human leg. This is good news because it lets us take something that has been covered in hundreds of tutorials and that is set up to be a reverse foot for the character. The problem, though, is that because of the proportion changes and the kind of control we want over the leg, a normal reverse foot, as we find on a human character rig, does not work well.

The difference here is that in order to make a stable rig for this character leg we need to run an IK Handle across what would be thought of as the ball of the foot on a biped, but is really more like the ankle on this character. In doing so, we limit control over this part of the character that an animator might want control over. XSI has a very nice "Dog Leg" IK solver and Alias Motionbuilder also has a very fine quadruped rig, both with specially coded IK Solvers designed to deal with the unique problems that come up when trying to rig for a character like this. Maya does not have this kind of solver coded for it, so we have to fake it.

There are several ways to set up this leg so that the animator has good control over the leg. The first and most simple way is just to draw a single chain down across the three joints in the leg. This works fine, but you don't really have much control over those three joints. The joint stiffness can be adjusted to help control the solver, or adjusting the preferred angles of the joints can work as well, but both of these have drawbacks. The problem with the stiffness setting is that it slows down the IK solve of the joints, it's hard to control, and it can cause the joints to lock or jump. The preferred angle does not have that problem of slowness that the stiffness setting does, but you either have to set it and leave it, or you can animate the preferred angle, but this can only be adjusted a slight amount before the IK snaps and freaks out. This can be used if you just need a bit of extra flex on your joints, but be cautious when you use it.

The regular reverse foot rig method also works—you rig the leg just like a normal foot standing on its tiptoes. Then the animator only needs to animate two controls all the time instead of one; otherwise the foot looks stiff and can tend to look unnatural. It does not give you the feeling of a full set of muscles all working together to hold up a character, but instead looks like the upper leg and lower leg are disconnected at the ankle, which is not what we want.

The last way to set up the leg involves a mix of techniques that gives the same three joint IK solve that we wanted from the first method, but will have extra controls for "flex" or "force" at the ankle and knee.

To figure out how this rig was going to work, we did a quick and simple test on the joints without worrying if it was fully working or even on the real skeleton. In Figure 7.10, you can see a quick NURBS curve sketch of the leg that was skinned to the skeleton. Doing this let us go in and do a quick animation to see if things held up, and it was a fast way to check for any flipping or unstable action on the rig since the skinned curve would reflect that action better than joints alone. The use of the Maya IK FK blending was also planned and now was a good time to test it. Also note that the foot is not set up, as this is just a test for the leg right.

Rigging the Pig Leg

1. To start, we will work on one side at a time, so in this case hide the right leg joint (see Figure 7.11).

2. Next, duplicate the left leg and move it back so that the legs are not stacked on top of each other (see Figure 7.12).

3. Delete the "prxy" mesh and the foot and toe joints so that it looks like Figure 7.13.

   This new joint chain becomes the driver for the original leg chain. Color it so that it is bright yellow. That way it's easy to see, and you know that if the joints are yellow it's a rig joint and not part of the original pig skeleton. We will also name this new chain with a prefix of "ctrl_" with the Prefix Hierarchy tool. This method is just another way to help keep the file organized, but you can use whatever kind of naming scheme you prefer (see Figure 7.14).

The Notes part of the Attribute Editor should be taken advantage of when creating your rig. It is an easy place to store notes and rigging details for objects in a name-independent way, and you can export these notes to a single file, if needed, with a little bit of Mel scripting. You can also use the notes to store custom data for game assets. The Max equivalent of Notes is User Properties. This feature also lives on each object and can be used for the same things.

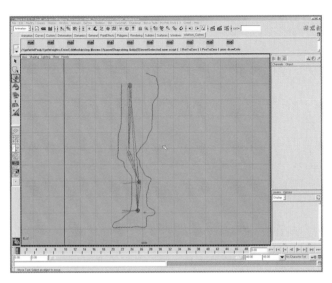

Figure 7.10
Quick test leg.

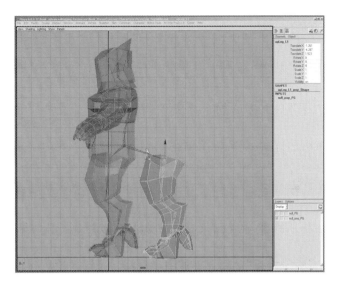

Figure 7.12
Duplicated leg.

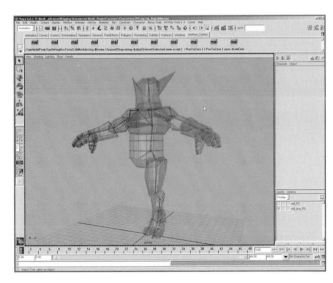

Figure 7.11
Skeleton and mesh ready to begin rigging.

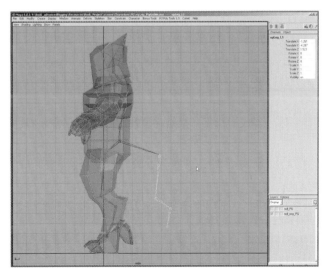

Figure 7.13
Duplicated leg moved back from the character.

7. Stable, User-Friendly, Flexible Rigs

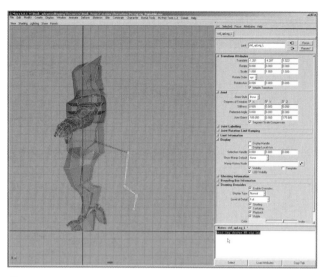

Figure 7.14
Rig leg colored and notes added.

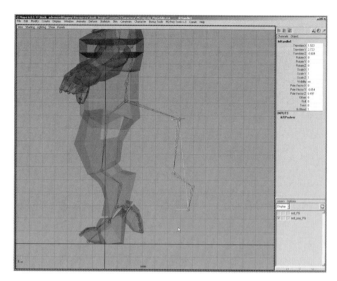

Figure 7.15
Full leg IK.

4. Now we'll add our first IK Handle onto the "ctrl" skeleton from the top joint to the bottom. Name this new handle "ik_fullLeg_L" and remember the "effector" that is also created when you make an IK Handle also needs to be named. Rename it "ef_fullLeg_L." See Figures 7.15 and 7.16.

5. Next, add the IK Handle to the original leg from the "upLeg_L" to the mid leg and then one more from the "foot_L" to the ankle of the mesh, the "ball_L" joint. Name them like you did previously, "ef_jointname_L" and "ik_jointname_L" (see Figure 7.17).

6. Snap the "ctrl" leg over to the original leg so you can attach them together. You will also have to snap the ik_fullLeg_L handle to the original position (ball_L). See Figure 7.18.

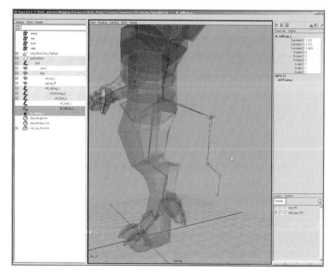

Figure 7.16
Renamed IK and effectors.

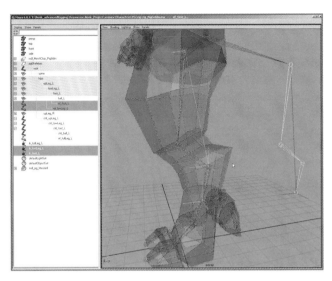

Figure 7.17
Two more IK chains that will give you extra control over the leg.

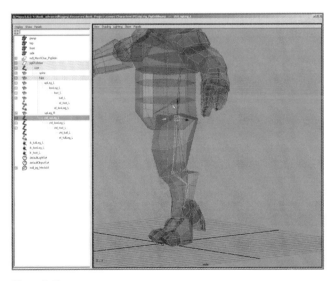

Figure 7.18
Duplicated leg snapped back into position at hip.

7. Parent the "ik_lowLeg_" under the "ctrl_lowLeg_L" joint and the "ik_foot_L" under "ctrl_foot_L," using the drag-and-drop parenting in the Outliner. Once they are parented, the handles will turn yellow showing you they are under the right joints. Test it by selecting "ik_fullLeg_L" and translate it; the two skeletons should move together (see Figure 7.19). Undo to get the leg back into position.

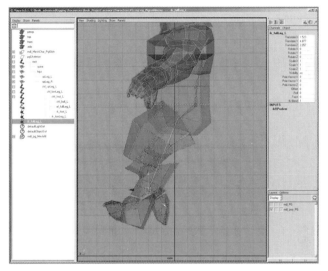

Figure 7.19
Testing new leg IK.

For the sake of keeping our rig zeroed out as much as possible, we will go ahead and group the IK Handles to make them ready to animate and freeze transforms. Remember to parent/group first and then freeze transforms so that you don't cause them to be unfrozen if you parent them again, since you then change what space they were zeroed out in.

1. Select the "ik_foot_L" and freeze transformations so that it is zero.
2. Select the "ik_lowLeg_L" and group it once. The group pivot will go to the location of the IK Handle's parent, but we need to move it to the ankle location (see Figures 7.20 and 7.21).

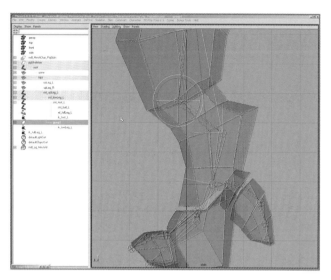

Figure 7.20
Grouped IK Handle.

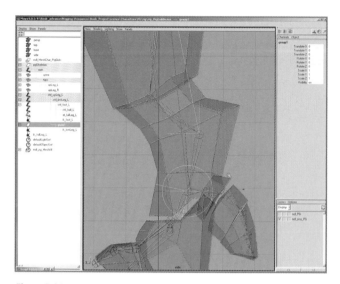

Figure 7.21
Proper pivot location for the "force" group node.

3. Rename this group "ctrl_force_lowLeg_L" and this will become the driver for the flexing or force (to keep taking from Mike Isner), once we add a control onto it with our parent shape trick a little later.

4. Pick the "ik_lowLeg_L" again and freeze its transformations as well.

5. The last thing to do is make sure that the "ctrl_force_lowLeg_L" local rotation axis is set up so that positive Z rotation is forward so it's consistent with the rest of the rig. Select the "ctrl_force_lowLeg_L" and display its LRA. Then select and rotate the LRA interactively (rotation snap on), until the LRA is rotated 180 degrees around X.

6. You can also do the same thing using only the Attribute Editor. In the Attribute Editor, first set the Rotate Axis attribute to -180 in X. Then set the Rotate X attribute to 180. If you test the rotation now, it is still producing negative rotations, but it's easy to fix by setting the Rotate Order to be ZYX and not XYZ. This worked because we had the LRA oriented correctly; then we just had to change how the rotation matrix added the Euler channels together to get the positive rotation value in Z. Figure 7.22 shows the final settings for the "ctrl_force_lowLeg_L."

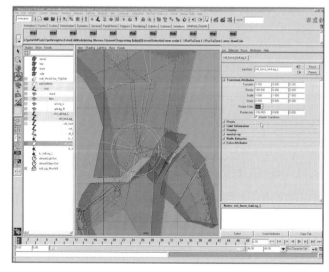

Figure 7.22
Final settings, including rotation order and RotateAxis.

Zeroing the Controls

If you are worried about the 180 rotation being left on the control once it is locked and hidden, it really doesn't have any side effects to leave it that way, but let's look at two other ways to fix this problem.

1. The first way to fix this is to group the "ctrl_force_lowLeg_L" once and name it "ctrl_force_lowLeg_Zero_L." It will be used to orient and zero the real control object.

2. Rotate "ctrl_force_lowLeg_Zero_L" 180 in X, and make sure that its child "ctrl_force_lowLeg_L" is now zeroed both in Rotation and the Rotate Axis. This time the Rotation Order can be left XYZ. Continue down to the IK Handle and make sure it is zeroed out as well. If you now rotate the "ctrl_force_lowLeg_L" in positive Z, it should flex the leg forward (see Figure 7.23).

3. The second way is to use a single joint. By using a joint object as the parent of the "ik_lowLeg_L" instead of a regular group, you can use the Rotate Axis and the Joint Orient to fix the Z so that its rotate ions are positive, while still keeping the rotate values all zeros. In this case, the Rotate Axis is set to 180, Joint Orient is set to −180, and the Rotate Order is left alone. This is the way we will leave it since it has fewer nodes to compute.

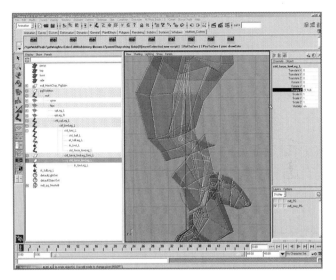

Figure 7.23
Positive Z rotation on the controls as well as the FK skeleton.

After you decide on the way you want to control your "force" attribute, you will set up rotation limits so that the force controller cannot rotate the leg past a point where it will pull away from the other leg chain. In this case, you will set up the Rotation Limit Z to be -30 min and 45 max. You can decrease or increase these values as needed, but this works well to keep the leg from breaking while still giving a wide range of movement.

1. We will group the "ik_fullLeg_L" controller to itself; adjust the pivot point so that the new group pivot is at the same spot as the IK Handle, and then freeze transformations on both the group and the IK Handle.

2. Name this new group "ik_fullLeg_Zero_L."

3. For now we will hide the ctrl leg until we are done with the foot rig. We will also create the control shape for the "force" node while we are creating the foot control shapes.

> You might have noticed that so far we have not locked out anything. We save this for a last pass once you know that you will not have to do major changes or tweak the rig, saving the time to unlock/unhide attributes when you're in the middle of a rig build. The other advantage of waiting until the end of the rig process is that you can quickly store/record the Mel for locking and hiding all the attributes you did for the rig, making it fast to undo or reapply in your procedural rig process.

Pig Feet Rigs with Pivot Nodes

This section will cover the reverse foot that every one knows and loves with a bit of a different approach from how the regular reverse foot is usually done.

1. Like all the other reverse feet, we need to add some IK Handles to the foot joints. Name them "ik_toe_L" and "ik_toeTip_L" and do the same for the end effectors (same names with "ef" in front instead of "IK").

2. Now group each new IK Handle and name the new groups like we did before for the zero nodes, "ik_toe_Zero_L," for example. Snap the group pivot to the location of the respective IK Handle.

3. The tip of the toe will be adjusted to be at the base of the toe mesh and not where the IK Handle is, in this case, because of the location of the toe end joint and the angle of the foot (see Figure 7.24).

> The good thing is that because this is a rig layer, we don't have to adjust the skeleton location in order to get the animation controls to be at the proper location to work correctly. If we had to move the skeleton, then the skin skeleton and rig skeleton would get out of sync, causing us problems later. They can also get out of sync due to changes in the mesh after the skeleton was created or improper initial placement of the mesh or joints. With the non-linear way that production works, dealing with these kinds of changes is part of every Character TD's job. Creating separate layered rigs that work with skeletons helps allow for small changes without breaking the rig.

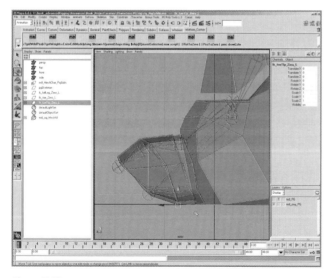

Figure 7.24
Toe pivot location.

Most reverse foot tutorials only let the feet have a set of controls that work for basic walking motions but do not allow them to add more flexibility, which can quickly complicate the animation controls and create a lot of keys to manage.

Feet provide a lot of movement and are the base of the character. Most of the time when watching 3D characters, the feet look locked off, or they don't look like they are interacting with the ground properly. This is mostly the animator's responsibility, but you must provide a rig that allows for a more complex movement.

1. You will parent the IK groups together to make the normal reverse foot hierarchy first and then expand the control with extra groups (pivot points) where needed.

2. Pick the "ik_fullLeg_Zero_L" and parent it to the "Ik_toe_Zero_L."

3. Parent "Ik_toe_Zero_L" to "Ik_toeTIp_Zero_L" so you end up with a hierarchy like Figure 7.25.

   This lets the foot roll forward but not off the heel. We will group the "Ik_toeTIp_Zero_L" once and place its pivot at the heel of the foot, where the mesh is (see Figure 7.26).

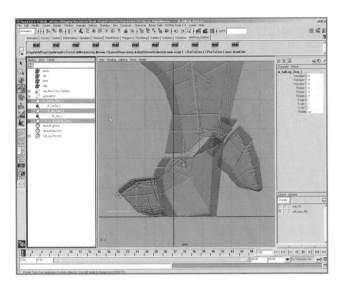

Figure 7.25
Final parenting of the foot IK.

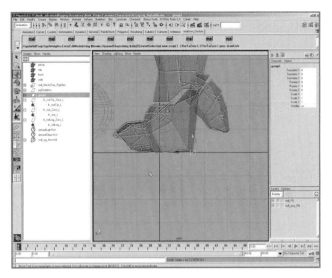

Figure 7.26
Location of heel pivot.

4. Name it "ik_heel_Zero_L." (Even though it does not directly control an IK Handle, it controls all the handles so, to keep the naming consistent, we name it "ik_heel.")

   Since we have decided on a preferred rotation plan for the character's skeleton, we need to make sure that our controls for our IK system work the same way for rotation. We want the animator to have a consistent mapping of rotation for any control that rotates, so keeping this in mind, we need to make sure that a control like the "ctrl_foot_L" has a rotation mapping that matches the FK skeleton rotation. In our case, positive Z rotation is forward.

5. Using the same techniques as you did on the "ctrl_force_lowLeg_L" to create the proper rotation orientation, you will create the foot control with a joint.

   Create a new joint and set it to the origin, 0 0 0. Name the joint "ctrl_foot_L."

6. Group it once and name the group "ctrl_foot_Zero_L" and snap the group to the ankle location.

   If you freeze the group nodes' transforms, it will zero them but pass the translation offset onto the child joint, which is not what you want. You want them both to be zero.

7. In order to make the joint have its main transform be zero after you relocate it to be at the ankle, from the Channel Control, unhide the "rotate pivot translate" attributes on its parent "ctrl_foot_Zero_L."

Copy the translate value to the equivalent "rotate pivot translate" value and zero the "translate" attribute. Now the joint will be zero and at the proper location. Just hide or lock the rotate pivot translate values when done and make a note, that this is where the translation lives for this object in the Attribute Editor Notes.

The end result is that the foot control is zeroed out, and its local rotation matches the FK joint. This can help later if you have to transfer the rotation values from the FK rig to the IK rig, and it will let you mirror the IK rig rotation controls. The only difference is that the control is oriented at 90-degree angles, so X is not aligned to the joint like the real ankle joint is.

8. We need to make a control handle for the foot. This can be any shape you want. We will use a spherical shape that is three NURBS circles with the shapes all parented under "ctrl_foot_L." You could also use a curve shaped like a foot that is on the ground plane instead.

9. Name each shape "ctrl_Foot_L_Shape" (see Figure 7.27).

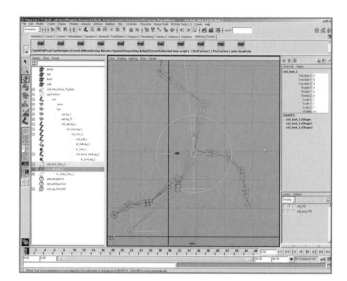

Figure 7.27
The new control shapes parented under the foot control.

This becomes the parent of the "ik_heel_Zero_L." Having the foot control at the ankle works best, allowing full control of the foot once it's off the ground, leaving the other rotation pivots for foot control when it's in contact with the ground. On other rigs, the main foot control is often at the ball of the foot or at the heel of the foot, and it can cause unwanted or extra movement that must be counter-animated.

10. Finally, set the rotation order to ZYX so that it is more stable during rotations, since the X value will later drive the leg twist and this will help keep the knee from twisting unexpectedly due to gimbal rotations.

Expanded Reverse Foot

The next set of steps and the whole foot hierarchy could be simplified with using the ability to animate the pivot point of a node, but for software compatibility of rigging concepts and for a bit more flexibility over how we blend or mix the foot poses, we will rig them in the standard way with each pivot point being a node in the hierarchy.

1. First, let's add the additional nodes needed for the side to side rocking of the foot. We want the extra nodes to tilt the foot while still being relative to the rest of the foot movement.

2. Select "ik_toe_Zero_L" and group it twice. Name the two groups "instep_pvt_foot_L" and "blade_pvt_foot_L" (see Figure 7.28).

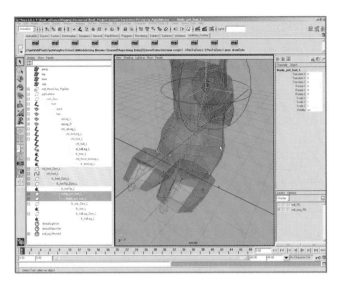

Figure 7.28
The pivots in the hierarchy of the foot rig.

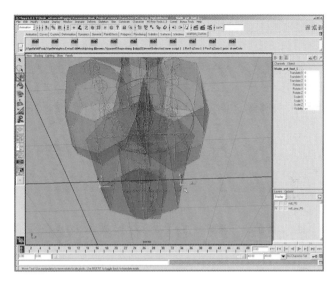

Figure 7.29
The pivots for the edge and blade of the foot.

The main point of rotation for these two points should be around the balls of the feet since that is where the solid points of contact are with the ground. Place the two group nodes' pivots at this location, the "blade_pvt_foot_L" on the outside of the foot, and the "instep_pvt_foot_L" on the inside of the foot (see Figure 7.29).

Once you are happy with the location of these pivots, rotate them to make sure they are rocking the foot side to side. At this point, this foot has a lot of controls that, while giving a lot of flexibility, create way too many nodes for the animators to work with and manage keyframes on. To fix this, we will borrow our interface simplification ideas from Jason Osipa by creating a foot roller joystick control.

3. Create a locator or null object and snap it to the ankle joint and freeze its transforms. Name it "ctrl_foot_roller_L." This will become our driving control node (see Figure 7.30).

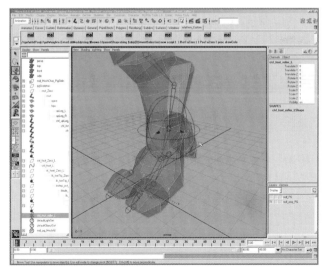

Figure 7.30
Roller control.

4. We will use Set Driving Keys to drive all the rotate nodes on the foot from the roller controls translation.

> Max and XSI have the same kind of ability to drive other objects' attributes with curves; in Max, they are called *reactor controllers*, but take a bit more work to set up. Max 7 has adjusted the interface, and the reactors are more streamlined to work with.

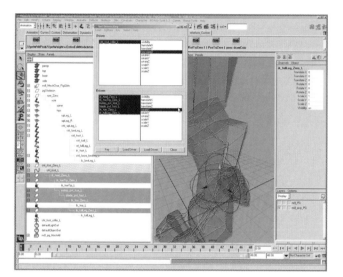

Figure 7.31
Foot Set Driven Keys.

Open the Set Driven Key window and pick the "ctrl_foot_roller_L" as the driver. Select the rotation nodes for the foot, as seen in Figure 7.31, and load them as driven. Translate Z of "ctrl_foot_roller_L" will control the forward and backward roll of the foot; rotate X for your other driven objects.

5. The first object you will control is "ik_toe_Zero_L," keying it so that as you move the foot roller forward, it will rotate to bend the foot at the ball and then at the toes. You can adjust how much you want to have the foot flex and at what distance you move the "ctrl_foot_roller_L" in positive Z or negative Z to have the foot react. Keep the distance short and in whole values so it's easy to control and edit. In this case, .5 in Z for "ctrl_foot_roller_L" will rotate the ball of the foot all the way forward about 50 degrees on X. You can easily adjust when the foot bend happens by adjusting the SDK curves. Adjust to desired foot roll feel.

6. Next, you will link up the translation in X to the rotate in Z on the "instep_pvt_foot_L" and "blade_pvt_foot_L" in order to have the foot tilt side to side. Load the "ctrl_foot_roller_L" and the "instep_pvt_foot_L" and "blade_pvt_foot_L" into the Set Driven Key window.

7. Set the first key with all controls at 0, then set the "ctrl_foot_roller_L" to -1 in X, and then rotate the "instep_pvt_foot_L" to 55 degrees and key. Do the same for the "blade_pvt_foot_L" with values of 1 and -55 for the controls this time.

8. Parent the "ctrl_foot_roller_L" to "ctrl_foot_L." You will see the foot jump because of translation values that were applied to the roller control; to fix this, just freeze the transforms on the roller control, and it will fix the offset.

9. Now, you will limit the controller movement to the 1×1 grid using translation limits in the Channel Box (see Figure 7.32). Also, notice that we set the limit for Y to 0; this is something that adds an extra layer of protection to a rig component that just locking and hiding attributes does not do.

In Max, limits are the only way to make sure that objects are locked down because there is no concept of lock and hide attributes. Unfortunately, unless you're using bones, limits in Max are only on/off locks or zero limits and do not allow you to set min and max values. A cool trick with maxscript: it's possible to ask the object what limits are set on it and use that to control what kind of keyframes are set on that object. For example, if the object has translate limits and scale limits turned on, only keyframes for rotation will be set.

10. You should now be able to translate the control anywhere in XZ within a 1×1 square area to mix and blend the main movements for the foot. This will be fine for most animation, but we have to allow the animators control over the rig without having to come back and request changes from the Character TD or trying to dig into the rig on their own to fix something. We will use some more advanced connections and nodes to quickly scale the values of the current rig and add in the extra controls that are going to be needed for the rest of the foot.

    Using a multiplyDivide node, you will create a way to amp up the amount that the roller control distance affects the amount of foot roll in all directions. To keep the node count down, you will create only two multiplyDivide nodes and then use all their X,Y,Z channels on both nodes to give six independent channels without needing six separate nodes.

11. You will take the SDK curve output and map it to the multiplyDivide node input1x. Then take the output and send it to the "instep_pvt_foot_L." Continue with the other SDK nodes to the other channels until all the connections are made, as shown in Figures 7.33 and 7.34. The reason we do the connection from the SDK output and not before the SDK is because we want to amplify the end result of the SDK and not change the value that the SDK reads from the roller controls translation.

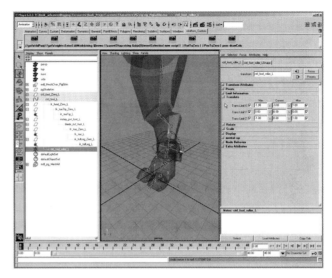

Figure 7.32
Limiting the "ctrl_foot_roller_L" translation.

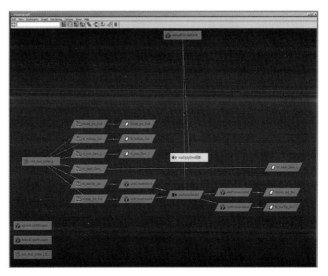

Figure 7.33
Picking the output of the multiplyDivide node.

7. Stable, User-Friendly, Flexible Rigs

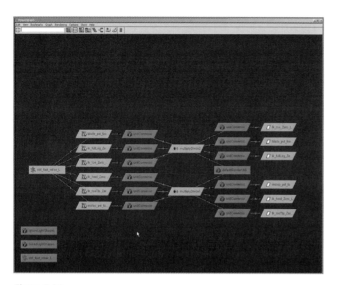

Figure 7.34
The final connections of the mulitplyDivide node.

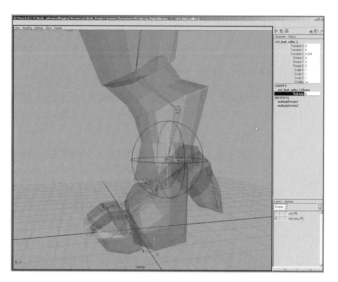

Figure 7.35
The custom attribute on the shape node of the controls.

12. Create a custom attribute named "rollAmp," with a default of 1 on the "ctrl_foot_roller_L," a shape node for the control. This keeps it easy to access but away from the attributes that we want keyframes on (see Figure 7.35).

13. Now you will connect this attribute to the multiplyDivide nodes in the input2, so that you can scale the numbers from one attribute and control the amount of roll. Lesser values make the foot move less, letting you limit the range of the rotations, if needed.

14. The next override control you want to have is the adjustment of when the foot rotation happens so you can control when the ball of the foot stops rotating and the toes take over. Again, this extra control will go on the shape node so that it does not interfere with the main keyframes for the animation control.

15. Add a new attribute called "rollBallAdjust" with a default value of 1 as before.

16. Use the Mel command `createNode multDoubleLinear` to create a node that will adjust the roll between the toe rotation and the ball rotation.

17. Then using Mel again, connect the roller control translate Z to the multDoubleLinear input1:

    ```
    connectAttr ctrl_foot_roller_L.translateZ multDoubleLinear1.input1;
    ```

18. Then do the same for the ctrl_foot_roller_LShape.rollBallAdjust, connecting its output to the input 2 on the multDoubleLinear:

    ```
    connectAttr ctrl_foot_roller_LShape.rollBallAdjust multDoubleLinear1.input2;
    ```

7. Stable, User-Friendly, Flexible Rigs

19. Finally, pipe the output of the multDoubleLinear to the "Ik_toe_Zero_L_rotate" X SDK node.

    Figure 7.36 shows the final graph all connected. Notice that this time we added the node before the SDK, because in this case, we want to keep the same movement from the SDK, but we want to control when that movement happens, if at all.

> The next steps could be added to another locator and set up to control the foot like the foot roller control, but in this case we want to keep the keyframes on as few controls as possible. The main foot animation is completely possible without going to the Channel Box, but we still put attributes that are needed less often in the Channel Box. They are good to have accessible, but might not get used in every animation.

20. There are a few more controls for the foot that we will add to allow for twisting motions, such as putting out a match or just pivoting off the ball of your foot to turn around. And we will also add a heel pivot and a toe tap control.

21. Create three new custom attributes on the Foot Roller control. The first attribute will be "toeTap" for animating the up-and-down movement of the toe joint; then continue adding the other two "ballTwist" "heelTwist." Once those are added to the "ctrl_foot_roller_L," you will hook them up to the appropriate groups to control the rotation.

22. First, pick "ik_toeTip_L" and group it, name the group "toe_pvt_L," and set the pivot point for this group to the ball of the foot (see Figure 7.37).

23. Now connect the "toeTap" attribute to the "toe_pvt_L" rotate x. This connects the two, but at a one-to-one value mapping, making the attribute slow to rotate the foot. We can adjust the unitConversion node that Maya auto-inserted between the attribute and the rotation channel, and increase its value to make a smaller change on the "toeTap" attribute and have a greater effect on the toe.

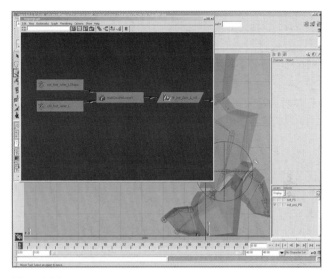

Figure 7.36
Node graph of the foot break control.

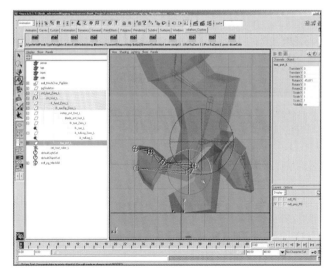

Figure 7.37
Toe pivot in action.

24. Select the "toe_pvt_L" node and graph the connections in the Hypergraph. You will see the unitConversion node. Select it and open the Attribute Editor. The conversion factor should be 0.018, and you will change this to .5, letting the animator move the mouse less to get the same result. The other step is to make sure our positive animation values still make sense. Positive numbers should cause the toe to rotate up but right now it rotates down. To fix this, place a - sign in front of the .5 so that it will rotate up.

25. Continue the connections for the other attributes: "ballTwist" to "Ik_toeTIp_Zero_L" rotate Y and "heelTwist" to "ik_heel_Zero_L."

> The unitConversion node can be used instead of the reverse node and does not suffer from the value off-setting that the reverse node suffers from. Maya uses this throughout the software for dealing with connections, and Character TDs should take advantage of this in their own rigs.

You can rig up as many different layers of control as the animators want and need, and as long as your hierarchy is solid and you understand how to add to the rig with extra group nodes or by using math nodes to layer in the offsets, you can create a very fast, stable, and flexible foot rig or any part of the character rig for that matter. On your own, try to create a new set of controls for the foot rig that work over the top of the current system. You can create all the individual attributes like other foot rigs, and using the plusMinusAverage node, animate the foot with just these attributes, and the joystick-like roller control will still work (see Figure 7.38).

> To help avoid extra nodes, try placing them right after the multiplyDivide nodes so the connection is between the multiplyDivide node and the unitConversion node. This will eliminate extra conversion nodes being placed if you were to connect the plusMinusAverage node between the unitConversion node and the final rotate node, like "toe_pvt_L," for example.

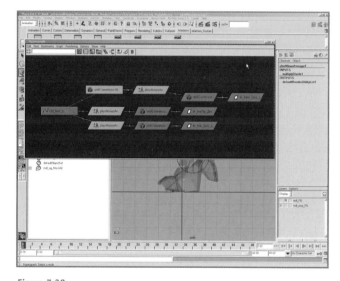

Figure 7.38
The extra attributes being fed into the plusMinusAverage nodes for layered control.

Toes and Cleanup

Up to now, we have only been dealing with what we will call *coarse controls*, the leg and the foot—both of which are needed for rough animation and posing. What we need to do now is rig up the controls for the toe joints to allow for finer control.

To finish off this foot rig, we will add some auto toe controls over the top of the FK controls that are there, again trying to keep the keyframes in the same location, if possible, and allowing for animator flexibility. We also need to add an easy-to-pick shape node to the "ctrl_foot_roller," instead of just the locator cross-shape, and add in a control shape for the leg flex or force node we created earlier.

1. First, let's create a quick control for the flex node on the leg. It is up to you how you want to control this, either with a selectable control in the scene or with a custom attribute. We will use a custom attribute on the foot control (see Figure 7.39).

2. Next, make a better selection shape for the foot roller locator. For this control, using an orient control shape from the comet scripts that is scaled flatter works great (see Figure 7.40). This hides the extra attributes we put on the shape node, which is not a bad thing since they were more for the Character TD to adjust than for the animator to really mess with. Just pickwalk down and hide the original locator shape node. Name the shape node "xtraAttrs" for clarity.

3. To control the toes, you will use SDKs linked to "toe curl" and "scrunch" attributes for the toes. Because the joints rotate, channels should remain unlocked for FK. You need to do something a bit different with these joints in order to have them work with the custom attributes.

4. Create a second layer of joints for the toes to get SDK driven. Duplicate the "bigToe" chain and delete the shape geometry from the joints.

5. Suffix the new joint chain with "_Layer" using cometRename.mel or similar renaming script to speed up the process.

6. Parent the toe joints so that each joint is now the child of its corresponding layer joint. This adds a layer onto the joints that keep the SDK from locking the FK joints directly. Figure 7.41 shows the new layer joints in the proper hierarchy and name.

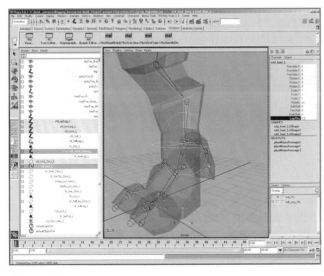

Figure 7.39
Leg flex attribute.

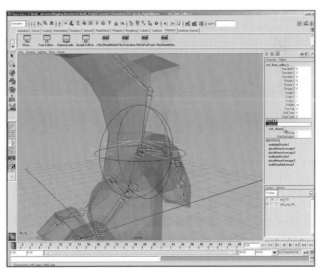

Figure 7.40
Rename shape node; this will be done for any secondary attributes.

7. Stable, User-Friendly, Flexible Rigs

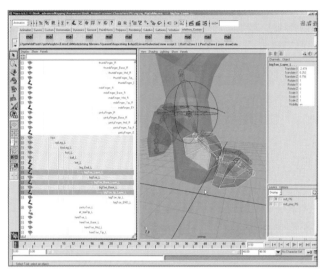

Figure 7.41
Layered joints for the toes.

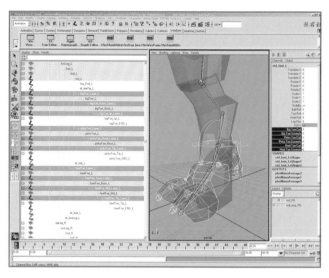

Figure 7.42
Final toe attributes.

7. Now create the custom attributes on the "ctrl_foot_L" node and Set Driven Key them into the curl shape you are happy with. Remember it's better to allow the control to over-rotate the joints and let the animator decide what is too far to push the pose, rather than impose artificial limits in the rig. Do the same process for the rest of the toes. Figure 7.42 shows the final rig for the toe controls.

8. Before you continue let's clean up the Outliner real quick. Pick the "pgSkeleton" and the "ctrl_foot_Zero_L" and parent them to a new curve control named "pgWorld." This control will be the world space for all your characters' controls and allow you to transform your entire rig to any palace in the scene and still keep all your controls zeroed (see Figure 7.43).

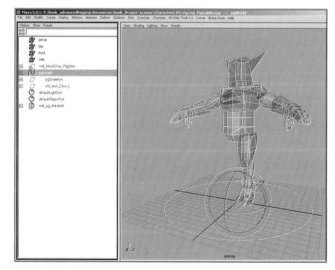

Figure 7.43
Quick cleanup in Outliner by adding the pgWorld control.

7. Stable, User-Friendly, Flexible Rigs

Foot and Leg, Leg Twist, and Centralizing IK/FK Controls

The knee control on this leg will be linked to rotate with the "ctrl_foot_L," and we will have an offset attribute that lets the animator animate on top of the leg twist. There are a lot of ways to connect the objects, but in this case Set Driven Keys are fast ways to connect them, so we can have two attributes drive the IK twist.

1. To make sure that the twist and rotation allow for full rotation, set both the "ctrl_foot_L" rotate X to 360 positive and negative and do the same for the IK twist on "ik_fullLeg_L" and set up the SDK for this.

2. Next, add a custom attribute to the "ctrl_foot_L" called 'kneeOffset" and link its value to the "ik_fullLeg_L" twist as well. Again, allow a full 360 rotation, but map to the attribute value between -10 and 10. For consistency, make the positive value of the custom attribute turn the leg to the outside of the body. (You can make this a wider range so that it's not as quick to respond or hold the Ctrl key when you middle mouse drag, so you get finer control over the values.)

3. Last, we need to set up the IK/FK switching for the leg and make the FK joints have the option to inherit or not inherit the rotation from the body. (If you were at the Alias master class for hyper-real character rigging, this FK inherit switch will not be a new concept for you.)

4. The default Maya IK/FK controls work great, but they are limited to single IK Handles with only one chain like an arm, for example. Our leg has a more complicated set of IK Handles and joint chains, so we have to take care of the IK/FK controls, but still use the IK/FK blending without having to use the standard three skeleton blending with constraints.

5. First, create a single "IkFk" attribute on the "ctrl_foot_L" with a default of 1 and a range of 0 to 1 and connect it so that it drives all the IK Handles on the foot and leg, except "ik_fullLeg_L." That controls the "ctrl_leg" and will remain in IK the whole time.

6. Next, select all the IK Handles that are in the leg rig and turn off the snap attribute so that they do not jump to the end of the joint chain they control, pulling away from your control object and causing an offset. Test that it works by setting the "IkFk" attribute to 0 and then you should be able to rotate the leg by selecting the mesh and rotating it.

FK Inherit Switch

The other step we need to do in order to make the leg a broken hierarchy is to set up a way to blend the rotation inheritance between its parent and a world node.

1. Just duplicate the "upLeg_L" joint and delete its children. Once that is done, name the new joint "ctrl_upLeg_ori_L" and this will be what controls the rotation inheritance from the rest of the body on to the FK leg.

2. Duplicate the new joint again and name it "ctrl_upLeg_ori_Local_L."

3. Duplicate this again and name it "ctrl_upLeg_World_ori_L" and parent it under the "pgSkeleton" node and group it once. Name this new group "fkWorldOri_GRP." This new group will hold all the duplicate joints that will have the other "ori" joints constrained to, once we create them.

4. Parent the "upLeg_L" to the "ctrl_upLeg_ori_L."

5. Orient-constrain the "ctrl_upLeg_ori_L" to both the world and local joints. Set the constraint "interp type" to shortest to keep the leg from flipping.

Now when you set the weight between the local or world, the FK joint will either inherit the movement of its parent, or it will maintain its orientation in world space. Again, we just need to make this easy for the animator to turn on or off.

To continue exploring how great utility nodes are in a rig, we will use the reverse node to do a switch value for us to control the orient constraint's weight value.

1. Create a locator and call it "ctrl_fkOri." This node eventually will hold all the custom attributes for the FK inherit switching for all the body parts. Add a custom attribute to this locator's shape node and name it "legL" with a default value of 0.

2. Now use a variation of the parent shape trick to create a kind of instance of the shape node from the locator to, in this case, "upLeg_L" so that when the animator picks the leg to FK animate, he can also just set the inherit value from there without having to jump to another object to set it.

3. We will use Mel parent -add -shape ctrl_fkOriShape upLeg_L to attach the shape node of the locator to the leg.

   Figure 7.44 shows the attribute and the shape added to the leg

4. Now connect the "legL" attribute to the "ctrl_upLeg_ori_World_LW0." Then connect the output of "legL" to a reverse node and connect the reverse node into the "ctrl_upLeg_ori_local_LW1."

   This works along the same idea as a character node in Maya where you create a collection of attributes in one location, but the attributes live all over the rig.

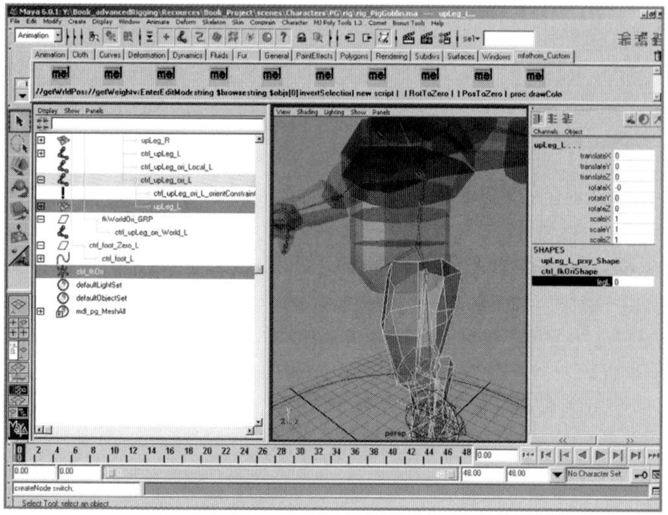

Figure 7.44
The instanced attribute holder shape.

This idea of instanced attributes is not just a Maya only workflow. In Max it works very well with instanced modifiers and instanced controllers. By layering the empty modifiers and having different attributes on the different modifiers again, you help control what gets keyframes and what does not, and it helps keep the animators working from rough to fine control without overwhelming them with slider after slider of controls.

XSI also has some unique ways of aliasing attributes and grouping them for in-view port editing based on what you select, and it does not have to have the attributes directly on it to display them.

Mirroring Controls, Rigging the Other Side of the Body

Since this whole rig is only for one side, the left side, in this case, getting the rig set up on the right leg involves the same steps with a few adjustments for things like control orientation so the IK rig behavior is mirrored as well as the FK rig. We will not go back through the entire rig process step-by-step for the other leg, but we will point out a few ways to speed up the process. One way is that because we used joints for our main control objects, those can be mirrored with the Mirror Joint tool and will give you the option to mirror with behavior, letting the IK controllers animate in a mirrored fashion when rotating.

1. Mirror the "ctrl_foot_L" with the Mirror Joint, and it will mirror the orientation for the most part. Then you need to adjust the rotate axis so that it's facing the correct direction to get positive Z rotation values (see Figure 7.45). We also get all the hierarchy nodes below the control as a bonus. To finish fixing the right foot controllers, do the following steps.

2. Group the "ctrl_foot_R" and call it "ctrl_foot_Zero_R" and parent it under "pgSkeleton" and do the same process for zeroing translation as before, using the rotate pivot translate to do the offset and keep the controls at zero.

3. Select the child nodes and display the LRAs so you can realign the control pivots to the proper locations on the foot and resnap them into the proper place on the foot.

4. Mirror over the control leg and remove any extra IK Handles or effectors in the hierarchy that were duplicated; they will be replaced by the new IK Handles on the right leg. Add the IK Handles onto the right leg, name them, and parent them back under the matching zero nodes.

5. Make sure to rename all the objects to the correct side, fixing any L or R swaps and hidden nodes like the end effectors.

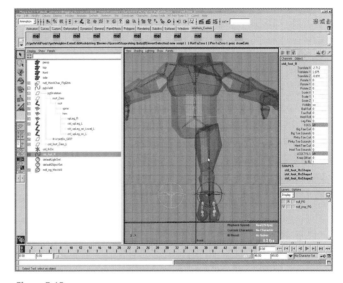

Figure 7.45
Initial mirroring of the leg controls.

The real trouble of trying to mirror a rig like this by hand is that you have to rebuild all the node networks and set up all the SDK connections again, including poses for the feet. This should show a very clear example where taking the time to build a script for creating a rig or even components of a rig will always pay off later even if you only have this one character to rig. For practice and to make sure that the underlying rigging concepts are clear, we will continue to work out the right side of the rig by hand.

Figure 7.46 shows the current rig state of the two feet: the top graph shows all the connections on the left foot and the bottom graph shows the right foot without the needed rigging. Lucky for us, we can do some tricks like duplicating most of the nodes from the left foot and reconnecting them into our own graph on the right foot.

For the initial easy connections of custom attributes, we will connect them as we did previously in the chapter, hooking up each custom attribute to its correct connection. After that, we will duplicate our more complex graph and connect up the rest of the foot rig.

1. Duplicate the "ctrl_foot_L" with the duplicate setting of "Duplicate Input Graph." This will create a copy of all the connections, including our SDK nodes.

2. You can then connect your "ctrl_foot_L" attributes into this graph and remove any of the nodes that are duplicates afterwards. It will be easier if you do the inputs first because there are fewer nodes to work with, and then you can work on the outputs from the graph to the right leg and foot joints and nodes.

3. Finally, re-parent the shape node "ctrl_fkOri" with the Mel `parent -add -shape ctrl_fkOriShape upLeg_R` and add the "LegR" custom attribute onto it and do the connections for the switch like it was done earlier.

> You can keep using the reverse node until it's out of inputs and outputs, in order to keep node numbers down and keep your connections organized.

4. Now that you have finished with your connections, clean up the duplicated objects by running File-Optimize Scene Size-Options with all the boxes checked. Save your file before you run it, just in case it removes something you wanted; then you can get it back.

5. At this point, a side effect of rigging the leg with only using the IK twist attribute is that we set the IK pole vector values to 0 0 0, allowing the IK to rotate freely without flipping. The problem is that the hips or root when rotated will also cause the legs to rotate as if they were controlling the pole vectors for the leg IK Handles. We will fix this later when we create the hip control

Figure 7.47 shows the final set of mirrored controls and the hierarchy you should have when done.

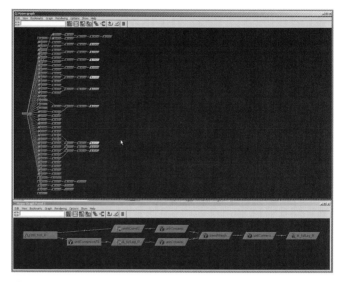

Figure 7.46
Final foot graph that we want.

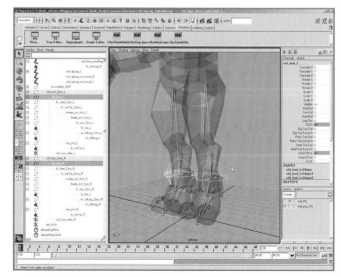

Figure 7.47
Final leg controls.

Shoulders, Arms, and Hands

The face, hands, and arms are some of the most expressive parts of the body. Combine those parts with our wide range of motion on the shoulders, and you get a very powerful communication tool on a character (if you make sure that the animators can control these body parts). There are some basic core ideas that all arm and hand rigs need to accommodate in order to make your animators happy. These basic ideas do not include squash and stretch control over the arms, but that could be added in on top of this arm rig.

Here is a list of the core ideas that make up a good arm rig.

◆ IK/FK switching

◆ FK separation of motion from main body at the shoulder

◆ Easy-to-control elbow

◆ Wrist control that allows the hand to blend between world or local inherited rotations, like the shoulder

◆ A blending switch for the IK control between world, body, and upper body transformation space

◆ One additional blend space for the arm to blend out to an auxiliary control that can be attached to any object, such as a weapon

◆ Auto-clavicle with animator control, defaulting to off

◆ Finger and hand controls simple and flexible

◆ Basic pose controls for the entire hand and override on top for fine-tuning

◆ Quick access to a pose system for managing and recording the poses of the hands and the ability to share poses from one hand to the other

◆ An easy way to switch between the transformation spaces without jumps or pops, either with scripts built into the rig or using a shelf button

The setup of the arm will be a lot like the leg rigging, so most of the repeat material will not be explained here in detail. If you are having problems, look back to the leg section for help.

1. Starting with the left arm, add an IK Handle to the arm joints "upArm_L" to "hand_L" and name it "ik_arm_L;" then group it once, naming the group ik_arm_Zero_L (see Figure 7.48).

When doing a rig for a symmetrical body part like an arm, the best two options are to either build each component for both sides as you go so that there is not a lot of work to duplicate over the rig in the end (like the foot) or to script the creation of the rig and then adjust the script to build a mirrored version. The script is the best option, but often on tight deadlines or quick ones—use rigs, building both sides as you go is a better choice. This tutorial covers building the rig for the left arm only, but you can keep both ideas in mind as you go. Which order to create the rig in for a tutorial is not always what works best in production.

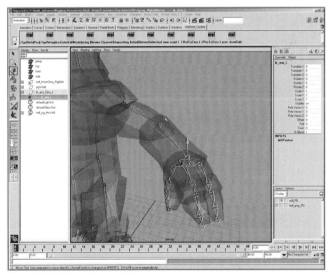

Figure 7.48
Arm IK Handle grouped and named.

2. Snap the pivot point from the origin to the location of the IK Handle and then freeze the transforms on the "ik_arm_L" handle. We also want to set the pole vector value to 0,0,0. Hide the handle for now while you work on other parts of the arm.

3. Using a curve, create a shape that looks like a locator or use cometScripts to create a shape. This will become the control for the arm position and display its selection handle. Using this instead of a curve shape or some other kind of selection device keeps the rig as clutter-free as possible and because it only has one main function, which is to translate the arm, you don't need to make it stick out in any special way. We just want it to be easy to select. Try to make a visual difference in the controls that only translate, compared to ones that both translate and rotate.

4. Name it "ctrl_arm_L" and group it. Name the group "ctrl_arm_Zero_L" and snap it to the wrist location and freeze transforms on this node.

5. To hook up the "ik_arm_L" to the control, you need to create a node that will be point-constrained to the "ctrl_arm_L" for now. Select "ik_arm_L," group it once, and name it "aux_blend_L." Make sure that its pivot is snapped to the same location as the "ik_arm_L" and its transforms are zero.

6. Create a pole vector control for the arm so you can control the elbow. Create a curve locator like we did for the wrist and name it "ctrl_elbow_L." Group it and name the group "ctrl_elbow_Zero_L."

7. A trick to get the elbow pole vector not to cause the arm to jump when you constrain the IK Handle to it is to make sure that the pole vector target is in the same plane that the IK will solve in. Because this character's arm is off axis and the plane is hard to locate by hand, we will do a few steps to place the object in the right plane.

8. Select the three arm joints "upArm_L," "lowArm_L," "wrist_L," and "ctrl_elbow_Zero_L" and do a point constraint. This finds the center of the IK plane for the arm joints.

9. You need to find a direction vector to translate the group along so that the pole vector is away from the arm, keeping it from flipping. Pick the "lowArm_L" and "ctrl_elbow_Zero_L" and do an aim constraint. When you translate the "ctrl_elbow_Zero_L" on X, it will translate in the plane of the IK solver. Once the control is in place, you can delete the constraints and set the "ctrl_elbow_Zero_L" rotations to zero and freeze transforms.

10. Now constrain the "ik_arm_L" to the "ctrl_elbow_L" with a pole vector constraint. You should not see the arm move or jump. If it does, then the control was not in the correct plane and needs to be checked. Figure 7.49 shows the location of the arm pole vector, and the rest of the nodes are hooked into the arm, which is what you will do next.

> You can also set the *group options* for the *group pivot* to be *center* since this can help speed up your pivot placement when grouping one object, as it centers the pivot at the bounding box center point and not the origin.

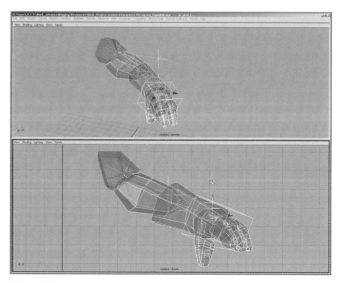

Figure 7.49
Elbow pole vector.

11. To clean up a bit before moving on, let's make sure that you parent your control under the "pgWorld" node. The next step creates a system where the pole vector will follow the arm wherever it goes. This might seem strange, but it creates a system where the pole vector can be set out of the character's way and keyframed as an offset from itself to cut down the amount the pole vector gets in the way during complex moves. We will have an option to stick it in world space as well if this following action is not wanted.

12. Create a locator and call it "ctrl_elbowAttach_L" and vert snap it to the top of "upArm_L" and parent this to "shoulder_L." Then freeze the transforms on the "ctrl_elbowAttach_L." This will be the upper point that your next control will be constrained to, both this point and the wrist locator.

13. Create one more locator and name it "ctrl_elbowFollow_L" and constrain it to both the "ctrl_elbowAttach_L" and the "ctrl_arm_L" and for now, parent it under the "pgWorld" node.

14. Select the "ctrl_elbow_L" and group it once and name this group "ctrl_elbowLocate_L." Then parent-constrain this node to the "ctrl_elbowFollow_L" and parent-constrain the node to the "pgWorld," letting you blend between following the arm or sticking in the world. By default, you will set this to follow the arm, but you can set it to stick in the world, if needed.

15. You will interface this just like we did the other blending of constraints by adding a custom attribute to the shape node of the "ctrl_elbow_L." Name the shape node "elbow_attrs_L." Add an attribute named "followArm" and make it a float with a min at 0 and max at 1 and its default at 1. Using our reverse-node trick and the Connection Editor, hook up the attribute to the parent constraints on "ctrl_elbowLocate_L."

> The idea of the pole vector or up vector following the arm might seem strange, but it offers a unique advantage compared to its world space counterpart because it stays out of the way but with the character. The problem with the pole vectors that stick in the world or just move the root of the character is that they move when you don't want them to, but it also makes sure that the elbow motion is always an offset from the current arm position. It might be a bit strange at first to see the locator following the arm, but once you get used to being able to just set and forget the elbow for most of a move, you will find yourself looking for this on rigs that don't have it.

16. You have the start of an arm rig; there are a few more things you need to do in order to make this a full working rig, though. The next step is the same process that you did for the leg to create the FK Inherit switch, but you want to do the same thing for the arm. Remember to add the switch attribute to the "ctrl_fkOriShape" and call it "armL" and connect it to the "ctrl_upArm_ori_L" constraints to blend between the "ctrl_upArm_ori_Local_L" and the "ctrl_upArm_ori_World_L" nodes. Parent the shape node with the –add flag, like in the leg to the "upArm_L" node.

17. Check and make sure you set up the connections with the right attribute by setting the arm IK Handle blend to 0 and trying to rotate the body of the character. If the arm follows by default, it's good. When you set the armL attribute to 1, it should not rotate with the body. If you have a problem re-creating this rig component, refer back to the leg section where we did the same process.

Final Pass on the Arm and Hand: Adding in Options and Controls Over the Limb

The arm is coming together and like the leg, you need to rig up a few more items such as IK/FK blending, IK twist, space blending between local and world, a wrist control for the hand that will also need to inherit local or world rotation from the arm, finger controls, and then setting up an auto-clavicle that will react when the arm is raised to a certain point.

IK/FK

1. Rig up the IK/FK switch by adding a custom attribute to the "ctrl_arm_L" and name it like you did on the foot, ikFk, 0 min, 1 max, default of 1. Connect it to the "ik_arm_L" Ik Blend attribute on the IK Handle.

2. The IK twist is also just as easy. By adding attributes and doing a direct connection, you can control the arm twist separate from the pole vector. A trick here is to tweak the unit conversion node between the two connections to make the value on the Arm Twist drive the IK twist much faster so you don't have to scroll the mouse as far. A value of 1 or 1.5 in the unitConversion node works very well.

3. There are some rigs that drive the twist off a rotating object placed at the shoulder or the elbow of the character and this works as well as or in place of the twist attribute, but it spreads the keyframes out onto several objects, and causes lots of extra selections and tool switches, so it tends to work better if it's an attribute. If you do want to have the twist controlled by an icon, then place it close to the main hand control so that it is fast to grab and is easy to control, not off axis from the arm joint or hidden in the arm geometry.

   Space-blending or transform-inheritance for the arm is a great feature to use throughout the rig; the arms use it the most, but you can add this to the legs, if needed. This kind of feature will usually be set at the start of an animation and left in one space or the other, but it will be able to blend between the spaces smoothly.

4. Using text for the node targets is fast and easy and lets the animators know what each node is and how it is affecting the arm. Create some text using Arial with capital letters "W" and "L." This creates curve shapes and group nodes that you can use for the world and local space-switching. The local space control will get hooked into the hip rig at a later time since the "L" keeps the arm in the same space as the upper body, but outside of the shoulder/chest, while the world control is to remain outside the character space and can be animated to attach to another character or create an off-set on the arm, if needed.

   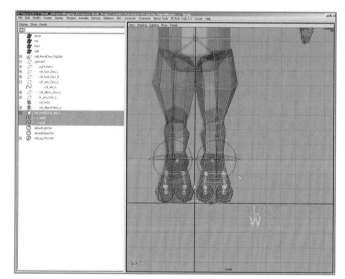

   Figure 7.50
   The new nodes in the proper place for this part of the rig.

   Figure 7.50 shows the naming and location for the world and local curve controls. Once they are in place and named, you can take the "ctrl_arm_Zero_L" and parent-constrain it between the two curves. We will set up a custom attribute to do the blending between the world and local controls like our constraint switches.

5. Rename the "ctrl_arm_L" shape node from "curveShape1," as it is called in our file, to "xtraAttrs," like you did on the foot roller control. Add the custom attribute called "worldLocal" and make the world space the default. Because this switching attribute is part of the main animation controls, we put it on the shape to keep it from being animated by mistake.

Auto-Clavicle

Rotations vs. translation for our controls is something that comes up quite a bit when deciding how to allow an animator to interact with the rig. In most cases, translation is a bit more intuitive to pose without the problem of gimbal lock, but rotations can be easy to edit and understand in the Graph Editor. Since we already have the nice FK skeleton and mesh set up to pick the clavicles and animate them, you could just add an extra layer of control to do the auto-clavicle and have a way to turn off or amp up the result.

1. Start with selecting "clav_L" and group it once. This will get controlled later for your autoRig. Name it "ctrl_clav_AutoClav_L." It will be connected to rotate with a Set Driven Key based on the position of the "ctrl_arm_L."

2. The "ctrl_arm_L" will be the driver and the "ctrl_clav_AutoClav_L" will become the driven. Standard SDK workflow is to key the zero pose and then lift the arm up into a reaching overhead position where the arm is at or past its limit, rotate the AutoClav node up in Y so that the arm and clavicle look good for the position, and set your next SDK key. Do the same process for the Z translation on the arm, pulling it forward and rotating the "AutoClav" node forward in X. You can adjust the keyframes and SDK curves to get a nicer feeling motion from the clavicle.

   Figure 7.51 shows the SDK curves for the "ctrl_clav_AutoClav_L."

3. Now that you have the automatic part of the clavicle done, the animators need to have control over it. You will use the same technique to do this as you did for the "Roll Amp" adjustment for the feet. Simply add a new custom attribute called *autoclave* to the "ctrl_arm_L" shape node "xtraAttrs" where you placed the World Local attribute.

4. Next use the Mel command `createNode multDobuleLinear` and duplicate the new node once. With both of them selected, select the "ctrl_clav_AutoClav_L" node and graph them in the Hypergraph so that you can do your connections. Hook up the multDoubleLinear nodes between the SDK curves and the "ctrl_clav_AutoClav_L" rotation values. Then take your "autoclave" and connect it to the open slot on the multDoubleLinear nodes (see Figure 7.52).

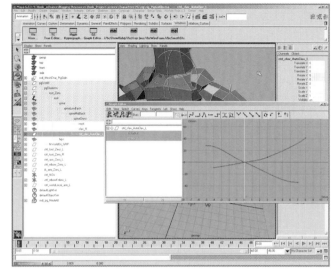

Figure 7.51
SDK curves.

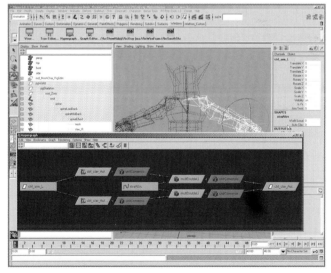

Figure 7.52
The final connections for the nodes.

Remember that since we added the multDoubleLinear nodes after the SDK connections we can either scale their effect to 0, turning off the automatic movement of the clavicle, or amp the value so that the clavicle has a bigger range of movement. You can even give it a negative number and the shoulder will pull away from the arm as you translate the control forward, not practical unless something is pulling on his hand and he tries to pull away.

5. One thing to keep in mind is that when you switch to IK from FK, the auto-clavicles will no longer work. This is not a big problem to deal with though; you just blend the value off during the switch back and forth. Most animators will not want the automation turned on anyway, but there are times when it's nice for quick blocking or game moves that have tight turnaround.

Scapula Rig

In order to create a rig for the scapula, we have to make sure that it meets a few requirements. Its main requirement is to offer control over deformations following the clavicle and at the same time be animated for things like muscle tensing and subtle motion. In order to work out the details of the rig, setting up a quick test file outside of the main character rig to test ideas is a great way to go. It gives you a small file you can mess up all you want, and you don't have to worry about contaminating your real rig file. Once you have something working the way you want, you can build it clean in the rig file (see Figure7.53).

Looking at the joint placement of the test rig, the key to get this to work is that the rotation point for the scapula must be in the center of the mesh where, when rotated, the joint end arcs along the surface of the mesh. This makes sense because the scapula floats over the rib cage, and we need to emulate that motion. We also need to allow the joint to translate up while rotating out, such as during an arm lift over your head.

This process will happen in two stages. You will create the joints in the rig file, and then you will transfer them back to the template skeleton file and skin file.

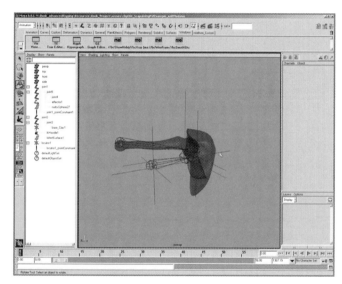

Figure 7.53
This is a quick test rig for the scapula rig.

1. In the rig file, we have a reference to the character high-rez mesh that we will turn on in order to place the new joints more easily. Just hide the head so you can focus on the rib cage/shoulder area. Figure 7.54 shows the location of the shoulder blade rotator, in the top view, letting it rotate along the surface of the rib cage.

2. Next, using a rough shoulder blade model with the location of where the shoulder blade pivots for its twist, marked by a red arrow, you will scale and move it into the position where you think this character's shoulder blade would be. When you are happy with the size and location of the shoulder blade, rotate the end joint to align with the scapula twist pivot (see Figure 7.55).

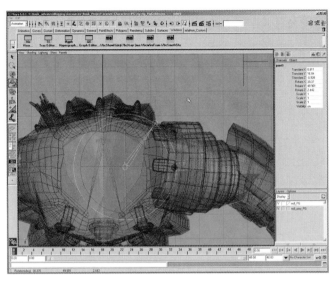

Figure 7.54
Pivot location for the shoulder blade rig.

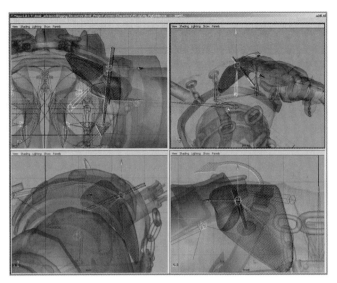

Figure 7.55
Scapula joint location.

3. Now snap new joints over the top of these temp joints and end on the end of the clavicle joint, creating three new joints total. Name them starting at the root, "ctrl_autoScap_L," "ctrl_autoScap_Attach_L," and "ctrl_autoScap_END_L." Adjust the "ctrl_autoScap_L" LRA to match that of the clavicle.

4. Create one single joint that will be used for skinning and snap this new joint to the pivot location of the scapula, name it "scap_L," and parent it under the "spineChest." This joint will receive both translation and rotation data for it to move correctly. Parent "ctrl_autoScap_L" to the "spineChest" joint. Figure 7.56 shows the new rig joints and the new scapula joint.

5. This joint is what you will save out and put into the other template and skeleton files. Remember to set the LRA to be consistent with the rest of the skeleton, positive rotation in Z is forward and negative is back, with X being the twist axis so it gets aimed down the direction of the scapula twist and at the proper angle. Make sure they have a name for Trax. Mirror the joint over once you're done. Figure 7.57 shows the joint with the proper LRA alignment.

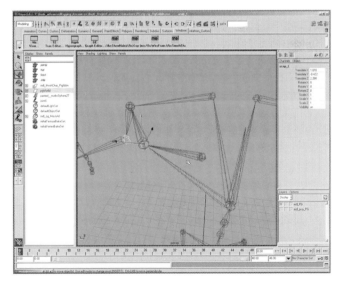

Figure 7.56
Scapula joint and rig joints.

Now unparent them and export the two scapula joints from this file and load them into the skeleton file and template file. Re-parent them in the rig file after the export is completed.

6. Add an IK Handle from "ctrl_autoScap_Attach_L" to the "ctrl_autoScap_END_L" joint and name it "ik_scap_L" and its effector "eff_scap_L." Parent it to the "clav_L" joint.

7. So that you can see what the effect of your rig will have on the scapula joint, parent-constrain the "scap_L" joint to the "ctrl_scap_Attach_L" joint so that they move together. Then just parent the scapula mesh under the "scap_L" joint so you can see its movement easily.

8. To finish the connections and make the scapula follow the clavicle for the full range of motion, you need to set up a rotation and translation connection for the scapula control.

9. Create a locator and snap it to the "ctrl_autoScap_L" location, parent it to the "clav_L," and name it "ctrl_scapPos_Attach_L." Freeze the locator's transform so that the locator is zeroed out.

10. Create and snap another locator to the same location as before and name it "ctrl_scapPos_L" to translate in Y when the clavicle rotates up. Freeze the locator's transform so that the locator is zeroed out.

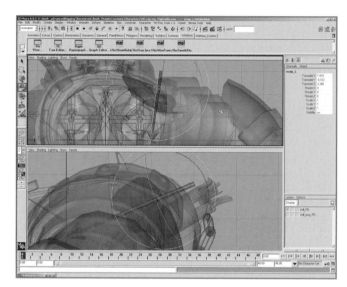

Figure 7.57
Scapula joint and rig joints with proper LRA alignment.

11. Group it and parent the group to "spineChest" and name the new group "ctrl_scapPos_Zero_L."

12. Parent "ctrl_autoScap_L" to the locator "ctrl_scapPos_L."

13. Point-constrain the "ctrl_scapPos_L" in Y only to the "ctrl_scapPos_Attach_L" node. This will allow the shoulder blade to translate up the back as the clavicle rotates up.

14. Now connect the "clav_L" Z axis to "ctrl_autoScap_L" Z axis so that when the clavicle rotates front to back, the scapula will slide around the rib cage and give a very nice natural motion to the scapula without the animator having to animate it.

If you have the Maya 6.0.1 bonus tools installed, you can Ctrl right-click on the selected attribute in the Channel Box and add it as a driver, then select the driven object, Ctrl right-click again, and pick the New Attribute Driver from the list. Then just clear them once you are done. It is faster than going through the Hypergraph or the Connection Editor when you all you need are simple direct connections.

In Maya 6.5 bonus tools, this functionality is turned off by default, but can be activated by uncommenting the code in the publish command in the userSetup.mel.

15. The one wrinkle is that it needs one more connection for it to work with the auto-clavicle. Remember an advanced rig is one in which the Character TD has made sure all the separate systems work together; you're creating a tool for animators to use, not just a feature list. When the arm is pulled forward, you are causing the rotation to happen on the "ctrl_clav_AutoClav_L" and not the "clav_L" joint, which is what the scapula forward-back rotation is hooked to.

16 You will use your trusty utility nodes once again in order to mix both rotations into the "ctrl_autoScap_L" Z rotation axis.

17. Select the "ctrl_autoScap_L" and a new plusMinusAverage node and graph them. Connect the "clav_L" rotate Z to the input 1D[0] of the plusMinusAverage and then take the output of it to the Z rotation of the "ctrl_autoScap_L."

18. Now take the "ctrl_clav_AutoClav_L" output for rotate and feed that into the plusMinusAverage node, input 1D[1]. Then take the unitConversion node that goes between the "ctrl_clav_AutoClav_L" and the plusMinusAverage and set it to –, so that the "autoScap" node rotates the correct direction, and name the unitConversion node to "unitCon_clavReverse_L" so that we know it is being used in the rig and is not just a default Maya-created node (see Figure7.58).

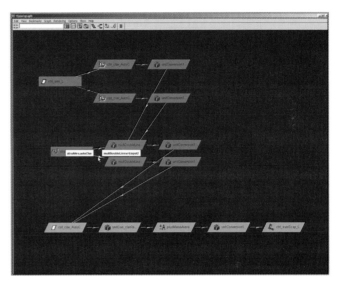

Figure 7.58
Final connections for the auto-clavicle.

If requested by the animators, you can add a twist control for animating the rotation of the scapula joint or go in and adjust the position of the "ik_scap_L" for a more extreme movement of the scapula, but we will not do that for this tutorial.

Wrist and Fingers

For the wrist control and hand, you will create a joint like you did for the ankle so that you can mirror the rotations from one hand to the other without problems and the rotations will be zero.

1. Create a new joint, group it, and snap it to the wrist joint. Name the joint "ctrl_wrist_L" and the group "ctrl_wrist_Zero_L."

2. You want to match the wrist control to the wrist joint so that they rotate the same. Parent the "ctrl_wrist_Zero_L" to the "lowArm_L" and freeze the transforms. In order to get the joint to match the wrist, you can do a few things, but a fast way using a new feature of Maya is the Presets button inside the Attribute Editor. First, pick the "wrist_L" joint and go to the Presets button and save a new preset. Then select the "ctrl_wrist_Zero_L" and go to Presets-wrist_L-replace, which will match the control wrist joint to the real wrist joint perfectly.

   The rest of the wrist setup will work just like the FK arm and leg inherit rigging where the wrist is able to follow the arm when it's rotated, or it will blend into world space where it does not inherit the rotation from the arm.

3. Duplicate the "ctrl_wrist _L" joint twice and name one "ctrl_wrist_ori_World_L" and the other "ctrl_wrist_ori_Local_L." Parent the local control to the "lowArm_L" and parent the world node under the "fkWorldOri_GRP".

4. Orient-constrain the "ctrl_wrist_Zero_L" to the world and local joints. (Make sure the constraint settings are reset to default).

5. Next, create a box rotator shape and parent the shape node under the "ctrl_wrist_L." You need to adjust the rotation order on the wrist so that it works better for animation and rigging. Because the twist on X is something that affects the entire forearm and wrist, X needs to be the first master axis, then Z for side-to-side movement, and then Y as the up and down movement. This order also helps avoid gimbal lock by separating the axes that are used most by an axis that rotates the least; in this case, the side-to-side movement on the wrist is limited in its range of motion. That is why picking a rotation order of YZX for the wrist control works well. This is also the reason that the rig has this extra layer of complex joints instead of just controlling the "wrist_L" joint with FK directly. Figure 7.59 shows the wrist rig and its controller (the control shape must still be added). We can have one control adjust two skeleton joints on the rig, the wrist and the hand joint for more natural movement in the hand. Figure 7.60 shows the hierarchy and nodes for the orient-switching.

In order for the rotations to map correctly, you need to change the rotation order of the skeleton joints as well. (Remember to make the same change to the skin skeleton file as well; while this is not necessary, it's good to keep them matching.)

6. Attaching the rotation from the "ctrl_wrist_L" to the "bn_wirst_L" and "bn_hand_L" will be straightforward. Using direct connections, rotate XYZ on the control to the XYZ on the joints. The slight change is that you cannot connect the X axis on the "bn_hand_L," which keeps the twist from happening below the wrist, but allows the up/down and left/right rotation to use both joints. This setup places the wrist rotation out past the end of the ulna and radius joint and will give the skin the look of sliding over the joint once animated.

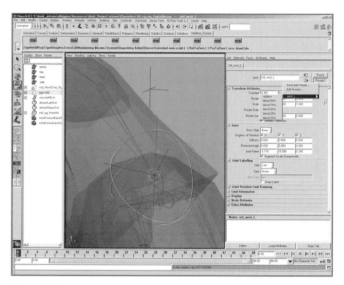

Figure 7.59
Wrist control joint without curve shape.

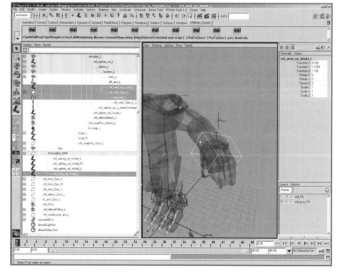

Figure 7.60
Wrist switching nodes.

7. Stable, User-Friendly, Flexible Rigs

7. Now select "ctrl_wrist_L" and name the shape node "xtraAttrs." Create a custom attribute and name it "wristFollow" default of 1. When it's set to 0, it will be off. This is your control to blend on and off the inheritance. The rigging will be set up the same way you did all the other blend controls with a direct connection and a reverse node (see Figure 7.61).

Fingers—Pose-Based Hand Controls for FK Hands

The easy and most direct way to rig the fingers is to leave them all FK. Hands require a level of dexterity and control that is much greater than that of the feet and toes. That being said, hands present a problem for animation because the large number of joints produce a lot of keyframes to manage and adjust. One way around this is to use some kind of pose script/library for the hands so that you can have all the attributes set, and you have fewer to pose each time. Another way is to set up controls with attributes like the toes were set up, having a layer of joints that an attribute can control for things like curl, spread, and so on.

Unique approaches to dealing with complex sets of joints are to use scripts to store and manage the poses that live in the file right on the controls themselves. We have already mentioned the use of scripts like the zooTriggered or the zooObjectMenu script for doing things like this. A very fast way of setting up the zooObjectMenu with poses is by using the bonus tools—Store Pose scripts generate quick sets of Mel that can be placed in the zooObjectMenu as right-click menu selections. This works great for keeping the poses stored with the character. A shelf or custom Mel script stored with the character works very well also. A variation on using the Store Pose tool is to add in the zooObjectMenu controls to create and edit custom dagPoses for things like fingers.

Just to offer some variety, we will set up some custom attributes and show you another way you can interface your controls for the hand. It's a way to just speed up selection and manipulation of the fingers by using a script job.

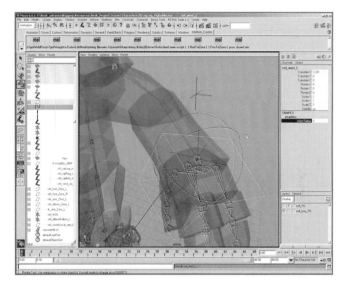

Figure 7.61
Wrist custom attributes on the "xtraAttrs" shape.

For Max users, the script from Paul Neale called Pen_Attribute_Holder is a great tool for this since it allows you to add custom attributes to the scripted modifier (node in Maya), and the Pen_Attribute_Holder lets you save poses, copy and paste, and blend the influence of the pose across the attributes that are on the holder. You can get the latest version from his Web site at http://paulneale.com. He is a very talented character setup artist and has some great work and examples on his site, including some very good DVD training material for a character rig done in Max, which by coincidence happens to be similar to the rigging done in our book.

We will go over two ways to approach this; the first is inspired from the *Character Rigger's Cookbook* from the GDC talks by Steve Theodore. The second is a variation on this that allows the same functionality but makes the process a bit more streamlined and multi-character friendly.

> You can find the entire *Character Rigger's Cookbook* at this Web site http://www.radgametools.com/cookbook/cookbook%20 final.html. It is a very well-rounded look at the pros and cons of rigging and has lots of cross software examples. It's a very good site for character artists of all skill levels to check out.

We will create a few attributes on all the fingers where we will connect them in order to speed up selection. Since they will be connection-based, name changes to the skeleton should not affect it.

1. Add the first set of attributes to the all the fingers minus the end joints and name it "selHand" and set it to string so that it is hidden from the Channel Box.

2. Next, create a control shape that will become the node that will select the hand shapes. Using annotations makes for easy to label and selectable controls for our example. Annotate the "ctrl_wrist_L" and then parent the annotation under the wrist control. Name the annotation "fingerAll_selHnd_L." The "_selHnd" will tell the script that it's the kind of object it should look for connections on.

3. Add a custom attribute to the "fingerAll_selHnd_L" just like we did to the fingers. Name it "selHand" and set it to string.

4. Connect the output of "fingerAllsel.selHand" to the entire fingers ".selHand" custom attributes. These connections are what will let the controller node find all the objects it needs to select once we have the script set up.

5. One more attribute we need to add is a switch to turn on and off the select script. Create an attribute on the "pgWorld" and call it "autoSelect" and make it a boolean (see Figure 7.62).

6. Now open up the Expression Editor. We are going to use a script node to run our script and let our script live in the file with the character. Once the Expression Editor is open, set the "Select Filter" menu to "By Script Node Name."

7. In the blank for Script Node Name call it "autoSelect" and add a comment "//this is our auto select script" so that you can click the Create button, and it will have text in it to create a node with. If you leave it blank, it does not create a scriptNode. Figure 7.63 shows the newly created script node. Change the "Execute ON" to "Open/Close." This will start the script when the file is opened. The script below goes in the "Before" section.

The final script looks like this:

```
//this is our auto select script
//sets up our script job and makes it look for a Maya event,SelectionChanged
// check out the script job command in the Maya help file for details
scriptJob -killWithScene -compressUndo 1 -event "SelectionChanged" "selectHnd";
global proc selectHnd()
```

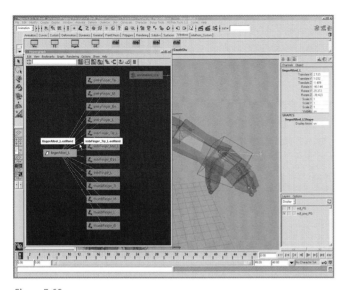

Figure 7.62
The hand with the attributes on it connected up.

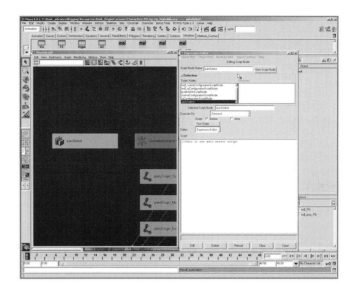

Figure 7.63
Newly created script node.

```
{
    if (` getAttr pgWorld.autoSelect` == 1) {
        string $selectHnd[];
        $selectHnd = `ls -sl "*_selHnd*" "*:*_selHnd*" `;

        if (`size $selectHnd`) { select `listConnections .selHand`;
        RotateTool;// switch the tool to rotate mode after objs are selected

        select -d  `ls -sl "*_selHnd*" "*:*_selHnd*" `;
        }
    }
}
```

Now you can take this further by having an extra set of attributes, connections, and conditional statements in your script job so that you can have a custom multi-selection handle for just each finger and not the entire hand at once, for example. You could use this same technique to create an IK FK swapping system, name independent systems to replace quick selection sets, and so on—the options are wide open. This is a basic and low-tech version compared to the zooTriggered scripts, but if you just want to have a few controls like this in your file and you don't want to use a script that you have to install to make this work, this is a good option to keep the rig all in one package.

> The ability to turn on and off this script is not currently reference-friendly and will error out. It also is not multi-character friendly since it is calling a getAttr on a specific node name.

Multi-Character and Reference-Friendly Script Node

We have talked about making sure that you plan for your pipeline and build your rig in such a way that maintains its flexibility during production. The previous finger selection method was based on another person's work and modified and while it is functional, it's not flexible as it was not designed for our pipeline. This is a common problem the Character TD must deal with when rigging, trying to make sure that what works in a single file holds up once it is placed into the pipeline.

The problem with the previous script was that in this line " if (` getAttr pgWorld.autoSelect` == 1) {" the script was looking for a specific node name and if that name were to change, then the script would break. Referencing a file or having more than one of these characters in a file will cause that "pgworld" node name to change, so how do we fix it?

1. First, borrowing a trick from Jason Schleifer, you will use .message attributes to connect your "fingerAll_selHnd" controls to the "pgWorld" node. By doing this you can then change your script to look for "pgWorld.autoSelect" without needing to have the name. By using the listConnections Mel command to check .message connection from the world node to the selector controls, you can then extract the name of the world node and check that the ".autoSelect" attribute is on or off.

2. Add a message attribute to the "pgWorld" node called "selectors" using this Mel command:
   `addAttr -ln "selectors" -at "message."`

3. The "selectors" attribute will be connected to a "world" attribute that will be added to the "fingerAll_selHnd" L and R nodes.

   Select each of the "fingerAll_selHnd" nodes and run this Mel: `addAttr -ln "world" -at "message"`

4. Now you need to connect the "selectors" attribute on the pgWorld node to the "world" attribute on the "fingerAll_selHnd" nodes. Use the Connection Editor or the Mel command connectAttr:
   ```
   connectAttr pgWorld.selectors fingerAll_selHnd_R.world;
   connectAttr pgWorld.selectors fingerAll_selHnd_L.world;
   ```

5. The other change from the first method of hooking up the selection control to the fingers to select is that you will now use selection sets instead of having to put a custom attribute on each node that you want to select.

6. Pick all the finger joints in the right hand and make a quick selection set called "pgSelect_fingers_R" and do the same for the left hand.

7. Add a message attribute called "selectNode" to both "fingerAll_selHnd" L and R nodes. You will connect this attribute to the selection sets so the script can find the nodes you want to have selected when you pick your controls.
   `addAttr -ln "selectNode" -at "message"`

8. Now add the selector's attribute to each selection set just like you did with the "pgWorld."
   `addAttr -ln "selectors" -at "message."`

> Selection sets are like any other node in Maya and can have custom attributes assigned to them. While normally you might just associate adding custom attributes to transform nodes or shape nodes, using selection sets to store custom attributes opens up a lot of possibilities. For example, linking custom attributes to lots of objects without having to actually have the attribute live on those objects as we have done here.

9. Connect the attributes from the "fingerAll_selHnd_L" to the "pgSelect_fingers_L" and do the same for the right side.

```
connectAttr fingerAll_selHnd_L.selectNode pgSelect_fingers_L.selectors ;
connectAttr fingerAll_selHnd_R.selectNode pgSelect_fingers_R.selectors ;
```

10. Set up the new script node like before but with the new code.

```
//new script////////////////////////////////////////////////////////////////////////////////////////////////////
//this is our auto select script
//sets up our script job and makes it look for an maya event,SelectionChanged
scriptJob -kws  -compressUndo 1 -event "SelectionChanged" "selectNode";
global proc selectNode()
{
//get selected node
string $sel[] = `ls -sl`;
//loop over the nodes looking for our custom attribute
for($node in $sel)
//make sure the object has the attribute
    if(`objExists ($node+".selectNode")`)
        {
        //get the world node that is the parent of the selection controls
        string $worldCon[] = `listConnections ($node+".world")`;
        //check the world node to see if the user wants the selection control to function
            if(`getAttr ($worldCon[0]+".autoSelect")`== 1)
            {
            // get the connections to the selection sets and then select those items
            string $root[] = `listConnections ($node+".selectNode")`;
            select -add $root;
            // deselect the selection contorl
              select -d $node;
            // switch the tool to rotate mode after objs are selected
            RotateTool;
            }
        }
}
//new script////////////////////////////////////////////////////////////////////////////////////////////////////
```

11. Finally, test out the system and make sure all the connections are working as before. You can now rename the "pgWorld" to "ugly" and the selections should still work as expected, regardless of the name. Make sure you set the name back to "pgWorld" before continuing.

Head Rig

The head on this character is going to be a bit different than you would find on other characters that do not have a heavy leather strapped-down helmet like our character. We will still rig this head like we would if the helmet were not there, because you never know if the helmet might need to come off. The animators will just have to be careful about how much the head moves with the helmet on.

The head and neck of a character have some simple design requirements. The head needs to be able to blend between world and body space like the other body parts. The head should have one control that controls the neck as well as the head, both translation and rotation. You could have the head and neck

7. Stable, User-Friendly, Flexible Rigs

follow an aim target that then changes from local to world space, but this kind of control can be more limiting and slow to work with since it gives you rotation only control.

1. Start by adding an IK Handle from the "neck" to the "head" joint. Name it "ik_head" and "eff_head."

2. Create a duplicate of the head joint and name the duplicate "ctrl_head," then delete the end joint and shape node. Unparent the "ctrl_head," zero its translations so it moves to the origin and group it. Set its Rotate Order to YZX.

3. Snap the group to the "head" joint and name the group "ctrl_head_Zero."

4. Parent the "ik_head" to "ctrl_head" and then orient-constrain the "head" joint to "ctrl_head_oriTarget."

5. To connect the twist of the head to control the neck, you will first add a custom attribute to the "ctrl_head" shape node called "neckTwist." This will be an override and limiter to control the neck twist. Create a multDoubleLinear and connect the "ctrl_head" rotate to the multDoubleLinear node and then to the "ik_head.twist."

6. Connect the "ctrl_head.neckTwist" to the open connection on the multDoubleLinear. Set the "neckTwist" to .5 so it will halve the rotation on the neck so that as the head turns side to side it does not rotate as much. A value of 0 will turn off the neck twist, or the animator can animate the value, if needed.

7. Next, the head controls need to be hooked into the skeleton so that you can do the local world space rotation switching and have the head controls stay with the body.

8. Create two empty groups and name the top group "ctrl_head_ori_Local_Zero" and the child "ctrl_head_ori_Local." Create one more empty group named "ctrl_head_ori_World." Parent the local zero node to the "spineChest" and parent the world node to the "fkWorldOri_GRP."

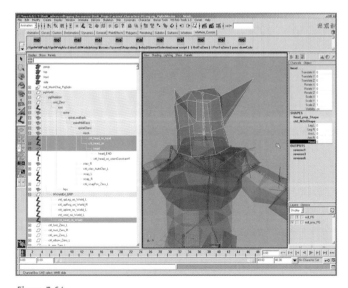

9. Orient-constrain "ctrl_head_Zero" to both world and local nodes to set up the orient-switching. Figure 7.64 shows the head rig before attaching it to the rig.

9. To make this rig work, you need to have the head control follow the chest, group the "ctrl_head_Zero" to itself, and name it "ctrl_head_Attach." Parent it to the "spineChest."

10. Add the custom attribute "head" to the "ctrl_fkOri" node that contains the attributes for the other inherit switches. Use the Mel `parent -add -shape ctrl_fkOriShape ctrl_head` to parent the shape node under the "ctrl_head". Then hook up the "head" attribute to the "ctrl_head_Zero_orientConstraint" weights.

You will now be able to rotate the back controls and the main character node while the head stays level with the ability to switch to follow with the body.

Figure 7.64
The head with the orient control shape attached. Notice it has all the FK orients on it.

Spine Rig

The spine of your character should be easy and quick to pose without a lot of controls. The animator should not have to fight to get good arcs or counter-animate the back when needing to tweak a pose, but the pose needs to interpolate well during animation. Most spine rigs come down to two methods, IK or FK, or a mix of both. While currently this character has a usable FK back and is able to pose the hips separate from the upper back, and since we have the ability to isolate the head and arms, it is not a lot of work to adjust a pose that we want. Depending on your animators, you might find that this is all they need.

Case in point, Character Studio has a back solver that is FK, but it allows you to pick multiple spine joints and additively rotate them, something that Maya users take for granted when rotating a chain of joints or hierarchy. For Max animators, this functionally is not part of the default Max software, however, so having that feature is considered advanced for Character Studio.

> There is a Max script that lets you do this kind of additive rotation outside of Character Studio. It works in Max 6 and it should work in Max 7. It is called *Rotate Chain 1.1*, created by Shawn Lewis. It is available at www.scriptspot.com.

Based on the number of joints and the joint placement on this character's spine, we get very good rotation during front/back and left/right side bends. Twisting down the spine is a problem, but splitting out the twist rotation to extra helper joints for skinning works very well and is also well documented. Take a look at the *Character Rigger's Cookbook* for more details if you need them.

For our spine rig, we will take full advantage of the built-in spline IK advanced twist controls. This back rig is inspired by David Walden, who did a very nice spine tutorial, the only one I have seen on the advanced twist control. He also has it set up automatically with his dwRiggingTools as an added bonus.

> The dwScripts can be downloaded from http://www.davidwalden.com, including a very cool Attribute Manager script for Maya that gives you a lot of control over working with custom attributes, including those that are already rigged. His skinning tools are also very good and save a lot of time running around the Maya interface.

> XSI has a very powerful spine solver that works past the 180-degree rotation without flipping and has some nice advanced controls to adjust the lumbar bend and flexibility and also pushes it back out of the way as it compresses so it does not collapse. Max has a spline IK that works OK for limited applications, but flips and snaps too easily to make it of use for this exact kind of rig we are doing in Maya. However, there are several alternatives that are possible that act like spline IK, but are not using the Max spline solver.

Back Rig Requirements and Design

The center of the body involves controls for the root, hips, spine, and the influence of the spine in the surrounding area of the chest. Most spine rigs offer a lot of control at the cost of animation speed and counter-animation or fast rough posing without the finer control over the back, giving a negative result to the animator. We want a rig that is equal at speed to pose with power to tweak.

Basic back rig requirements break down to these qualities:

◆ Independent hip and chest movement, rotation, and translation provide separate animation reactions.

◆ Pose refinement without counter-animation

◆ FK posing and animating for better whip action

◆ No movement in chest when waist is moved, same for waist when chest is moved.

◆ Twist distribution from both hips and chest (with ability to animate twist offsets).

◆ Squash and stretch on back with ability to dial down or turn off.

In order to accommodate this kind of functionality, we will use the Maya spline IK with a combination of advanced twist parameters, constraints, and utility nodes.

> Because we are going to be scaling the spine joints, we need to make sure that the scale effect is limited to only the spine and not spread into children joints of the chest. If you notice this happening when just scaling the joints by hand, then the local scale axis has gotten out of sync with the LRA and needs to be fixed. On a finished back, you have to unhook any connections to the spine joints, running the Mel `joint -e -zso` on each joint and re-rigging the back. You want to make sure that the scale axis is correct from the start before getting too far into the rig. Having the rig scripted helps as well, if you have time.

To start, you need to create a second set of joints that will be the FK skeleton for this rig. You want this to be the same as the back joints so you can create new joints or just duplicate off the back joints, removing other nodes besides the core trunk joints "spine" through "spineChest." Prefix the new spine with "ctrl" and remove the 1 from the end of "spine1."

1. Hide the "ctrl_spine" temporarily until you get the IK set up on the real back.

2. Create a spline IK chain from the "spine" to "spineChest" with Auto Parent Curve off and Number of spans set to 2. This curve will be rebuilt to allow you to limit the influence of the spline into the upper chest and waist. Name it "ik_spine," effector to "eff_spine," and name the curve, "ik_spineCurve."

3. Pick the curve and Ctrl right-click; you will have the option to cluster the curve. The default Maya auto cluster script creates relative clusters, so you need to uncheck the relative flag on each cluster.

> The fastest way to do this is to remove the relative check from the script that came with Maya. It's called *clusterCurve.mel* in the main Maya scripts directory under *C:\Program Files\Alias\Maya6.0\scripts\others*. Copy this script and put it in your *My Documents\maya\6.0\scripts* folder; then edit it to remove the `-relative` line from the cluster command.

4. Now let's create our controls for the back. These shapes will control the translation, rotation, and the twist of the back. Create the first cube-shaped curve and group it. Name the group "ctrl_chest_Zero." Snap the group pivot to the "spineMidBack." Freeze its transforms. Adjust the curve cvs until the shape fits the body, as shown in Figure 7.65.

> You might be wondering why we placed the chest control so far down the spine. What we have found is that most rigs that use a spline IK work best if the control rotates around the point where the ribs attach to the spine instead of at the separation point between the neck and chest. It gives the animators more control and causes them less counter-animation.

5. Later on, you will be orient-constraining your chest joint to the chest control. To make sure that the control and the FK joint are the same, you will duplicate off your clean "ctrl_spineChest" joint and make it a child of the "ctrl_chest_Zero."

6. Name the curve "ctrl_chest" and zero out its translation. Then parent the control curve shape node under the "ctrl_chest."

7. Select and group the top two cluster handles, in this case "cluster4Handle" and "cluster5Handle." Center the pivot and name this group "ctrl_upperBack_Zero." Finally, parent it under the "ctrl_chest."

8. You now have rotation and translation control over the top of the spine, but the chest still rotates when you translate the "ctrl_chest." To fix this, orient-constrain "spineChest" to "ctrl_chest."

9. Repeat this process for creating the hip controls. Just switch the name "chest" for "waist" and use a joint that matches the "root" joint for the control instead of the chest joint.

10. Group the last three clusters, name the group "ctrl_lowBack_Zero," and parent them under "ctrl_waist."

11. Name all the back cluster handles in order from the bottom to the top "ctrl_Back_Cluster_#" with # starting at 1 and to 6.

12. Now point-constrain the "root" joint to the "ctrl_waist" (see Figure 7.66).

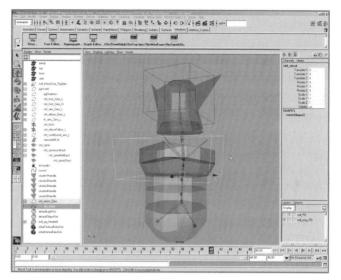

Figure 7.65
Back rig shapes and Outliner showing the clusters and IK handle.

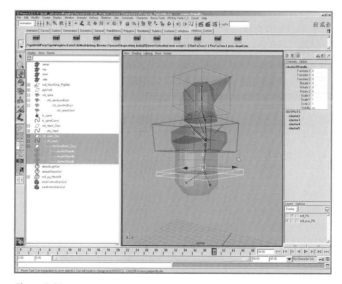

Figure 7.66
The current rig state with the clusters under the waist control.

13. Last, you want to orient-constrain the "root to the "ctrl_waist."

14. Hook up your twist for the back now so that when you twist your spine controls, it will twist the back. Select the "ik_spine" and go to the Attribute Editor. Under the IK Solver Attributes→Advanced Twist Controls, check Enable Twist Controls and set the World Up type to Object Rotation Up (Start/End). Put the names of the "ctrl_waist" and "ctrl_chest" in the WorldUp Object blanks (see Figure 7.67).

15. The final stage to get the IK and FK working is to orient-constrain the real spine joints to the control joints you duplicated at the start of the tutorial. The fast way is to pick the "ctrl_spine" and then the "spine" joint and do an orient-constraint. Then just pickwalk down and press the G hotkey (repeats last menu command) to finish constraining the rest of the spine joints. (For Max users, if you put the Constraint menu in your quad menu, you can run the command once; then just picking the top of the quad will redo the last command done in the quad, but we recommend a script to emulate the Maya style of picking objects and then constrain instead of the Max tool approach first.)

16. The next thing you need to do is to add some custom attributes to the chest control to adjust the IK/FK switching. Add the attribute ikFK, min 0 max 1 and default to 1 to the "ctrl_chest." Connect it to the "ik_spine."

Squash and Stretch Back

Adding the ability for the spine to squash and stretch helps keep the chest and hips from pulling apart and also adds in an extra layer of subtle or exaggerated control for the animators. There are a few ways to set this kind of rig up. As the Character TD, you will have to decide whether or not you want to have the back joints scale or translate, if you want it to be limited to a scale range or just indicate it by colors or some other warning, if you need it to scale in both FK and IK modes, and if you want to be able to turn it off and on. This last part, like every other automated thing in the rig, should have a switch to turn it off, regardless of how you set it up. (For a game engine, you also need to find out if your game can support scale or if translation is a better option.)

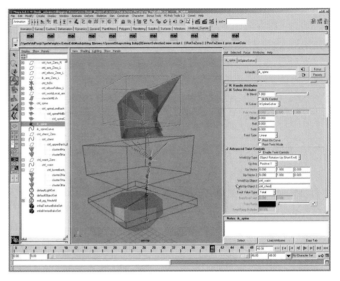

Figure 7.67
The settings for the twist controls.

When possible, it's nice to use automation or built-in tools as a starting point, but you should make sure you understand what the script is doing so you can make it fit your rig. The Bonus Tool script creates the stretch by using a distance node instead of an arch length node to control scale. The joints use the scale limits to control how much they can lengthen and compress, while the scale is driven through a multiplyDivide node to have the Y and Z react to the Xvalue and then into a plusMinusAverage node where the values of the multiplyDivide are subtracted to produce a value of 1 for scale at rest. The other thing that running this script does is hide the translate attributes from the spine joints. The script is straightforward, and I encourage you to look over its construction so you understand how it works.

1. For the squash and stretch on this rig, you will use scale on the joints to create the squash and stretch using the built-in Bonus Tools-Stretchy IK. Pick the "ik_spine" and run the script; X is pointing down the back so you will chose X in the UI that pops up. (The more use the Bonus Tools get, the better since there are a lot of tools in there that should be fully built into Maya.) You could also use the squash and stretch spine rig from Chapter 2 in place of the bonus tools script.

2. After running the script, you have to do some changes because of how your spine is rigged so far. First thing is to unparent the distance locators, because the current parents are causing dependency cycles. You also want to name the locators. The bottom locator gets named "ctrl_ikScaleLow" and "ctrl_ikScaleUp." Name the distance node "ik_spine_ScaleDistance."

3. Parent the "ctrl_ikScaleLow" to the "ctrlWaist" and "ctrl_ikScaleUp" to "ctrl_chest." This fixes the dependency loop and puts the scale distance check onto the real back controls. Freeze the transforms on the two locators.

4. As mentioned earlier, there is no quick way to just turn off or dial down the stretch effect. The cool thing about what we rig up next is that we can control whether or not just the hips or just the chest scale the back or both of them together.

5. Create a new custom attribute on the "ctrl_chest" shape node called "squashStretch" (you can name the shape node xtraAttrs if you want).

6. Next, create a new pairBlend node (createNode pairBlend). Ctrl-select the distance node and the "ctrl_chest" in the Outliner and graph them in the Hypergraph (see Figure 7.68).

7. The pairBlend node will be placed between the input from the "ctrl_ikScaleUp" to the "ctrl_ikScaleDistance" node. Our chest control custom attribute "squashStretch" will drive the pairBlend.weight attribute and that will blend to any value you put in the pair blend node, tricking the distance node into thinking that the distance has not changed. Figure 7.69 shows the connection to the pairBlend node, and Figure 7.70 shows the final connections of the pairBlend in to the distance node.

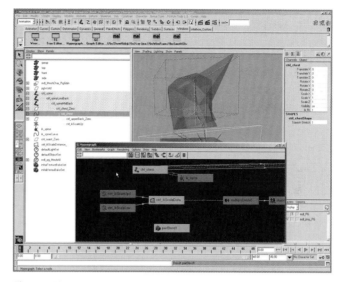

Figure 7.68
The new node and the graph that the stretchy IK script created.

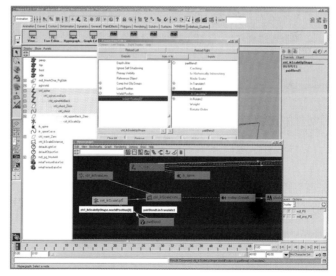

Figure 7.69
Connecting the pairBlend node.

Figure 7.70
Final connections.

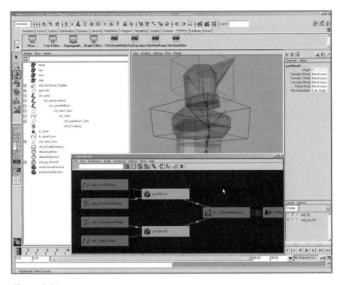

Figure 7.71
Both upper and lower connections into the back distance node.

8. We need to add in our default blend value so the spine thinks the distance is the same. Select the pairBlend node and open the Attribute Editor. Set the In Translate1 values to be equal to the In Translate2 values at rest. Your stretchy spine override should now be finished. Test it by pulling the back up and then dialing down the "squashStretch" attribute. The spine should return to its default length, leaving the back with a value of 1, 1, and 1 for the scale.

9. If you notice you have only done the upper locator, this squash and stretch value only works to control the upper back from causing the spine to stretch; the waist control will still stretch the back. We do the same process for the lower back. This gives us a lot of control over how the spine reaches its maximum stretch (see Figure 7.71). The spine squash and stretch effect also works with the FK controls as well.

> If you were doing this setup in MAX, you could use the Measure tool instead of the Distance tool, along with using the list controller weight to blend the influence of the scale on or off.

Final Back Controls and Outliner Cleanup

To finish up the back rig, you need to add one more control shape that will be the master control for the upper body.

1. Create a new control object just like the chest and hips using a joint and curve shape. Call it "ctrl_master" and group it to create a zero group.

2. The location of the new control will not be at the base of the back, although it will be at the center of gravity. You can guess where this is easy enough, but it's quick and easy to do using some quick constraining. Select the "root" and both hips and then the "ctrl_master_Zero" node. Then Constrain-Point and right after that do Constrain-Remove Target. The "ctrl_master_Zero" node will now be in the center of the pelvis.

You can even move it a little closer to or in direct line with the hip joints, depending on how you want the control to work. This control, when animated, will be the same action as if you were keeping your legs and pelvis still and leaning forward. Notice that your pelvis rotates around the location of the leg socket while your pelvis pushes back so that you don't fall over. This movement is very distinct and different than rotating from the base of the spine like a pelvic thrust or twist. This rotation point is also very visible when you're sitting down or have your butt on a hard surface.

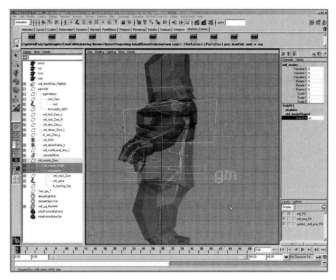

3. Group the "ik_spine," "ik_spineCurve," and the "ik_spine_ScaleDistance" and name the group "ik_backrig_Grp."

4. Parent the "ctrl_spine," "ctrl_waist_Zero," and "ik_backrig_GRP" to the "ctrl_master."

5. Because you parented the "ik_splineCurve" to the control that also controls the clusters that move the curve, you have created a double offset. This is easy to fix. Pick the curve and go to the Attribute Editor and uncheck the Inherits Transform option. This is an easy way to keep your deforming geometry in groups that make sense for organization, but would cause problems if they were moved.

6. With the range of movement that the "ctrl_Master" can go through, the rig needs to have an extra layer of control to avoid gimbal lock. Just group it once and name the new group "ctrl_master_Gmbl." Create a curve text object letter "gm" for gimbal master and parent its shape node under the "ctrl_master_Gmbl."

7. Create an extra attribute on the shape node of the "ctrl_Master" that is called "gmblCtrl." Make it a boolean value. Connect the custom attribute to the visibility of the "ctrl_master_Gmbl" curveShapes so that the animators can use it if needed, but it's not visible to select. If you connect it to the visibility of the control transform node, then the entire back rig would be hidden (see Figure 7.72).

Figure 7.72
The finished back rig with custom attributes for the gimbal control.

You might find you need to create extra controls like this on other parts of the character, such as the wrists or any node that needs to rotate a full 360-degrees on more than one axis. Just follow the same procedure to create other rotation override controls.

7. Stable, User-Friendly, Flexible Rigs

Arm World Local Switching

With the back rig set up, we can now go back to our world and local nodes for the arm and parent or parent-constrain them under the proper controls. The world control should remain in the character's world space so it will stay where it is. The local control will get parent-constrained to "ctrl_chest." You can constrain it to a few body parts like the head and then let the user blend between what local space he wants to use.

Depending on how you want the rig to work with the other local and world inheritance switching on things like the arms and head, you can use the parent constraint on them so that the world space is under the "ctrl_master" and not the full world node. Remember we have all our world orients under the "fkWorldOri_GRP."

Attribute-Driven Visibility Switching

A few more visibility switches are in order while we are on the subject. Make the "ctrl_arm_L|xtraAttrs.worldLocal" switch value control the visibility of the L and W nodes. Giving your animators as uncluttered a file as possible is part of the rig UI design and should be done where possible. In the case of making an on/off visibility switch for something that is a blending attribute, you want to make sure it's clear to the artist when it is blending or only on world or local. Using Set Driven Keys is the fast and easy way to rig this, but it's possible to do with condition nodes, too. When the switch is at 0, it's in world space and the L should be hidden; when it's at 1, the arm is in local space and the W should be hidden. Any blend value in-between both L and W should be visible.

You will do this same kind of process to the "ctrl_back" to show when the animator is in FK or IK, but you will do it with colors and not visibility since the back can be controlled by FK or IK at the same time—a color change can help the animator figure out what keyframes are having an effect on the rig. Drive the color on the "ctrl_chestShape" under Display Overrides with a simple Set Driven Key to switch the control from default blue to the light blue when in FK mode. It's subtle but enough to give a quick hint as to what the control is set to. Look for the Override Color attribute on the shape node to do the SDK.

These concepts can all be used or just partially implemented; the idea of animator feedback is the same. The longer it takes someone to figure out what a rig is doing once animated, the longer it will take to animate with or fix it if the rig breaks. One last way to help control the rig is to control the selectability of objects by driving the reference override value, still staying away from layers to keep the character self-contained to be easily referenced or imported multiple times into a file or even saved to be sent offsite for outsourcing of animation.

Additional visual indicators, such as lines connecting floating controls like pole vectors for arms, are also handy and easy to create with either clusters and a two-point curve or using something like the annotate command to create an arrow and text labels for a control.

> Here is a tip for Maya users. You have the ability to clean up the display of joints that are branching at places like the hips or the chest. Set the Draw Style for the joint that is the parent of all the branching nodes to be Box and not Bone, and this cleans up the file visually very quickly and with much less effort.
>
> New to 6.5 is the ability to control the joint size per file and per joint, allowing further cleanup and tweaking compared to 6.0, where these settings were global from file to file.

Rigging the Right Arm

It might seem strange that we left the right arm rigging until now. Since the arm rig is one of the more complex systems on the character because of its connections to so many other parts of the rig, it's easier to complete one entire arm and make sure it works and then mirror it for the other arm or rig the other arm from scratch. For the book, we recommend that you do it from scratch so that you have a better understanding of the rigging process, or you can go through a way to mirror-over part of the rig if you feel confident you understand the rig.

Mirroring-over a rig as complex as this arm can take a lot of work in order to get the connections set up again between the constraints, custom attributes, and utility node networks. As stated at the start, the best thing to do is automate this process if possible. This next section will walk you though doing a rig mirror with a little work in the Hypergraph and a clean mirror file to start with. While you work on creating a mirror of a rig, it works better if you can clean out anything that does not belong directly in the arm rig. The first step to getting the arm rig mirrored is to look at all the nodes that make up the arm and also check the connections in and out of the arm components.

1. Use the Outliner to filter for only things named "*arm*"; this will show all nodes that are related to the arm rig and their parent nodes. Go ahead and remove anything that is not part of the arm system, legs, head, controls IK, and so on (see Figure 7.73).

2. Since you are working in a new file for the right arm, go ahead and search and replace the names from L to R. You also want to remove any constraints or connections to your new controls. The connections will be done in the final file, and you want to make sure that only clean controls import in and not ones that will bring extra-connected nodes with them. Do an Edit-Delete All by Type–Constraints to clear them out (see Figure 7.74).

3. Next let's move over the easy bits like the "ctrl_worldLocal_arm_R." Since the pivots will stay the same for the controls, you will just grid-snap the vertices of the control shape over to the right eight units to create your mirrored version.

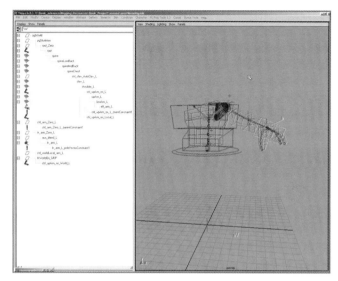

Figure 7.73
Starting point for mirroring the arm.

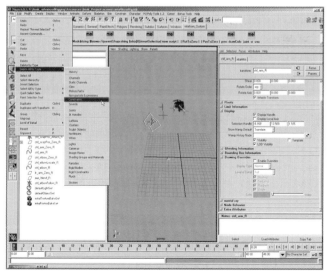

Figure 7.74
Removing all constraints and other nodes you don't need.

7. Stable, User-Friendly, Flexible Rigs

141

4. Next, you will mirror what joints that you can, including the joints are orient-constraint targets.

5. Group everything that is left in the file except any joints (you will have to unparent controls that are joint based), and negative-scale it on X to flip all the nodes. In order to freeze the transformations, you need to break all connections on the nodes. Then freeze transforms and unparent everything from that group node. Save this file.

6. Load this clean file into the master rig file. Start adding IK Handles to the right arm skeleton and to the scapula rig and name them to match the left IK Handles. Since you have brought in all the transform nodes from the mirror process, you can parent the new "ik_arm_R" under the "aux_armZero_R" that will then get parented into the "pgWorld" node. Parent the "ctrl_armZero_R" under the "pgWorld" (see Figure 7.75).

7. Constrain the "ik_arm_R" with a pole vector constraint to the "ctrl_elbow_R" and also point-constrain the "aux_blend_R" to the "ctrl_arm_R" just like you did on the other arm.

8. Continue re-parenting and constraining the right arm nodes until they match the left arm. Once that is done, you can hook up all the custom attributes and node networks. (Sometimes, the rotation or the joint-orient of the mirrored joints will have to be fixed or re-matched to the original joints after parenting, so just watch that your joints rotations remain zero during this process.)

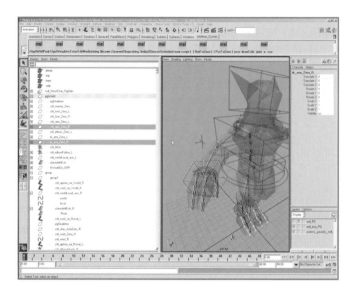

Figure 7.75
New arm nodes parented into main hierarchy.

This process can be very tedious, but it's good to know how to mirror a rig that is somewhat complex. Again, though, we stress the importance of having a scripted system if you have to do more than one rig or even a single rig that you might have to adjust or fix later.

After all the nodes have been parented in and constrained, then you will be ready to hook up the custom attributes that were mirrored-over with all the controls.

9. Working from the outside in, start with the hand controls and pick both the right and left control and graph the connections. This will let you see what nodes and attributes are connected, and you can duplicate the utility nodes from the left hand and hook them into the right. Depending on the attributes you're driving, you might have to add in "–" (negative) signs to the unitConversion nodes so that the attributes values produce the same result.

10. To add the auto selectability to the right hand, you just need to add an annotation node like you did on the left and add the "selHand" string custom attribute to the hand annotation node and connect the attribute on the fingers. (Because you mirrored the joints, the custom attributes will be on the joints already.)

11. After you have gone through and finished all the attribute and node connections, you should have a graph for both arms that looks like Figure 7.76. A few things to note—you can duplicate the Set Driven Key nodes, but for them to work on the right arm, you just need to scale the values -1 in the Graph Editor, flipping the values.

Leg Fixes: Separating Out Rotation Inheritance from the Hips

Looking back to where you rigged up the legs, everything works great except that because of how we edited the pole vector not to let the leg flip, the side effect is that the leg's parent node causes the legs to rotate. This points the knee in the opposite direction of our foot control and causes the animators to counter-animate the leg. To fix this problem, we are going to take away any rotational influence the hips have over the leg joints.

1. Create an empty group and parent it to the "bn_hips." Name it "ctrl_leg_GRP_R."

2. You will need to snap the group node to the top of the leg joint and freeze transformations.

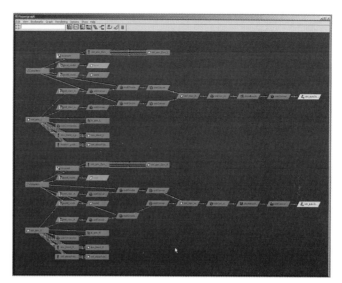

Figure 7.76
Matching graphs of the two arm controls after all the reconnecting by hand.

3. Select "ctrl_upLeg_R," ""ctrl_upLeg_ori_Local_R," and "ctrl_upLeg_ori_R" and parent them under "ctrl _leg_GRP_R."

4. We don't want the legs to be affected by the hip's rotation. To fix that, start by creating an empty group or null object.

5. Name the new null "ctrl_legs_Ori;" this will be what the orientation of both legs is attached to. Parent it to the "bn_hips" and freeze transformations on it; then parent it to "pgSkeleton." That will match the orientation for the next step.

6. Orient-constrain "ctrl _leg_GRP_R" to "ctrl_leg_Ori," which will remove the "bn_hips" influence from the legs.

7. Test it by rotating the hip controls; the top of the leg should move, but when you rotate the hips right and left, the knee should stay pointing straight ahead.

8. After you have the right leg working, repeat the steps for the left leg, replacing R for L where needed.

Rig Wrap-Up

With the main rigging components complete and hooked together, the file is functionally done, but is still not ready to hand off to an animator until it is cleaned up. Cleaning a file requires that you do the following steps:

◆ Finish any visual cues for control switching like IK/FK blending.

◆ Create final groups and finish cleaning up the Outliner.

◆ Hide and limit the visibility/selectability to only those objects that will be allowed to be animated.

◆ Lock and hide any attributes that will not be animated.

◆ Create selection sets for both animation controls and rig sets that make sense for the Character TD to look at.

◆ Set the controls to automatically select the kind of tool that should be used on them—rotation mode, translate, or both when selected.

◆ If needed, set up a custom "pickwalk" system so that the animators can "pick walk up and down" without selecting a control that is not meant to be grabbed.

> Remember as you hide and lock attributes that it's good to copy and paste the Script Editor contents into a text file. That will be the quick way to hide or unhide all the rig bits so that you can adjust or tweak the rig later without a lot of extra unnecessary work. New in Maya 6 is the ability to filter the output not to include all the results, info, warning or error messages so you can create a very clean copy-paste script.

Visual Feedback

The first stage of cleanup will be to finish adding in the color switches to the arms to let the animators know when they are in a certain mode, just as we did for the back controls. Because the proxy geometry is on a layer, you have to break the connection to the override color in order to link it to the IKFK attribute. This causes the mesh not to be associated with the layer anymore, but you can just reassign it to the layer, since the color has an incoming connection. The color switch will still work because the layer was not able to break the SDK connection.

One other simple way to show what state a control is in is to have text or annotations turn on and off, depending on the attribute value. For example, for the arms you could turn visible a small text object that says "IK" in a bright color that stays with the IK arm control, so that it's very clear what mode the rig is in.

In whichever way you, as the Character TD, want to provide feedback to the animator, the key is that you do something to communicate the state of the rig so it's easy to work with and animate.

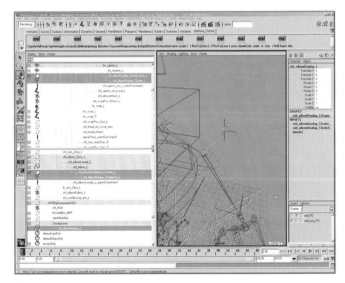

Figure 7.77
Display lines.

To make a simple, visual connection between a floating control like the elbow control and the joints it controls, create a degree one curve. Degree one curves only need two vertices to create a line. Cluster the two points of the curve and parent one under the upper arm joint and the other under the elbow control. Now, wherever you move the elbow control, it gives a very clear connection to what part it is controlling, keeping it separated from the other elbow control. In our file, the nodes are named ctrl_elbowDisplay_L or R.

Outliner Cleanup

Because the cleaner the Outliner and the hierarchy of the file are, the faster the rig is to edit and work on and the easier it is to animate, you want to make sure that items are all grouped and ordered properly. In Maya, changing Outliner order also serves to control selection order; for example, bringing nodes closer to the top of the Outliner causes them to get evaluated first in the scene graph. This has direct effect over how items are selected and evaluated so you want to try and keep control objects higher in the tree than non-control objects. Figure7.78 shows one possible way to group and order the Outliner. You can see the skeleton, controls, and extra bits that people should not touch are each under a node. The controls group is higher in the list than the skeleton or the "do not touch" nodes because we want the controls to be what get checked for selection first when objects are overlapping them.

Lock and Hide

The final cleanup stage involves cleaning off every node in the rig, so that only the attributes that should be animated will get animated, and the channels that are not supposed to be keyed don't get keyed. This does not keep animators from unhiding and unlocking these attributes, but it does do a good job in pre-

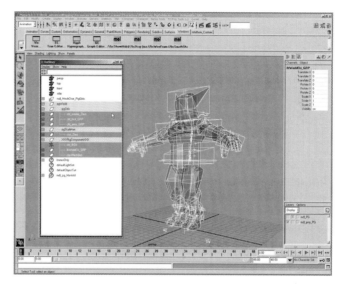

Figure 7.78
Cleaned up Outliner groups.

vention. If you can or do use file-referencing of your rig, then anything you have locked and hidden cannot be changed by the animator, and it also protects the SDK curves and connections from being deleted by mistake. The other benefit of doing this is that fewer keyframes mean less curve data, fewer nodes, and fewer connections and that all keeps the rig fast. On some controls, if being able to see the object's attribute value for feedback could be of use, then just lock it and don't hide it. For controls that are well hidden, I will usually just lock them and not hide the attributes. For any control the animator will touch, then I lock and hide the attributes.

Remember to turn on and filter the output of the Script Editor for all the attributes that you have locked and hidden or objects for which you have turned the visibility on or off. Doing that makes it very quick to copy and paste the script to toggle everything on or off that is supposed to be hidden/locked when you have to get in and edit the rig. To unhide everything, you just need a quick "for" loop to run through all the nodes and make them visible and unhide and unlock the main attributes.

7. Stable, User-Friendly, Flexible Rigs

Beyond locking and hiding the attributes, you need to lock and hide the parts of the rig that should not be selected by animators. The quick way is to just throw things on a layer and be done. The problem with this is that the first thing people do when they open a file is to unhide all. Animators use hide and unhide all the time to view only certain parts of a character and because of this we have to do some creative hiding. To hide any object and defeat the show-all problem, you need to make sure that you lock the visibility attribute of an object. On some objects, you might have to make the visibility attribute visible in the Channel Box first and then lock it.

At this point, you can also set any joints that are bright yellow back to default colors for their part of the body since they were turned yellow just to make it easy for us to rig the objects. Still, you should record this in the show bits script so you get the rig back to its starting state.

Part of cleaning up the mesh is to make sure that the animators don't select the parts of the mesh that are only there to be proxy mesh and not for controlling FK animation. Because we have all the mesh on a layer, we can keep the layer there, but we need to break the connection that the layer is controlling that lets us set the value to template or reference for each mesh object. Below is the simple "for" loop used to do the breaking on all the selected mesh shapes.

```
//kill layer connection
{
string $sel[] = `ls -sl`;
     for ($obj in $sel) {
     CBdeleteConnection  ($obj + ".ovdt");
     }
}
```

After you run the script, use the channel control to move the overrideDisplayType to the keyable section and keyframe it for now to lock the layer from connecting to it once we reassign the mesh to the layer. This way the layer still controls the visibility, but we have control over the display type. If you don't want to use the layer at all, then you can create a master attribute on the mesh that drives the visibility of all the mesh shapes for the proxy geometry. Now that you have control over the mesh, you will set the mesh to be a reference for anything that will not be used as a FK control.

You need to keep an incoming connection on any nodes you want to set as reference to still use the layers. We can leave the keyframes, but those have a chance of being deleted by mistake. Instead, just make a simple custom attribute on the "pgWorld" that is an Enum and create three values of Normal, Template, and Reference and name the attribute "prxyViz." Connect the values to the inputs on the proxy geometry displayOveride attribute. This lets us control them from one place on the rig and keeps the layer from having the control. To remove the layer altogether for the proxy mesh, you can also add a prxyVisiblity attribute on the "pgWorld" and hook it to all the prxyShape visibility attributes.

Selection Sets and Character Sets

Creating selection sets for your controls can be much better than just expecting that grouping and names alone will keep the rig easy to edit. The problem with that is that in trying to keep everything in proper groups, you can cause extra work for yourself by needing to add more constraints or figure out how to connect controls when really the node just needs to be parented into part of the rig. Since sets are hierarchy-independent, they are the perfect tool for grouping your rig components. At a minimum, you want to create a set for each system in the rig, examples like the entire spine rig, arms, and legs and head selection sets. This keeps the file easy for you to edit and for someone else to edit without having to look through the entire hierarchy to find all the rig components.

Character sets will be set up to help both for Trax-compatibility later on and also to allow for grouping all the animation data, regardless of hierarchy. Again, this is very handy and frees you from having to worry about some of the keyframe management issues that can happen with lots of controls. This is especially important when trying to keep something like the IK/FK arm-switching in sync. We recommend that you build a character set or subset of all the nodes that are required to be animated for the IK and FK arm and any other nodes that can influence the arm switch, including the elbow pole vector and the clavicle nodes. Another set of nodes that would be good for setting up a subcharacter for would be the fingers. This lets you manage, pose, and track all the keyframes for the fingers more easily.

> A note about naming—because we have some attributes that have the same name on nodes that are the same name, you will want to make sure that there is at least an L and R on any nodes that will live at the same level in a character node, or you will not be able to tell the attributes apart very well. This is an easy fix to apply later if needed.

Auto Tool Select and Custom Pickwalking

One of the best ways to make a rig quick to work with is to set up the controls so that they automatically switch to the proper tool that should be used on them. FK controls are rotation and should, when selected, switch your current manipulator to be the Rotate tool. Translate controls should switch you to the Move tool, etc. Maya has a multi-manipulator that will let you do rotate and translate together and should be set up on nodes like the leg controls and the head where one control is allowed to rotate and translate. This is one of the best ways to help visually reinforce what the selected character control does.

Using the built-in Maya method requires you to work with the manipulator mode selected and that you set up your tool switches per object using the showManipDefault attribute that can be set by Mel or in the Attribute Editor under Display.

The other way to do this is by using a script job like we did with the hand rig where the script job sees a custom attribute, or it could even read what the manip setting is on the showManipDefault attribute so you cover both bases. The script can just set the Rotate, Translate, or Scale tool directly so you don't have to be in manipulate mode. We actually do this in the script for the hand rig by calling RotateTool command.

> For Max users, there is a script called SMART SELECT v0.1 by Martijn Van Herk, and it is available at http://www.scriptspot.com. It lets you do the same thing as our script job would do, but in this case, you put text commands in the user properties of an object that will trigger your Scale, Rotate, or Translate tool. (User properties of an object in Max are the same as the Notes area in the Attribute Editor in Maya.)

Here is the Maya equivalent script job that was posted to the Highend 3D listserv by Shahar Levavi (http://www.levavi.net/). To use, add a custom attribute to each control of the rig (arm, hips, legs etc...) and name it defaultTool.

7. Stable, User-Friendly, Flexible Rigs

That attribute is an Enum with 3 options 0, 1 and 2 (or "move", "rotate", "scale"). Then add a script node that executes each time the file was launched.

In the script node place this script.

```
//////////////////////////////////////////////////////
global proc SL_toolSwitch()
{
scriptJob -e "SelectionChanged" "whichTool";
}
global proc whichTool()
{
string $gTools = `currentCtx`;
string $obj[] = `ls -sl`;
        if (size($obj) != 0)
        {
                if (`attributeExists "defaultTool" $obj[0]`)
                {
                string $tool = `getAttr ($obj[0] + ".defaultTool")`;
                switch ($tool)
                        {
                        case "0":
                                $gTools = "moveSuperContext";
                                break;
                        case "1":
                                break;
                        case "2":
                                $gTools = "scaleSuperContext";
                                break;
                        }
                }
        }
setToolTo $gTools;
}
//////////////////////////////////////////////////////
```

Figure 7.79 shows the final rig with the character sets, final groups, and selection sets.

The completed rig is never really finished. Once in production, the rig will go through changes and revisions, and the rig will get fine-tuned. Hopefully, the ideas and concepts discussed in this chapter and throughout the book will allow you to create a stable, fast rig that is a solid foundation for you to build on.

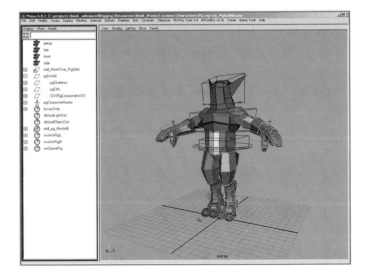

Figure 7.79
Final Rig.

chapter 8
Props and Interactive Accessories

Props have been a challenge since 3D animation began. The hierarchical nature of 3D animation made it difficult for characters to simply pick up and put down objects. As 3D animation software has advanced, different tools have emerged to make prop management easier. The development of constraints has allowed objects to transcend the limits of hierarchy. So now that the tools exist, new issues arise. What is the best way to organize props?

Before tackling a prop, it is important to do some homework and ask some questions. In the case of props, the first thing to ascertain is the permanence of the prop: Is it something that is an integral part of the character? If you are setting up a character such as "Hellboy," who always carries a specific weapon, that prop is always going to be with the rig, and its setup will probably be designed to go with the character on a permanent basis. Other props may be interacted with on a scene-by-scene basis, such as a can of soda a character drinks from and then sets down.

A Simple Prop Constraint Switch

Many times as a character rigger, you will come across situations where you will need to constrain one object between two others and allow the object to switch easily from one to the other. In the case of props, this could be a simple setup designed for one shot, as well as a basic control on the character itself. Maya's constraint and node system is adept at switching an object between two locations via a constraint switch. This section will cover creating such a switching system using Maya constraints. In later sections, we will look at switching a constraint between multiple points.

To begin, let's take a look at setting up a constraint system that can easily switch between two targets.

1. Open the file reverseConstraint_start.ma (see Figure 8.1). You can find this file at http://www.courseptr.com/downloads. You should see a simple

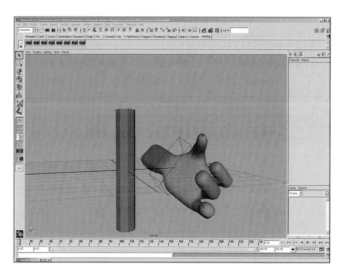

Figure 8.1
The reverseConstraint_start.ma scene.

hand, a cylinder, and a world space controller represented by a NURBS curve. The idea is that the cylinder "prop" will be set up to blend between a position on the hand and the NURBS curve, which acts as a controller.

2. Select the cylinder. It should be located at the origin. Press "Ctrl+g" to group it. Rename this new node "prop_pivot." This node will serve as an offset node—it will be capable of being animated, and it will come into play if the animator needs to make adjustments to the prop.

> Notice that the prop geometry is grouped under the "prop_pivot" node. This allows the geometry to be replaced at any time with a bit more ease should the need arise. This single piece of geometry can be replaced by a group of objects, and the actual pivot of this group is not important—it only needs to be positioned with respect to the "prop_pivot" node.

3. Press "Ctrl+g" to group the "prop_pivot" node again. Rename this new node "prop_attach." This is the node that will be constrained. The hierarchy should resemble the one in Figure 8.2.

4. Now it is time to set up the position where the prop will attach to the hand. Create an empty group using Create→Empty Group (or simply press "Ctrl+g" without anything selected) and name it "prop_wrist_null."

5. Select the "wrist" joint. This is the joint the prop will be constrained to. Since the object will be held in the palm of the character's hand, we want it to move whenever the node responsible for deforming the hand moves. Shift-select the "prop_wrist_null" node and create a point constraint and an orient constraint.

6. Create a locator and name it "prop_wrist_attach." With the locator selected, Shift-select the "prop_wrist_null" node and press the "p" key to parent them.

7. In the Channel Box, set the translations and rotations of the "prop_wrist_attach" node to 0.

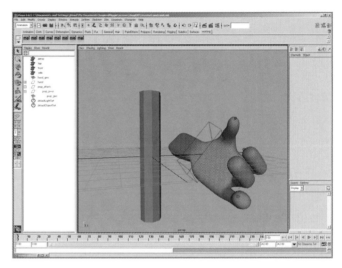

Figure 8.2
The hierarchy that controls the prop geometry.

> Notice that this constraint target is not connected to the hand IK controller. It is very likely that, in animation, the IK controller may not be used and would therefore not match up with the deformations of the character. Always attach props to the transforms that deform the geometry to minimize problems.

8. Use Create-Empty Group to make a new null node. Rename it "prop_wrist_offset" and parent it under the "prop_wrist_attach" locator. Set its rotations and translations to zero.

9. Using the File→Import menu item, import the nurbSplineCube.ma from http://www.courseptr.com/downloads. Rename the "curve1" node "prop_ctrl."

10. Now create another empty group and rename it "prop_ctrl_offset." This will be the node the prop assembly attaches to on the NURBS curve controller. With the "prop_ctrl_offset" node selected, Shift-select the "prop_ctrl" NURBS curve and press "p" to parent them. Set the translations and rotations of the "prop_ctrl_offset" node to 0. When you have finished, your Outliner should resemble the one in Figure 8.3.

11. With nothing selected, select the "prop_ctrl_offset," the "prop_wrist_offset," and finally the "prop_attach" nodes. Create a point constraint and an orient constraint using the Constraint menu.

12. Now it is time to build a control attribute for the prop. The placement of this attribute is a matter to be decided between the rigger and the animator. For this example, the control will be placed on the NURBS curve.

13. Select the "prop_ctrl" NURBS curve. Press "Ctrl-a" to reveal the Attribute Editor. Create an attribute called "toHand" that has a minimum value of 0.0 and a maximum value of 1.0. This attribute will control the switching of the prop.

14. Open the Hypershade window. Select the "prop_ctrl" curve and the "prop_attach" nodes and graph the input and output connections. You should see the nodes and the constraints in the Hypershade window.

15. From the General Utilities section of the Create Maya Nodes bin, create a reverse node. Rename the reverse node "prop_reverse."

16. Using the right mouse button, connect the "prop_ctrl.toHand" attribute to the "inputX" attribute of the reverse node, as in Figure 8.4.

17. Connect the "prop_ctrl.toHand" attribute to the "prop_wrist_offsetW1" attribute of the point and orient constraint nodes.

18. Connect the "outputX" attribute of the reverse node to the "prop_ctrl_offsetW0" attribute of the point and orient constraint nodes.

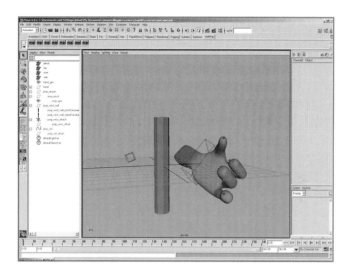

Figure 8.3
The hierarchy for attaching the prop to the palm of the hand and the prop world space controller.

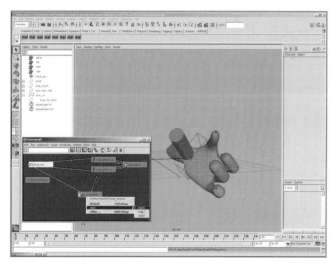

Figure 8.4
Connecting the "prop_ctrl.toHand" attribute to the "prop_reverse" node.

19. Set the "prop_ctrl.toHand" attribute to 1. Notice that the prop goes to the center of the wrist geometry. Select the "prop_wrist_attach" node and move it so that the prop fits in the hand. When you are satisfied with the placement, use Freeze Transforms on the locator to make this its rest position (see Figure 8.5).

> When you are positioning the "prop_wrist_attach" locator, make sure you adjust the "prop_ctrl.toHand" attribute to see how the prop is blending to and from the hand. Many times, the rotation of the locator is such that the prop will sweep out a 360-degree arc when transitioning, which is usually not desirable as it prevents a smooth transition from the prop controller to the hand. This can be corrected by rotating the "prop_wrist_offset" locator to a more agreeable position. Usually, rotating this node by 180 in the Z-axis will correct the problem. It may take some experimentation to find the best blend. If the locator cannot be changed in order to keep proper alignment, try changing the "ctrl_prop_offset" node's rotation to make a smoother transition.

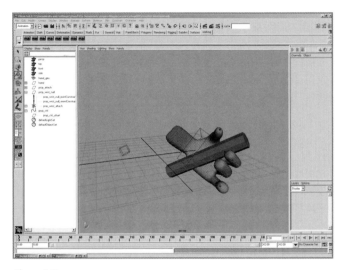

Figure 8.5
The finished reverse constraint system.

The constraint is now finished. If you change the value of the "toHand" attribute, the prop will blend between its controller and the attach locator on the palm. Notice that the entire prop exists outside of the hierarchy that controls the deformation—there was no parenting to any of the joints. This is advantageous as it allows the prop system to be deleted at any time without affecting any of the deformations. The prop can be grouped under a node that simplifies the process of locating and editing it.

Another thing to notice is how the prop transitions between its locations. With the orientConstraint, it is possible that the prop flips unacceptably when the weights are adjusted. This is due to the nature of rotation resolution within Maya. When rotations are resolved, Maya converts rotations form Euler to quaternions to compute the rotation. The result is converted back into Euler rotations. The flaw with this is that the quaternion solver will sometimes pick an alternate set of Euler rotation values as the proper target. To alleviate this problem, select the orientConstraint and set its "interpType" attribute to "shortest." This will usually eliminate unwanted flipping, as long as the two orient targets are rotated with respect to each other.

You may have also noticed that you really do not need to have extra offset nodes under the locator and the prop. The offset nodes are an extra layer of flexibility that you may never actually need to use. They do take up some memory and some computing power, but their overhead is pretty low, and it is usually better to err on the side of caution. Were this a scene with hundreds of props, it would be worth going through and stripping them out.

A One-Handed Prop System

So the simple reverse constraint works well for props that will only have two attach locations, but for some props, more complex behavior will be required. Throughout this book we have been working on a fantasy character, so let's take him and give him a weapon. Our imaginary director has dictated the character needs a wicked knife to slice his enemies. Looking at the storyboards for the shots where the character uses the knife, it is determined that the knife only needs to fit into the character's right hand and a sheath on his belt. However, anticipating the needs of the project, we will add the ability for the knife to be free in the world. The rule of rigging is not to overbuild, but in this instance, it will not take that much more effort, and it is easily possible that the knife will need to be free.

Now that we know what the prop needs to do, we want to look at the geometry of the prop and the hand that is meant to hold it. In this case, it is pretty straightforward: the knife has a handle, and the character has hands that are well-suited to grasping. The character's hand will fit comfortably around the handle, so a lot of shifting will not be necessary.

The technique we will use to control the prop will involve constraining it to different attachment nodes. Maya has parent constraints that allow objects to be dynamically parented, and these are very useful for quick, simple prop setup. However, for this prop, which is going to be heavily used, the parent constraint has a few drawbacks. For one, when switching from one controller to another, there is no guarantee of the location of the prop. To maintain consistency in production with a character that is going to be used by many animators, you want as few chances for misalignment as possible.

1. Open the knife_start.ma file. This file is located at http://www.courseptr.com/downloads.

2. Import the knife.ma file from the same Web site. You should see the knife and sheath geometry in the Maya scene. In the Outliner, a new node called "knife" should be present. If you examine the knife group, you will see it contains the two nodes that make up the knife geometry. The knife will come in at the origin (see Figure 8.6).

3. Create another Empty Group and rename it "sheath_geo_offset."

4. With the "sheath_geo_offset" node selected, Shift-select the "sheath_geo" node. Create a pointConstraint and an orientConstraint.

5. Using the Move tool, position the "sheath_geo_offset" so that the geometry of the sheath is next to the torso of the character. Once it is in position, do not Freeze Transformations—this will set the sheath to an incorrect orientation.

6. Using the File menu, import the nurbsSplineCube.ma. This is the NURBS curve you will use to control the sheath. You can find this file at the Web site mentioned previously.

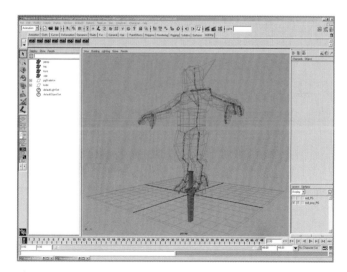

Figure 8.6
The imported knife geometry.

7. Select the newly-imported "curve1" and rename it "sheath_ctrl."

8. Select the "sheath_geo_offset" node and then Shift-select the "sheath_ctrl." Create a pointConstraint and an orientConstraint to align the "sheath_ctrl" to the geometry. Delete the constraints and use the Move tool to position the "sheath_ctrl" curve relative to the sheath for selection, as in Figure 8.7.

9. Create a new Empty Group. Rename it "sheath_ctrl_Zero."

10. Select the "bn_hips" node and Shift-select the "sheath_ctrl_Zero" group. Create a pointConstraint and an orientConstraint.

11. Use Window→General Editors→Channel Control to bring up the Channel Control window. Make the translate, rotate, scale, and visibility attributes of the "sheath_ctrl_Zero" node unkeyable.

12. Select the "sheath_ctrl" and Shift-select the "sheath_ctrl_Zero." Press the "p" key to parent them.

13. Use Freeze Transformations on the "sheath_ctrl" node.

14. Select the "sheath_geo_offset" node and Shift-select the "sheath_ctrl" node. Press the "p" key to parent them.

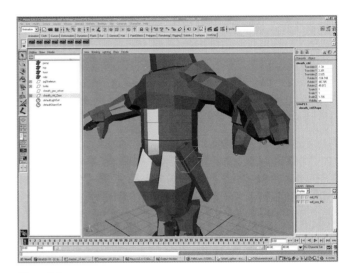

Figure 8.7
Positioning the sheath control curve.

The purpose of the "sheath_geo_offset" node is to offset the rotations of the sheath geometry, so it need not be in a rest position at 0 0 0. The "sheath_ctrl" node should be at a rest position, but the Freeze Transform command will freeze all the transforms in a hierarchy, which will affect the rotation of the geometry with respect to the "sheath_geo_offset" node. Therefore, rotational fixes should be done after the "sheath_ctrl" node has been Freeze Transformed.

15. Select the "sheath_geo_offset" node. Select the channels in the Channel Control and lock them with the right mouse button menu.

16. Create an Empty Group and rename it "knife_geo_ofset."

17. Select the "knife_geo_ofset" node and then select the "kinfe_geo" geometry. Create a pointConstraint and an orientConstraint. Ideally, the knife geometry should be zeroed out with respect to the origin, so that when the constraint is made, the geometry does not move.

The purpose of this node is only to be a constraint target for the geo—if the geo is ever replaced, it can be constrained to this node and the node can be repositioned, if necessary.

18. With the "knife_geo_ofset" node selected, press "Ctrl+g" to make a new group. Rename this group "knife_pivot."

19. Import the nurbsSplineCube.ma file again. Rename the imported "curve1" node "knife_ctrl."

20. Using the Move, Rotate, and Scale tools, position the "knife_ctrl" curve in a place that relates well to the knife geo for proper selection, as in Figure 8.8.

> In this section, a lot of the work with the props takes place around the origin. To facilitate this, toggle the visibility of the character's layer and hide the joints from the Show menu on the modeling panel.

21. With the "knife_ctrl" node selected, use Modify→Freeze Transformations to zero out the control.

22. Select the "knife_pivot" node and Shift-select the "knife_ctrl" curve. Press the "p" key to parent them.

23. With the "knife_ctrl" node selected, press "Ctrl+g" to group it again. Rename the resulting transform "knife_ctrl_Zero."

24. Now, it is time to build the constraint system. Create an empty group and rename it "knife_handR."

25. With the "knife_handR" node selected, press the "g" key to group it. Rename the new group "knife_handR_attach." You should have two empty groups in a simple hierarchy.

26. Duplicate this hierarchy and rename the top node "knife_sheath_attach" and the node beneath it "knife_sheath."

27. Duplicate the hierarchy again and rename the top node "knife_world_attach" and the node beneath it "knife_world."

28. At this point, you should have three hierarchies of empty groups, as in Figure 8.9. Notice that all of these nodes are prefixed with "knife_." If you were to have more than one prop, this would prevent having multiple nodes names "world" or "handR." In the Outliner, press the [+] next to

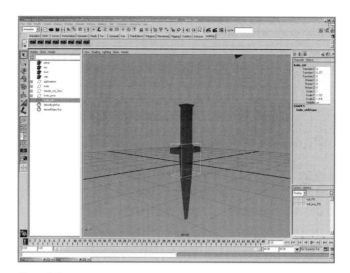

Figure 8.8
Positioning the knife control curve.

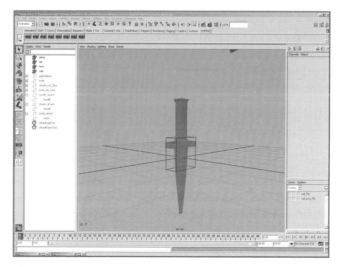

Figure 8.9
The prop hierarchies.

each group to open the hierarchies. Ctrl-select the "handR," "sheath," "world," and "knife_ctrl_Zero" nodes in that order. Use the Constrain→Point and Constrain→Orient commands to create both a point and orient constraint.

29. In the Outliner, press the [+] gizmo next to the "knife_ctrl_Zero" node to open its hierarchy. Select the "knife_ctrl_Zero _orientConstraint1" node and, in the Channel Box or Attribute Editor, set the Interp Type to "Shortest." This will prevent unwanted flipping when switching between the targets.

30. Select the "knife_ctrl" node. Open the Attribute Editor and create three new attributes called "handR," "sheath," and "world." The attributes should be of type float and have minimum and maximum values set to 0 and 1. The default values of the attributes should be 0 except for the "sheath" attribute, which should be set to 1—this will be the default location of the prop.

> It is up to the technical director and animators to determine which location should be the default. It is always good to determine an appropriate default, as it prevents the prop from being in an undesirable position when the file is distributed. For example, if the knife's default were "world," every time the file was sourced for a new animation the prop would have to be manually set to "sheath" or "handR," which is just another detail that would need to be tracked.

31. This next step is best accomplished in the Hypergraph. In the Outliner, Ctrl-select the "knife_ctrl_Zero," "knife_ctrl_Zero_pointConstraint1," and "knife_ctrl_Zero_orientConstraint1" nodes. In the Hypergraph window, graph the input and output connections using the "pod racer" button. Using the right-mouse context menu, connect the "knife_ctrl_Zero.handR" attribute to the "handRW0" attribute on the "knife_ctrl_Zero_pointConstraint1" node. Repeat this process to connect the "knife_ctrl_Zero.handR" attribute to the "handRW0" attribute on the "knife_ctrl_Zero _orientConstraint1" node, as in Figure 8.10.

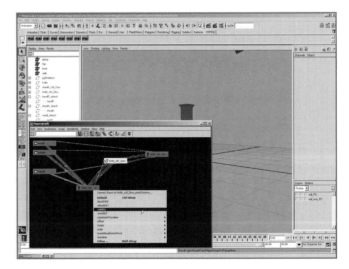

Figure 8.10
Connecting knife_ctrl_Zero to the constraints.

> The order in which you select the constraint targets affects the name of the attribute that controls the weight on the constraint. The first target node's name will be suffixed with "W0" when the constraint node is created. The second target will be suffixed with a "W1," the third with "W2," and so on. When setting up and controlling multiple constraint targets, it is important to give them meaningful names because this may be the only way to keep track of them as you control the weights.

32. Repeat this process for the other attributes on the "knife_ctrl_Zero" node. Connect the "sheath" attribute on the node to the "sheathW1" attributes on the point and orient constraints. Also connect the "world" attribute to the "worldW1" attribute on the constraint nodes.

33. At this point, you can control which target the knife goes to by adjusting the values on the "knife_ctrl_Zero" node. It is a good idea to hide the attributes that are being overridden by the constraints. Use the Window→General Editors→Channel Control command to open the Channel Control window. Highlight the translate, rotate, and scale attributes (and visibility, if you so desire) and make them non-keyable by pressing the Move button at the bottom of the window.

34. Now it is time to adjust the prop locations. Select the "knife_ctrl_Zero" and set all the values but "sheath" to 0. Set the "sheath" value to 1. The knife should be near the origin where the empty nodes are.

35. Select the "sheath_ctrl" node and Ctrl-select the "knie_sheath_attach" node. Create a point and orient constraint. You should see the knife move over towards the sheath, but it is not accurately positioned.

36. Select the "sheath" node and, using the Move and Rotate tools, position the knife so that the blade is in the sheath, and it appears as if the knife is securely holstered, as in Figure 8.11.

> Do not Freeze Transform the "sheath" node—remember it is not a control, it is an offset node and does not need to be zeroed out.

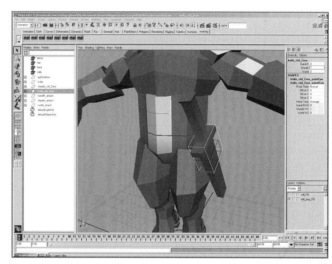

Figure 8.11
Positioning the knife constraint target.

37. When it is in the proper position, select all of the channels in the Channel Box and use the right mouse button menu to lock them. Use the Window→General Editors→Channel Control menu item to bring up the Channel Control window. Select the keyable channels for the "sheath" node and make them unkeyable by pressing the Move button.

38. Select the "knife_ctrl_Zero" node and set all of the attributes except "handR" to 1.

39. Select the "hand_R" joint and Ctrl-select the "handR_attach" node in the Outliner. Create a point and orient constraint.

40. Select the "handR" node and use the Move and Rotate tools to position the knife so that its handle rests in the palm of the warrior (see Figure 8.12).

Take a moment to verify that the knife will transition smoothly from its sheath position to the hand position. Even with the orientConstraint interpType set to "shortest," if there is a substantial difference in orientations between the "sheath" and "handR" nodes, the prop can still rotate undesirably.

8. Props and Interactive Accessories

These next few steps will go through the process of refining the constraint targets to create a smooth blend.

1. Pose the character such that it appears to be drawing the knife from the sheath. Since there isn't a formal rig on the character, go ahead and rotate its joints to get this pose. Use Figure 8.13 for reference.

2. When the character is in position, select the "knife_ctrl_Zero" node. Set the "sheath" channel to 1 and the other channels to 0. Make sure the time slider is at 0 and save a keyframe by pressing "s."

3. Move the time slider to frame 10 and set the "handR" attribute to 1 and the others to 0. Save another keyframe.

4. Now scrub the time slider back and forth between frames 0 and 10. If all goes well, you should see a smooth transition. If this is not the case, look at on which axis the twisting occurs. In this case, it is the Y axis. Select the "handR" node and rotate it along the Y axis 180 degrees. For example, if the "handR" node is at 35 degrees, try rotating it to 215 (180+35). Scrub the time slider back and forth to check the results.

5. Now that the orientation is set, delete the keyframes set on the "knife_ctrl_Zero" node. Go ahead and lock the channels for the "handR" node. Use the Channel Controls window to make the channels unkeyable.

6. Select the "world_attach," "sheath_attach," "handR_attach," "sheath_ctrl_Zero," and "knife_ctrl_Zero" nodes. Press the "g" key to group them together. Name this group "knife_rig."

Now the prop is set up. By animating the changing of the weights, the prop will shift from the hand to the sheath to the world. This shifting is by design, as it may be helpful for the animation to be able to "fudge" the actual transition point of the prop from one target to the other.

Easing the Transition

So the prop is all set up for switching, but setting all those ones and zeros is kind of a drag. Hey, they hired you so that animators wouldn't have to keep track of all the ones and zeroes, right?

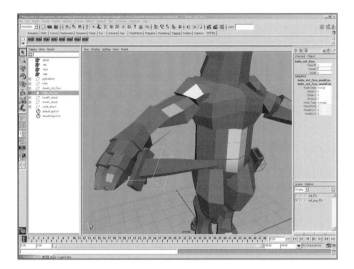

Figure 8.12
Positioning the knife with respect to the hand.

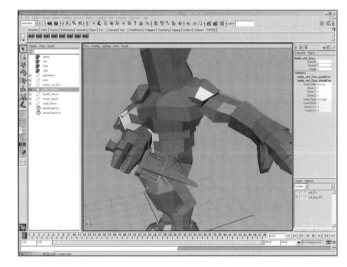

Figure 8.13
Posing the character to refine the knife's transition from sheath to hand.

Really, though, it would be tight if you could automate the prop switching such that, if you want it to move to the hand, you don't have to set all the other attributes to zero manually, especially since it is doubtful that any animated scene will require the prop to be caught halfway between the hand and the sheath. It would be handy to set up a system where setting one target "on" will switch the other targets "off."

One solution would be to have an integer drive the constraint weights via a Set Driven Key. The integer could be an enum attribute added to the "knife_ctrl_Zero." The drawback to this is in the animation. Let's say, in the enum, the sheath target is "0," hand target is represented as a "1," and the world target is represented by a "2." In an animation, a transition from the sheath, or 0, to the world target, 2, will require a pass through position 1, the hand.

A way to get around this is to create an interface that will set the attributes of the prop automatically. If the only keyable attributes on the prop are the target weights, it is a simple matter to set all the attributes to zero except the target that is desired. To do this, Maya has some tools that make such custom manipulation possible.

In this next exercise, we will set up a smooth, automated switch system for the prop.

1. Continue from the previous section or open the file /chapter_08/scenes/knife/knife_part2.ma.
2. Select the "knife_ctrl_Zero" node.
3. For this next part, you will use the Script Editor, so make sure it is open. Use Edit→Clear All to clear the input and history panes.
4. In the Channel Box, set the "handR" attribute to 1. Set the other target attributes ("sheath" and "world") to 0. You should see the commands echoed in the Script Editor—they should be as follows:

```
setAttr "knife_ctrl_Zero.handR" 1;
setAttr "knife_ctrl_Zero.sheath" 0;
setAttr "knife_ctrl_Zero.world" 0;
select -r knife_ctrl;
```

The select command in this script is optional. Since the knife_ctrl node will probably not be animated heavily, it may not be necessary to select it in the script. This decision should be made by the animators and character riggers.

Now, we need to create some scriptNodes to manipulate the knife's control attributes.

1. Select the commands in the history field and copy them to the clipboard with "Ctrl+c."
2. Use the Window→Animation Editors→Expression Editor to open the Expression Editor. Use the Select Filter→By Script Node Name to switch the editor to edit script nodes.
3. In the Script Node Name field, enter "toHandR." In the Script pane, paste the commands you copied from the Script Editor. The Script Editor should resemble Figure 8.14.
4. With the Script Node window open, select the "knife_ctrl_Zero" node. Change the "handR," "sheath," and "worth" nodes 1. Press the "Test Script" button to verify the commands work.

5. Press the "Create" button to create the Script Node. Its name should be added to the list.

6. Create a locator and name it "hand_switcher." Press the "g" key to group the locator and name the resulting node "hand_switcher_Node."

7. Select the "hand_R" joint and then Shift-select the "hand_switcher_Node." Create a point constraint.

8. Select the "hand_switcher" locator and use the Move tool to offset it from the wrist joint.

9. On the command line, enter the following: buttonManip "scriptNode -executeBefore toHandR" "hand_switcher. "

10. In the Expression Editor, copy the commands from the "toHandR" script node by selecting them and pressing "Ctrl+c".

11. Press the "New Script Node" button to clear the settings in the Expression Editor.

12. In the Script field, paste the commands by pressing "Ctrl+v".

13. Change the values of the setAttr statements to set the "knife_ctrl_Zero.sheath" attribute to 1 and the other attributes to 0, as in the following code listing:

```
setAttr "knife_ctrl_Zero.handR" 0;
setAttr "knife_ctrl_Zero.sheath" 1;
setAttr "knife_ctrl_Zero.world" 0;
select -r sheath_ctrl;
```

14. Again, the decision to auto-select the sheath_ctrl node is optional.

15. In the "Script Node Name" field, enter "toSheath."

16. Press the "Create" node to create the new script node. The name should be "toSheath" (see Figure 8.15).

17. In the modeling environment, create a locator and name it "sheath_switcher." Group this node by pressing the "g" key and rename it "sheath_switcher_node."

18. Select the "sheath" node and Shift-select the "sheath_switcher_node." Create a point constraint.

19. Move the "sheath_switcher" locator so that it is offset from the body.

Figure 8.14
Creating the "toHand" script node.

Figure 8.15
Creating the "toSheath" script node.

20. In the command line, enter the following command: buttonManip "scriptNode -executeBefore toSheath" "sheath_switcher_node."

21. Select the "sheath_ctrl" node and Shift-select the "sheath_switcher_node." Create a pointConstraint using the Constrain→Point menu item.

22. Select the "sheath_switcher" node and position it so it is outside the geometry, as in Figure 8.16.

23. Go back to the Expression Editor and press the "New Script Node" button. In the Script Node Name field, enter "toWorld."

24. In the Script pane, add the following commands;
```
setAttr "knife_ctrl_Zero.handR" 0;
setAttr "knife_ctrl_Zero.sheath" 0;
setAttr "knife_ctrl_Zero.world" 1;
select -r world_attach;
```

25. When switching to the world, it is probable that the world node should be selected, simply because it is likely the node will need adjustment.

26. In the modeling environment, create a locator and name it "toWorld_switcher."

27. At the command line, enter the following command: buttonManip "scriptNode -executeBefore toSheath" "toHandR1."

28. Select the "worldSwitcher_Node," "sheath_switcher_Node," and the "hand_switcher_Node" and the manipulator nodes in the Outliner. Finally, Ctrl-select the "knifeRig" node and press the "p" to group the nodes.

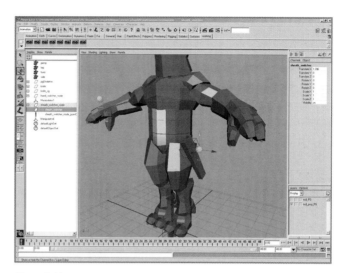

Figure 8.16
Creating the "toHand" script node.

The buttonManip command creates a sphere that, when clicked, executes the command in the first argument. The second argument is a transform with which the sphere moves. The script node holds the commands to set the weights of the constraint. When the attribute values are changed, the changes can be recorded via setting keyframes on the "knife_ctrl_Zero" node.

ButtonManips are best utilized when linked to a transform. When the transform is moved, the buttonManip goes with it. The control has one drawback: the sphere that is the button cannot be scaled and always maintains a constant size in the modeling windows.

It is important to know the reason behind the use of the buttonManips. In Maya, it is possible to use a reverseNode and create a simple alternating weight control. When one weight is at 0, the other is at 1 and vice versa (see the reverseNode section of Chapter 2 for more information.) When balancing between three or more weights, however, things increase in complexity. It is possible to layer reverse and multiply nodes to control more than two targets, but you will still end up with multiple attributes that need to be set to 0 or 1. The buttonManip and scriptjob solution make this easier to manage—you can make as many scriptjobs as you need for as many targets as necessary. In our Maya setup, we usually work with autokeyframe on—if this is not your style, you may want to add a setKeyframe command to the scriptjobs to save a keyframe when the targets are switched.

This situation is a bit more controllable. Instead of a constant connection, the scriptNode manually sets the attributes just as if they were manipulated in the Channel Box.

Adding Some Polish

Now that the basic prop system is set up for the knife, a few more touches will make the system cleaner. For one thing, the buttonManips, while very useful, take up a bit of screen real estate. For this character, the knife is more of a secondary prop, so it makes sense to hide the controls in order to simplify things for the animator. For the knife prop, the main control is the "knife_ctrl_Zero" node, so it will also control the visibility of the prop controls.

The following steps illustrate how to set up visibility controls for the buttonManips.

1. Open the Outliner.

2. Select the "knife_ctrl_Zero" node and open the Attribute Editor.
   Using the "Add Attribute" menu item, add a boolean attribute called "knifeSwitchControls."

3. Open the Connection Editor. In the left panel, load the "knife_ctrl_Zero" node. In the right panel, load the "knifeRig" node. Make sure the button in the middle is set to "from→to".

4. Connect the "knife_ctrl_Zero.knifeSwitchControls" attribute to the visibility attribute of the "knifeRig" node (see Figure 8.17).

Now the animator has control over making the controls visible without searching through the Outliner. Because the "knife_ctrl_Zero" node is the root-level node of the prop, it is a logical place to put special attributes that affect the functioning of the control. Also note that the "knifeSwitchControls" attribute is keyable. Ideally, it would not be, but this would prevent it from being displayed in the Channel Box. Every production is different, but, for our preference, the ease of access overrides the potential annoyance of having nonrendering controls animated on and off.

Figure 8.17
Adding visibility controls for the knife-switching.

Now the prop is set up, but let's say the character is going to put the knife down on a table. When switching from the right hand to the world space, there is an unnatural shift. This could be corrected by eye or by creating some temporary constraints, but it might be beneficial to build that functionality into the prop system itself. In order to do this, we will need to make use of a script that was developed using some of the material from Chapter 3—a script called snapArgs. SnapArgs accepts as an input two node names, and it snaps the second node to the first, much like a constraint. No permanent connection is made, however, as the script merely sets the attribute values.

The behavior we want to enact is this: whenever the prop is switched from the hand or the sheath to the world space, the world space node should align itself to the position and orientation of the current attach node. For the knife, all of its position and rotation data are provided by the "knife_ctrl_Zero" node. This is the transform that is constrained to the "handR," "sheath," and "world" nodes. If the "worldCtrlWorld" node is moved to the position of the "handR" node when the prop is switched from the hand, the prop will not appear to shift and the transfer will be smooth. In order for this to be smooth, use the following steps:

> It is important to keep in mind which transforms are affecting the prop. In order for this process to work smoothly, the "ctrlKnife" node needs to have its rotations and translations zeroed.

1. Select the "knife_ctrl_Zero" node and open the Attribute Editor.

2. Use the Attributes→Add Attributes menu command to add a boolean attribute called "worldAutoSnap."

3. Use the Window→Animation Editors→Expression Editor to open the Expression Editor window.

4. Use the Select Filter→By Script Node Name command to put the editor into script node editing mode.

5. Select the "toWorld" node from the Script Node panel.

6. In the Script pane, add the following lines before any of the setAttr commands (see Figure 8.18).
```
if(`getAttr knife_ctrl_Zero.worldAutoSnap`)
{
    select -r knife_ctrl_Zero knife_ctrlWorld;
    snap();
}
```

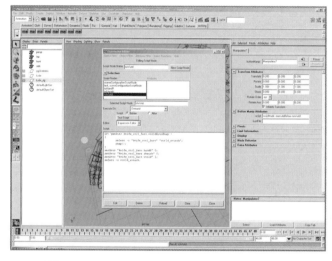

7. The first line checks to see if the world space node should snap to the position of the prop when the switch is made. The second line uses the snap MEL command from Chapter 3 to make the snap happen. A copy of the snap command can be found on the Web site at http://www.courseptr.com/downloads.

Figure 8.18
Adding a snap command to the "toWorld" script node.

8. Press the Edit button to commit the changes to the script node.

9. Select the "knife_ctrl_Zero" node and set the "worldAutoSnap" attribute to "on."

Now, if you click the buttonManip for the hand or the sheath, the prop moves. If you click the world buttonManip, the world space control snaps to the location of the currently active prop. It's really snapping to the current location of the "knife_ctrl_Zero" node before it changes the weights on the constraints.

Two-Handed Props

So, a one-handed prop is pretty straightforward. Now we will look at a two-handed prop. A two-handed prop introduces more questions. How will the prop be controlled? Will the prop drive the motion of the arms? How will the arms drive the prop?

Many animators prefer forward kinematics solutions wherever possible. Keeping this in mind, it is reasonable that, when designing a two-handed prop, the main action of the prop can be locked to a main arm. The other arm can be constrained to a point on the prop. This is a simple solution and works well as long as the prop does not need to switch hands.

Let's look at giving our character a spear.

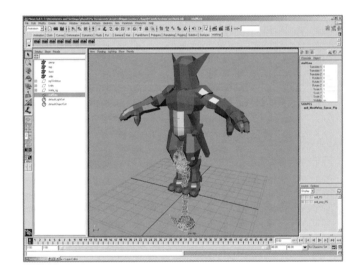

Figure 8.19
Importing the character's two-handed prop.

1. From the URL http://www.courseptr.com/downloads, download the staff_start.ma file.

2. Use the File→Import command to import the /chapter_8/scenes/ staff/staff.ma file. You should see the character's staff centered around the origin.

3. Create an empty group and rename it "staff_geo_offset."

4. Select the "staff_geo_offset" node and Shift-select the "staffGeo" node. From the Constrain menu, create a pointConstraint and an orientConstraint.

5. From the File menu, select Import and import the nurbSplineCube.mb. Rename the "curve1" object "staff_ctrl."

6. Select the "staff_geo_offset" node and Shift-select the "staff_ctrl" curve. Press the "p" key to parent them.

7. Select the "staffCtrl" node and group it with Ctrl+g. Rename the group "staff_hand_L_attach."

8. Import another control curve. Rename the "curve1" node "staff_hand_L_ctrl." This will control the left hand once it is attached to the staff.

9. Select the "staff_hand_L_attach" node and Shift-select the "staff_hand_L_ctrl" node. Press the "p" key to parent them.

10. Select the "staff_hand_L_ctrl" and parent it under the "staff_ctrl" node.

11. Select the "staff_hand_L_ctrl" node. Use the Move tool to move it farther down the shaft of the spear. It is not necessary to position it precisely at this point, as we are just preparing the hierarchy. When you are finished, the two controls should be positioned on the staff, as in Figure 8.20.

12. Now, we will create the attachment nodes. First, create an empty group and rename it "staff_r_hand_offset." Group this node and rename it "staff_r_hand_offset_attach."

13. Select the "bn_hand_node." Shift-select the "staff_r_hand_attach" node. Create a point constraint and an orient constraint.

14. Create an empty group and rename it "staff_world_offset." Group this node and rename the resulting group "staff_world_space."

15. Select the "staff_r_hand_offset," "staff_world_offset," and the "staff" nodes. Create a point constraint and an orient constraint.

16. Select the "staff_ctrl" node and open the Attribute Editor. From the Add Attributes menu, create an attribute called "toWorld" with a minimum value of 0.0, a maximum value of 1.0, and a default value of 0.

17. Open the Hypergraph. Select the "staff_ctrl" and the "staff" nodes. Graph the upstream and downstream connections.

18. Connect the "staff_ctrl.toWorld" attribute to the "sWorldW2" attribute on the "staff_pointConstraint1" node and again to the same attribute on the "staff_orientConstraint1" node.

19. Open the Hypershade from the Create tab, select Maya Utilities, and create a reverse node. Rename the node "staff_reverse."

20. In the Hypergraph or Hypershade, select the reverse node and the "staff_ctrl" node. Graph the connections.

21. Connect the "toWorld" attribute of the "staff_ctrl" node to the "inputX" attribute of the "staff_reverse" node, as in Figure 8.21.

22. Connect the "staff_reverse.outputX" attribute to the "r_HandW1" attributes on the "staff_pointConstraint1" and "staff_orientConstraint1" nodes

23. The staff should be aligned with the "r_Hand" node on the right arm. Select this node and use the Move and Rotate tools to position the staff so it is visually aligned with the right hand.

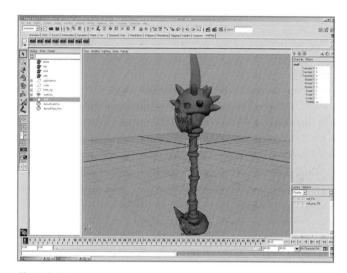

Figure 8.20
Creating the staff control geometry.

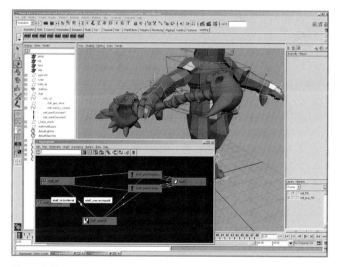

Figure 8.21
Connecting the staff_ctrl.

For a one-handed staff, like a walking stick, this setup would be sufficient. For the PigGoblin, we are going to hook the left arm into the staff to make it more interactive. What we want to do here is set up the left hand so that it will blend between its normal animation rig controls and controls that place it on the staff. This means the attachment point for the left hand on the staff will have point and orient constraint targets to hold the left hand.

1. Pose the figure so that the staff and the left hand are in contact in a natural way. You may want to take this opportunity to reposition the "staff_ctrl" so that it is near the attachment point. If you do this, be sure to use Freeze Transforms so that the rest pose for the control is established. See Figure 8.22 for placement reference.

2. Now it is time to make the first weapon target. Select the "ctrl_wrist_ori_local." If you have difficulty locating it, enter it in the selection box or type "select –r staff_hand_L_ctrl" on the command line.

3. With the node selected, press Ctrl+d to duplicate it. Rename the node "ctrl_wrist_ori_Staff_L."

4. Leave the node selected and Ctrl+select "staff_hand_L_attach" node. Press the "p" key to parent them.

5. Select the "ctrl_wrist_ori_Staff_L" node and Shift-select the "ctrl_wrist_Zero_L" node. Use Constrain→Orient Constraint to add the duplicate node as a new orient target.

6. Select the "ctrl_wrist_L|xtraAttrs" node. From the Attribute Editor, use the Add Attribute menu item to create a new attribute called "weapon." Give it a minimum value of 0.0 and a maximum value of 1.0. The default value should be 0.0.

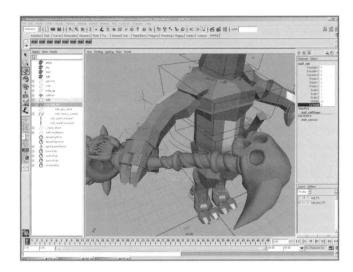

Figure 8.22
Adjusting the position of the "staff_ctrl" node.

7. The weapon attribute will control the blending between the left arm controls and the staff. This attribute will hook into the various constraints that control the arm orientation by means of some utility nodes. In the Hypershade, create a reverse node. Rename the node "staff_orient_reverse."

8. The next few steps are best completed in the Hypergraph or Hypershade windows. Connect the "ctrl_wrist_L|xtraAttrs.staff" attribute to the "ctrl_wrist_Zero_L_orientConstraint1.ctrl_wrist_ori_Staff_LW2" attribute. This will set the weight of the weapon target to 1.

9. Connect the "ctrl_wrist_L|xtraAttrs.staff" attribute to the "staff_reverse.inputX" attribute.

10. In the Hypershade, create a multiplyDivide node. Rename the node "staff_constraint_dampen." This node will be used to scale the values of the original hand targets to 0. When the "ctrl_wrist_L|xtraAttrs.staff" attribute is set to 1, both of the other weights of the world and local orient targets will be multiplied by a 0, which will set them to 0.

11. Connect the "staff_reverse.outputX" attribute to the "staff_constraint_dampen.input2X" and the "staff_constraint_dampen.input2Y" attributes, as in Figure 8.23.

12. Connect the "ctrl_wrist_L|xtraAttrs.wristFollow" attribute to the "staff_constraint_dampen.input1X" attribute.

13. Connect the "reverse5.output" attribute to the "staff_constraint_dampen.input2Y" attribute. These are the sources that control the local and global weights on the wrist orient.

14. Connect the "staff_constraint_dampen.outputX" attribute to the "ctrl_wrist_Zero_L_orientConstraint1. ctrl_wrist_ori_Local_LW0."

15. Connect the "staff_constraint_dampen.outputY" attribute to the "ctrl_wrist_Zero_L_orientConstraint1. ctrl_wrist_ori_World_LW1" attribute.

16. At this point, the orient constraint override is in place. It is now time to create the translation override. Select the "aux_blend_L" node and duplicate it. Rename the node "aux_blend_staff_L."

17. With the "aux_blend_staff_L" node selected, Shift-select the "staff_hand_L_attach" node. Press the "p" key to parent them.

18. Select the "aux_blend_staff_L" node and Shift-select the "aux_blend_L" node. Select Constraint→Point Constraint to add the "aux_blend_staff_L" as a target for the point constraint.

19. Create a reverse node and rename it "staff_point_reverse."

20. Connect the "ctrl_wrist_L|xtraAttrs.staff" attribute to the "aux_blend_L_pointConstraint1.aux_blend:staff_LW1" attribute.

21. Connect the "ctrl_wrist_L|xtraAttrs.staff" to the "staff_point_reverse.inputX" attribute.

22. Connect the "staff_point_reverse.outputX" to the "aux_blend_L_pointConstraint1.ctrl_arm_LW0" attribute.

Now the blending setup is complete. The character should resemble Figure 8.24. When the "ctrl_wrist_L|xtraAttrs.staff" attribute is set to 1, the other weights of the point and orient constraint are multiplied by 0, which drops their value to 0.

Figure 8.23
Connecting the "staff_orient_reverse" node to the "staff_constraint_dampen" multiplyDivide node.

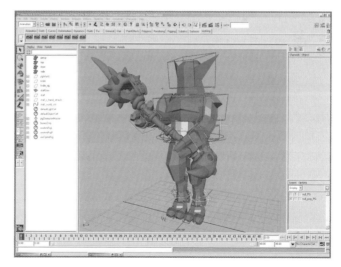

Figure 8.24
The finished prop.

In creating the targets for the left hand, notice that it is easier to duplicate and re-parent a target, especially if you are using a joint as a target. Joints with their custom orients can be tricky to match. You will also notice that the prop did not have to be in the rest position to be utilized as the target. As a matter of fact, care needs to be taken when setting up a two-handed prop because they cannot be set up in the normal rest position. One way to ensure that you preserve the rest pose is to save a keyframe for all the animation controls at frame 0 and do your posing setup at a different frame.

Caleb Owens

chapter 9
Focus on the Face

We have two sections in this chapter to talk about facial rigging. Facial rigging and modeling could take an entire book to cover properly and has been done so by Jason Osipa in his book "Stop Staring." We were lucky enough to get an interview with Art Director Caleb "cro" Owens who did some early groundbreaking work while at Digital Domain on projects like the "Digital James Brown" and then later for nVidia with the entirely real-time facial demo "Zoltar." In addition to this interview, we have a fantastic tutorial by Josh Carey, character artist at "The Animation Farm," who was taught by Caleb Owens. The Pig Rig tutorial by Josh covers both Caleb Owens' and Jason Osipa's of style facial rigging to allow you to choose which style of rigging will fit your characters best.

Interview with Caleb Owens

Caleb "cro" Owens is a multifaceted artist, designer, and musician. For almost 15 years Cro has worked professionally and extensively in every aspect of computer graphics, including commercials, forensics, education, interactive, feature films, and large format film.

In the fall and winter of 1999-2000, Owens was Lead Technical Director on the Experience Music Project at Academy Award-winning, visual effects studio Digital Domain. Owens led a team of artists in creating a 3D computer-generated facial replacement of James Brown. Utilizing the latest technology, such as Maya and subdivision surfaces, as well as new techniques in artistic and design approaches, his efforts helped set a new standard for photo-real facial animation and the creative application of 3D computer graphics.

In October of 2000, Cro was again part of a revolutionary jump in CG. Working with world-leading 3D graphics hardware gurus and the force behind the X-Box nVidia, Caleb designed, constructed, and animated a fully 3D character for the groundbreaking launch of nVidia's new geForce3 product. Expanding on his work with James Brown, Owens again set a new standard—this time in the realm of real-time animation.

Caleb's partial credit list includes the following: Film: *The Life Aquatic, Peter Pan, iRobot(previs), Loony Tunes, Astronaut's Wife, Inspector Gadget.*

Owens holds a Bachelor of Fine Arts from Florida Atlantic University. Aside from his day job, Caleb is owner, designer, and builder for a custom motorcycle shop, cro customs inc., and trademark owner of mumbo jumbo. For more info, go to www.crocustoms.com and www.mumbojumbotunes.com.

The Interview

Let's start with a brief introduction. Your biography is great, and we plan to ask you about the James Brown and nVidia projects. What do you do currently as a daily job routine?

At the time of this interview, I just accepted a job at EA (Electronic Arts) as Technical Art Director. My role here is not only to help create art assets for next generation games, but also to assist other artists in direction and troubleshooting.

When someone says "facial rig," the first thing I think of is your James Brown that I was lucky enough to get a glimpse of when you taught the Maya class that I was in. As impressive as that was, what other projects have you worked on since then that match or surpass that awesome quality of facial animation?

That was a milestone, and I was very fortunate to have that opportunity. As impressive as the work was, I think it could have been so much better. At that time, we were talking about things people really had not addressed yet, and we were only able to get about 30 percent of those ideas in the work. I was very happy with the work I did for nVidia on the Zoltar character. While not film, the overall 3D foundation was similar and in some regards better than the James Brown work. Zoltar was a speaking performance instead of singing, and while the model was based off a scan of me, I distorted it and made it more of a caricature.

The Zoltar character was very cool, especially since it was real-time. What technical complications did you come across while doing that project? Can you talk a little about any adjustments that you had to make in order to do a real-time project involving facial animation, compared to your previous film experience?

That is what was so cool about that particular job. The nVidia guys said, "Make it look as cool as possible, and we will figure out the technical details with regard to real-time rendering." So I used all the techniques I would use in film on that project as well. The good and bad thing about the gig was that I did the entire project from concept to completion, completely on my own in my house in Malibu, CA. nVidia had an artist modify the texturing to fit their particular needs for the real-time demo. The good thing was that I had total control over the production, the mocap session, and integration; the bad thing was that I only had three months and 20+ pieces of dialogue to deliver. It was a challenge to deliver that amount of work at a level I was happy with and nVidia was expecting. Bad, because of

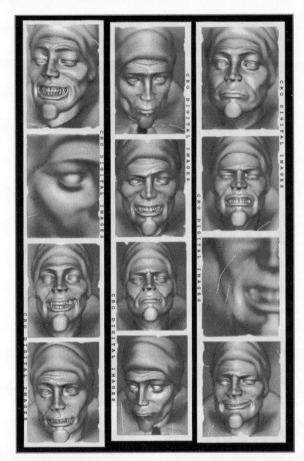

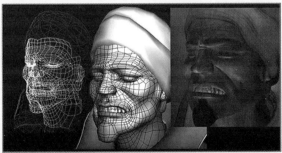

all the same reasons it was good…(laughing). In the end, the guys at nVidia really loved the work and even though I would have liked more time to tweak the animations, I was happy with the final result and the response it got.

As far as style goes, what appeals to you more—photo-realistic or stylized?

Both really. What appeals to me are good character development and believability that the character has life. There was a push several years back that I was part of, for this digital clone idea. The digital clone idea was interesting to most people because of its technical challenges; for me, it was more of the aesthetic challenges that very few people spoke about. It is my strong opinion that lots of people miss the boat on this one. Way too much focus is put on the technical aspect of complex work of this nature and the aesthetic, even at the most minute level, suffers. While doing all my research before the James Brown work, this stuck out as the biggest aspect of photo-realistic facial work that was missing.

Can you talk a little more about aesthetics, and what it takes to achieve that next step? Obviously, it takes years of practice and studying to take notice of all the small details. What would you say is the hardest challenge to overcome when going to the next level?

Developing an "eye" is the hardest, most elusive and misunderstood attribute. An "eye" for composition, an eye for detail, etc. Some of the greatest fine artists and filmmakers of our time have an "eye," people like Ansel Adams, Kubrick, and so on. When you see their work, you know it, and very few people argue that their work is not only great, but also memorable. Developing an eye is having the ability to slow down, look, and look at things that others may overlook. Over time, it becomes automatic. For me, it goes back to that simple idea of "think or look at the simplest things first." In our industry, it used to be that finding technically savvy people was difficult, then it was hard to find tech savvy people with an artistic background, and now, in my opinion, it is *very* difficult to find truly intelligent visionaries in the arts since aesthetics are as much a science as they are ostensibly subjective.

How do you approach a project that involves realistic facial animation?

First and foremost, I focus on the aesthetic; then I think in the simplest terms first. What is the fastest, most immediate way to accomplish this task, while at the same time creating movement that is believable? I set a foundation that is clean, then build on it making sure not to over-engineer things.

How often do you get to do R&D to try new techniques on facial rigging? Have there been any new techniques that you've tried lately that you can talk about?

Hard-core facial projects are rare these days, but when I have had the time I do experiment with ideas. I am most interested in things that can be done that don't involve a software team. Most large studios like Sony, ILM have teams of people that support other teams of artists in these tasks. Most recently, I have been playing with simulating skin using a series of constrained cloth simulations.

Sounds interesting… Does this also involve using muscle meshes to drive the skin so you can get a nice sliding skin? What tools or techniques have you found useful in trying to get the appearance of sliding skin?

I have played around with lots of cloth ideas. Syflex and Maya, for instance. It isn't really anything groundbreaking or new, but the idea of trying to build something usable, fast, and believable is the challenge, and it can be fun.

Speaking of new techniques, have you looked at the Paul Ekman FACS system that was the foundation for the Gollum face rig and is being used by Valve for the new Half-life game?

Mr. Ekman's research is very well known. I did read quite a bit of his work and, of course, those ideas are incorporated in my work as well. I also did lots of research that dated much earlier than Mr. Ekman. One of the most interesting things I read, some of it actually covered by Mr. Ekman, was about studies funded by the CIA in the early 50s. I found these docs archived deep in the law library at UCLA. Don't ask how I found them because I don't even recall. I remember my Dad telling me when I was really young about how these CIA agents could tell if you were lying by just looking at you. That just popped in my head, and I starting looking. The idea that very small muscle movements in the face are controlled only neurologically, and are impossible to re-create consciously, was just fascinating. Feelings, or emotional responses, can be read through microexpressions in the face. The nuances are everything. Even if we don't outright see them, we can recognize if they are not there.

I find that to rig or animate a face, the amount of controls and keyframe to manage it can get to a point of diminishing returns. How do you like to approach interfacing a face rig for both fast-posing and low-level controls for fine-tuning?

I tend to take a layered approach. Broad strokes, key emotional states, then subtle emotional states, large muscle groups, small muscle groups, each group then isolated. I tend to use these layers or groups to build phonemes; this way, depending on punctuation and emotional performance, the phoneme can be tweaked and won't ever be the same way twice.

I've seen lots of talk about layered controls lately. Disney talked about that some at Siggraph this past year (2004) in their amazing Chicken Little *presentations. Of course, the amount of controls available was huge—hundreds even. As an example, what would you classify as primary controls vs. secondary controls on a human face?*

There are no real hard-and-fast rules, but again, clean and simple works well for me. Primary controls may be emotionally driven, i.e., happy, sad, curious, etc. Some other primary controls may be phonemes or large muscle groups; secondary controls would be muscle isolations, squints, furrows, things like that, fine controls for areas around the mouth, thus avoiding twinning issues.

What methods do you use to get the subtleties in facial animation (your rigging or animation methods)?

Muscle groups, subtle wrinkles, shapes used only as secondary deformations. Modeling goes hand-in-hand with skinning. I used a poly cage to sub-d approach.

What makes for an efficient pipeline? How do you handle changes or fixes to rigs in the middle of a production?

This is a case where scripting is handy. The ability to swap a model out in the middle of production can be very important. As long as the base foundation of the rig is clean and easy to get at, changes are not a huge hassle.

Do you feel it's important for Character TDs to get their fingers dirty and do modeling so they understand how the mesh affects the rig?

Absolutely, that goes for modelers as well. It is important to know all aspects and to understand how one affects the other.

To follow up the last question, do you have a view on the workflow between an animator, rigger, and modeler on how they need to work together in making a production rig?

That is a loaded question. It varies from show to show, from people to people. Teamwork. Be receptive to new ideas and be open to change. Be smart enough to know how much you may not know.

How often do you use scripted setups (autorigging) for body or facial rigs?

That is becoming more and more common, especially in game development. But, if you need something specific to really develop a character, a custom rig is the way to go.

When doing a face rig, do you feel that it is important to follow the realistic muscles in the face—and to have controls to simulate those muscles? Or do you feel that going by prebuilt combinations of expressions, visimes, etc., is a better approach?

My opinion is, if you use the muscles based off of stress lines or the contour of the face, you will always end up with a better result. No matter what method, if it is linear in nature, that is not good.

Have you worked with motion capture or facial motion capture?

Yes, and for me it is a tool to the end result of getting a good performance. If the goal is realism, the mocap can be very good; if the goal is cartoon, then it may not be a good choice, but it can still be used. Mocap should not be used as a crutch or replacement; it is just another tool in the director's box to tell a story.

In regard to rigging, what advances in software do you look forward to, or want to have? What is still harder or more work than necessary because of off-the-shelf software?

I never see limitations anymore. Really, it is all about execution and the aesthetic now. The software is there, the tools are mature, and it is down to the performance and execution of the artist.

If you have any final thoughts or tips and techniques that you could offer the readers, feel free to add them here.

When a character is on-screen delivering a piece of dialogue or a compelling emotional experience, no one sees all the nifty buttons and complex scripts, all they see is the performance. Character TDs are the unsung heroes of animation, but at the same time if they lose sight of the end goal, they can be the brunt of a lot of mad animators!

In addition, while I have had some great experiences and have been part of some great Character TD work, it is my time to step aside and let the younger, smarter cats do better work. I have moved more toward the art direction end of production and hope to learn more about all the new developments and tools and use them on some challenging projects in the future.

What made you want to take the next step (career-wise, moving from TD to AD)? And what do you feel is necessary for someone to make that move—after a whole lot of experience, of course?

Well, the truth is, my ideas for a career have always been "art" driven. I sort of fell into the CG thing so I guess it is a natural progression of sorts. In addition, when you get a little older maybe you just get a little burnt on keeping up with all the latest CG trends as they relate to a TD's job or the like. In addition, I felt that my jobs started to become more technical and less art-driven than when I first started out. For me, it has gotten to be so much so that I do not want to lose touch with those aesthetic sensibilities. But, in a lot of ways I am still trying to figure it out. Like you say in the dailies... "It's a work in progress."

PIG RIG—The Bacon and Eggs of Pig Facial Rigging

The following is written by Josh Carey, a Character TD at The Animation Farm in Austin, Texas. While his main title is a Character TD, Josh also deals with modeling, animation, and any technical problems during a production. He has had experience in rigging for productions of all kinds—from games to films, from cartoony characters to realistic creatures and humans. Josh has also reviewed software and plug-ins for CGChannel.com. He can be reached at his Web site www.vfxcreator.com.

In this chapter, he will talk about an internal short that was created at The Animation Farm and share some production experiences about body and facial rigging. He will also go over some concepts about facial rigging in different methods, so you can choose which method would be best for you.

The Production

The short film about this pig began during some downtime here at The Animation Farm. Our concept artist, Tom Heimann, had created several 2D cartoon farm animals for the company in the past, so we decided to start creating them in 3D, and eventually, make a short with them. After the pig was modeled, and his personality was starting to show with the early version of the rig, we decided to use this as a chance to get the rest of the studio up-to-speed with Maya, as we were mainly a Max house (see Figure 9.1).

Before I moved on to rigging, I gave the model an evaluation. Does the face have enough loops? Where will he need to bend, move, and *how* will he move? After discussing it with the art director, we decided to keep it as simple as we could get it, since after all this was to train the guys up in Maya. So after the model was done, I threw on a first pass of a skeleton—just a rough placement of where I want things to move and how (Figure 9.2)

Ignoring the face for now, I concentrated on the body—mainly tail, razorback hairs, legs, and the "hips." I say hips in quotes because, well, where are the hips on this guy? The hairs on top get a joint or two each. I ended up with one joint because we really didn't need to have them move all that much after thinking about it. The tail, being a curly little thing, could have gone two ways:

◆ A joint chain following the geometry, forming a curled joint chain
◆ A joint chain straight out as if there were a straight tail there, not worrying about the curl

I ended up with option two, simply because we didn't see any need to uncurl the tail. Looking back, I think it would have been really cool to make it like a super-stretchy tail, perhaps with either a splineIK or a wire deformer. We'll get into that a little bit later.

Now for the legs. I applied a simple reverse foot rig, even though there was no ball or toe—somewhat similar to how a game rig with limited joints might be. The green joints here are the skinned joints (thigh—knee—ankle—toe). The purple joints are the control rig joints (ankle—toe—heel). Just like a human reverse foot, the ankleIK is parented to the ankle rig joint, and the ball (or toe) IK is parented to the heel rig joint. As you can see, it's easy to use the same techniques when you want a similar effect (see Figure 9.3).

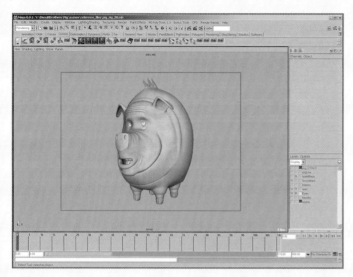

Figure 9.1
The finished model posed. Image copyright: The Animation Farm 2005

For the body, I wanted at least a COG control, a head control, and some kind of hip/rolling control. I decided to take the root and parent the two rear leg bones to it, while keeping the front two parented to another joint under the root (called *pelvis*).

This now acts as a roll/hip joint, as you can see the rotations that it provides. Take note of where the pivot for the actual control is located as well. If the pivot would be on the joint itself, we wouldn't get the desired rotations. Also note that there is no skinning on the root (this is pretty common for most of my rigs). See Figure 9.4.

As the production progressed, we also realized that we wanted to be able to break the rig—to make some stretchiness happen and to break the rules about what is actually seen on camera. Since the pig basically has no neck, it's hard for him to put his head down to eat without avoiding a lot of crashing. Depending on the camera angles for these specific shots, we had to be able to break the rig to fake his lack of maneuverability.

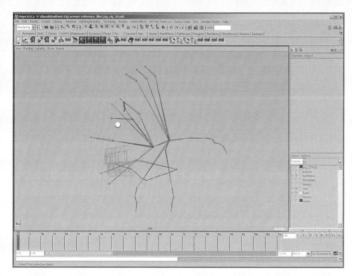

Figure 9.2
Rough skeleton pass. Image copyright: The Animation Farm 2005

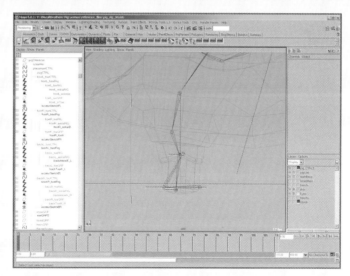

Figure 9.3
The pig reverse foot. Image copyright: The Animation Farm 2005

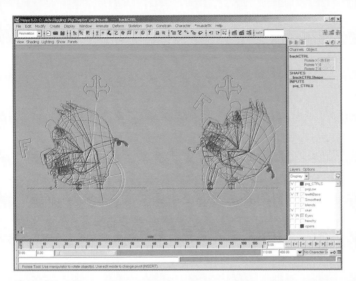

Figure 9.4
Range of motion. Image copyright: The Animation Farm 2005.

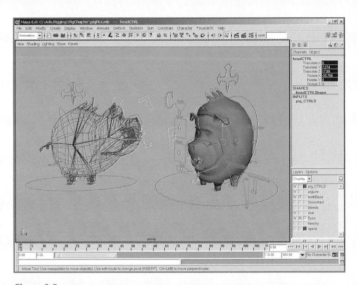

Figure 9.5
Breaking the neck. Image copyright: The Animation Farm 2005.

Figure 9.5 shows what I did for the head. I simply made the original head CTRL (which was rotate only before) have a constraint on the head joint, and then made sure the skinning would still be correct as the joint translated outward. I also added some SDK in there for some bulging skin as the head compressed inward.

Another break was done on the thigh joints to get the legs not to be affected by the COG control. This can simply be done by hand keying them (grab the joints and set a key in the correct position), or you can set up a controller for the thigh and set it up to inherit the parent joint or the world coordinates. Here's a quick rundown of what to do for this:

1. Make your controller.

2. Align it to your thigh joint—parent it under the thighJNT, freezeTransforms, group it, and unparent the group from the joint.

3. Now you can point-constrain the thighJNT to the controller, and it is now locked down to the world.

4. To set it up for choosing world or root, you can then constrain the group of the new controller to the root (or whatever the parent joint would be), and you'll be able to animate that constraint to be on or off, which would be root or world. You'll probably want to make this constraint easily reachable for an animator; for example, add a custom attr to a controller that would make sense for this, and either direct-connect it or SDK the constraint.

Time for a Facial

OK, so enough of the easy stuff—let's get down and dirty with the face. My initial thoughts about the face were to do my usual wire/cluster setup. This is just a mix of techniques that I've picked up and developed over the years, stemming from Cro's techniques. After thinking about it, I wanted to stay as simple as possible, so I ended up basing the face rig on Jason Osipa's method. Yes, the oh-so-lovely joystick controls as some people call them. I'm a big fan of optimizing workflows and eliminating the need for sliders anywhere gets a big plus in my book.

So, for those unfamiliar with the Osipa style facial setup, this involves making blendshapes. Not just any old blendshapes, but really kickass ones. Now, thanks to Mark Behm of Blue Sky and Harry Michalakeas of ReelFX, there is a script called blendTaper (v03) that is available for blendshapes that lets you model the full blend (left and right side), and the script will spit out a left- and right-side mesh for you. Nice and handy! Unfortunately, sometimes it's a hassle to model both sides at the same time, or you cannot do things symmetrically for any reason.

In this case, I actually whipped a script together to automate the making of the right-side blend, after I modeled just the left side. I've noticed that similar scripts are out on highend3d.com and other personal sites, so I'll just mention the process here. It may or may not work as well when you have largely asymmetrical meshes, and it is certainly not an exact method as it does not dig into things at a vertex level.

Here is the rundown of the procedure:

1. First, you have your original head and your left- or right-side blend (Head and Smile_L, for example)
2. Duplicate your original head and name this the right side blend (Smile_R, for example)
3. Duplicate the original again and name it tempMirror (or anything that makes sense to you to use as a temporary mesh)
4. Now grab Smile_L and tempMirror, and create a blendshape deformer. Keep the blend at 0 for now.
5. Making sure the pivot for all these meshes are at their center, scale tempMirror in X by -1.
6. Now select Smile_R, Shift-select tempMirror, and create wrap. Note: Smile_R and tempMirror must be right on top of each other.
7. Now just crank the Smile_L blend on tempMirror up to 1, select your Smile_R, and del history. Quick and easy mirrored blendshape!

Now, hooking the blendshapes up is a simple process. Since I chose to go with Osipa's method for hooking them up to the "joystick" controls, the main function used in these expressions is the clamp function. Clamp just limits values, in this case between 0 and 1, and is also used to limit the additive blends. Osipa goes over the whole process in depth in his book, so I'm not going to repeat that all here.

One thing that I'd like to add, in addition to using the clamp to keep things between 0 and 1, is that you shouldn't let that limit yourself. I recently made a "poo" control on the pig to make a full "Poo" shape, which consisted of about five blendshapes together. In that case, the clamp was used to limit each one between 0 and 1 in the end result, because that's what goes into the blendshape, but within the expression, I was clamping between 2 and 3, 3 and 4, etc. The control was then going from 0 to 4 in local space to make the whole "Poo"—sucking in, pursing lips, puffing cheeks out, puffing lips out, then releasing the ooo sound. So just remember, there are no limits!

To Blend or Not to Blend

Now for the blendshape creation process, I will sometimes create a temporary rig to help make the blendshapes faster. As with all these shapes, we have the option to make them either a blendshape, or make them controllable via joints. For instance—the eyelid blinks. We can put in joints to the actual rig and drive them with the same controllers that we would use to drive blendshape attributes. Sometimes, the joint option is more desirable since joints work on arcs—blendshapes are linear (unless you make inbetweens).

An example of this with the pig rig versus Ospia's method is that I used a jaw joint in the rig instead of having an openMouth or closedMouth blendshape. I simply connected the rotation of the jaw to the same Sync control as the Smile/Narrow controls via SDK. The problem that can show up with not creating this openMouth blendshape is that the corners of the mouth may not be perfect with just a jaw joint rotation. In case you need to make that adjustment as the jawJNT rotates down, you can make a cluster with the corners of the mouth and cheeks, and SDK the scale of that cluster to the jaw rotation. I also made a jaw control that controlled the rotateY of the jawJnt, with a simple translateX on the control. I could have added a translateY to this same control to add the rotateZ of the jaw, but I decided to make that rotation connected to a hands-on control on the face itself (see Figure 9.6).

Another control that I used joints for instead of blends was the nose. We couldn't simply say that this is a "sniff" blendshape—the use of rotations in all three axes added to the animation, as opposed to a single blend. Having joints there also allows for some really nice cartoony dragging action (see Figure 9.7).

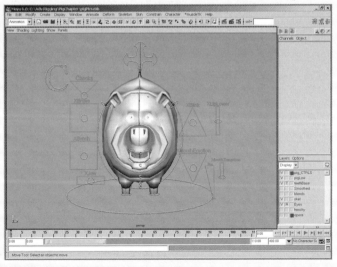

Figure 9.6
The facial controls. Image copyright: The Animation Farm 2005.

Figure 9.7
Don't be so nosey. Image copyright: The Animation Farm 2005.

The Alternative Face Rig

The facial setup on the pig is pretty much on the opposite side of the spectrum compared to past facial rigs that I've done. Usually, I would have finer-tuned controls that would act as either skin controls or muscle controls, and then have blendshapes as a secondary option "just in case." This goes hand-in-hand with what Cro talks about in the interview previously in the chapter—the layered approach. Make your major muscle groups/controls and then have smaller, finer-tuned controls to layer in with. Let's take an example with an older model/rig (see Figure 9.8).

This setup is actually quite simple if you break it down. Looking back at it, it would be an ideal rig if I had my joystick controls with blendshapes, plus these extremely fine-tuned controls. Of course, it will always have to depend on your production time and purposes. A facial rig like this by itself is still good enough for lip sync; you just have to be able to be patient enough to animate all the controls. Some will like it, others will not (see Figure 9.9).

For the face control rig, I duplicated the deforming wire controls (which I'll get to in a bit) and set them in their own group node, making sure they were not connected in any way to the actual deforming rig. I then moved these aside to what you see as the templated curves next to the head in Figure 9.9. Each of these curves was then clustered (each CV was selected and made into a cluster). Maya 6 has a nice handy shortcut for doing this—select a curve, then hold Control and the right mouse button down. The marking menu will have an option for "cluster," which makes a cluster on each CV of the curve.

I then made the control boxes, named them accordingly, and positioned them to where I wanted them—most likely snapping them to each of the corresponding clusters. After that, I simply parented the clusters under their proper control box and hid the clusters. Then I made the wires templated. I should

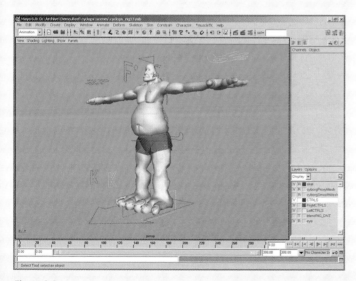

Figure 9.8
Cyclops complete with facial rig.

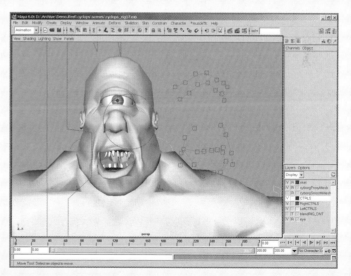

Figure 9.9
A closeup of the facial rig.

note that when parenting the clusters under the boxes, they were grouped to preserve position—something that we'll use when we hook this control rig up (see Figure 9.10).

You can now group the control boxes under a main facial control so you can move that group wherever you want in the viewport. You could also attach a camera to that group and make a pop-up interface that is locked to the face control cam.

Now for hooking it up, which is just as simple as the preceding. I did the following to a blendshape, which was always "on" when plugged into the rigged Cyclops model. I like doing that because there is always that "just in case" that could happen; you may need to change something, or you may not like something, or any number of things could happen. So, to this blendshape, I made some facial curves going in the direction and control that I wanted (the very ones that I duplicated previously). I applied these as influence objects, along with a couple of joints (that were separate from the actual Cyclops rig). With the curves as influence objects (as opposed to wire deformers), you can now paint their influence with the Paint Weights tool.

You can probably see where this is going at this point. After you have the weights painted out, you can cluster these influence curves. Now, you can animate with these clusters, or put these into the control rig to animate with, but I like controls to be clean and not so directly connected to the heart of the rig (like joints). That is why I built the control rig from the duplicated joints. All you have to do now is to directly connect the translations of these influence curve clusters to either the control curve clusters (that are parented under the squares), or directly connect them to the squares themselves. Either way, everything should be zero'd out to avoid any trouble spots (see Figure 9.11).

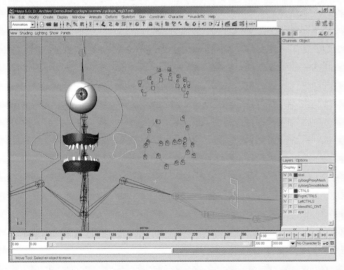

Figure 9.10
The facial controls with clusters showing.

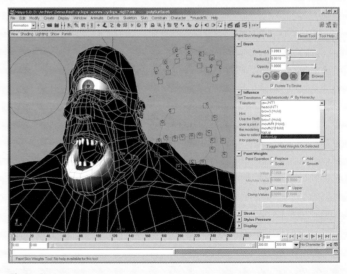

Figure 9.11
Painting the influence curves.

This is the basic rundown of the facial rig, though there are other techniques here and there. One problem you'll need to watch out for is double transformations, especially when you start connecting up the clusters. You can use wire deformers instead of influence curves to get a different effect. You can also use joints to get some pivot action going, as well as using just clusters (or soft mods) on the original mesh, and control all these in the same type of control rig. Mixing and matching techniques is up to you. As a TD, you figure out what works best for you, the animators, and for the production as a whole.

Jumping Back to the Pig Production—Production Issues

As the production progressed and shots/demands were changed, the rig had to change as well. Using file-referencing made this possible. If you haven't used file-referencing or are not sure what it is, I highly recommend you look it up in the docs and see what it's all about. If we didn't have referencing available, any changes to a rig, background, prop, and so on would have to be updated in every scene file throughout the production. You can imagine what a headache that would be!

So, with referencing, I was able to add blends and rig fixes/changes throughout the entire production—even as we were doing the final touches and rendering tweaks! For instance, our lead animator preferred to have IK on the ears instead of the FK controls that I had set up. Another easy and quick fix was needed when we decided the pig needed to chew things and that required some extra lip movements. I simply went into the rig file, added some clusters (soft selection deformers would have worked just fine as well), made sure the deformation order was correct, and attached some easy to use controls (see Figure 9.12).

Other fixes included blendshape changes and bulging/geometry crashing issues. I even had to make a blendshape that stayed on all the time, since we decided to make some changes to the pig's creases. The fixes for the crashing issues were done with clusters or blendshapes that were SDK'd to certain joint rotations. Since the initial writing of this chapter, we've used the pig for some animations on a children's show on PBS, and I have added several things to the rig, including stretchy legs, several new facial controls to hit even more expressions, more blendshapes as alternative expressions, multiple costumes and props, new UVs to handle certain maps, and minor tweaks and fixes found along the way.

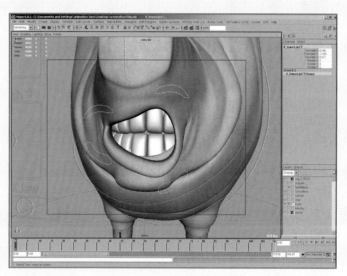

Figure 9.12
Pig Chew controls that were added far after the rig was completed and animated. Very similar to the previously mentioned technique for fine-tuning controls on the Cyclops. Image copyright: The Animation Farm 2005.

Even as we continue with the PBS project and other projects, I still would like to play with some ideas for the pig and other cartoony rigs that I'll be making in the near future. Inspired by Disney's display of *Chicken Little* footage at Siggraph 2004 this past year, I would really like to explore the possibilities of taking rigs into a more cartoony and stretchy direction—something that really pushes the limits. Breakable rigs and super-stretchy limbs are sort of a hot topic in the TD world right now, and it's something that I'm sure we'll be seeing for a long time.

Figure 9.13
Final render of the pig in The Pig Review. Image copyright: The Animation Farm 2005.

SECTION 3

Advanced Rigging

chapter 10
Automation

As productions that utilize computer animation grow more complex, it is important for the character rigger to explore and understand ways of making the rigging process easier and more reliable. Maya provides a great tool for automation in the form of MEL.

It is tempting to view automation with skepticism. After all, even for a technical director, 3D rigging is a creative field that requires a certain eye for anatomy and aesthetics. Truly, 3D rigging is a complex field and there is no automated system that will rig a character for you. However, there are certain benefits to automation that are invaluable to the modern character rigger, including the following:

◆ **Automation is reliable.** As character rigs grow in complexity to meet the demands of production, the opportunity for human error to creep into the process is magnified. Automation can greatly reduce the time a rigger spends digging though the nuts and bolts of a rig.

◆ **Automation is efficient.** Most of the cases where automation can be applied with greatest impact are repetitive operations.

◆ **Automation is educational.** There is no better way to learn how software works than to take it apart at the component level. Maya's graph-based architecture provides a great deal of access via MEL commands that make it possible to see exactly what Maya is doing.

Principles of Automation

Selecting a good process for automation is tricky. It is too much work to try and automate everything—a technical director must make thousands of decisions about how to rig characters, and each character is different. Trying to make one script that will automate everything is probably not efficient or desirable.

The processes that benefit most from automation are simple processes that can be time-consuming. These are usually components of a larger process, little areas that take time to complete but are not overtly complex. In the process of rigging characters, pay attention to processes you do repetitively because these are often good candidates for automation. Other candidates include Maya functions that are not easily accessible. For example, to see an object's Local Rotation Axis, one must select the object or objects and access the command through the Display→Component Display→Local Rotation Axis command in the main menu. This process is time-consuming for a character rigger, who will often want to toggle the display of rotation axis, which makes this function a prime candidate for automation.

As you gain more experience with rigging characters, you will begin to amass your own toolbox of shortcuts that make life easier.

When looking at how to automate a process, one obvious method to take is to open the Script Window and start going through the steps of your process. Maya will echo all the commands into the script window, and after the process is done, these commands can be copied into a text file or a MEL file and be executed on demand in Maya. The commands as echoed in the Script Editor are specialized, however, and will need some refinement to be turned into editable scripts.

This functionality is very useful, but there is a great deal more power available to someone who is familiar with MEL and its inner workings.

Converting MEL from the Script Editor to Executable Commands

The Script Editor is a great reference for dissembling the steps that must be taken to create a desired effect. Since every command is echoed to the Script Editor, it is easy to see the arguments that Maya passes to the commands.

One of the things you will notice in the Script Editor is that the commands echoed do not list the object names. When Maya executes a command, it pulls its arguments from the selection list or the list of objects that are currently selected in the modeling environment. When you select an object and constrain it, for example, you will see the Script Editor echo the following (see Figure 10.1):

```
pointConstraint -offset 0 0 0 -weight 1;
```

This command is effective, but it requires that the proper objects be selected in the proper order. This adds some overhead to the script writing process, as it requires the addition of several select statements. It is much easier to call the objects by name in a script:

```
pointConstraint -offset 0 0 0 -weight 1 objectA objectB objectC;
```

So how does one translate the Script Editor's output into MEL commands? When you execute a command such as the one above, Maya takes the global selection list as the arguments for the command. The global selection list is, as its name implies, a list of all the objects that are selected in Maya. To see the selection list, enter the following MEL at the command line.

```
ls -sl;
```

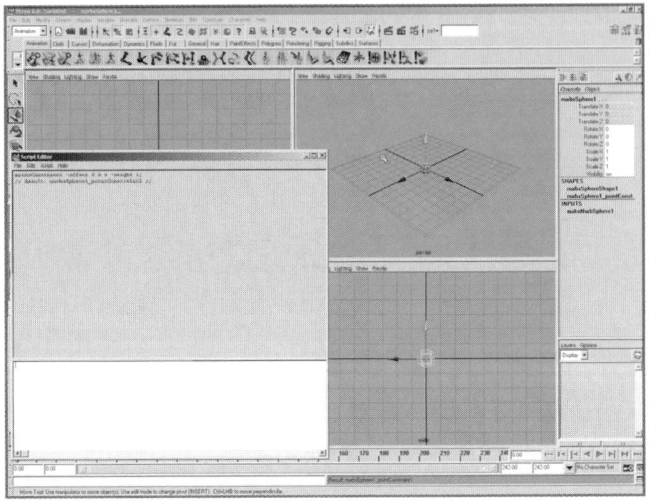

Figure 10.1
Maya commands are echoed to the Script Editor.

The result of that command is a string array of the objects that are selected. If you were to paste the output of this command onto the end of the command from the Script Editor, you would get a version of the command that would execute correctly, regardless of what objects were selected.

1. Start with a new Maya scene.
2. Create a locator. Move it away from the origin.
3. Create another locator and move it away from the origin and the first one.
4. Create a polyCube.
5. With nothing selected, select the first locator, then Shift-select the second locator, and then Shift-select the polyCube (see Figure 10.2).

In the Script Editor, enter the following:

```
pointConstraint -offset 0 0 0 -weight 1 `ls -sl`;
```

You will see that the polyCube is constrained to the locators. This illustrates the way commands are echoed to the Script Editor—the selection list is taken as the arguments of the MEL command. Another way to effect the same command would be the following:

```
pointConstraint -offset 0 0 0 -weight 1 locator1 locator2 pCube1;
```

Many of the commands in Maya will take an array of objects as an input, and special significance is attributed to the last node selected. The extrude command, for example, requires the path to be the last curve selected. The ikHandle command requires that the last node is the end-effector.

So how do you know which arguments are important and what order they need to be in? The answer is in the MEL Command Reference. You can find the reference by using the Help→MEL Command Reference menu item. The MEL command reference contains all the information on all of the MEL commands used by Maya, including what arguments they expect. Figure 10.3 shows the Maya MEL command reference.

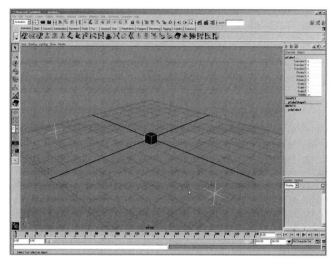

Figure 10.2
Select the locators and the polyCube .

Figure 10.3
The MEL command reference.

10. Automation

187

Working with Maya Names

No discussion on automation would be complete without a rundown on how Maya handles naming objects. The names of nodes are of utmost importance in Maya because the names of objects are used to organize all the objects in a scene. In addition, every MEL command uses Maya names to determine which objects it is acting upon.

When a node is created in Maya, it is given a name, either by default or by an "-n" command flag. At this time, Maya looks at the hierarchy where the object exists. If there are any other objects in that level of the hierarchy, Maya renames the object, appending a number on the end. If this is the second object to attempt to use an unavailable name, Maya appends a "1."

Now here is the catch—when an object is created, Maya *only* looks at the hierarchy where the object is made. This is usually the "world," the top level of the hierarchy. It is possible, however, for an object to have the same name, but be located under a different parent node. For example, you could have a hierarchy called "shoe" in Maya, and under "shoe" is a surface called "lace." It is possible to create a new node in the world and call it "lace."

This functionality becomes very important in automation because when there are two or more objects in the scene that share the same name, Maya cannot select them merely by name. If you were to type: select –r "lace;" in the previous example, the Select command would error out, as in Figure 10.4. The only option to select the object now is to resolve a path to tell Maya which node to select. A path in Maya traces the hierarchy of an object from the "world" node to its current location using the "|" character to separate each level. The path to the "lace" node under the "shoe" node would be "|shoe|lace." All Maya's commands will work fine with this argument, but it creates a lot of extra work for the creation of scripts, as you constantly have to take object names and strip off the path. This can be tedious and add a significant level of effort, and it is one of the many reasons that character riggers have adopted the following rule:

No two significant nodes in a Maya scene should share the same name.

We define significant nodes as all transforms and utility nodes, or any node you will ever want to select and manipulate. We recognize them as significant because there are many secondary nodes in Maya that you will never manipulate, and therefore you never need to know their names. Ensuring the uniqueness of each node will prevent errors, such as the one illustrated in Figure 10.4.

The following example illustrates the potential perils of Maya's naming mechanism in a simple script.

1. Start with a new Maya file.
2. Use the Window→General Editors→Script Editor to open the Script Editor.

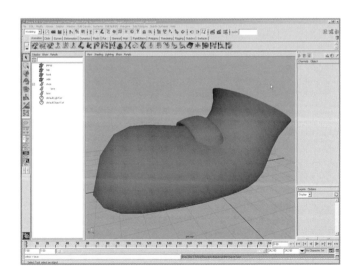

Figure 10.4
The Select command will error out when two objects in the scene have the same name.

3. Create a locator, rename it "target1," and move it away from the origin.

4. With the locator selected, press Ctrl+D to duplicate it. Maya should rename this locator "target2" and move it to another area of the scene.

5. Create a polygon cube.

6. Deselect the cube. Select the "target1" node, Shift-select the "target2" node, and finally select the "polyCube1" node. Use Constrain→Point to create a point constraint.

7. In the Script Editor, you will see all these commands echoed (see Figure 10.5).

What you will notice about the commands is that they proceed in a linear progression, tracking each step you completed in the previous example. But, let's assume you wanted to make simple rigs like this. The next step would be to take these commands and use them to create a duplicate, as in the following example:

1. Select all the text in the Script Editor, not including the "file –f -new" line.

2. Copy the commands with "Ctrl+C" and paste them into the Script Editor.

3. Press the numeric Enter key to execute the commands.

Open the Outliner—it should look similar to the one in Figure 10.6. If you select the "target1" node and move it, you will see that "pCube1" moves, as it is constrained between the "target1" and "target2" nodes. If you select the "target3" node and move it, nothing happens. The second polyCube sits at the origin, unaffected.

This is another result of Maya's usage of node names. Almost every function in Maya is dictated by the name of the node it is operating on. This is why it is so crucial that no two objects in a scene share the same name. Let's look briefly at how Maya's node-naming mechanics affected this example.

When Maya replayed the commands, it created a new locator. It attempted to name this locator "target1," but a node with that name already existed, so Maya tried to name it "target2." This name was also taken, and the node was named "target3." The same thing happened for "target4"—Maya tried to rename it

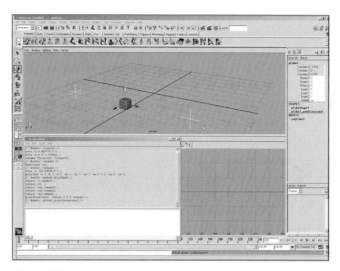

Figure 10.5
The commands echoed in the Script Editor.

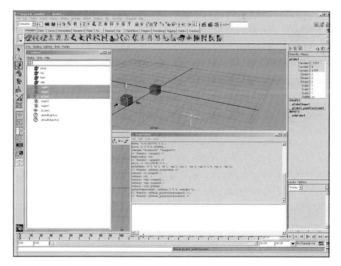

Figure 10.6
Attempting to make a duplicate rig.

10. Automation

189

"target2," then "target3," and finally "target4." This renaming mechanism of Maya is all at once very handy and troublesome, as you will see as you go through this chapter.

Another way in which Maya's node handling broke was when it attempted to create the pointConstraint. The MEL commands that led up to the constraint command had Maya select the "target1," "target2." and "polyCube1" nodes in that order. Then it executed the pointConstraint command. This simply tried to re-create the constraint that already existed on pCube1. There was no way for Maya to know that it was supposed to constrain the new cube to the new locators. As you go through the next few sections, you can see how potential naming problems are circumvented.

The Hidden Voodoo of the Character Rigger

One of the most valuable tools you will use in automating your rigs is the MEL Command Reference. This indispensable set of docs outlines all of Maya's MEL commands and goes into detail about what each of the flags used by a command menu can do. You will notice as you begin putting scripts together that the commands Maya echoes in the Script Editor are not in a usable format for a script. When you execute a command in Maya, it operates on the objects that are selected and utilizes their values at that point in time. In order to streamline your automation scripts, you will not want to be dependent on these factors, and this is where the MEL Command Reference comes in (see Figure 10.7).

When using MEL scripts, another command that is very useful is the "whatIs" command. WhatIs identifies the source of a command, whether it is a MEL script or a run-time command. If it is a script, whatIs will report its location or whether or not it was entered interactively. This command is extremely useful for debugging pipelines with a lot of custom scripts.

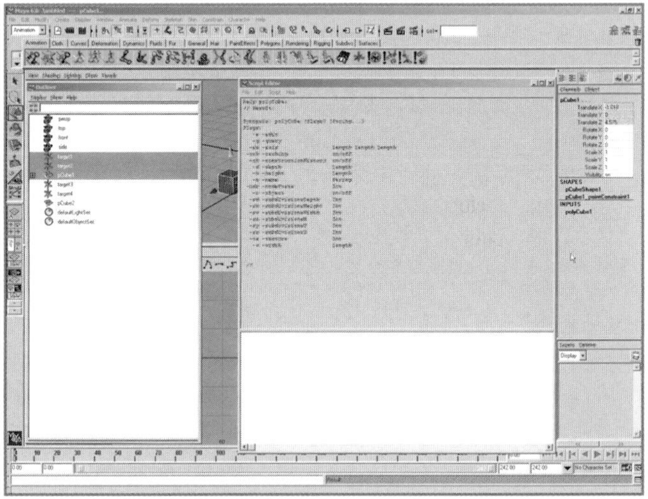

Figure 10.7
The "help" MEL command.

An Automated Rigging Tool

Let's look at creating some automated tools for rigging. In *Inspired 3D Character Setup*, the authors covered some simple MEL ideas, such as getting the list of selected objects and going through that list using variables. This example takes those ideas and builds upon them.

One of the more repetitive tasks of the character rigger is the creation of IK Handles for characters. You will often find that many of your characters are similar in their structure, especially since most of the characters you create are bipeds. Since this is a repetitive task, it could stand to be streamlined by some MEL automation.

The key to this automation is the idea that most of the IK system's setup on a chain follows a similar pattern: there will be an IK Handle that controls the leg from the thigh to the ankle, another from the ankle to the ball of the foot, and a final handle that runs from the ball to the tip of the toe. To take advantage of this, you can use the ikHandle MEL command. Let's look at this command in a simple script:

1. Open the scenes/chapter12/legSetup.mb file.

2. Open the Script Editor or a text editor. Enter the following script:

```
global proc setupIK()
{
    string $sel[] = `ls -sl`;
    ikHandle -sj $sel[0] -ee $sel[1] -n "myIK";
};
```

3. Enter this script in the Script Editor. To ease editing, use Ctrl+A to select all the text before pressing the numeric Enter key. This will enter the text from the editor without clearing it, which makes further editing easier.

4. Select the "thigh" joint and the "ankle" joint. At the command line, enter "setupIK" and press Enter. You should see output similar to Figure 10.8.

You will see an IK Handle appear, as in Figure 10.8. The ikHandle command takes several arguments that are preceded by flags. Flags are identifiers that are preceded by a dash ("-"). Flags generally set the options for a command. Normally, when you perform operations on objects in Maya, you open the option box. For the ikHandle command, you have two flags. The "-sj" flag, which is short for "startJoint," tells the ikHandle which joint to start from. The "-ee" flag tells the command which joint is the "endEffector" of the ikHandle. On the command line, each of these flags should be followed by the name of a Maya object. In the script, however, the names are passed from the selection via the "$sel[0]" and "$sel[1]" variables. The "-n" flag tells Maya what to name the IK Handle. As you can see, the argument supplied is a string, since it is in quotes. The names of all Maya objects are strings.

It is strongly recommended that you use a text editor to perform the exercises in this chapter. While the Script Editor is versatile, it is easy to lose the script you are working on by entering it accidentally or possibly hanging Maya with a simple mistake. Keeping your work in a separate application makes it easier to save edits to disk and provides insulation against mishaps. To move scripts to the Script Editor, simply copy them from the text editor and paste them in the Script Editor.

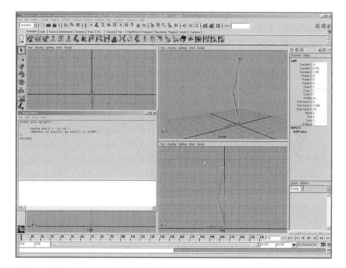

Figure 10.8
A scripted IK Handle.

Now that the basic function of the script is working, it can be expanded upon. Let's set up the script to do more than one IK Handle:

1. Select the IK Handle "myIK" and delete it.

2. In a text editor or the Script Editor, edit the text to mimic the following:

```
global proc setupIK()
{
    string $sel[] = `ls -sl`;
    ikHandle -sj $sel[0] -ee $sel[1] -n "ankleIK";
    ikHandle -sj $sel[1] -ee $sel[2] -n "ballIK";
    ikHandle -sj $sel[2] -ee $sel[3] -n "toeIK";
}
```

> Whenever you re-enter a function in Maya with the same name, the old function is overwritten with the new instructions.

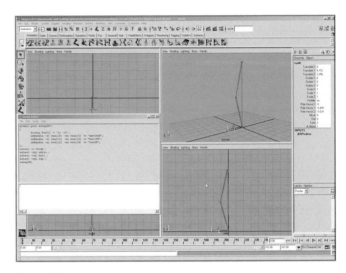

Figure 10.9
Scripting the construction of multiple IK Handles.

3. Select the "thigh," "ankle," "ball," and "toe" nodes, in that order.

4. Execute the "setupIK" command. You should see output resembling Figure 10.9.

Three IK Handles! Now we're talking. Notice that the order in which the joints are selected is important. The variable $sel is used often, each time with a different number. The first entry is 0, and that is taken by the "thigh" joint when the joints are selected in the correct order. The script also gives the IK Handles proper names, which is already a great time-saver for the character rigger on the go.

Adding Simple Error Correction

In the script above, the number of objects selected is important. Let's say the script is executed when only the "thigh" and "ankle" joints are selected. What will the script do when it tries to access the "ball" joint or "$sel[2]" in the script? There is no object on the selection list in "$sel[2]," so the script will cause an error. Take a look at the results:

1. Select the ik handles in the scene and delete them.

2. Select the "thigh" and "ankle" nodes only.

3. Execute the "setupIK" command.

You will see the feedback line turn red and the message "Error: line 5: Selected objects are not valid." You will also see that only one IK Handle has been created. When an error occurs, the script stops executing where it is. This is usually undesirable, as it is difficult to ascertain just which actions have been performed in a complex script. Since you know that the script requires four objects to be selected, it may be a good idea to check to see how many objects are selected when the script runs. Here is how to do it:

1. In the Script Editor or your text editor, insert a line so that your script looks like the following:

```
global proc setupIK()
{
    string $sel[] = `ls -sl`;
    if(size($sel) != 4) error("Please select only 4 joints");
    ikHandle -sj $sel[0] -ee $sel[1];
    ikHandle -sj $sel[1] -ee $sel[2];
    ikHandle -sj $sel[2] -ee $sel[3];
};
```

2. Press the numeric Enter key to register the new script.

3. Select the "thigh" and "ankle" nodes only.

4. Execute the "setupIK" command.

An error message appears indicating that there are not enough objects selected. This error message is different, however—it was put in there in line 4. The "if" statement checks the size of the "$sel" variable. If four objects were selected, the size of the "$sel" variable would be four. If the size is anything other than four, the error command will stop the execution of the script and display the text "Please select only 4 joints." In essence, you have told the script to abort if a condition that you know is essential to the proper function of the script is not present. Notice that the text sent by the error command doesn't merely report an error, but it informs the user what the correct input is for this script: four joints. It is a good idea to make error messages as informative as possible. You can see the results of the error in Figure 10.10.

As you begin making your own automated tools, it is a good idea to take a moment and think about who will be using them. If you are writing a quick tool for yourself, the issue of whether or not it requires four objects to be selected may be moot. If it is a quick fix you will use to do something highly repetitive, you can squeeze by without any error checking. In many cases, though, other people may use your script, or you yourself may put a script aside for a long time, forgetting the details of its function. While it is difficult to perceive all error conditions, it is a good idea to eliminate at least the obvious ones.

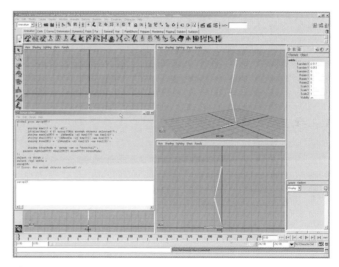

Figure 10.10
Some simple error checking can save a lot of time.

Adding Some More Controls

So now you have a handy little script that sets up some leg IK Handles and names them. This is pretty good, but let's say you want to expand it, in order to make it more useful. Let's add a node that controls the rotation from the ball of the foot. This node will be used further in a more complex rig, but for now, setting up the ball node will be enough. It will require some changes to the script:

1. Open the scenes/chapter12/legSetup.mb file or delete all of the IK Handles in the scene.

```
global proc setupIK()
{
    string $sel[] = `ls -sl`;
    if(size($sel) < 4) error("Not enough objects selected!");
    string $ankleIK[] = `ikHandle -sj $sel[0] -ee $sel[1] -n "ankleIK"`;
    string $ballIK[] = `ikHandle -sj $sel[1] -ee $sel[2] -n "ballIK"`;
    string $toeIK[] = `ikHandle -sj $sel[2] -ee $sel[3] -n "toeIK"`;
    string $footNode = `group -em -n "footCtrl"`;    parent $ankleIK[0] $ballIK[0] $toeIK[0] $footNode;
}
```

When you execute this script, you will see all the IK Handles have been grouped under a node that was created with the "group" command (see Figure 10.11). Whenever you want to create a null or a pivot with no geometry, you can use the "group" command with the "-em" flag. The "parent" command places a list of nodes under the last node specified in the hierarchy.

You will also notice that all of the creation commands are preceded with a variable declaration. When the objects are parented in the last line, they are called by the variable instead of the name assigned with the "-n" flag. The reason this is done is to make the script more robust. Whenever you use the "-n" flag, Maya attempts to give the object the name you specify. If, for some reason, an object already exists with that name, Maya will have to alter the name the object receives. For example, if there is already an object named "footCtrl" at the world level when you execute the script, Maya will name the node the script creates "footCtrl1." If your script is looking for the "footCtrl" object, it will manipulate the wrong one.

To prevent this, you can use variables. Whenever Maya creates a node, it returns the name of that node as a string. If you create a locator, the name of that locator is returned in the Script Editor. In this script, when Maya creates the objects, the variables catch the real names of the created nodes. The variables are string arrays for the ikHandle commands because when Maya creates an IK Handle, it returns the name of the handle and the name of the end-effector. The handle name is first, so it occupies the 1st position, which is the index 0 in the string

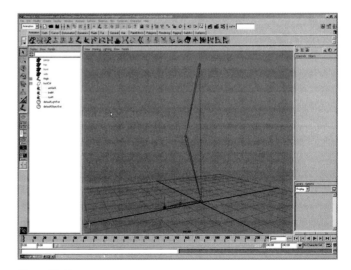

Figure 10.11
The results of the automated setupIK script.

array. The end-effector is never really used, but if you try to catch the result with a regular string, Maya will throw an error. Whenever the IK Handle variables are accessed, notice that the script is accessing the 0th variable using the subscript, i.e., "$ballIK[0]." This is because the actual name of the ik handle is in the 0th spot, while the 1st spot is the name of the end-effector. Notice that the "$footNode" variable is a single string—when Maya creates an empty group, it only returns the name of the group. The majority of creation commands in Maya return more than one node.

You will also notice that the IK Handle creation statements are enclosed in evaluation marks (`). When a statement is enclosed in these marks, Maya evaluates it first in the environment and returns the result to the script. It is not always necessary to use these marks, but there exists ambiguity about when exactly they are needed and when they are not. We find that it is better to use them when in doubt, as they only serve to clarify the instructions to Maya.

With the variables in place, it doesn't matter what other objects exist in the modeling environment. To try it out, delete the IK Handles from under the "footCtrl" node and run the command on the joints. The script will create a "footCtrl1" node and put the handles underneath it.

Dealing with xforms

With the basics in creating the IK Handles, empty nodes, and parenting down, there is only one feature needed to create a proper hierarchy. In order to position the nodes automatically, we need a way to get the position of the components. In the previous example, when the "footCtrl" node was created, it was created at the origin. For practical use, we would want that group to be positioned at the same spatial location as the ankle, or any other joint, for that matter.

To get the position of the joints, you can use the "xform" command. xform can be used to query almost any aspect of a joint's transformations, from its position to rotation to scale. xform returns an array of floating point numbers, so the proper variable must be declared.

```
global proc setupIK()
{
    string $sel[] = `ls -sl`;
    if(size($sel) < 4) error("Not enough objects selected!");
    string $ankleIK[] = `ikHandle -sj $sel[0] -ee $sel[1] -n "ankleIK"`;
    string $ballIK[] = `ikHandle -sj $sel[1] -ee $sel[2] -n "ballIK"`;
    string $toeIK[] = `ikHandle -sj $sel[2] -ee $sel[3] -n "toeIK"`;
    string $footNode = `group -em -n "footCtrl"`;
    float $position[] = `xform -q -ws -t $ankleIK[0]`;
    move -a $position[0] $position[1] $position[2] $footNode;
    makeIdentity -a 1;
    parent $ankleIK[0] $ballIK[0] $toeIK[0] $footNode;
}
```

The "$position[]" variable is created and the location of the "$ankleIK[0]," or IK Handle, is queried by the xform command. These numbers are then used to move the "footCtrl" node to an appropriate spatial location. You will also notice that the "footCtrl" node has been zero-transformed in its new location. The "makeIdentity" command can zero the transforms of an object, and the "-a" flag ensures that the object maintains its current position and orientation when being zeroed-out.

Making a Helper Command

Moving nodes around seems like something a technical director would do a lot, especially when one is considering an automatic foot setup tool. The MEL code that does this is relatively bulky and repetitive. For every ik handle you want to snap a node to, you have to get its position, move the node, and zero the transforms. This is three lines of code, but since you are doing it for multiple nodes, it adds up. With every repetition in the script, the possibility for mistakes is greater. This looks like a great candidate for a helper function.

A helper function is simply a small function that does a repetitive task usually in the service of another procedure. As procedures grow in complexity, the number of operations you will need to perform on an object can increase. To put all of these operations in one procedure can lead to excessive errors and make it difficult to read the script later. By using helper functions, scripts become more manageable. A script that handles the positioning will probably have another use, but for now, it is a component that will streamline this script.

What we are looking to create is a function that takes two objects, moves one to the other, and freezes the transforms. It will pretty much mirror the code in the script used previously, but we'll use variables to make it a more general case. The script is as follows:

```
global proc positionAndFreeze(string $source, string $dest)
{
    print("positionAndFreeze "+$source+" "+$dest+";\n");
    float $pos[] = `xform -q -ws -t $source`;
    move -a $pos[0] $pos[1] $pos[2] $dest;
    makeIdentity -a 1 $dest;
    print("// Result: "+$source+"\n");
}
```

To use this script, enter it into the Script Editor or a text editor and save it into the Scripts directory with the name positionAndFreeze.mel. You will notice the MEL commands are very similar to the code in the previous example, except the object name variables have been replaced with variables in the declaration of the procedure. If the "setupIK" script is edited to use this new script, it will look like the following.

```
global proc setupIK()
{
    string $sel[] = `ls -sl`;
    if(size($sel) < 4) error("Not enough objects selected!");
    string $ankleIK[] = `ikHandle -sj $sel[0] -ee $sel[1]`;
    string $ballIK[] = `ikHandle -sj $sel[1] -ee $sel[2]`;
    string $toeIK[] = `ikHandle -sj $sel[2] -ee $sel[3]`;    string $footNode = `group -em -n "footCtrl"`;
    positionAndFreeze($ankleIK[0], $footNode);
    parent $ankleIK[0] $ballIK[0] $toeIK[0] $footNode;
}
```

One line, the call to the new procedure, replaces three. This is a good savings, especially when this script will create five or so nodes when completed. Anytime you can save the repetition of MEL code, it's a good idea to implement a helper function.

Notice the print statement in line 3 of the "positionAndFreeze" script. This will print a line in the Script Editor every time the procedure is called. The purpose for this is to help track down errors. If Maya encounters an error, it reports only the line number of the error. If you are using a helper script that is embedded in another script, it can be difficult to determine which script caused the error. In this example, the script echoes its name and the arguments it was called with to the Script Editor. If an error occurs, the execution of the script will stop, as will any script that has called it. It is then possible to examine the error and the state of the Maya environment at the time it occurred.

The print statement echoes the command to the Script Editor window in the same format that it can be entered at the command line. There is also a print statement at the end of the function that prints a result. The purpose of this statement is to better determine the location of the error. It is possible that an error might occur immediately after the successful completion of a "positionAndFreeze" command. The result statement indicates that the command completed executing—however, if the error occurred in the helper script, the results would not be echoed to the Script Editor.

Now all of the tools and techniques needed to rig the hierarchy of the reverse foot have been covered. All that remains is to give Maya the proper instructions to create, position, and parent all of the nodes needed.

Putting It All Together

So now all of the tools are ready: you know how to use the relevant MEL commands, and you have a function that will aid in manipulating objects. Now it is time to complete the script, creating and organizing all the nodes in the hierarchy of the foot.

```
global proc setupIK()
{
    string $sel[] = `ls -sl`;
    if(size($sel) < 4) error("Not enough objects selected!");
    //create ik handles
    string $ankleIK[] = `ikHandle -sj $sel[0] -ee $sel[1]`;
    string $ballIK[] = `ikHandle -sj $sel[1] -ee $sel[2]`;
    string $toeIK[] = `ikHandle -sj $sel[2] -ee $sel[3]`;

    //create rig nodes
    string $ballNode = `group -em -n "ballRIG"`;
    positionAndFreeze($ballIK[0], $ballNode);

    string $toeNode = `group -em -n "toeRIG"`;
    positionAndFreeze($ballIK[0], $toeNode);

    string $heelNode = `group -em -n "heelRIG"`;
    positionAndFreeze($ankleIK[0], $heelNode);

    string $toeTipNode = `group -em -n "toeTipRIG"`;
    positionAndFreeze($toeIK[0], $toeTipNode);

    string $footNode = `group -em -n "footCtrl"`;
    positionAndFreeze($ankleIK[0], $footNode);
```

```
//parent ik handles
parent $ankleIK[0] $ballIK[0] $ballNode;
parent $toeIK[0] $toeNode;

//parent rig nodes
parent $ballNode $toeNode $heelNode;
parent $heelNode $toeTipNode;
parent $toeTipNode $footNode;
}
```

The results of the latest setupIK script should resemble Figure 10.12. Notice that the technique of using variables instead of actual object names is carried throughout the script. Using variables to capture the returned names of nodes prevents unusual results in the event that there are two or more nodes in a scene that share the same name. Notice also the addition of the comments, preceded by the "//" characters. As scripts grow in complexity, comments become more essential to understand quickly how scripts work. In the script, each major step is delimited by comments describing what they do. The amount of commenting used in a script is usually at the discretion of the scriptwriter, but more is usually better.

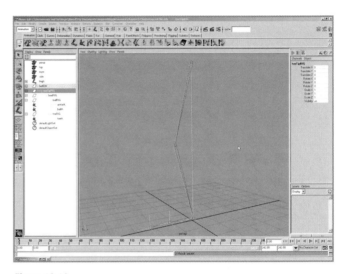

Figure 10.12
The complete hierarchy of the reverse foot is built using the script.

One of the caveats of this script is that, based on the geometry of the character, the placement of the heel node is inexact. In order to make the script work, we just take the position of the ankle joint and use that as the heel location. Once the script is run, the heel pivot may be repositioned to match better the geometry of the particular character. In setting up automation in your rigging, you will never be able to fully automate the need for human judgment. While there is no easy way to reliably place the heel automatically, it is much faster to use the rigging script and reposition the heel than to build the whole thing by hand.

Adding Complex Behaviors

In the previous section, MEL automation was used to manipulate the names and hierarchies of objects in a foot rig. In this section, we are going to take that a step further and add some set driven keys to the rig.

The first step in fleshing out the automated foot is to add some attributes to the "footCtrl" node. The attributes will control the toes of the foot rig. Adding attributes in this manner is a two-part process. The first step uses the "addAttr" command to add the attribute to the control. The second part is to make that attribute keyable, so that it appears in the Channel Box for the animator to manipulate.

To add the attributes, the following lines will be added to the setupIK script.

```
//add control attributes
addAttr -ln roll -at double -min -10 -max 10 -dv 0 $footNode;
setAttr -e -keyable true ($footNode+".roll");

addAttr -ln toe -at double -min -10 -max 10 -dv 0 $footNode;
setAttr -e -keyable true ($footNode+".toe");
```

You will notice that the variables are used with string-concatenation to access the variables. The string arguments can be passed to any MEL function that requires the name of an attribute. One key thing to remember when using the string concatenation is that the attribute name must be separated from its object by the "." character. You will also notice that the argument for the concatenation is surrounded by parentheses. This prevents any misinterpretation of the argument by the MEL script. It is always a good idea to isolate these arguments with parentheses.

Now that the attributes are added, it is time to hook in some set driven keys. The thing to remember with automating rigging is that you will run into many variations of creatures and characters, so it is unlikely that one automated rigging solution will work 100 percent for all possibilities. However, a rigging script can shave a lot of time off.

In the case of set driven keys, Maya's regular interface or creating them is a bit cumbersome, so it is often easier to create the keys and edit their values in the Graph Editor. In the case of this particular setup script, the set driven keys will be created with default rotation values that have just been derived from observation.

The setDrivenKeyframe command sets the driven key values. The following lines added to the MEL script will add the Set Driven Keys.

```
//add standard driven keys
setDrivenKeyframe -cd ($footNode+".roll") -dv 0 -v 0 ($ballNode+".rotateX") ;
setDrivenKeyframe -cd ($footNode+".roll") -dv 5 -v 30 ($ballNode+".rotateX") ;
setDrivenKeyframe -cd ($footNode+".roll") -dv 5 -v 0 ($toeTipNode+".rotateX") ;
setDrivenKeyframe -cd ($footNode+".roll") -dv 10 -v 30 ($toeTipNode+".rotateX") ;
setDrivenKeyframe -cd ($footNode+".roll") -dv 0 -v 0 ($heelNode+".rotateX") ;
setDrivenKeyframe -cd ($footNode+".roll") -dv -10 -v -30 ($heelNode+".rotateX") ;
setDrivenKeyframe -cd ($footNode+".toe") -dv 0 -v 0 ($toeNode+".rotateX") ;
setDrivenKeyframe -cd ($footNode+".toe") -dv -10 -v -30 ($toeNode+".rotateX") ;
setDrivenKeyframe -cd ($footNode+".toe") -dv 10 -v 30 ($toeNode+".rotateX") ;
```

Notice how all the variable names are incorporated into the attribute names. As stated before, these default driven keys may not work exactly for the geometry of the particular character, but the idea is that adjusting these values via the Graph Editor is a bit easier than setting all of the keys with Maya's Set Driven Key window. Also, in the case of very similar characters, it is possible to find values that work well for most cases and use those values to set up a large group of different characters. When added to the script, the "footCtrl" node will appear as in Figure 10.13.

Another thing you will notice is that all of the set driven keys have a key for the driver value of 0. This is to ensure that, at a value of 0, the objects driven by the attribute are in their rest pose, which usually has all of the objects' rotations set to 0. This pose corresponds to the bind pose, and it is necessary to easily put the character back in its bind pose for skin editing. If values were to be set for only the maximum and minimum values, there is no guarantee that when the driver attribute is set to 0, the driven attributes will be at 0. Since set driven keys are channel connections, they cannot be disabled by the Modify→Evaluate Nodes→Ignore All command. If the 0 position did not correlate to the bind pose, the connections between the set driven key curves and the joints may need to be broken to put the skeleton back in its bind pose.

Setting Up the Knee

Now that we have a good automated foot setup script with rolling heels and moving toes, let's look at hooking the knee into all this goodness. In *Inspired 3D Character Setup*, the authors go through the process of creating a knee control that manipulates the pole vector of the leg IK Handle.

The first step is to create the knee control. Until now, we've been working mostly with nulls. Now we will use the circle MEL command to create a circle that will be the geometry of the controller. The circle command will return a string array of the nodes that are created. In this case, it will return the name of the transform and the name of the NURBS curve generator node. For this reason, we will set up a string array to grab that information and use it to create the rest of the knee rig.

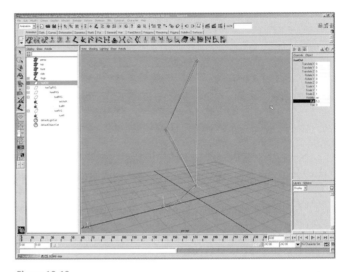

Figure 10.13
The leg setup with setDrivenKey controls.

```
//add knee control
string $kneeCtrl[] = `circle -n "kneeCtrl"`;
string $kneeCtrlGrp = `group -em -n "kneeCtrlGRP"`;
parent $kneeCtrl[0] $kneeCtrlGrp;
positionAndFreeze($sel[0], $kneeCtrlGrp);
```

We will also want to translate the circle forward on the Z axis a bit and move its rotation pivot back to the location of the hip. First, we can use the "positionAndFreeze" script to properly position the controller group. After positioning, the "kneeCtrl" node is translated forward on the Z axis.

```
xform -r -t 0 0 5 $kneeCtrl[0];
makeIdentity -a 1 $kneeCtrlGrp;
makeIdentity -a 1 $kneeCtrl[0];
```

Finally, the constraints are created.

```
pointConstraint $sel[0] $kneeCtrlGrp;
poleVectorConstraint $kneeCtrl[0] $ankleIK[0];
```

At this point, the controller for the knee is set up. All that remains is hooking the foot rotation to the "kneeCtrl" node. In *Inspired 3D Character Setup*, the authors used an expression to do this. We will use a utility node to do the same thing.

```
//connect knee control to foot
string $kneeRotateNode = `createNode -n "kneeRotateMulti" multiplyDivide`;
connectAttr -f ($footNode+".rotateY") ($kneeRotateNode+".input1X");
setAttr ($kneeRotateNode+".input2X") .7;
connectAttr -f ($kneeRotateNode+".outputX") ($kneeCtrlGrp+".rotateY");
```

You will notice the use of the "connectAttr" command. This is the MEL equivalent of using the Connection Editor. The "-f" flag tells the command to override any connections that exist on those attributes in favor of the new connection.

Making It Name Safe

Now that the "setupIK" script is working for one leg, it would add a lot of functionality to expand it to work on two. As a character rigger, you may need to set up the rigs for several models that have been weighted to skeletons. While it is possible to create one leg rig and duplicate it with the upstream graph, this can disrupt the weighting present on the model. It is much easier to adapt the script to work on a scene with two separate legs.

If you were to run the "setupIK" script on two identical leg chains, you would get an error similar to the following:

```
// positionAndFreeze ballIK ballRIG;
// Error: line 4: More than one object matches name: ballIK //
```

First, notice that the error doesn't print out which procedure encountered the error. Was it "setupIK?" A quick look would indicate otherwise. In this case, however, it is easy to see that the error occurred when the "positionAndFreeze" script tried to move "ballRIG" to the location of "ballIK." Now that we know where the error is, we can assess what caused it.

The reason for the error lies in the mechanism Maya uses to manipulate and organize object names. Maya's name-resolution system prevents any two objects that share a parent from having the same name. It does allow objects with different parents to have the same name, however. Whenever this is the case, an error occurs when a MEL script attempts to access them by name. When the "setupIK" script is run for a second time, Maya attempts to re-create all of the nodes that were created in the first script. Because many of the nodes are in the "footCtrl" hierarchy, Maya allows the new nodes to have the same name as the old ones. When the MEL calls "positionAndFreeze," it doesn't know which "BallRIG" node to select.

The solution to this problem is simple—no two objects in a scene should ever have the same name. After running the script, the thigh node could be selected and Prefix Hierarchy Names menu option in the Modify menu could be used to rename all of the nodes that the script created. This will work fine, but requires extra interaction, which makes the script a little less automatable. To do this, we'll add an argument to the procedure statement that will be appended to the names of all the created nodes.

```
global proc setupIK(string $prefix)
```

With the argument in place, the "$prefix" variable can be integrated into the "–n" flags of the commands. When the script is run, all that is needed is to provide a unique prefix to prevent the leg assemblies from containing members with the same name. This prefix variable is then appended to the names of the created nodes in the script. The final script will be like this:

```
global proc setupIK(string $prefix)
{
    print("//setupIK\n");
    string $sel[] = `ls -sl`;
    if(size($sel) < 4) error("Not enough objects selected!");

    //create ik handles
    string $ankleIK[] = `ikHandle -sj $sel[0] -ee $sel[1] -n ($prefix+"ankleIK")`;
    string $ballIK[] = `ikHandle -sj $sel[1] -ee $sel[2] -n ($prefix+"ballIK")`;
    string $toeIK[] = `ikHandle -sj $sel[2] -ee $sel[3] -n ($prefix+"toeIK")`;

    //create rig nodes
    string $ballNode = `group -em -n ($prefix+"ballRIG")`;
    positionAndFreeze($ballIK[0], $ballNode);

    string $toeNode = `group -em -n ($prefix+"toeRIG")`;
    positionAndFreeze($ballIK[0], $toeNode);

    string $heelNode = `group -em -n ($prefix+"heelRIG")`;
    positionAndFreeze($ankleIK[0], $heelNode);

    string $toeTipNode = `group -em -n ($prefix+"toeTipRIG")`;
    positionAndFreeze($toeIK[0], $toeTipNode);

    string $footNode = `group -em -n ($prefix+"footCtrl")`;
    positionAndFreeze($ankleIK[0], $footNode);

    //parent ik handles
    parent $ankleIK[0] $ballIK[0] $ballNode;
    parent $toeIK[0] $toeNode;

    //parent rig nodes
    parent $ballNode $toeNode $heelNode;
    parent $heelNode $toeTipNode;
    parent $toeTipNode $footNode;

    //add control attributes
    addAttr -ln roll -at double -min -10 -max 10 -dv 0 $footNode;
    setAttr -e -keyable true ($footNode+".roll");

    addAttr -ln toe -at double -min -10 -max 10 -dv 0 $footNode;
    setAttr -e -keyable true ($footNode+".toe");

    //add standard driven keys
    setDrivenKeyframe -cd ($footNode+".roll") -dv 0 -v 0 ($ballNode+".rotateX") ;
    setDrivenKeyframe -cd ($footNode+".roll") -dv 5 -v 45 ($ballNode+".rotateX") ;
    setDrivenKeyframe -cd ($footNode+".roll") -dv 5 -v 0 ($toeTipNode+".rotateX") ;
    setDrivenKeyframe -cd ($footNode+".roll") -dv 10 -v 30 ($toeTipNode+".rotateX") ;
    setDrivenKeyframe -cd ($footNode+".roll") -dv 0 -v 0 ($heelNode+".rotateX") ;
```

```
setDrivenKeyframe -cd ($footNode+".roll") -dv -10 -v -30 ($heelNode+".rotateX") ;
setDrivenKeyframe -cd ($footNode+".toe") -dv 0 -v 0 ($toeNode+".rotateX") ;
setDrivenKeyframe -cd ($footNode+".toe") -dv -10 -v -30 ($toeNode+".rotateX") ;
setDrivenKeyframe -cd ($footNode+".toe") -dv 10 -v 30 ($toeNode+".rotateX") ;

//add knee control
string $kneeCtrl[] = `circle -n ($prefix+"kneeCtrl")`;
string $kneeCtrlGrp = `group -em -n ($prefix+"kneeCtrlGRP")`;
parent $kneeCtrl[0] $kneeCtrlGrp;
positionAndFreeze($sel[0], $kneeCtrlGrp);
xform -r -t 0 0 5 $kneeCtrl[0];
makeIdentity -a 1 $kneeCtrlGrp;
makeIdentity -a 1 $kneeCtrl[0];
pointConstraint $sel[0] $kneeCtrlGrp;
poleVectorConstraint $kneeCtrl[0] $ankleIK[0];

//connect knee control to foot
string $kneeRotateNode = `createNode -n ($prefix+"kneeRotateMulti") multiplyDivide`;
connectAttr -f ($footNode+".rotateY") ($kneeRotateNode+".input1X");
setAttr ($kneeRotateNode+".input2X") .7;
connectAttr -f ($kneeRotateNode+".outputX") ($kneeCtrlGrp+".rotateY");
}
```

When it is executed, you should see results similar to Figure 10.14.

As you can see, the $prefix variable has been inserted into every node that is created with a name flag. The final result is a procedure that can save tremendous time with creating similar setups in the same file.

Batch Processing

One of the things a technical director will want to do, especially on a large project, is batch processing. There are many times on a project where, for technical reasons, adjustments need to be made to all of the assets. If the production is using a good pipeline and all of the assets conform to its standards, it is possible to make global changes with a MEL script and use batch processing to apply the script to the files in question.

Batch processing can be a challenging process. A good batch-processing script would have very robust error checking and reporting. Ideally, the batch script would keep a log file or text file of all the errors or warnings encountered when the batch process executes. This makes it easier to track down any problems that may arise.

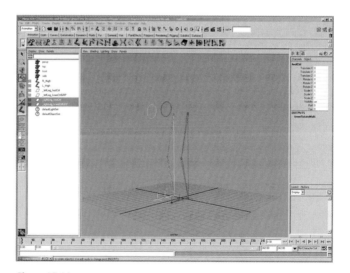

Figure 10.14
The setupIK script made name safe—both the left and right leg have been set up with the same script.

10. Automation

203

The first step in batch processing is assembling the list of files that are to be processed. Basically, Maya will need the path and the names of the files themselves, both of which are handled as strings. The list of filenames will usually be an array, as there will be more than one file to process.

To begin, we will create a procedure that is designed to process multiple files.

```
global proc batchProcess(string $path, string $fileList[], string $command)
```

The procedure will take a string for the path and an array for the files to be processed. The final argument is the name of the MEL procedure that is to be run on each of the files.

At this stage, it is important to note that, in order to streamline the batch processing, the MEL command that is to be called should not require any arguments that are to vary across the scenes to be processed. For example, let's say you needed to change the color of a character's eyes in a series of files. You create a MEL function called "colorEyes" that takes a string as the color. The script can accept "blue," "green," or "brown" as arguments and will change the color of the eyes accordingly.

In this situation, you could run the batch process with "colorEyes(\"brown\")" as the string for the $command variable. This would set the color of the eyes to brown for all of the files. If you wanted some files to be green and others to be blue, however, the process for setting these values would have to be included in the MEL script.

Now that the procedure has been defined, a simple for loop is created to go through the files.

```
for($file in $fileList)
{
    file -f -open ($path+$file);
    {
```

This part of the script uses string concatenation to put the path and the file strings together to get the proper full path for the file command to open. The next line will execute the command:

```
    eval $command;
```

In order for the MEL command outlined in the script to work, it must either be saved in one of Maya's script directories or it must be sourced. Since this batch script uses a currently open and running interactive session of Maya, it is only necessary that the script be sourced in the Maya environment. If the command can be entered at the command line and executed correctly, it will work with the batch script.

Finally, the script saves out the changes.

```
File -f -save;
}
```

When completed, the script should look like this:

```
global proc batchProcess(string $path, string $fileList[], string $command)
{
    for($file in $fileList)
    {
        //open the file
        file -f -open ($path+$file);
        //process it
        eval $command;
        //save it out
        file -f -save;
    }
}
```

Now the batch script is ready. To try it out, copy the sample directory called "batchSamples" from the Web site at http://www.courseptr.com/downloads to an easily locatable location on your hard drive. (We recommend "c:/batchSamples.") In production, the path you use will probably be more complicated, but the idea is the same. Let's begin by passing a simple command to test the batch process. At the MEL command prompt, enter the following:

```
batchProcess("c:/", {"a.mb", "b.mb", "c.mb", "d.mb"}, "sphere -n testSphere")
```

If you open the files, you will see that a sphere has been created in each one. You can remove the sphere with the following command:

```
batchProcess("c:/", {"a.mb", "b.mb", "c.mb", "d.mb"}, "delete testSphere")
```

Now the spheres are gone. Just for kicks, run the last command again. You will see that Maya error is out, because the sphere in that scene has already been deleted. It is important to observe this behavior—if you are executing a batch process on a hundred scripts and Maya encounters an error on the 73rd file, it will stop exactly where that error occurred. This makes it important to write robust scripts for batch processing whenever possible.

OK, a sphere is rather boring. Let's look at using the batch process script to do something much more useful. In the previous section, you constructed a MEL routine that set up character controls automatically. This is something the batch processor can be used for.

When using the setupIK script, the joints in a leg are selected in a certain order. If you look at the Maya files in the "batchProcess" folder, each one has a set of leg joints. All of the leg joints have the same name. To build the ik for a set of legs in one of the files, all you need to do is execute the following MEL commands:

```
select LHip LAnkle LToe LToe_tip;
setupIK("L");
select RHip RAnkle RToe RToe_tip;
setupIK("R");
```

To use these with the batch process, it is easier to wrap them in a MEL procedure. This procedure can be saved into the Scripts directory, or if the batch process is being run in an interactive session of Maya, it can be entered into the Script Editor. For this example, we will just execute it interactively. Enter the following script into the Script Editor:

```
global proc batchIt()
{
    select LHip LAnkle LToe LToe_tip;
    setupIK("L");
    select RHip RAnkle RToe RToe_tip;
    setupIK("R");
}
```

If you open one of the files in the batchProcess directory and execute the "batchIt" command, the IK system for the legs should be built. Now we simply need to pass this function as an argument to the batchProcess script as follows:

```
batchProcess("c:/", {"a.mb", "b.mb", "c.mb", "d.mb"}, "batchIt")
```

Now if you examine the Maya files, you will see that they have all been set up with their IK systems.

As you can see, Maya provides a very powerful and flexible scripting environment that provides many opportunities to speed production workflow through automation. As the demands placed on computer-generated imagery grow, it will be important for character setup artists to develop and enhance their toolsets with automation.

chapter 11
Tail Rigging for *Paul and his Bananas*

Paul the monkey is the star of the upcoming Bishop Animation short film, *Paul and his Bananas* (see Figure 11.1) While this is an educational short film for children, we wanted to put our all into the development of the project. There is a lot of very simple (and quite frankly, not very good) children's educational content out there, and we wanted our project to be different. Therefore, when it came time to build Paul, we wanted him to be able to do everything a real monkey could do, and use those abilities in the short. After studying monkeys at the zoo for a while, it became apparent that the tail could be a nightmare if not done correctly.

Monkeys use their tails for many different purposes. The tail can lag behind, allowing for some very nice secondary motion. The tail can be moved using forward kinematics, acting like another arm or leg. The tail can also wrap itself around a branch, allowing the monkey to hang and swing from the tail. We needed a tail rig that would allow for all of these functions, as well as combinations of the three (see Figures 11.2 and 11.3).

Here is a little bit of what we did to achieve Paul's tail rig.

1. First, we created the bones for the tail.
2. We created a joint per every row of geometry (or every two, in order to have a lighter skeleton).
3. We checked out that LRAs (local rotation axis) are all the same.
4. Then we duplicated the whole thing three times, and we named one BIND, second one FK, third one IK, and fourth one FullFK.
5. Next, we created layers and hid all of them except Full FK skeleton for now.
6. We created our control curves for each joint, renamed them CTRL_tail_base, start, mid, end.
7. Then we created a null group and duplicated it, so we had a null group for each controller.
8. Then we point- and orient-constrained the nulls to the joints, one by one, and deleted the constraints, so that they had the same position and rotation information with the joints.

Figure 11.1
Final image of monkey.
"Paul and his Bananas" written and directed by Floyd Bishop
Character Design by Benjamin Plouffe
Character Model created by Tristan Lock
Character Rig by Firat Enderoglu
Character materials and fur by Floyd Bishop
TM & © 2005 Bishop Animation

Figure 11.2
Default model posed in its ready-to-rig state.

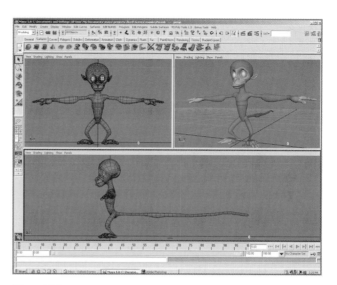

Figure 11.3
Default model posed in its ready-to-rig state wireframe view.

9. Then we parented the curves under each null group and did freeze transformations on them so that they would get the rotation information from the null group while keeping their rotation values 0.

10. Now we have one curve for each joint positioned at the same place with the same rotation information as the joint. Then we opened the Connection Editor and connected the rotations of the curves to the joints, one by one (we can do the same thing in a dependency graph).

11. Now, we have all the curves that rotate the joints. Starting from the very last curve, we started parenting. We took the null group above the last curve and parented it under the adjacent curve and then took its null group and parented it under an adjacent curve. So it's like Null1<-Curve1 <-Null2 flCurve2. By doing that, if we selected all the curves together and rotated them, it would make a curl.

12. And finally, we parented the very top node under Hip Null node and locked/hid translates and scale attribs on the curves. Then we hid FulllFK (see Figure 11.4).

Figure 11.4
Basic FK rig.

This time we turned on the FK tail and did a similar thing without using direct connections.

1. First, we created three or four controllers and placed them with equal spaces along the length of the tail and then did a freeze transformation on them.

2. After that, we opened the Set Driven Key window and took the curve control as the driver and picked the joints that were close to that curve control as driven. Then we set drive the rotations of all those joints to that curve control so that when you rotate the single control, several joints will rotate together.

2. We did the same thing for the other two curves and then parented them under to the first joint that they controlled.

3. Then we made only the IK tail visible and created an IK Handle from the beginning of the tail to close to the end, about 3–4 joints until the end.

4. Next, we created an empty node, pointed- and orient-constrained it to the first joint after the IK part, and deleted constraints.

5. We created a curve and placed it on top of the IK Handle, parented it under that empty node and did freeze transformations, and then in the Connection Editor connected the rotations of that curve to the very first joint's rotations (the one after the IK part). Then we parented the IK Handle under that curve to finish it off (see Figure 11.5).

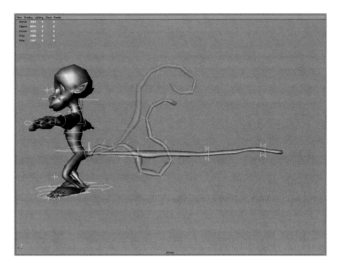

Figure 11.5
Detailed layer of FK joints allow for more extreme poses.

For the last 3–4 joints left, we used the same method that we used on FullFK tail.

1. We create d3–4 curves and 3–4 empty nodes and then point- and orient-constrained them to the joints and deleted the constraints.

2. We parented the curves under the empty nodes.

3. We did freeze transformations on the curves.

4. We connected the rotations under the Connection Editor or dependency graph.

5. Starting from the last one, we parented the curve's group node under the adjacent curve.

6. This time, we parented the main group node (the one above the curve that controls IK Handle) under the placement node of our full skeleton.

Now that we had all our different tail rigs with all working controllers, the last thing we needed was to have all these rigs control the bind one that we hadn't touched yet, so we could switch between these rigs easily. We wanted to orient-constrain the BIND skeleton joints to all these rigs.

First, we have FullFK and BIND on our Hypergraph or Outliner. Then we selected the first joint on fullfk and then selected the same joint on bind skeleton and orient-constrained it. We did this for every joint. After that, we did the same thing with IK and FK skeletons. So now we had all the BIND joints orient-constrained, and under the Channel Box we had three attributes to control the weights on each constraint (such as FullFKw0, IKw1, and FKw2). We wanted to create a float attribute on any controller, such as the hips or on the main controller of the character and name it tail switch (or whatever). We restrained that attribute's values to -5 to 5, or -10 to 10. Then we are opened the Set Driven Key window and loaded that attribute as driver and loaded *all* the constraints under the Bind skeleton as driven. We keyed on the last three attributes on the constraints (the ones that should have W-and number). See Figure 11.6.

If we wanted-5 FullFK, 0 FK, 5 IK modes, while the driver was at -5, we would adjust the constraint weights on all of them (fkW* and ikW* ones are going to be 0 and fullFkW* will be one) and Set Driven Key them. We will do the same thing for FK and IK modes and that's it. One last thing we could do is to set drive the control curve's visibilities to the controller attribute so that when we switch we won't see the other rig's controllers (see Figure 11.7).

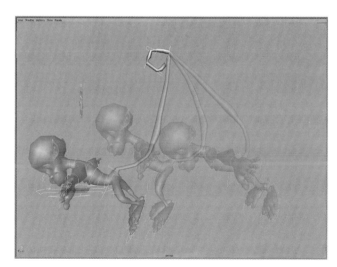

Figure 11.6
IK tail allows us to be able to lock the end part of the tail.

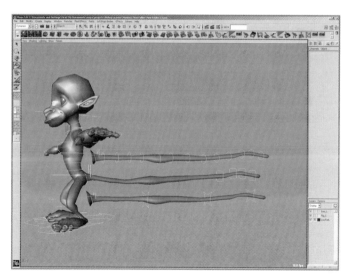

Figure 11.7
The final rigs for the tail split apart to be viewed more easily.

11. Tail Rigging for *Paul and his Bananas*

Additional Characters and Rigging

In addition to Paul the Monkey, character rigging for several other characters was required for this short. Below we look at some of the rigging for the Magicians' hat. Figure 11.8 shows the final rendered character and the base mesh for the model is shown in Figure 11.9. You can see the exaggerated base pose and the edge flow resulting from using Maya Sub-D surfaces.

www.bishopanimation.com

BISHOP
ANIMATION

Figure 11.8
Final image of magician.

Figure 11.9
Base mesh of the magician.

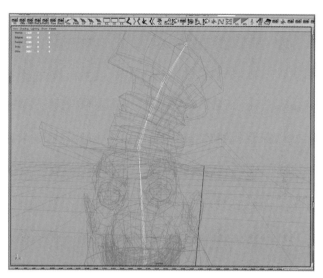

Figure 11.10
Hat mesh and joints.

Here is a quick soft body tutorial for the magician's hat. This same technique can be used for many things like coat tails, long ears, or belt straps on your characters.

1. Create the bones for the hat. Make sure to add an extra joint as a spacer to limit the effect of the spline IK and to allow the hat to be removed, if needed (see Figure 11.10).

2. Create a spline IK from the base to the tip.

3. Now select the spline Ik curve only from the Outliner or Hypergraph.

4. From the Dynamics→Soft/Rigid Bodies→options box set the creation option to Duplicate Make Original Soft and turn on "make non-soft a goal." This way the spline IK curve will have particles in place of the CVs and those particles will follow the duplicated curves' CVs.

5. Then create clusters on the non-softbody curve's CVs for extra control over the animation. You can parent the clusters under extra FK control hierarchy for direct animation control. Additional control over the effect can be hooked up by painting or editing the goalWeight to control the floppiness.

6. With any automated control, hook it up to a custom attribute that can override the dynamics and turn off/on or can be set to some percent in-between blending between the dynamics and the hand key-framed animation (see Figure 11.11).

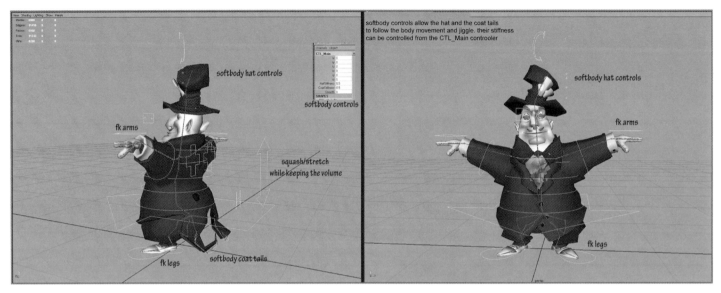

Figure 11.11
Custom attributes setup and the final rig controls.

Figure 11.12 shows the Banana character rig, using the combination of basic rigging controls and mixing in the softbody rig for the banana peels.

Thanks to Bishop Animation Studios for putting together this behind-the-scenes look into their character rigging process. Be sure to check out http://www.bishopanimation.com/ for the latest updates on this film.

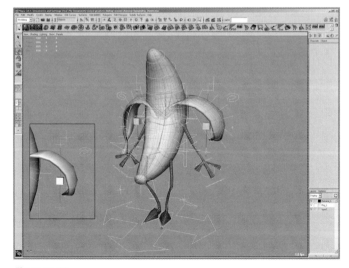

Figure 11.12
Additional character rig and skeleton—a quick view inside the Banana character.

11. Tail Rigging for *Paul and his Bananas*

Rick May

chapter 12
Interview with Rick May of
TOONSTRUCK ANIMATION

We have mentioned several times in this book about the importance of talking over the design of a character rig with your project's supervising animator or animation director. Rick May was kind enough to give us some insight into how he likes characters set up both as an animator and supervisor.

Rick May has been working in the animation industry for more than 15 years, much of that time in the Los Angeles and San Francisco areas. Starting out as a technical director, May got his chops using Prisms and Wavefront software in the late 80s. After several years doing vfx and the occasional character animation work on commercials and features, he decided it was time to dedicate his full-time attention to character animation. Quitting his cushy job, he bounced around from project to project in the Los Angeles area working as a freelance character animator and animation supervisor. In the late 90s, May moved up to the San Francisco area and formed Toonstruck Animation, an animation studio to other animation studios. Toonstruck has been providing character design, modeling, rigging, and character animation assistance to other facilities that need help on their commercial and film projects.

Make sure to check out Rick's current project called "'Till Death Do us Part." At http://www.toonstruck.com/shortfilm, you can read over the plog, or production log, for the film where more details from technical to artistic will be posted during the length of the production. For more information go to http://www.toonstruck.com/.

What kind of controls/interface do you like for a character? You mentioned on the CGCHAR Web site that when you rig a character, you like to have a small floating interface for the selection of controls. Do you prefer this to in-view port controls?

Ideally, it would be nice to have both. There are times it is easier (and faster) to grab a NURB curve; however, at other times it is simply too difficult to find a buried curve because of some convoluted pose the character is in. Because of that, an interface can come in handy. I'm partial to a floating interface that is actual geometry and sits in your workspace, as seen in Figure 12.1 The interface needs to have adjustable transparency, be easily turned on and off, and have the ability to scale up or down in size and move around the display. Another advantage for the floating interface is that it is extremely quick to mouse-over and make your selection without covering much real estate since you can locate it right next to where you are working. I've seen some very nice Mel interfaces, and there is nothing wrong with such an interface; however, my biggest complaint with these are that they use up too much screen space (generally speaking).

I do like in-viewport controls, but just like the character curves, they can cause clutter as well or be at an angle that is hard to select. Do you have the interface aim only at the main camera or do you have a more complicated system to aim at whatever view you're looking through? Also, how do you deal with the clutter?

You would never see it at a funny angle; it can be connected to whatever camera you are presently using by just pressing a hot key or clicking a shelf button, and so on. If you really wanted, you could have Maya do it for you automatically when you switch cameras.

There are icons that perform various common functions that I like to have easy access to while animating. If you click on the head icon, you can rotate and translate the character's head, but if you click on a small icon near the head, the body interface disappears entirely and the face interface replaces it (see Figure 12.2). Now you can adjust facial controls. The same thing happens when you select an icon near the character's hand—a new "hand interface" replaces the body interface, and you can fine-tune hand/finger poses. It certainly isn't rocket science, just a clutterless way to select objects and perform various common animation functions. If there are multiple characters in the file, I generally give the interface the ability to swap out for the other character or to open multiple floating interfaces.

For the selection handling, do you use a custom script job or some other system like the zooTrigger tools that let you set up the selection and keyframe events?

I initially used zooTrigger, but I started developing my own scriptJob system when I needed a way to program the interface on the fly (so that the interface could quickly be adapted to new characters). Later on and after an email exchange with Hamish, I learned that zooTrigger would work for what I needed to do, but at that time I already had my own thing up and going. For anyone wanting to put something like this together, I suggest first looking at zooTrigger to see if it will work for you. It is a great script and will most likely fit your needs.

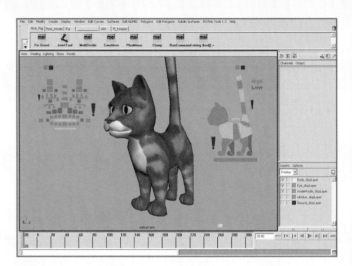

Figure 12.1
Example of viewport controls.

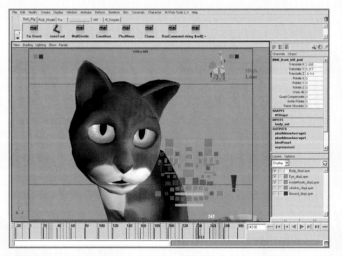

Figure 12.2
Here the face controls are the focus and the body and other High/Low switch controls are off to the side and out of the way.

I know you like to use the Maya character sets to help with keyframe management. Can you talk about your workflow?

I generally block a shot out by posing an entire character and then step key that whole character at once via its character set. I only get out of character set/step keymode after I've pretty much nailed down the timing and posing for the shots, including breakdowns. Now, this method can vary quite a bit depending on what the shots require. There are many instances that I won't even use a character set because it isn't the most efficient process.

The character sets are built in a layering approach—for instance, an overall set that will include the whole character, a subcharacter set that is for his body, and another for his head. Inside of the head subcharacter set are more subcharacter sets that break down the eye controls, mouth controls, and so on. This way I can easily see where keyframes are for the entire character or just a subset of that character. This makes me more efficient in the early blocking stages.

I know that there have been some complaints that character sets can slow down a file or are prone to breaking. Have you found this to be a problem either with the speed of the rig or any other things that the TD or animator should be aware of when working with the character sets?

I've never run into any of those problems. I'm not sure what I'm doing differently. Maybe I'm not trying hard enough.

Do you use file-referencing of one master rig or do you use a new rig in each file and then just copy the motion to a final, render-ready file?

Generally, I have the character referenced into each shot file (or a Maya scene file that includes multiple shots). That source file has the character rigged to a very basic skeleton. There is no IK, there are no joint limits, and there is nothing but the basic skeleton and its weighting. The more complex rig is built on top of that basic skeleton for each shot file via running a script. It is at this time that IK is added, expressions and nodes are connected, character sets are built, and so on. This way you can fine-tune the rigging for each shot if it is really needed.

I like the idea of using custom rigs per shot, but I find that it can be almost more work to accommodate and troubleshoot files so that each could have different rig options compared to knowing that each file is the same rig. In the system you're describing, can you talk about keeping files compatible with each other, like if the animation needs to be transferred to another shot but the rig needs to be different? Or even something like training the animators on what controls they need to use to make a rig work when it is different in each file? Or do you still have the Character TD do the rig but use the custom rig builder with input from the animator?

I may have given the wrong impression. Although the controls are built for each shot (or group of shots), they aren't drastically different from animator to animator. It is a system that allows one person to have slightly different options than another animator if there is a need. You cannot vary these things too much because it will cause too many problems down the road. However, some things can be changed without disrupting too much. For instance, maybe an animator likes character sets to be set up a little differently. With a few changes to a script, he can have what he needs.

I used to build IK or FK arms per shot, depending on the needs of that shot and the animator. However, that caused too many problems and now all rigs have an IK/FK arm system that is always IK and FK at the same time (no switching needed).

What are some things that you find Character TDs don't think about or miss when making a rig for you to use? Or along that same line, do you see the same kinds of problems in the rigs you have animated? Do you live with the problem or have it fixed?

The biggest problems I see in rigged characters are that some TDs tend to make them overly complex. Most animators like things easy and organized. Don't weigh us down with an excessive amount of controls when the same thing can be accomplished with less. This doesn't mean to slim the controls so far that we can't get the performance out of them that we need. Just don't overdo it. Take the foot, for instance. You don't need a separate object to control the toe, ankle, and heel. Put them all on the same controller—it is so much easier to deal with when you are animating. Same thing goes for the hand. I've seen countless rigs with cumbersome finger and hand controls. Some even go so far as separate controls for each joint on each finger. Arghh. There is certainly nothing wrong with the idea of having the ability to go in and fine-tune a finger pose, but for 99 percent of the hand/finger animation that needs to get done, you should be able to do it from one controller.

Also, don't build the rig in such a way that it causes that animator to do a lot of counter-animation. For instance, allow the head to both rotate with the shoulders or not with the shoulders (animator can pick as they go). Double up head rotation controls so that a character's head movements can be animated as usual, but if he is talking, the head movements to emphasize his lines can be added on top very easily on that second control. Another thing I like is a head that cannot only be rotated, but also translated (if cartoony, you need some scale, too). Even on the more realistic characters, translating a head can come in handy.

Interesting idea about the layered head controls—that is something I had not heard of before. This lets you essentially keep the dialogue head movement as an offset from the head pose that is needed for the overall posture of the character.

Yeah. My workflow for a dialogue shot varies depending on my mood. Nevertheless, occasionally I will animate the step key version with the head accents intact. When it comes time to clean it up, I wipe out those head accents and then reapply them down the line. When you reapply, it helps to have that additional control to layer on top.

Hands and fingers have always been something that can be very difficult to work with since they contain so many joints and can have so many keyframes. Can you expand on what you think are the minimal controls that the hands and fingers should have to keep the workflow fast but still give the animator control over a very expressive body part?

I like to set up hands so that you grab the wrist and rotate it as usual. However, in that wrist object, there are extra attributes to control that hand's fingers—for example, individual finger spread, curl for each finger (rotates everything but the knuckle), and then a knuckle rotation for each finger. Set up the attributes in an order where you can select the knuckles and curl them together to easily curl the whole finger. I find it very important to have the knuckle rotation kept out of the finger curl; you cannot get the same poses if you combine those. I used to include the thumb rotations in that same wrist controller. However, there is so much involved, I now give it a separate control.

A setup similar to this seems to take care of most needs. It is also nice to have an attribute in the wrist controller to hide/unhide individual finger joint controls. Sometimes, you need to push them a little farther than what the basic control allows.

How do you feel your understanding of rigging and animation work together? Does it hurt or help your work?

That is hard to answer. I've been rigging characters for as long as I've been animating, so I probably wouldn't have a very objective answer. However, I do believe that because I am an animator, it helps me to make animator-friendly rigs. So, yes, I think it does help your work. Conversely, I'm not so sure that my rigging background makes me a better animator. It just makes me more frustrated when I'm working with a rig that isn't very intuitive.

Thank you for your time and input, Rick.

chapter 13
The Pipeline

Y ou don't get far in the world of character rigging nowadays without hearing about pipelines. Over the years, cg productions have become increasingly broad and the need to organize huge amounts of data has become paramount. *The Lord of the Rings Trilogy* involved thousands of digital soldiers and creatures that needed to be built, rigged, and animated. To manage the production of all these assets requires the design of a pipeline, or standardized process, for the creation and preparation of digital assets.

The term "pipeline" is a very broad term that encompasses almost all aspects of a cg production. It is not unusual for pipeline considerations to cover the rigging of characters, the naming of nodes, the location and format of files, and the rendering process. Since the focus of this book is character rigging, we will look at the areas of the pipeline that deal directly with that area.

File Structures

One of the most basic aspects of a pipeline is the file structure. Choosing a proper file structure will help organize the data for the project and help keep everyone in sync with where assets can be found.

Maya provides a basic file structure in the form of its workspaces. For many projects, especially small ones, this file structure is perfectly usable. When projects begin to scale up, however, they usually depart from the Maya-style structure. In interactive entertainment, for example, the organization of data usually results in central locations for textures and other data separate from the characters themselves.

While file structures tend to change based on a project's needs, there are some principles that can help guide pipeline design. One of those principles is organizing characters as complete entities. In the standard Maya project, there is a scenes directory, a texture directory, and so on, which hold all of the data a character needs. If that character needs to be moved or updated, however, artists must look in several different folders to locate the proper data for editing. If the character needs to be backed up or duplicated to create the basis for another character, files must be tracked down again.

Instead of this disparate layout, an efficient way to organize characters is for each character to have its own directory structure. The top level directory is the character's name. Beneath that are directories for the model, the rig, the textures, any animations the character may have, and other data. Then, if the character needs to be moved or duplicated, all of the character's information is duplicated at once. Figure 13.1 shows a sample hierarchy.

This structure is very similar to the way data is organized for games—generally, a character is a complete unit, with its animation, rig, and model data all existing in the same chunk of memory. Encapsulating the texture data is an additional step on our part, and is not necessarily as feasible, depending on the strategy used by the programmers to manage their texture data.

In any pipeline, there are usually two sides that mirror each other—a creation side and an export side. The creation side usually contains the models, rigs, textures, and so on that make up an animated scene. The export side will contain the processed animation, the results of muscle simulation, etc. These assets are high resolution and usually maintained in a state very similar to the final rendered output: simulations have already been run and the results cached, animation has been baked into skeletons, and so on. These files are kept in case there are minor changes or re-rendering to be done. If there are five characters in a scene and the animation on only one needs to be adjusted, there is no sense in running cloth/muscle simulation on all the characters that do not change.

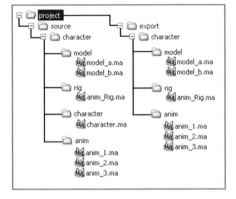

Figure 13.1
A sample pipeline hierarchy.

In interactive applications, the export side is often the compiled or exported data that is ready to be read into the game engine. Many times this structure contains files that have been converted into different formats by game software. In these types of pipelines, it is often beneficial to treat the exported animation as "rendered" and to keep a copy of the baked animation, which consists only of the joints and the model in a state before it gets sent through the exporter. In this situation, the animation is effectively exported twice—once to a file that has only joints and mesh, and from there to an alternate, engine-ready binary format. This may seem excessive, however, it can provide a good deal of insight into any problems that may arise in the export process. Having this type of pipeline in place can also facilitate the management of multiple characters in cinematic scenes.

When building a pipeline, the simplest solution is often the best, and in this case, it is best if the source and export directory structures mirror each other as closely as possible. For example, if you are using the character-directory layout discussed previously, the exported version of the character should be a directory under which there is a model directory with the game model, a texture directory with the downsampled/processed texture, the animation directory with the in-game animations, etc. This structure greatly simplifies the amount of work needed to develop tools for importing, exporting, and otherwise managing data. By enforcing similar file structures, it is possible to bring more scripting support to bear when handling file I/O. Offloading file functions to a script can streamline production and eliminate human error.

The first component of a pipeline is a simple function that gets the export path for the data you are working on. For any scene file, you can query its path using the "file –q –sn" MEL command. This command returns a string of the file's full path and its full name, which will be something like this:

C:/topDirectory/project/scenes/source/characters/char1/char.mb

> In Maya, the filenames are resolved using forward slashes on Windows, IRIX, and Linux systems, which makes porting more feasible and avoids the nasty need to escape the backslash character when used in strings.

If a simple mirrored structure is maintained, this path can be used to provide a suitable destination path. The following script is found in the getDestPath.mel file at http://www.courseptr/downloads. Let's go through it step by step:

```
global proc string getDestPath(string $source, string $dest)
{
    string $sourceFile = `file -q -sn`;
```

The result of the file command is the full path to the current scene, including the scene name. Since we just want a destination directory, the dirname command can be used to remove the file from the path.

```
    string $sourcePath = dirname($sourceFile);
```

Now, in a production pipeline, you are going to have a set directory structure that you can code into the script. You can use the substitute command to replace the parts of the directory structure that need to change.

```
    if(!`gmatch $sourcePath ("*"+$source+"*"`) error ("Source dir not in file path");
        string $newPath = `substitute $source $sourcePath $dest`;
```

This is where the work is done—the directory passed in by the $source string is swapped for the directory passed in via $export. Notice the if statement with the "gmatch" command. Should the command be sent to a source directory that does not exist in the scene's path, the substitute command would have no effect. The script would then return the name of the source directory. If you are using this script to export data, you may end up writing over the original file. It is better to trap any such mistake and have the script throw an error.

This code is pretty helpful, but it can be made a bit more useful. If you use the code on a file that has no mirrored path, Maya will throw an error because the destination directory does not exist if you try to save to that destination. A small routine can be added to the getDestPath script to automatically create a destination directory if one does not exist. To do this, add the following command before the return statement:

```
if(!`filetest -d $newPath`)
        sysFile -md $newPath;
    return $newPath;
}
```

The string result is the full path and name of the export file. Since we are not working with an exporter, Maya's file command will serve as a substitute. For the specific needs of your pipeline, you may need to modify the actual name of the file itself. The substitute command is excellent for this purpose. Take a moment to test out the script.

1. On your local hard drive, create a directory called "samplePipeline." Under that directory, create a directory called "sampleSource" and under that another one called "sampleChar." Finally, create a "sampleAnim" directory.

2. In Maya, open the Script Editor and source the getDestPath.mel script, which is the one that was just built. The file can be found at http://www.courseptr/downloads.

3. Create a polyCube using the Create→Polygon Primitives→Cube command.

4. Use File→Save As to save the scene as "testAnim.ma" in the "samplePipeline/sampleChar/sampleAnim" directory. The file structure should resemble Figure 13.2.

5. Once the file has been saved, enter the following command at the command line:
```
getDestPath("sampleSource", "sampleExport");
```

6. In the Script Editor, you should see output like the following:
```
C:/samplePipeline/sampleExport/sampleChar/sampleAnimation
```

7. This is the string that is returned when the command executes. You will notice that the path is the same, except the "sampleSource" has been replaced with the "sampleExport" directory. If you open up a file browser, you will see that the directories have been created for the export path.

Figure 13.2
A sample character animation file in a sample pipeline.

Maya is always case-sensitive, even though the Windows operating system isn't. If you pass the command "samplesource," the command will error out.

The getDestPath.mel script will not overwrite or delete a directory that exists.

With the getDestPath script in place, it can be incorporated into a simple export script. Generally, when exporting an animation scene, whether for interactive or narrative purposes, you will need to extract the destination filename, destination path, and generally run an export function of some sort. The following example builds an export script using the Maya file command to export data.

The first part is, of course, the procedure declaration. The $source and $export variables are there to make the script more universal—they are passed onto the getDestPath procedure.

```
global proc exportCurrentScene(string $source, string $export)
{
```

The next line uses the getDestPath.mel script not only to build the export path, but also to return it for the export command.

```
    string $exportPath = getDestPath($source, $export);
```

The next step is to get a filename for the export. Maya provides the "basename" command to strip the file's name from the full path.

```
    string $exportFile = basename(`file -q -sn`,"");
```

Finally, the export command uses the path and filename to export the data.

```
    file -op "v=0" -typ "mayaAscii" -pr -ea ($exportPath+"/"+$exportFile);
}
```

Now, try out the new script. Enter it into the Script Editor or source the file from the exportCurrentScene.mel file found at http://www.courseptr/downloads.

1. Open the /samplePipeline/sampleSource/sampleChar/sampleAnimation/ testChar.ma file from the previous exercise.

2. At the command line, enter the following command:
   ```
   exportCurrentScene("sampleSource", "sampleExport");;
   ```

3. Using the File→Open command, open the exported file /samplePipeline/ sampleSource/-sampleChar/sampleAnimation/testChar.ma. The file should be located in an export directory, as in Figure 13.3.

The exportCurrentScene command from the exercise could be copied to a shelf button for any particular project. On an interactive game project, the Maya file command could be replaced with a call to a custom export command.

Having a simplified file structure can save a great deal of time browsing through directories and can allow for the creation of simple utilities to aid the artists in their work. By having the script determine the export paths, you also prevent human error, which can occur with surprising frequency on projects where you end up working until 2 a.m.

Figure 13.3
The export path created by the "getDestPath" script.

Referencing

Maya's file referencing is a powerful feature that many approach with trepidation. Referencing is inherently complex, and it can be intimidating to troubleshoot the errors that accompany it. In 6.0, the referencing features have been revamped and upgraded. Referencing has been brought into the production pipeline in film and interactive applications.

The main appeal of using file referencing is its ease of updating. Let's say a model and its rig are referenced for animation for many shots in a production. The animators begin working on scenes with that character. It is then determined later that some aspect of the character needs to change. Since all of the animations reference the same model and rig file, any changes to that file will propagate through the pipeline to each of the scenes that reference it the next time the scenes are opened. This ease of editing and making global changes are the key elements of referencing.

There are other benefits to referencing. When a file is referenced, Maya loads a read-only copy into memory. When the current scene is saved, the referenced data is not saved with it—only the file reference is saved. For example, if a fully rigged character were loaded into a scene and animated, when the scene is saved, the model, the rig, and the animation curves would all be written out to a file. If the character and rig were referenced, Maya would only save out the animation curves in the file. This yields smaller file sizes and faster saving times.

Another benefit of file referencing is that all nodes from referenced files are read-only. This means that any node from a referenced file cannot be deleted. In addition, nodes that were locked in a referenced file cannot be unlocked and keyable state of attributes cannot be changed. File referencing is not entirely foolproof because connections can still be broken. If the connected attributes are made unkeyable, they cannot be broken via the Channel Box, but they can still be deleted in the Hypergraph. However, most accidental deletions, such as destroying all Set Driven Keys with the Delete→All By Type→Channels operation, can be avoided. When it is desired, the reference can be imported, at which point all of its nodes will be fully editable.

A reference can be created via the Create Reference command in the File menu. In the following exercise, you will learn how to create a reference.

1. Create a new Maya scene.

2. From the File menu, select the Create Reference options box. From the Reference Options dialog box, select Edit→Reset Settings to ensure the reference options are set to the default.

3. From the file browser, select the pigGoblin_low_res.ma. The file can be found online at http://www.courseptr/downloads in the sampleAnim.zip archive.

4. You should see the character appear, as in Figure 13.4.

Figure 13.4
A referenced file.

Notice that the icons in the Outliner have changed slightly. You will notice on each node in the Outliner a small square with an "R" in it. This indicates that the node is read-only, and that it cannot be deleted. You will also notice that each node name has been prefixed with the name of the file and a colon ":". This indicates that the node is in a namespace. A namespace is like a partition in that all of the nodes in a namespace must have the prefix and colon. Using namespaces makes it easier to keep track of the nodes created when referencing files. Whenever a file is referenced, it will always have a prefix appended to it, either the filename or a user-defined string.

The renaming aspect of referencing has a great impact on a production pipeline. Throughout this book, great care has been taken to make sure that names of nodes in scene files are unique. This is important to keep in mind because for many interactive content developers the names of geometry and joints in a character are relevant to other uses in the game engine, such as attaching objects or effects at runtime.

When implementing referencing, the peculiar necessity of appending a string at the beginning of all the nodes in a referenced file can actually be very useful in managing multi-character scenes, especially if, as in many games, there are multiple instances of the same character. When a file is referenced, Maya will use the filename or other string to append each of the nodes. If the file is referenced again to make a new character, Maya will not allow the same string to be used to reference the character. When the string is replaced, it is easy to keep the two characters separate, as all of their nodes will have different prefixes.

The naming characteristic of the referencing mechanism allows the easy selection of objects from a referenced file. Because the reference is guaranteed to have a unique prefix, commands that use the prefix as a wildcard can be used to select specific nodes. For example, if a character is referenced with a "char1_" prefix, and all of its animation controls end in "_ctrl," the command 'select –r "char1_*_ctrl"` will select all of the controls.

When working on interactive projects, the naming convention can interfere with the production pipeline if not taken into account. In many situations, the characters in an interactive project share the same skeleton and therefore require the names to be identical. When using referencing, the joint "shoulder" becomes "prefix_shoulder." When there are multiple characters that share the same skeleton in a scene, there can be multiple prefixes – "prefix1_," "prefix2_." and so on. In order to keep the names of nodes in order, files that are to be exported to an interactive engine require some preparation.

In this next exercise, we will look at taking a reference, importing it, and stripping the names from it. This section will use the "stripPrefix" procedure found in the stripPrefix.mel file. The stripPrefix command will go through all of the nodes in a scene and take off the first argument that precedes an underscore or a colon.

1. Download and unzip the sampleAnim.zip archive from
   http://www.courseptr/downloads. Open the file sampleAnim.ma.
   You will see an animated version of the PigGoblin (see Figure 13.5).

Figure 13.5
The referenced PigGoblin character. Notice the read-only flags on the node icons.

Both the sampleAnim.ma file and the pigGoblin_low_res.ma file should be in the same directory.

2. Open the Outliner. Shift-click on the [+] to open the hierarchy. Notice that all of the node names are prefixed with "def_".

3. From the File menu, open the Reference Editor. The Reference Editor displays all references in the current scene. You will see an entry in the window called "defRN." This is the node Maya uses to keep track of referenced files and the connections to them.

4. Select the "defRN" node. You should see the file fields of the Reference Editor change, listing the file path of the reference.

5. From the Reference Editor menu, select Edit→Import Reference.

6. Open the Outliner. You should see that the read-only tags are not on the nodes—they have been imported and are now editable and deletable.

7. Source the "stripPrefix.mel" script. At the command line, type "stripPrefix." You will see that all the nodes are renamed and the prefix is stripped off.

At this point, the file is ready to be exported. But this process is a bit time-consuming and unwieldy for a production environment, so we will look at automating it. For this example where there is one reference per file, it is pretty straightforward to convert it by using Maya and some simple scripts.

The first part of the export script is the declaration. Notice that like the previous export script, the $source and $export strings are there. Another string has been added—the $prefix string tells the function the name referencing prefix to strip off the names.

```
Global proc importRefAndRename()
{
    string $refFiles[] = `file -q -r`;
    for($file in $refFiles)
        file -ir $files;
```

The file command returns a string array of the files that are referenced—in this case, it is an array of one. The next step is to import it, which removes the referencing protection and makes the referenced nodes editable. The next step is to remove the prefix.

```
    stripPrefix();
}
```

Let's try out the script:

1. Open the file cubeAnim.ma, from the cubeAnim.zip archive at http://www.courseptr.com/downloads Web site. You will see an animated cube. The cube has been referenced and the animation added in this file.

2. At the command line, enter the following:
```
importRefAndRename;
```

You will see that the cube has been made editable and renamed. The stripPrefix command will loop through all the nodes in a scene, skipping the ones that do not have an underscore or a colon. It will strip the prefix off, regardless of whether or not the reference was imported using the namespaces option or not.

Building a Multi-Resolution Pipeline

One of the most straightforward ways to implement referencing in a pipeline is to create a file with the character model and the rig in a file and use referencing to load that into scenes where animation is applied. This is a good method, but referencing allows us to build upon this and create something more useful.

One of the major aspects of modern 3D production, especially with interactive content, is reuse. In games in particular, it is not unusual to have a limitation on the type and number of different skeletons in a segment of a game. Since the skeleton and animation data for a character consume a large amount of RAM, it makes sense to use the same skeleton to drive multiple characters. This creates a greater sense of diversity with minimal RAM impact.

In a more traditional pipeline, there would be several files involved—each variant of a creature would have its own model and rig file. There would be one "master" character that would be used to make the in-game animations, with special animations added to variants as needed. With referencing, this system gains an added advantage—the references can be replaced. So if you are using the same skeleton to drive a barbarian and a mage, in Maya the reference of the barbarian character can be replaced to see the same animation on the mage.

This pipeline certainly works, but it does limit the animator. It also starts to run into problems when the character needs to be upgraded. Many times, cinematic sequences are generated from in-game assets, so models are upgraded and soon there are multiple characters and rigs. Perhaps the production is geared more toward film—there could be several different levels of detail for a character. For example, you might have a low-resolution layout version, a higher-resolution medium shot version, or a fully detailed muscle system version. To speed the process of animation, it would be very helpful to animate the lowest resolution character and transfer the animation to the higher and then go back to the lowest.

File referencing can be used to separate the different levels of data. The main idea is to separate the animation controls from the actual model. To do this, we create two separate skeletons—one for the model, a deformation skeleton. The other skeleton is a rig skeleton, which is connected to animation controls. Once these separate entities have been created, we have a file that animators can use to animate while the modeling and fine-tuning of deformations occur on the other. The file-referencing mechanism keeps them both up-to-date. In addition, it becomes easier to implement alternate animation rigs for specific effects.

The following exercise illustrates how to create a reference.

1. Create a new Maya scene.
2. Use the File→Create Reference command and bring up the options dialog. In the "Name clash options:" section, change the text gadgets to "Resolve all nodes with this string:" Enter "def" as the prefix. Make sure the Use Namespaces check box is checked.
3. Click the Reference button and select the file pipeline/source/characters/pigGoblin/deform/ med_res.ma. You can download the pipeline directory structure from http://www.courseptr.com/ downloads. You should see a character model and a skeleton in the scene. The character has been bound by deformers to the skeleton. By default, the string "def_" should have been appended to the names of the nodes.

> When Maya uses a namespace, it appends the name of the space to the name of each node separated by a colon ":" instead of an underscore "_". If you are using references in interactive development and choosing not to strip off the prefix, you may want to avoid namespaces, as the colon can be unfriendly to animation exporters.

4. Use File→Create Reference options and edit it to Resolve "all nodes" with "this string" and use "rig" as the string. Press the Reference button and select pipeline/source/-characters/pigGoblin/rig/rig_pigGoblin.ma. You should see the animation rig for the character.

5. Source the "connectRig.mel" script. At the command line, type the following:

```
connectRig("rig_", "def_");
```

6. Press the Enter key. In the Script Editor, you will see a list of nodes. Select one of the animation controllers and use the Move tool to move it. You should see the deform model move with the rig. You should also see a new node called "constraints" in the Maya scene, as in Figure 13.6.

7. Select the "rig:ctrl_arm_L" node and use the Move tool to translate it. You will see that the deform skeleton moves with the animation rig.

8. One option you may want to use when working this way is to turn off the shading of the shapes that are used to select the joints. To do this, hold down the right mouse button over the "rig_mdl_prxy_PG" layer and select the Attributes entry in the context menu. In the Attribute Editor, make sure that the Shading check box is unchecked. Now the joint shapes are rendered in wireframe, allowing the animator to see the deformation model more clearly and still select the controls.

9. You can now save the file and have a basic character file that can be taken and animated. The "pipeline/source/characters/pigGoblin/character" directory has a saved version of the file.

The following exercises have been set up to use the directory structure in the pipeline.zip archive at http://www.courseptr.com/downloads. Download this archive and extract it to your local hard drive.

Figure 13.6
The referenced rig connected to the referenced deform skeleton.

The deformation rig is attached to the animation rig by constraints. Since both skeletons have the same joints with different prefixes, the MEL script simply goes through every joint in the deformation skeleton and connects it to its counterpart in the rig skeleton. You will notice a new node called "constraints" is created in the Maya environment. One of the limitations of referencing is that the hierarchy of a reference must remain intact. Any nodes parented into a reference hierarchy will prevent the use of the replace reference function. By default, constraints are parented under the constrain node. The connectRig script catches the constraints when they are created and pulls them out of the reference hierarchy.

The connectRig script is a pretty good start, but the fact that it relies completely on names can be a bit limiting. Also, there may be controls other than joints that need to be constrained, or attributes other than translate, rotate, and scale that need to be hooked up for custom deformations, like facial animation. To facilitate the inclusion of these nodes, the connectRig script has been upgraded to connectFull. This script will not only constrain the def nodes with the same name, but it will also connect any extra attributes on the def nodes to attributes on the rig node.

Great care must be taken when using custom attributes on the rig system. The system works in such a way that, should you switch to a deform skeleton with fewer custom attributes, the data should be saved.

It is possible to have multiple levels of deform model resolutions, from a light layout model to a fully simulated muscle system model. Swapping between these models can be accomplished via script, or merely by switching the reference in the Reference Editor. The following exercise reveals how to switch the resolutions for the deform model.

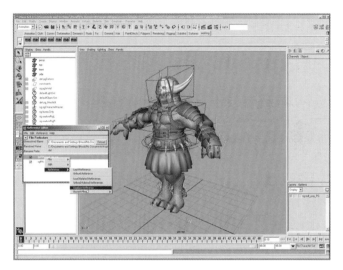

1. Open the pipeline/source/characters/pigGoblin/character/pigGoblin.ma, or if you have the file from the previous exercise, you can use that. You can get the file from the Web site at http://www.courseptr.com/downloads.

2. From the File menu, use the Reference Editor command to open the Reference Editor window. You should see the two references in the scene listed there. The first part of the reference listing is the prefix and the letters "RN," and the second part is the filename.

3. Select the "defRN" reference listing. You should see the different fields of the reference fill up with the path to the referenced file

4. From the Reference menu, select the Replace Reference command, as in Figure 13.7. From the file browser, select the pipeline/source/characters/pigGoblin/deform/hi_res.ma file.

Figure 13.7
Replacing a referenced file with the Reference Editor.

5. You should see the high-resolution deformation file replace the medium-resolution file.

In addition to swapping deformation rigs, the deformation skeleton can be unloaded. When a reference is unloaded, its nodes are removed from the Maya environment, but Maya retains memory of the nodes. An unloaded reference does not take any memory or CPU overhead, and it can be brought back into the environment at any time. This allows the animator to work with the lightweight animation rig only, maximizing the CPU and RAM of the workstation. The following example illustrates the unloading of references.

1. If you still have the Maya file open from the earlier example, everything should be in place. Otherwise, open the character.ma file.

2. Activate the Reference Editor from the File menu. You should see a listing for the rig reference and the deformation model reference. Beside each is a check box.

3. Uncheck the box for the deformation skeleton, "defRN" reference node, as in Figure 13.8. You should see the deformation skeleton disappear from the scene.

When a referenced file is unloaded, Maya remembers all the connections to the referenced file. For example, if you were to animate the PigGoblin and then unload the rig reference, the deform skeleton would no longer move. When the rig reference was reloaded, Maya would reconnect the constraint nodes and the animation curves to the rig, and the character would move again.

The key to this system is the skeleton—the skeletons between the two rigs must match, not just in name, but, ideally in joint orientation. In the case of the sample character, all of the joints in the rig that are to be connected start with "bn_," as do all of the joints in the deformation skeleton. It is possible to adjust the attachment system if the skeletons get out of sync, but this is not desirable as it creates a new point of failure for the pipeline. At all times, you want all assets of a pipeline to work together as uniformly as possible. You should strive never to have a special case model or rig—it will probably happen, but minimize it and document it as much as possible.

Now this file can be saved, and can be used as the basic character animation file. When necessary, the Reference Editor can be used to upgrade the deformation model so that the animator can check the deformation effects of the poses.

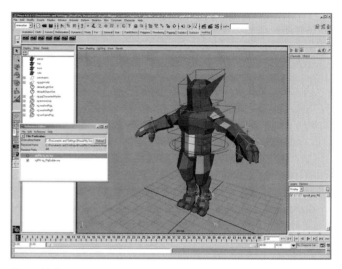

Figure 13.8
The deform skeleton is unloaded with the Reference Editor.

In addition, many different deform models can be connected to the rig, allowing diverse character models to use the same rig skeleton. When the time comes to export the animation for rendering, the motion can be baked onto the deformation system joints.

When creating this file where the rig and models are referenced, be sure to save it as a Maya ascii format. This can save a lot of time if the path changes to the referenced files. Should the files move, their paths can be edited in the .ma file to restore the reference. The alternative is to load the file and on file load Maya will ask what to do when it cannot find the reference. When you point Maya to the proper file, it will load it, but Maya will not remember the new path unless you replace the reference in the Reference Editor.

Referencing Pitfalls

While referencing is powerful, it is very important to understand how the mechanism works to avoid pitfalls. When editing a file that is referenced, it is important to know what type of edits will be accepted by the referencing system and which ones will cause unacceptable disruption to maintain the integrity of a pipeline.

The referencing mechanism relies heavily on node names. Let's assume you have an animation that uses a referenced character and rig. When the file containing the animation is loaded, Maya reads the referenced file and creates a read-only duplicate in the animation scene. Once this is done, all of the animation curves that control the channels are connected to the read-only nodes. If there are any channels that cannot be connected, Maya will throw a warning or an error. This is important as it can cause the referencing process to behave unpredictably.

The key point here is that referencing works off connections. If there is any disparity between the referenced file and the nodes that are in the animation scene that try to connect with it, problems will arise. In the case of our hypothetical animation, this means that changing the names of any of the nodes in the rig that have been animated in the scene will cause an error and possible undefined behavior. If the character file is opened and its model changed, this will have no effect on the animation. As long as all the nodes and attributes exist in the referenced model, the mechanism will have no problems.

Another aspect of referencing that can cause trouble is if the file being referenced is moved. When Maya attempts to load a reference and cannot find the proper file, it displays a dialogue that asks the user what to do. In order to load the file, press the Browse button and select the proper file, and Maya will continue to load the scene. Maya will not remember the new location of the reference, however. In order to get Maya to recognize the change in the paths, you must open the Reference Editor, use Replace Reference, and select the files.

Using Multiple Characters

The referencing pipeline works well with multiple characters. It is important to have a good plan when creating a scene with multiple characters. It is crucial to know how many characters will be in the scene because the Maya referencing relies heavily on names. When there are two or more characters in a scene, they cannot have the same names. To address this limitation, the characters in a multi-character scene are given distinct prefixes when they are referenced. The following example deals with using multiple instances of the same character in a scene.

1. Create a new Maya scene. In this scene, you will import two versions of the PigGoblin character and set them up for animation.

2. Activate the File→Create Reference command and bring up the options. Set the reference to "Resolve all nodes with this string:" and enter "rig1" as the string. Make sure the Use Namespaces check box is activated.

3. Press the Reference button and select the "/character/rig.rig_PigGoblin.ma" file. The animation rig should load and all of its nodes should have the "rig1_" prefix.

4. Repeat Steps 2 and 3, but substitute "rig2" for "rig1" in the Resolve settings. You should now have two versions of the PigGoblin rig, each with different prefixes.

5. Bring up the options for the File→Create Reference command.

6. Set the name resolution to resolve all nodes with the string "def1." Click the Reference button and select the /model/mid_res.ma to reference the PigGoblin deformation model.

7. Repeat the previous step using "def2" in place of "def1" in the Create Reference option dialog. You should now have two deformation skeletons with different prefixes.

8. At the command line, enter the following:

```
connectRig("rig:", "def:");
```

The deformation rig should align itself to the rig1 animation rig.

9. Enter the following at the command line:

```
connectRig ("rig1:", "def1:");
```

At this point, both of the deformation skeletons should be attached to their respective rigs, as seen in Figure 13.9

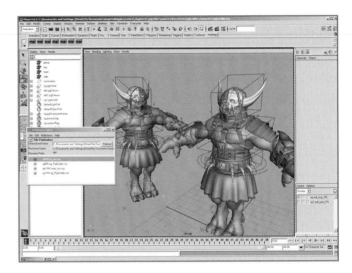

As you can see, the referencing pipeline takes a bit more effort—the character files cannot simply be imported or referenced. But by building them in the scene's layout, you can retain the functionality of deformation swapping. In addition, all of the loading and unloading capabilities of Maya's referencing mechanism remain intact.

Exporting the Deformation Skeleton

In a previous section, the character model and rig were all in one file, and it was targeted for a simple export path. In this more advanced pipeline, the export process must be revised to handle the multiple file references in a single scene. Exporting the animation of the reference pipeline depends on the target of the export. For rendering purposes, the character animation can be left on the animation rig and the file could be rendered as is. To optimize the process, the animation can be baked onto the reference skeleton.

Figure 13.9
Multiple references in the same scene.

Once the rig system has been created and animated, it is a simple process to export the animation to the deformation skeleton. When the animation is done, select the root node of the deform skeleton and use the Edit→Keys→Bake Simulation command to bake the animation onto the deformation skeleton. Make sure that the Hierarchy option is set to "Below." After the command completes, delete the constraints node to detach the deformation skeleton from its animation rig.

For interactive applications, more preparation is required. While the animation can be baked onto the deformation skeleton, many game engines use the joint names to order their data. In this case, the joint names may have to be renamed on export, which requires a bit more work.

In interactive applications, there are two types of animation: in-game animations and cinematic. The in-game animations are much like behaviors—run cycles, walk cycles, idles and attacks make up some of these anims. In cinematic, the animation is more traditional and narrative. In most cases, the character is an entity possessing a skeleton with specific names for the joints. When there are multiple characters in a scene, the requirements of naming them differently become problematic.

To solve the problem, a script is created that will prepare the skeletons for export. In this process, the reference of the deformation skeleton is imported, the animation is baked onto it, and its nodes are renamed. It is then exported to a secondary file that can be passed onto the exporter. This system allows any number of instances of similar characters in a scene to be exported to a skeleton with one set of names.

To facilitate the creation of this pipeline, it is first necessary to prepare the deformation skeleton files. Because multiple files are being referenced at one time, there is no way for Maya to know which file is the deformation skeleton for export and which is the animation rig. While you could spend a lot of time writing code to look for skinClusters in a file, there is no guarantee that there may not be a skinCluster in the rig file. The deformation skeleton should be grouped under one transform, and that transform should have an attribute called "skeleton," which the script will use to export it. The following exercise goes through the steps of setting up the deformation skeleton. It is optional—feel free to skip it if you feel you have a grasp of the preparation of the deform skeleton. The same thing needs to be done to the rig, only the attribute is called "rig," and it needs to be added to the top node of the rig.

1. Open the /pipeline/source/characters/deform/test.mb.

2. You will see that there are two top-level nodes in the deform model, pgSkeleton and MeshChar_PigGbln. To facilitate the pipeline, you will want only one top-level node in the scene. Select the two nodes and group them with Ctrl+g, and rename the node "pgDeform."

3. Open the Attribute Editor and use the Add Attribute menu to create an attribute called "skeleton." The type of the attribute is not important, as it will not be keyframed. Set the attribute type to boolean and uncheck the Make Attribute Keyable check box.

4. Save the file.

Now that the attribute has been added, you need to create a script that will isolate the deform skeletons and prepare them for export. When the character needs to be exported, all of the top-level nodes will be examined. Any of them that have the "skeleton" attribute will be baked and exported. This is accomplished with the MEL code that follows:

```
global proc string[] getExportNodes()
{
    string $result[];
    string $assemblies[] = `ls -as`;
    for($node in $assemblies)
    {
        if(`objExists ($node+".skeleton")`)
            $result[size($result)] = $node;
    }
    return $result;
}
```

This MEL script returns the name of the deformation skeletons. Once the names are ascertained, they can be selected and the results of the animation baked onto them with the following script:

```
global proc string[] bakeSkeletons(string $skeletons)
{
    float $startTime = `playbackOptions -q -min`;
    float $endTime = `playbackOptions -q -max`;
    bakeResults -simulation true -t ($startTime+":"+$endTime) -hierarchy below -sampleBy 1 -preserveOutsideKeys true -
sparseAnimCurveBake false -controlPoints false -shape false $skeletons;
    return $skeletons;
}
```

13. The Pipeline

The one last script needed is a function to delete the rig's information from the scene before export. This is simple enough—the script loops through all of the assemblies, and if they have a "rig" attribute, they are deleted.

```
global proc deleteRigs()
{
    string $assemblies[] = `ls -as`;
    for($node in $assemblies)
        if(`objExists ($node+".rig")`)
            delete $node;
}
```

The final piece of the puzzle is MEL code that will actually do the exporting. This script will need to import the reference of the baked deform skeleton. Once imported, the nodes can be renamed to match the original node names of the deform skeleton. There are a couple of helper functions on the http://www.courseptr.com/downloads folder that will facilitate this—the first is the importReference.mel script, which will import the reference of any selected node. The other is getPrefix.mel, which will return the prefix of the reference in order to facilitate renaming.

To put all of these elements together, we can create a script like the following:

```
global proc exporter(string $source, string $export)
{
    string $originalFile = `file -q -sn`;
    string $exportPath = getDestPath($source, $export);
    string $exportFile = basename(`file -q -sn`,"");
```

These first lines get the path of the original file and create the export path for this scene. The filename is retrieved with the "basename" call.

```
    string $temp = `internalVar -utd`;
    file -rn ($temp+"temp.ma");
```

These two lines are a bit of a safeguard. The internalVar command returns the temporary or working directory of the user. The call to the file command renames the current scene to "temp.ma." This is done so that, in the unlikely event an error is encountered and the script stops, the file will not be saved over the original.

```
    string $exportNodes[] = getExportNodes();
    $exportNodes = bakeSkeletons($exportNodes);
```

These two lines get all of the deform skeletons in the scene and bake the animation from the rigs onto the deform skeleton's joints.

```
    if(`objExists constraints`) delete constraints;
```

This line is just some bookkeeping—now that the joints have been baked, the constraints are no longer needed.

```
    importRefAndRename();
    stripPrefix();
```

These two lines have been used in earlier exercises to import the references and strip the reference prefixes.

```
$exportNodes = getExportNodes(); //names have changed
deleteRigs();
file -op "v=0" -typ "mayaAscii" -pr -ea ($exportPath+"/"+$exportFile);
```

Since the names have changed, another call to getExportNodes will grab all of the deform skeletons' root nodes. The deleteRigs call deletes all of the controls of the rigs, leaving only the deformation skeletons for export.

```
file -f -open $originalFile;
}
```

The final line of the script re-opens the original file. The way the exporter relates to the files is customizable. You may want to always save a scene before exporting, or automatically open the exported file after exporting is done. These decisions are generally made between the animator and the technical director.

Now let's try out the script:

1. Open the chpater13/scenes/pipeline/source/characters/pigGoblin/anim/anim.ma. You will see a simple animation of the pigGoblin character.

2. At the command line, enter the following command:
```
exporter("source", "export");
```

3. You should see the model go through the baking process.

4. Open the file /chapter13/pipeline1/export/characters/pigGoblin/anim/anim.ma. You should see the baked animation on the deformation model.

Open chapter13/pipeline1/source/characters/pigGoblin/anim/anim.ma and execute the exporter script. You should see the model go through the baking process and when it is complete, you will notice that the deform skeleton is no longer referenced and no longer has the "def_" prefix. All that remains is to export the deformation skeleton to a file. This is where the mirrored file system and the getDestDir.mel script come in very handy. The getDestDir script will swap the current open file directory for an export directory, and it will even create the necessary subdirectories if needed. In this example, the path to the character source files is something like the following:

```
C:/.../chapter13/pipeline1/source/characters/pigGoblin/anim/anim.ma
```

The destination of the export will be in the export subdirectory:

```
C:/.../chapter13/pipeline1/export/characters/pigGoblin/anim/anim.ma
```

13. The Pipeline

235

It really doesn't matter if these directories are in a project or on the C: hard drive—all that matters is that the path before the "/source/" directory is the same—that is, the export directory will be placed in the same folder as the source, and the path will be duplicated from that point down.

Problem Solving the Reference

So, the referencing pipeline has been set up. Things are going fine until a problem is discovered—perhaps a node has been named incorrectly, and it has to be changed in the skeleton. Since there is animation on the node, and the referencing system connects channels to animated nodes by name, changing the name in the referenced file will disrupt the animation file.

The solution is to ensure that the reference file contains an object with the correct attributes. When the reference file is loaded, the animation channels will be connected to the new object. They can then be copied to the correct object. Ideally, once the animation has been copied in all the files, the original temporary object can be deleted in the reference file. Obviously, this is a hassle if you have a hundred animation files. In such a situation, it is possible to use a batch process to correct the problem. This specific problem is covered in a later section called "The Fixit Script."

When referencing fails, the key to debugging it is in the Script Editor. All errors with the reference mechanism are echoed when Maya attempts to reference the file. Most referencing errors will involve clashing names and/or missing node/attributes. These errors are easily caught and fixed with some Script Editor scrutiny.

Implementing a Fixit Script

One of the advantages of the referenced pipeline is the ability to maintain the pipeline via scriptNodes. Because the character references the same base file, changes can be implemented in that base file and propagated through the system. Sometimes, the changes that need to be made are not easy to make by changing objects and connections in the referenced file—the problem of changing an animated node name was mentioned earlier. If a node that is animated needs to be changed, the referencing system will not know how to connect the renamed node to already created animation curves. In situations like this, a scriptNode can be used to execute script commands that correct a problem in the referenced file. The following exercise will demonstrate how a fixit script can be implemented in a referenced system.

1. Open the file cubeAnim.ma—you can find it in the cubeAnim.zip archive at http://www.courseptr.com/downloads. You will see a cube that has been animated. The cube is referenced from the file cube.ma.

2. Open the cube.ma file. Select the "pCube1" node. Rename it "polygonCube." Save the file.

3, Re-open the cubeAnim.ma file. You should get errors along the lines of the following:

```
// Error: line 1: Could not make connection; could not find destination plug 'cube_pCube1.v' //
```

4. The node has been renamed, so the referencing mechanism cannot function properly.

5. Re-open the cube.ma file. Use the Create→Locator command to create a transform. Rename the transform "pCube1."

6. With the "pCube1" node selected, press Ctrl+g to create an extra group. Rename this group "node_remapping."

7. Re-open the cubeAnim.ma file. You should not get any errors. In addition, you should see that the locator now has the animation the cube once had.

8. Select the "pCube1" node. Use the Edit→Keys→Copy Keys to copy the keys to the clipboard.

9. Select the "polygonCube" node and use the Edit→Keys→PasteKeys and bring up the options. Set the "Time Range" to "Clipboard." Click the Paste Keys button to paste the keys onto the "polygonCube" object.

10, Activate the scene playback. The "polygonCube" node now has the animation.

Since the referencing works off the node name, the animation is put on the new node named "pCube1." As long as the node names, the attribute names, and the attribute types match, the referencing mechanism will re-create the connections with the new node—as long as that node is the only one in the scene with that name. Having two nodes in two different hierarchies will cause problems, so make sure the renamed node is the only one.

The problem in this case is fixed, but in a pipeline it would be tedious to open each file and copy the keys by hand. In this situation, a scriptNode is a perfect solution. A script node is a chunk of MEL code that is embedded in a file. The scriptNode can be called directly or activated when certain events occur. To correct the animation problem, the scriptNode will be set to execute when the scene is opened.

1. Open the cube/ma file.

2. Use the Window→Animation Editors→Expression Editor command to open the Expression Editor.

3. Set the Select Filter menu item to By Script Node Name. This sets the Expression Editor to look not at expressions, but at scriptNodes, which are distinctly different.

4. In the Script Node Name field, enter "copyKeys."

5. In the Script: field, enter the following:

```
copyKey -option keys -hierarchy none -controlPoints 0 -shape 1 {"cube_pCube1"};
pasteKey -option insert -copies 1 -connect 1 -timeOffset 0 -floatOffset 0 -valueOffset 0 {"cube_polygonCube"};
```

These commands were taken from the Script Editor when the previous section was completed. In the copyKey command, the -time flag was omitted. This forces Maya to copy the entire curve and relieves the rigger from polling the start and end times of the animation for the copyKey command.

6. Set the Execute On setting to "Open/Close."

7. Press the Create button to make the scriptNode.

8. Save the file and open the "cubeAnim.ma" file. You should see the cube animated.

Every time a file is opened that references cube.ma, the copyKey scriptNode will be executed. If the cube were a character, this would happen for every animation in which that character file were referenced. As long as the script node does not reference any custom MEL commands, the file is easy to distribute because the MEL in the scriptNode is embedded.

The only drawback of this method is that the file-referencing mechanism prevents us from deleting the "pCube1" node once its purpose has been served. To keep things clean, it is stored in the "nodeRemapping" group. This is a small price to pay for having the functionality of self-correcting files.

There is no limit as to how a fixit script can be employed. Because the fixit script is located in the file that is referenced, there is only one source to consult should the script need to be edited. This makes it easier to keep the pipeline in order and prevents any special case files that can become a bookkeeping nightmare for anyone maintaining a pipeline.

SECTION 4

Skinning

chapter 14
Form and Function

Deformations are the final piece to the puzzle of being a Character TD. After all the time spent pulling your hair out, this is where it all comes together to bring the character to life. Creativity and an inventive spirit take precedence, because deforming a character requires intuition and a solid understanding of all of the options available to you (see Figure 14.1). While we could spend time dabbling in every one of those options, it would be better to focus on just a few and show you methods that have been tried and proven during production.

Introduction to Deformers

In general, when you refer to character deformations, you are talking about the systems used to move points of a mesh through space. We know that's very broad, but when you get down to the basic idea of it, all you're doing is moving points to make a 3D model look realistic when animated. The rig is the underlying control system for the skin and is the root of where all movement begins. If the underlying skeleton and rig structure doesn't work well or move properly, then getting good deformations is going to be quite a challenge.

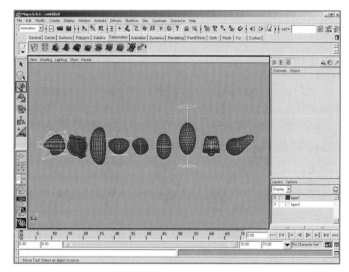

Figure 14.1
Deformer example.

Often, to make up for a poorly designed rig or to compensate for a bad model, technical artists will rely on extra tools and functions to correct deformation problems. This usually overcomplicates an already complicated process and requires more work than is necessary. If you have to constantly add to the solution in order to fix the original problem, then you were probably going about solving the problem the wrong way in the first place.

Thinking outside of the box is fundamental because when you're working under deadlines, any hit on the amount of time it takes to get the character looking good will cost everyone, not just you. This is a common problem, because people have the need to overcomplicate processes in order to feel justified in their efforts. In other words, if you have to keep trying harder, you're probably trying too hard. Never be afraid to start over.

Model Preparation

Maya has an entire arsenal of deformation tools. They get applied to the geometry of the model and are added into the history to be evaluated so you can see the resulting deformation. It's important to make sure there is no history on the model before you begin adding in deformers. History includes any tools you might have used during the creation of the model. Maya saves that information as an input onto the mesh (see Figure 14.2).

Deleting the history will delete the nodes in Maya connected to the input of the mesh and basically give the points a new default state. Freezing any transformations on the model pieces is also a good practice. While it won't affect the actual deformations, freezing the geometry beforehand is a good practice in case you need to go back and change anything later. You want the model to be tidy and optimized for the best functionality, like the Pig Goblin in Figure 14.3.

Optimization doesn't mean fewer polygons. An optimized model is one that has been created with the foresight of good deformations. A professional modeler will rely on communication from a technical director in order to make sure the model has been built well enough to deform correctly. Adjustments and tweaks will be made throughout, but as a starting point a model is ready to rig when it:

◆ Is in a relaxed pose with no areas of tension.

◆ Has proper edge loops defining the muscle flow.

◆ Has uniformly spaced geometry.

◆ Has a good quad topology, triangles only allowed in unobtrusive areas.

◆ Is frozen in space at the origin with no history.

You should allow for a period of adjustment between modeling and deformations. The model will most likely need tweaks in order to get the proper movements. This is especially true with highly detailed models such as a digital double, which may require extra attention to the way the mesh folds and wrinkles. Expect to receive guidance from an art director or character designer while determining deformations.

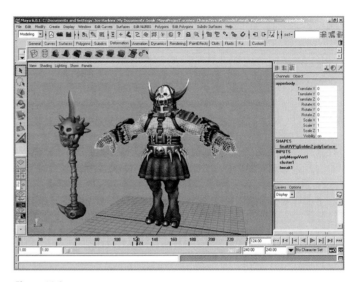

Figure 14.2
Mesh with history inputs.

Figure 14.3
Optimized model ready for deformation.

Deformer Relationships

The relationship between a deformer and the mesh it is deforming is very simple. The deformer is input into the model and the deformation is the result you see on-screen.

1. Create a sphere.

2. Select some of the vertices.

3. Using the deformer menu, create a cluster (see Figure 14.4).

4. Select the cluster handle and then translate it in space (see Figure 14.5)

5. Observe how the cluster affects the points on the sphere.

6. Open up the Hypergraph with the sphere selected and view the input graph.

7. Notice the cluster input on the model (see Figure 14.6).

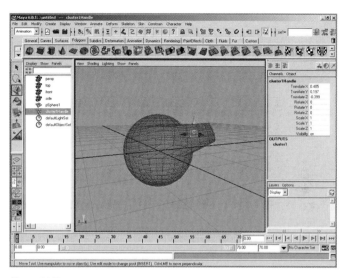

Figure 14.5
Cluster translated in space.

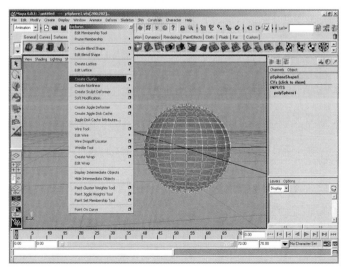

Figure 14.4
Cluster deformer creation.

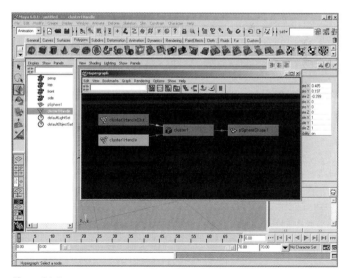

Figure 14.6
Hypergraph connections of the cluster.

This relationship is the basic premise behind all deformations in Maya. It is a push-pull system, one that relies on hierarchies and node-based connections in order to work. It is because of this system that we are able to use combinations of deformers in Maya to get a solid end result. Each system is evaluated according to the history input on the model. For example, you could have a character that is skinned to joints, has corrective blend shapes, and additional cluster controls on the mesh for refining movements. The model history allows you to continually add in more deformers as needed.

Deformer Types

In terms of the technology used to deform characters in Maya, many advances have been made over the years, giving us all of the available options. In addition to the standard Maya toolset, some studios are using proprietary muscle systems, skin solvers, and volume-based deformers. Some are using "off-model" deformers and developing tools to allow 2D animators to re-create the "line of action" using curve-based deformation plug-ins. These high-end tools require a good understanding of existing deformation systems in order to develop new technologies and ideas.

As a brief overview of what those options are, here's a list of the deformers available to you off-the-shelf in Maya along with their common uses. We will go over some of them in more detail later.

Skin Clusters

Skin clusters use joints for deformation (see Figure 14.7). They drive the skin using a weighted system, or envelope. Each point in the skin has a total weight of 1 that is distributed among the joints in the skin cluster node. Each joint will affect the points that are weighted to it based on the amount (from 0 to 1) that the point is driven. When smooth-bound, points can be weighted with falloff for a smoother deformation. Using a rigid bind, each point can only have one joint in the skin cluster driving it, as opposed to the smooth bind that allows for multiple joints to drive the same point using the weighted envelope.

Blend Shapes

Blend shape deformers let you change the shape of one object into the shapes of other objects (see Figure 14.8). Blend shape deformers let you deform a surface by creating target shapes for the main shape to change into. You can use blend shapes on a model with the same number of vertices (or CVs). In character setup, a typical use of a blend shape deformer is to set up targets for facial animation or to create fix shapes for problematic areas such as the shoulders.

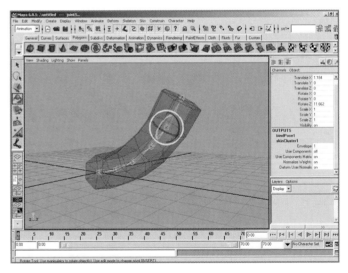

Figure 14.7
Example of a skin cluster deformer.

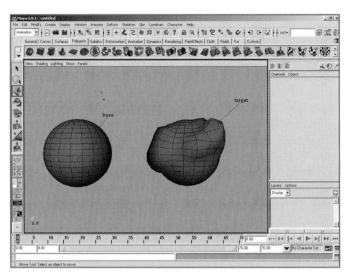

Figure 14.8
Example of a blend shape deformer.

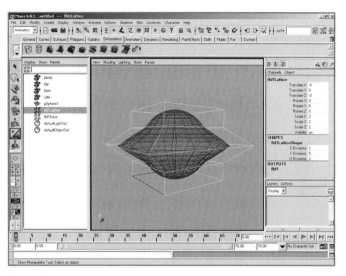

Figure 14.9
Example of a lattice deformer.

Lattices

Lattice deformers use a series of points connected together to affect the space inside (see Figure 14.9). The deformer includes two lattices: an influence lattice and a base lattice. By itself, the term "lattice" typically refers to the influence lattice. You create deformation effects by editing or animating the position of the points on the influence lattice. You can create a lattice around an entire group of objects to deform them together. They are also useful for getting that extra squash and stretch needed for cartoon style setups.

Clusters

A cluster node, much like a skin cluster, allows a selection of points to use a weighted envelope for deformations (see Figure 14.10). A cluster is used at the component level and uses Maya's set membership tools to define the vertices or CVs that will be included in the cluster. The weighted envelope will determine the cluster's influence on the mesh. Points on the mesh can be added and removed as needed. Weighting is done using the Component Editor or the Paint Cluster Weights tool.

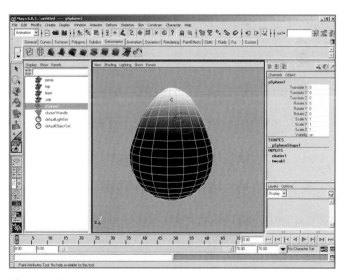

Figure 14.10
Example of a cluster deformer.

Bend, Flare, Sine, Squash, Twist, and Wave

More commonly referred to as non-linear deformers, this group can be used for specific types of deformation effects (see Figure 14.11). For example, you can use a squash deformer on a ball to help keep volume during a bouncing animation, or you can put a wave deformer on a plane and animate the attributes to make it look like water. They are typically used on cartoony setups, especially props.

Jiggle

The jiggle deformer affects points on a mesh by causing them to shake as they move (see Figure 14.12). For example, if you had a character with large rolls of fat that needed to jiggle, you could select the points you wanted to shake during animation and apply a jiggle deformer on them. The points will move according to how much they are weighted to the deformer. You can paint the weights or edit them manually in the component editor.

Wire and Wrinkle

Using a NURBS curve, wire and wrinkle deformers allow you to affect the points of a mesh by animating the CVs of a NURBS curve (see Figure 14.13). The relationship is much like a lattice in that there is a base and an influence wire. The deformation is determined by the space between the points on the base and the influence. You can change the attributes of the deformer to determine how much of the mesh you want to affect, and you can add and remove points affected by the deformer using the Edit Membership tool.

Sculpt

A sculpt deformer allows you to specify a shape volume that will slide underneath the affected mesh (see Figure 14.14). When the sculpt object is translated and intersects with the mesh, the points are pushed out by the underlying shape. This can be useful for faking the look of a muscle sliding underneath the skin or an Adam's apple moving in a throat. You can specify the underlying shape during creation.

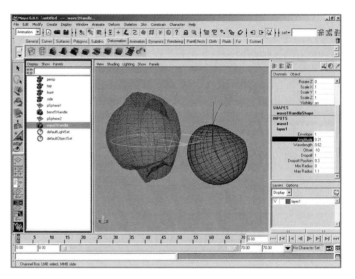

Figure 14.11
Example of non-linear deformers.

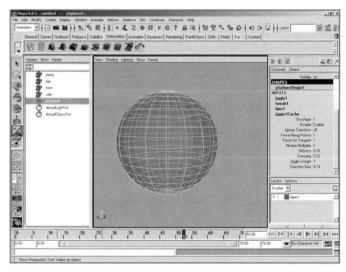

Figure 14.12
Example of a jiggle deformer.

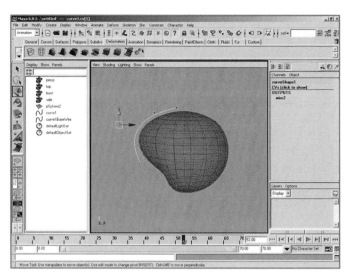

Figure 14.13
Example of wire and wrinkle deformers.

Wrap

Wrap deformers allow you to use a lower-resolution version of the mesh to drive the higher-resolution model (see Figure 14.15). The mesh driving the high-res skin can be bound to joints or other deformers and allows for easier editing because it is lower-resolution geometry. A wrap deformer can be difficult to use because of the amount of memory required to get the results, and you are also giving up control of some of the details in the higher-resolution mesh. This deformer is good for cartoony characters, but should be avoided if you're going for realism.

Plan Ahead

With all of these different options it can be difficult deciding what combination of them you need to use to achieve the look you're going for. Before you begin, take some time to research all of the available tools. Draw different poses of the character on paper. Draw arcs to see how the skeleton will affect the skin. Try to find the areas that are going to be difficult. Are there areas of fat, hanging skin, muscle masses? What are the challenges? If you plan ahead you will save yourself a lot of grief later down the line. Use a dry erase marker

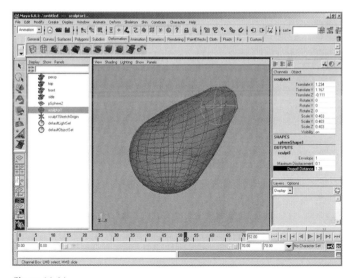

Figure 14.14
Example of a sculpt deformer.

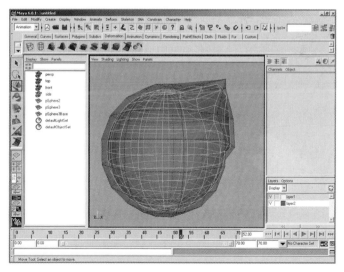

Figure 14.15
Example of a wrap deformer.

on your screen to help plan poses and see how wrinkles will deform (see Figure 14.16). If your creature resembles an animal, then examine a pet or go to the zoo and study how their skin and muscles work and move. Research is important! You must understand the anatomy of the character before you begin.

Research and Development

Once you've drawn everything out on paper and have a good grasp of the character in your head, then try to develop a deformation workflow. If time allows, do some R&D tests on areas of difficulty to find the best solution. Try to get input from supervisors and fellow co-workers on your results. Take all the criticism you can get and write down the bad points so you can make adjustments and fix problems.

Technical Considerations:

Another consideration you have to make during deformation setup is how your choices will affect the animators and other people who have to use the high-resolution model. While you want it to look great, you also want it to be fast and reliable for other people to use. High-resolution deformations take up lots of memory, and you're not going to get real-time feedback in Maya during animation playback. The fastest solution is not always the one you want to go with, but do try to keep the animators in mind when you're adding in those extra deformers.

Finally, before we really dig our heels in, remember that the ultimate goal is to push the limits of computer graphics. No matter what part of the industry you work in, chances are that you're always trying to make the finished product look better. By looking for new and better ways to do things, you're always going to be improving existing technology and pushing the look of the character you're working on (figure 14.17). Good deformations rely on great animators, modelers, and Character TDs working together as a team to help bring the character to life. If you do your job well, then your work will be transparent to everyone else, and the character will look great!

Figure 14.16
Drawing over screen captures is a helpful way to take notes.

Figure 14.17
High-resolution character ready for deformations.

chapter 15
Skin Cluster Deformer Applications

O ut of the box, Maya's skin cluster deformer gives you more modularity and versatility than any other deformation tool (see Figure 15.1). A setup relying solely on joints and a skin cluster can look great if used properly, but if done poorly, it can ruin a good model. In this chapter, we'll go over some tricks to help you better approach smooth binding, weighting, and editing skin clusters.

Binding Options

During the initial creation of the skin cluster node, you are given several options for bind settings. These settings are permanent once set, though they can be edited via a text editor or through a MEL script that allows you to change the initial bind settings.

When I use a skinCluster, I never bind using the "complete skeleton" option (see Figure 15.2). By using "selected joints," you can manually select all the joints in the character that will affect the skin. This will keep end joints and other joints that might not need to affect the skin out of the skin cluster node, and you won't have to worry about any vertices being weighted to them.

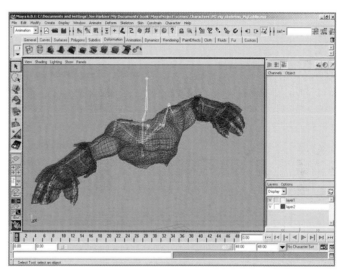

Figure 15.1
Skin cluster deformations.

We're going to attempt to explain what Maya calls "normalization." Each point on the smooth bound mesh must have a weight that adds up to 1. You can distribute the weighting among as many joints as you have set in the "maximum influence" during the initial bind. In my opinion, you would never need more than three influences for one point. One main influence and two for falloff weighting is the rule of thumb I stick to. You can turn off the normalization on a mesh, but it's not suggested.

During the weighting process, while you are changing the weights on the mesh, the remaining balance must be distributed to other influences so that the total influence equals 1. All of the joints in the skinCluster node are able to affect any point in the mesh that it is bound to (see Figure 15.3). You could end up with feet influencing arms during weighting if you're not careful. This means that if you don't pay attention to how the weight is being distributed, you will lose track of what points are weighted to what influences.

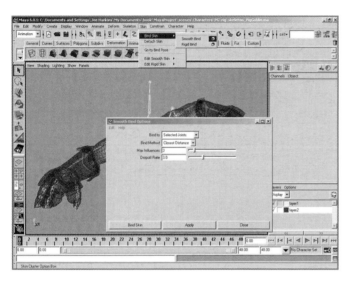

Figure 15.2
Skin cluster bind options settings.

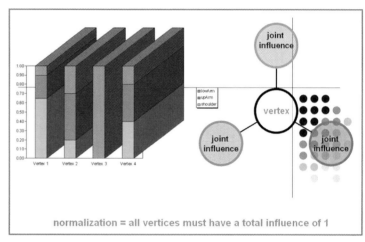

Figure 15.3
Skin cluster normalization diagram.

Setting the Dropoff Rate will determine the distance a joint will look for points on the selected mesh in order to determine default weighting. I usually set mine to 3. The Dropoff Rate can be set between 0.1 and 10. The higher you set this, the longer your initial binding will take to complete. Somewhere in the middle is usually a good starting place.

The last initial bind setting to cover is the Bind Method setting. You can choose between closest distance and closest joint. The differences are subtle, but I prefer closest distance. This, along with the Dropoff Rate, determines how the skin will be weighted at the initial bind stage. The default Maya weighting will almost always require editing in order to look good, so don't worry about which Bind Method you use.

Skin Cluster Weighting

Once your skin is bound to the joints, you need to edit the weights. This process can be done either by painting weights (see Figure 15.4), or through the Component Editor (see Figure 15.5). There are many people who swear by the Component Editor, but I'm not one of them. I rarely use it, and if I do it's only to set all of the weights on one joint to 0 or 1. I prefer to use a pen and tablet and paint the weights by hand. I highly recommend getting a tablet for

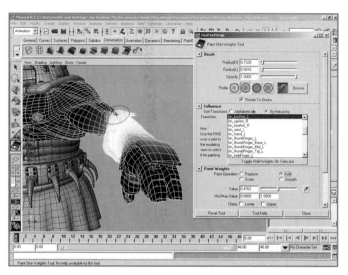

Figure 15.4
Painting skin cluster weights.

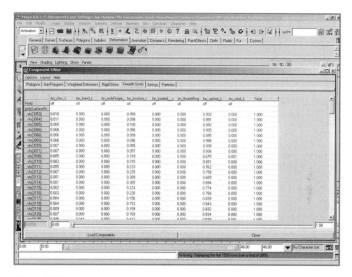

Figure 15.5
Point weighting in the Component Editor.

weight painting. It can change the whole process, and you'll have a much easier time getting the results you want with a pen and tablet as opposed to the traditional "bar of soap." To start out, I always weight all of the points on the mesh to the root of the skeleton. Starting from a clean slate allows you to work more efficiently and spend less time cleaning up after yourself later on.

Reverse Weighting

Reverse weighting, as I like to call it, is the process of weighting backwards. Instead of going through and weighting all the points from 0 to 1, I weight the points from 1 to 0, backwards. To start you have to weight all of the points to the root joint, usually the pelvis (see Figure 15.6).

The next step is to hold the weights on all the joints. In the Paint Weights options box, you'll see a button to hold the weights on a joint (see Figure 15.7). This will keep the weights from shifting around during painting and will allow you to remember what points are weighted to what joints without

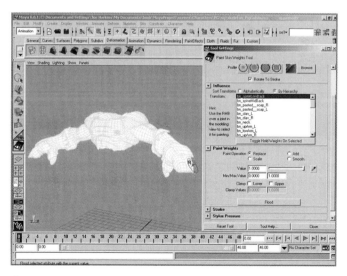

Figure 15.6
Replace flood quickly weights all points to one influence.

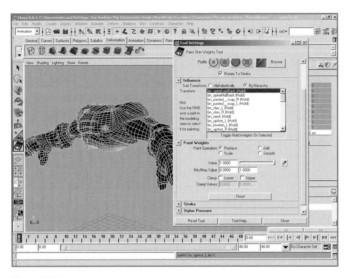

Figure 15.7
Toggle Hold Weights on selected in the Paint Weights toolbox.

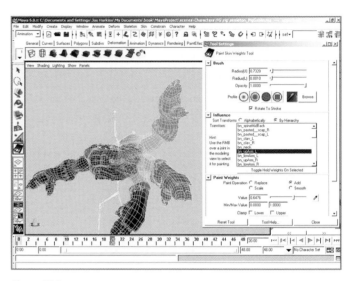

Figure 15.8
Animated joints help save time during weighting.

causing severe brain damage in the process. Put a hold on all of the joints, except for the root. This will keep the weights balanced between the root, the joint you're currently weighting, and the joints you've already weighted.

To keep from having to go back and forth between painting and testing movements, set keyframes on each joint to see how the skin will look when animated (see Figure 15.8). If you do this before you begin painting weights, you'll save yourself some time and won't have to keep opening the Paint Weights window. Also, consider setting a hotkey to get to the Paint Weights option box. I set mine to Ctrl+W so I can get to it quickly.

Since weight painting is mirrorable, you only need to paint one side of the character (assuming that the character is symmetrical). For painting, I suggest using the "add" and "scale" features. "Replace" is good if you want to wipe out any weights to other joints all at once. "Smooth" will relax the weights on the selected joint, but with other joints' weights on hold, Maya's automatic distribution might cause you a headache, so don't use the Smooth tool until later.

Remember that skinCluster weighting is normalized automatically, so each point must have a total weight of 1 at all times. The weighting will automatically be distributed to other joints, and it will require extra editing to get them distributed exactly as you want. Don't be discouraged by this process! Take your time and go through each joint slowly and methodically.

Back to the idea of reverse weighting—let's start by doing the fingers. Release the hold on "bn_spineLowBack" and the last joint in the left thumb, "bn_thumbFinger_Tip_L." With "bn_spineLowBack" selected, set your brush to replace mode. Set the paint value to 0 and paint out the "bn_spineLowBack" weighting over joint "bn_thumbFinger_Tip_L" (see Figure 15.9).

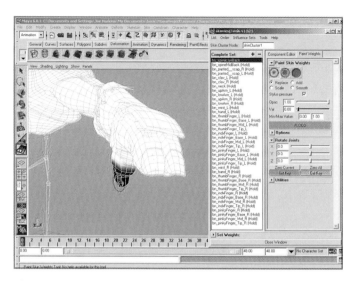

Figure 15.9
Remove the weights from the thumb tip.

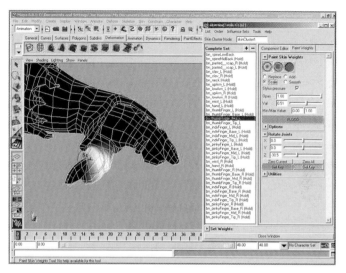

Figure 15.10
Weighting between thumb joints.

Select the "bn_thumbFinger_Tip_L" joint in the influence list. You should see that it is now weighted to the skin over the area you just painted. Now move up to the next joint in the left thumb and do the same thing by replacing the "bn_spineLowBack" weights at 0. Change the brush to scale and the value to .9.

Paint falloff influence between both thumb joints, as needed (see Figure 15.10). You'll need to leave the hold off these joints until you finish the weighting for all the joints that will affect the part of the skin you're working with. For the left thumb, you will keep moving up the chain until you get to the left hand joint. Once you have the thumb joints all weighted properly, you can set them to hold weights.

This is why you work in reverse—so you can control the weight distribution and not lose track of how each part of the character is affected. Working your way to the middle, you'll eventually have a pretty solid weight map on one side of the character that you can reliably mirror-over. Whether you choose to start from the middle of the character or from the extremities is irrelevant; it's a matter of personal working preference.

You absolutely must test the weighting and refine it as much as possible! Using only the options available to you during painting should get you most of the way there. Save tools such as Prune, Mirror, and Smooth for later. Once you've done one good pass at weighting and a refining pass, release the hold on all of the joints and mirror the weights.

15. Skin Cluster Deformer Applications

Fast Weighting—Add, Replace, Smooth:

If you're looking for a quicker solution, there is another solution to weighting. When given the time, my personal preference is to use the reverse weighting technique. Sometimes, though, a skinCluster will not be the primary deformer and only needs to be present with a basic pass at weighting. Other times, you may have only a few hours to weight a character. In this case, try using the previously mentioned bind settings, but do the painting differently.

Instead of weighting all the points to the root and then reverse weighting, just use the add, replace, and smooth features, respectively. For each joint, add to the area it is influencing so that it encompasses the entire area on the mesh you want it to influence; then go back in and replace with a value of 0 to areas that are being influenced by that joint that are not supposed to be. Finally, do a smooth flood on the influence a few times and then move on to the next joint in the hierarchy. This is kind of a cheat, because the weighting ends up looking very stretchy and smoothed, but if what you're going for is quick and dirty, then this is the way to go (see Figure 15.11).

Mirror, Smooth, and Prune

The Mirror Weights tool in Maya works by mirroring along two axes in the scene (see Figure 15.12). You'll want to mirror weights from the side you have weighted to the side you have not weighted, and weight across the plane your character is facing forward from (thank you, Captain Obvious!). The mirroring

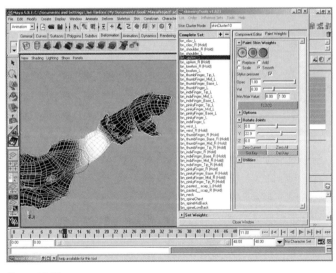

Figure 15.11
Fast weighting smooth technique.

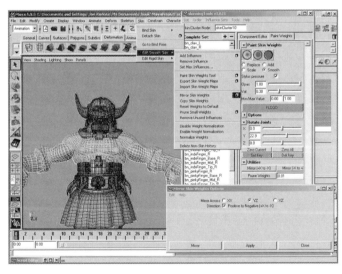

Figure 15.12
Mirror Skin Weights tool Options box.

process only works if the character is symmetrical as far as the number of points on each side of the character. The points can be moved in space, but the Mirroring tool works by searching for the relative point across the opposite plane and weighting to the respective opposite joint for you automatically.

After the weights have been mirrored, go through your test animations and make sure they worked properly. Any joints that did not have a mirror joint, such as the spine, neck, and pelvis, might need to be touched up along the center seam because Maya often has issues mirroring down the center axis appropriately. Use the Paint Weights tool to touch up any areas (see Figure 15.13).

The next step is to smooth and prune the weighting. I usually do three passes. With the Paint Weights window open, set the brush to smooth and the value to 1. Start from the top of the list and go through each joint and do a "flood." This technique will cause all points weighted to each joint to relax and smooth falloff between joints. This method only works properly if you did a good clean job of painting weights; otherwise, the smooth flood will wreak havoc and weight your points to joints you forgot existed. Once the smooth flooding is done, select the mesh and do a prune weights (see Figure 15.14). In the Options box, set the prune to .01 and apply it to the mesh. Go back and smooth-flood the joints again and do the pruning process two more times. Watch the test animations each time to make sure everything looks good.

Go through and paint any final touches, as necessary, using the Add and Scale options on the brush. The character should look good during the test animations, all of the joint rotations should cause smooth deformations, and any areas of intersections should be slight and look natural. A skin cluster can only take the character so far, so be reasonable with expectations.

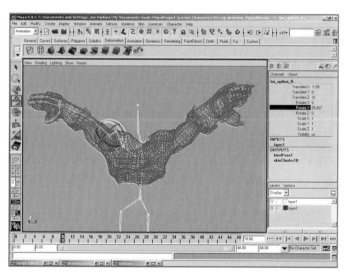

Figure 15.13
Check mirroring through animations.

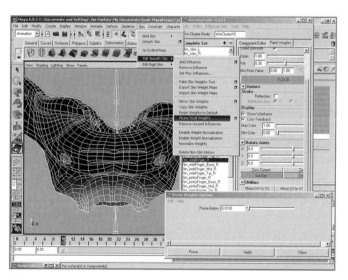

Figure 15.14
Prune Small Weights tool.

15. Skin Cluster Deformer Applications

255

Weight Storage Solutions

Weight maps in Maya can be saved to disk and reapplied to the character as needed. This means you can make changes to the joint placements and UV maps if you need to without having to worry about losing all of your work. The main thing to keep in mind is that you must not change your point count. You cannot delete vertices, add spans, create new edge loops, and so on. This will cause the weight map to be redistributed differently, due to Maya's arbitrary naming of vertices.

Maya's default way of saving maps is by using an image with black-and-white data to represent the 0 to 1 influences on the mesh. The two options are alpha and luminance (see Figure 15.15). The higher your character's resolution, the larger the image needs to be in order to save out all of the relevant data. Usually, 1024 or 2048 work well, but they can take a long time to save and load.

While Maya's built-in tools are decent, there are a number of scripts available to download for free online that will help you with smooth binding and the weighting process. Here's a list of the good stuff:

http://www.DavidWalden.com/

David Walden is a Character TD at Blue Sky Studio in New York. He has written some very useful rigging scripts, which he has kindly made available to the community online.

From his home page, follow the links to his MEL Scripts. The skinningTools MEL script is an all-in-one skinning toolset, packed with tons of features that streamline the skin-weighting process (see Figure 15.16).

The GUI is divided into the following sections:

◆ **Influence List:** Shows all influences affecting the selected geometry and gives the user basic, yet powerful, control over weighting selected points, toggling "Hold" for multiple influences, and so on.

◆ **Component Editor:** Like Maya's own Component Editor, yet shows only smooth bind information.

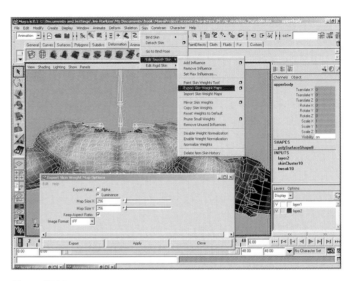

Figure 15.15
Maya's built-in Image Based Weight Exporting and Importing tools.

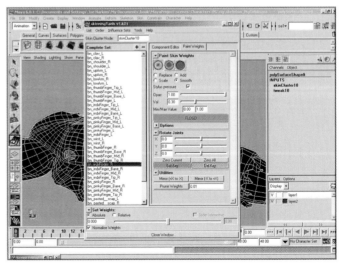

Figure 15.16
David Walden's skinning tools.

◆ **Paint Weights:** A more streamlined version of Maya's Paint Skin Weights tool. Here the user can take advantage of the Influence Sets menu, which isolates specific groups of influences for faster and easier weight painting. User can also quickly rotate joints to test skin weighting, while remaining in the Paint Weights context. The Utilities section offers additional tools.

◆ **Tools Menu:** Offers a variety of effective tools to help in the weighting process. For example, the user can quickly select all the points affected by a given influence. Transfer Weights will swap weight information from one influence to another. Add Influences is a quick way for adding multiple influences to your skinCluster.

◆ **Set Weights:** A fast-and-dirty approach for weighting selected points to highlighted influences in the Influence List. User can set skinPercent values of selected points either in absolute or relative mode.

http://www.highend3d.com/

From the main page go to Maya→MEL Scripts→Animation→aeSkinWeightsTransfer.mel

Written by Anders Egleus, this script will export and import skin weights by comparing the world space positions of the selection's points with the world space positions of the exported points. If it doesn't find an export point within proximity of the import point, it will average the weights of the export points in the vicinity of the import point.

cometScripts

On page two of the Animation MEL Scripts, you'll find Michael Comet's scripts, which include an updated "saveWeights" script from the "Big Idea," one he originally wrote. It now supports string search/replace, mirroring, pruning, and more. Other scripts include a quick Weight tool, Shape and Group creators, and other things to help for rigging.

If you go through the rest of the pages, you'll find a whole array of tools that other people have created to help with the skinning process. Opening the scripts in a Text Editor will give you more insight to commands such as skinPercent and the various inputs of the skinCluster node. You can also learn how these scripts parse through vertices and extract and apply weighting information.

Bind Pose

The bind pose is the pose that your character was in when it was initially bound to the skeleton. When you try to go in and add an influence, the skin and joints must return to the bindPose before allowing anything else to be added. You can delete the bindPose without problem, so if you are unable to get back to the bind pose for whatever reason, don't hesitate to select the bindPose node and just delete it (see Figure 15.17). With that out of your way, you'll be able to add as many influences as you like.

Adding Influences

If you need to add more joints to your skinCluster, you can do so by adding an influence. The easiest way is to set the influence automatic weighting to zero in the Options box so you can edit the weights yourself (see Figure 15.18). Adding a joint as an influence does not affect memory or create any new nodes in the scene; it simply adds a new connection from the joint to the skinCluster. Adding a geometric influence, on the other hand, can cause severe slowdowns in your scene, so avoid using geometry as an influence on the skinCluster if at all possible.

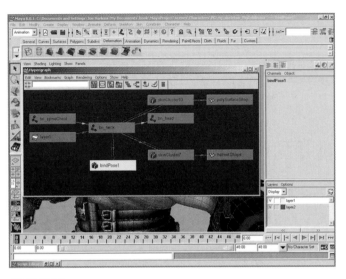

Figure 15.17
Bind pose node in the Hypergraph.

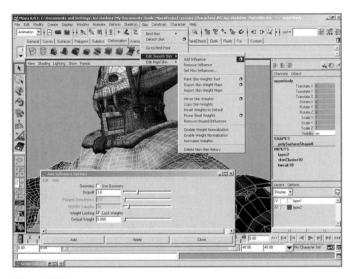

Figure 15.18
Add Influence Option box.

Layered Geometry

If your character has accessories or layers that need to be bound, then you're going to have to deal with those separately. Do not attempt to bind all of the geometry into one skinCluster, especially if you have overlapping pieces. Once you have the underlying skin bound and weighted, then you'll need to go through and apply corresponding weighting to the layers appropriately. In order to smooth-bind the layered pieces of geometry, you'll need to make sure they are similar in resolution and topology. If, for example, your character is wearing a coat that is half the resolution of the underlying body, then you are going to have a difficult time getting them to look similarly weighted.

A trick to getting two objects to deform similarly using skinClusters is to bind the overlapping object using the same influences and weighting as the underlying object. You can do this by using MEL scripting. By selecting the bound mesh and then Shift-selecting the mesh you want to be bound like it, you can use the following:

```
//list the selected geometry
string $sel[] = `ls -sl`;
//declare the first selected object as the main object
string $object = $sel[0];
//list the first objects history
string $hist[] = `listHistory -pdo true $object`;
//find the skinClusters in the history
string $skinClusters[] = `ls -type "skinCluster" $hist`;
```

15. Skin Cluster Deformer Applications

```
//declare the first skinCluster as the one to copy from
string $skinCluster = $skinClusters[0];
//list the influences in the skinCluster
string $infs[] = `skinCluster -q -inf $skinCluster`;
//list the number of influences in the skinCluster
int $numInfs = `skinCluster -q -mi $skinCluster`;
//go through the list of objects and influences and copy the skin //cluster settings to bind similarly
for($j = 1; $j < size($sel); $j++){
select -r $sel[$j];
for ($i = 0; $i < size($infs); $i++)select -add $infs[$i];
string $newSkinCluster[] = `newSkinCluster ("-toSelectedBones -ibp -mi "+$numInfs+" -dr 4")`;
copySkinWeights -ss $skinCluster -ds $newSkinCluster[0] -noMirror;
flushUndo;
}
```

You can make this into a procedure and add it into your shelf or create a hotkey to execute it. It will bind all of the objects selected like the first one, as long as they don't already have an existing skinCluster node. The weighting won't be perfect and will require you to go back and do touch-ups, but this should be a good place to start. Some of the above mentioned scripts available online also have great copying procedures for binding geometry similarly.

Modular Thinking

Because you have the ability to export and import weighting on a skinCluster node, you can save yourself some time by modularizing parts of the process (see Figure 15.19). Characters such as bipeds or digital doubles that are very similar and use the same joint systems will benefit from using the same weight maps. You should be able to copy over skinClusters from one character to another and do minor amounts of editing to get good deformations.

If you're looking for precision and are working under short time-frames, you can model characters using a standard generic mesh that you have weighted. Without changing the point count, you can alter the mesh to look like another character. You could then add additional clothing and accessories as needed per character and copy the weighting from the underlying geometry. It's always good to look for short-cuts in your deformation pipeline so you can spend more time doing the refining that makes the character stand out. This is just one small example. Many of the MEL scripts downloadable online have tools to help you create a solid pipeline and have been tried and tested in production, so don't forget to check those out.

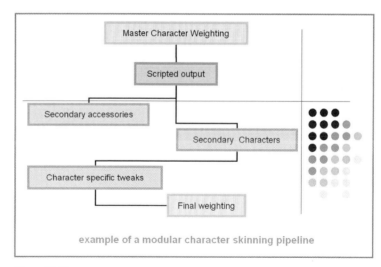

example of a modular character skinning pipeline

Figure 15.19
Modular character pipeline diagram.

For Maya pipelines, skinClusters are the most widely used solution for deformations. Relying solely on skinClusters can be risky, but it can and has been done. Game engines now support smooth binding, and characters you see in film and on television that were done in Maya are most likely using some form of smooth binding. Think of skinClusters as a good base you can add to. Since they are modular, you can go back and make changes early on as needed before you get into the refining details later down the pipeline. Weighting is a tedious and methodical process, but patience, understanding the tools available to you, and a little hard work will pay off.

chapter 16
Blend Shape Deformer Applications

This chapter will expand on what we've covered so far with skin clusters. A Blend Shape is a linear deformer that's great for fixing deformations and adding wrinkles or other subtleties into the character (see Figure 16.1). Assuming that you already know the basics of morph target systems and how they work, we're going to step right into the advanced applications of using these tools in a production pipeline. More specifically, we're going to focus on the why rather than the how, because that's what you really want to know. It's important to understand where and when to use Blend Shapes, in addition to knowing how to create them so you can better utilize their capability.

Layered Deformations

After you've skinned your character with a skin cluster and have everything weighted properly, you should be ready to add another layer of deformations. The history in Maya will allow you to add in as many deformers as needed. Blend Shapes are great for fixing deformations on problematic areas of the mesh. Two of the most difficult areas are the pelvis and the shoulders. These are the ball joints in the skeleton and the place where appendages join the torso. Due to the complex nature of the musculature and the way things

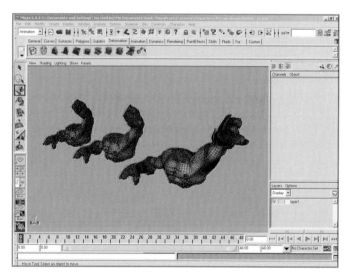

Figure 16.1
Blend Shape targets.

naturally work, we have a rather hard time duplicating those subtle movements in 3D without some added assistance. This is why we need secondary movement, additional deformers, and more ways to control the skin. A Blend Shape fix will allow us to get the exact shape we want and help those areas deform more naturally.

An understanding of how the Blend Shape node works will help you understand better how to make the deformer work for your character's needs. Because of the linear nature of the deformer, getting arcs and smooth transitions between shapes is difficult. Blend Shapes allow in-between shapes to compensate and let you sculpt a natural arc, but in reality it is still going from point to point, in a linear way. This is an exploitation of the Blend Shape deformer that is not to be overlooked! If you are trying to get realistic deformation and movements, then you must consider the use of arcs and smooth interpolation during setup.

Blend Shape Algorithm

A Blend Shape deformer is a linear deformer. You start with a base mesh and model target shapes that you want the base mesh to deform into. A Blend Shape node takes the position of the points from the base shape and subtracts them from the points on the target shape. This difference between the points, or offset you manually created, is multiplied by the Blend Shape node's weight value. The result is added back into the original mesh to give you the final shape. This entire process is linear; the points move from A to B via offsets in a straight line.

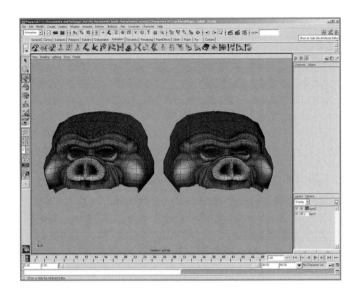

Figure 16.2
A linear eye blink target needs in-betweens for a more natural transition.

If you're not geeking out over the math stuff yet, here's what gets applied on a per vert level:

```
blendShape = (((new vert position - original vert position) * blendShape weight) + original vert position)
```

Additive Nature

Because a Blend Shape is linear, A to B, you must consider the result of applying more than one Blend Shape deformer at a time. If you have two target shapes that affect the same points on the base and you turn them both on at the same time, then you're going to get movement in the same vertices, twice.

> Base + Target = Target
>
> Base + Target + Target = New Shape

As an example, in Maya, create a polygon sphere:

1. Duplicate it twice and space the two spheres equally apart from the first one (see Figure 16.3). Do not freeze transformations!

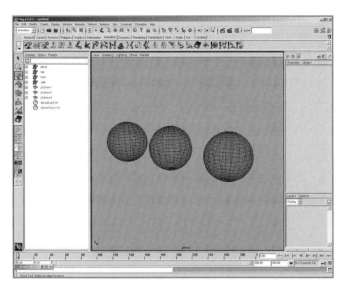

Figure 16.3
Polygonal spheres for Blend Shape targeting.

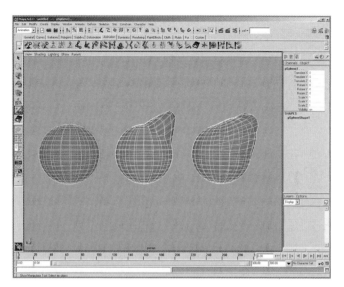

Figure 16.4
Modeled Blend Shape targets.

2. Deform the two duplicated spheres by selecting some of the vertices and moving them (see Figure 16.4). Deform the same area of the spheres for this test.

3. In order, Shift-select the two duplicated spheres and then the original sphere.

4. Create a Blend Shape with the default settings (Animation Menu→Deform→Create Blend Shape). See Figure 16.5.

5. Open up the Blend Shape Editor (Windows→Animation Editors→Blend Shape Editors).

6. Use the sliders to turn on and off each Blend Shape. Set them both to 1 and look at the result.

Notice how the points move once per target shape, creating a double-transform on points that are moved on both target shapes (see Figure 16.6). This is the result of the additive nature of a Blend Shape node.

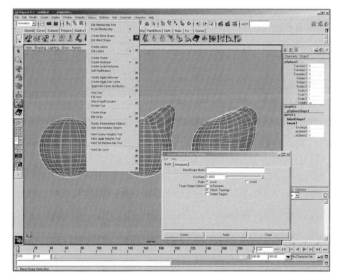

Figure 16.5
Create a default Blend Shape node.

It's important to understand how the system works before you start to use it. Each Blend Shape must count—each point being moved for a reason. The theories behind creating Blend Shapes differ, but they all must follow the same fundamental rules of the algorithm in order to work.

Pose-Based Deformation Fixes

Now that you understand the additive nature of Blend Shapes and the algorithm behind them, you can begin to make the system work for you. The most obvious use of a Blend Shape is to sculpt pose-based deformation fixes on parts of the model that deform poorly with just the default smooth binding. This is typically the larger areas of the mesh, such as the shoulders and the hips. They can also be used to refine the movement of arms and legs as they bend and crease.

You should be localizing your sculpt changes to specific areas on the mesh you want to deal with. You'll get a few benefits from this workflow, the first of which is it will keep things organized. Each shape will have a specific purpose; for example, if you needed a Blend Shape to create a flexing effect on the bicep when the arm is rotated up, then you could call that shape "bicepFlexRt." With each shape localized and named properly, then organizing into those categories and groups will be easy.

First, go through some test animations, calisthenics, and generic movements. Write down the problematic areas and prepare to address them one at a time. As an example, we'll do the left shoulder of our character.

1. Rotate the left arm and clavicle joints up to an extreme position, 30 degrees or so (see Figure 16.7).

2. Duplicate the high-resolution upper body in its deformed state twice and move them to the side (see Figure 16.8). Name them LeftShoulderFixA and LeftShoulderFixB.

3. Make changes on LeftShoulderFixB, leaving LeftShoulderFixA alone (see Figure 16.9). Do *not* freeze transforms! If you are a tablet user, we suggest the Artisan Sculpt Polygon tool. It has a smooth brush that can help relax points in creases and will allow you to paint changes. You want the shape to look natural, as if the muscle is flexed, but relaxed (see Figure 16.10). All of the creases should look natural and should look like folds, not intersections.

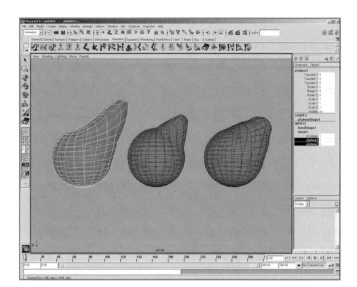

Figure 16.6
New shape created from two Blend Shape targets.

Figure 16.7
Character's shoulder posed in an extreme position.

4. Once you have LeftShoulderFixB sculpted into a shape that you feel is acceptable, Shift-select LeftShoulderFixA, LeftShoulderFixB, and the original deformed mesh (in that order).

5. Go to the Animation menu and go to "Deform→Create Blend Shape→" options box. With the Blend Shape tool open, select the advanced tab. Change the deformation order from "Front of Chain" to "Parallel," and then press the Create button (see Figure 16.11).

6. Next, open the Blend Shape Editor under Windows→Animation→ Blend Shape Editor. Set the LeftShoulderFixA Blend Shape to -1 and the LeftShoulderFixB Blend Shape to 1. With these set, rotate the clavicle joint back to 0. The original mesh will look strange, but that's good! (See Figure 16.12.)

7. Duplicate the mesh in its new state and call it "LfShoulderPosFix," short for Left Shoulder Positive Fix. You can now delete the other two shapes and the Blend Shape node associated with them.

Figure 16.8
Duplicate geometry for Blend Shape targets.

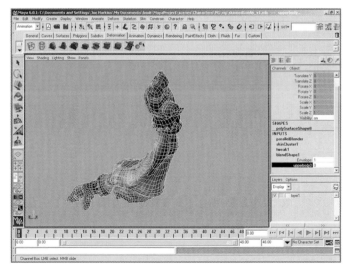

Figure 16.9
Original deformed geometry.

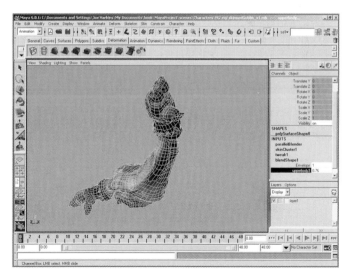

Figure 16.10
Sculpted Blend Shape target.

16. Blend Shape Deformer Applications

Figure 16.11
Parallel Blend Shape creation.

8. Create a new blend shape node by Shift-selecting LfShoulderPosFix and the deformed geometry in order, and make sure you're still set to parallel in the Advanced tab.

9. You can now use a Set Driven Keyframe to turn on and off this new corrective Blend Shape when the rt clavicle joint rotates positively. Open the Set Driven Keys window and load the left clavicle joint Y rotation as the driver. Load the new Blend Shape weight attribute as the driven. Set the joint rotation and Blend Shape weight to 0 and set key.

10. Rotate the clavicle joint to the extreme position it was in and set the Blend Shape to 1. Set key and close the Set Driven Key window. Test your settings by rotating the joint up and down to make sure the Blend Shape is turning on and off correctly (see Figure 16.13).

Now compare rotating the right and left clavicles by rotating the joints up and down and notice how much better the left clavicle looks with your new Blend Shape fix applied!

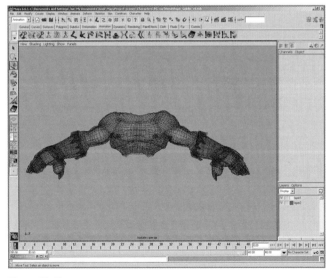

Figure 16.12
Pose-based fix new Blend Shape target.

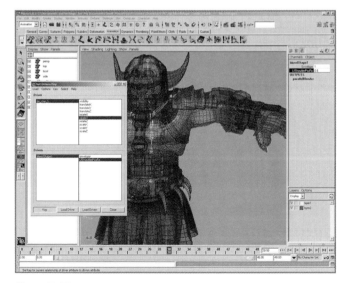

Figure 16.13
Set driven key on pose-based Blend Shape.

The extra steps we took to make a parallel blender allowed us to override Maya's rules that say we must create Blend Shapes from the default pose. By creating the Blend Shape from a deformed state and sculpting out the bad deformations, you are able to get better results. The process makes more sense and allows you to work logically through the model, fixing one piece at a time.

Mirroring Blend Shapes

Assuming that your model is symmetrical, Blend Shape fixes can be applied much like weighting. You can do one side and mirror your work over to the other side. This will cut your workload in half. It would be very difficult to get the same Blend Shape on both sides of the model without mirroring.

Our preferred method for mirroring Blend Shapes is to use a plug-in from HighEnd3d.com called "mirrorBlend." You can find it under the Maya plug-in section and download it for free. It includes a UI that will allow you to make symmetrical Blend Shapes by mirroring your deformed geometry.

The reason you can't just duplicate the model scale negatively and then freeze transforms is because of the way Maya assigns point IDs to the polygonal mesh. Even if you try to trick Maya, it still remembers the original point ID assignment, and your mesh will actually scale negatively when you turn the Blend Shape on. The only way to do it properly is to get the xform of each point you're mirroring and then use a script to find the opposite point across a specified axis and create a mirror shape. If you want to dig deeper, take a look at the previously mentioned scripts in a text editor to see how they work.

There are scripts that hack through some of Maya's other tools, such as the wrap deformer, to mirror Blend Shapes that way, but they are generally slower and are not practical to use on high-resolution geometry. Mirroring the Blend Shape geometry using a plug-in is much faster in our opinion. Don't try to mirror all the shapes at once, take your time and do them individually as you go. If you need to make adjustments later, you can do so and then mirror the changes back over as needed.

Pipeline Methodology

After you've created all of your pose-based Blend Shape targets, mirrored them over, and then named them properly, you are ready to apply the system to the deformed model from scratch. To do this, you'll first need to set up a directory structure for the Blend Shapes. Inside the directory that you are currently working from the character in, create a directory called "blendShapes," then create two directories inside of it called "body" and "face." The next step is to export each target shape into its own file within its corresponding subdirectory. If your mesh has more high-resolution parts, then make one directory for each part that you intend to make Blend Shapes for. The easiest way to do the exporting once you have set up the directories is to use MEL. This script will export each selected target shape into its own file in the directory you specify:

```
global proc exportSelectedObjects (){
fileBrowserDialog -mode 4 -fc "exportCallback" -an "Pick Your Blend Shape Directory";
return;
}
global proc exportCallback(string $path, string $mode){
print ("this is the dir path: " + $path + "\n");
string $all[] = `ls -sl`;
string $each;
for ($each in $all){
select $each;
```

```
file -es -type "mayaAscii" ($path + "/" + $each);
print "success! \n";
}}
```

Using this code, you can select all of your target shapes and run the "exportSelectedObjects" proc from the command line. You specify what directory the selected objects should be exported to using the fileBrowserDialog box that pops up. The objects are exported based on the names you give them, so make sure you name the Blend Shape targets properly before you run the procedure (see Figure 16.14). It will save over files of the same name automatically, so be sure that you are working in the proper directory and have everything named accordingly.

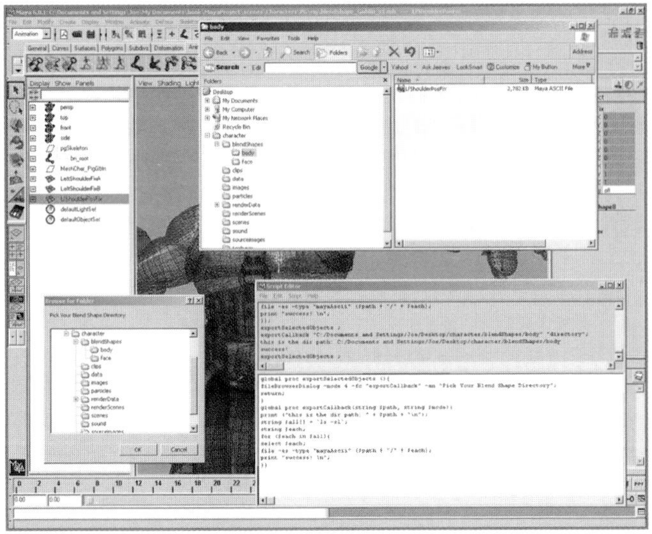

With all of your Blend Shapes exported, you should reload a previous version of your character, just in case you accidentally left any Blend Shape nodes or extra junk in the scene while you were sculpting fixes. Since everything is exported, all your work is saved and now all you have to do is import all the files and add them into the mesh as needed.

Figure 16.14
Exported Blend Shape.

Here's a script to import and create your Blend Shapes. First, you select the base mesh that the Blend Shape will be added onto; then you run the proc and select all of the target folders for the mesh. The proc then imports each file from the folder and adds the targets into a parallel Blend Shape for the base mesh. Once it's finished, it deletes the target geometry. The only thing it leaves behind is the Blend Shape node it created on the base mesh.

```
global proc importBlendShapes (){
fileBrowserDialog -mode 4 -fc "importCallback" -an "Pick Your Blend Shape Folder";
return;
}
global proc importCallback(string $path, string $mode){
//select the base mesh and list it
string $base[] = `ls -sl`;
// select all the top dag nodes in the scene, list them
select -ado;
string $before[] = `ls -sl`;
print ("this is the dir path: " + $path + "\n");
//get all of the files in the folder
string $folder[] = `getFileList -folder ($path + "/")`;
string $files;
//import each file
for ($files in $folder){
file -import ($path + "/" + $files);
}
```

```
//select the top dag nodes and list again
select -ado;
string $during[] = `ls -sl`;
//now compare the lists, the newly imported geometry will //be listed as a top dag node. Remove the first list //from the second
list
string $after[] = stringArrayRemove($before, $during);
// use the remainder for blendShape creation.
select $after;
select -add $base[0];
blendShape -parallel;
//delete the imported geometry
delete $after;
print "success! \n";
}
```

With these simple exporting and importing scripts, you are able to save all your sculpting work without having to worry about redoing it later. If you need to make changes to a particular shape, you can open the file for quick editing. Modularizing the processes as you go will help you save time and stay organized.

Driven Deformations

Each target will have a weight associated with it on the Blend Shape node that determines how much the base is influenced. For pose-based deformations, you can use Set Driven Keyframes to make sure each Blend Shape cooperates with its corresponding joint properly. To automate this task, you can use MEL scripting. The problem with automating this is that each Blend Shape target will most likely require a different range and might not use the same rotation axis. At the least, you'll probably have to do most of the Set Driven Keyframes by hand first and then if you need them again later, or if you have other characters that are set up similarly, you can use MEL to re-create the setup.

Another solution to driving the Blend Shapes is to use a utility node in Maya called "setRange." This node is brilliant, simple to use, and serves only one purpose: to change the range of one attribute and connect it to another attribute with a different range. Here's an example joint to Blend Shape setup with the setRange node. The only way to do this is through MEL:

```
//create the setRange node
string $sr = `createNode setRange`;
//connect the clavicle rotate Y into the setRange node
connectAttr "bn_clav_L.rotateY" ($sr + ".valueX");
//set the min and max driving range
setAttr ($sr + ".oldMinX") 0;
setAttr ($sr + ".oldMaxX") 30;
//set the min and max for the driven blendShape (0 to 1)
setAttr ($sr + ".minX") 0;
setAttr ($sr + ".maxX") 1;
//connect the setRange node to the blendShape
connectAttr ($sr + ".outValueX") "blendShape1.LfShoulderPosFix";
```

From the preceding code, you can derive that variables in place of the named attributes would be a good way to parse through the joints and connect the Blend Shapes. You can find specific information about the setRange node in the Maya Node Reference in the software documentation (see Figure 16.15). No matter how you choose to hook up your pose-based deformations, consider using MEL scripting to automate the procedure.

Pose-based deformations can be more complex than just one shape. You can go farther and add in-betweens for each shape, and even add in some more extreme shapes if you have time. Combining those together is still linear; there's no crossfade or blending. The kind of complexity we're talking about really only exists in one place, the face.

Priorities and FACS

The main challenge with Blend Shapes lies in making them work together in unison. Creating them, in my opinion, is the easy part. My favorite part is working with a really good modeler who understands the look of the character and can create shapes with amazing expressions. Animators are good at posing, but they must be given the right poses to key. It's like a piano—you start off one note at a time, then you progress to chords, and then you add bass and timing

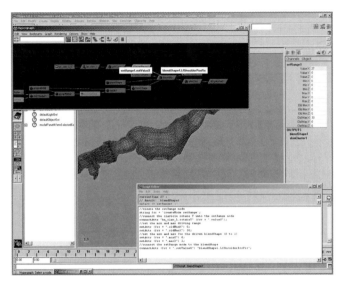

Figure 16.15
A setRange node driving Blend Shape.

and blend all the elements together to make a song. Blend Shapes have a similar complexity in terms of combining them together to look smooth.

A priority-based system basically tells each Blend Shape when it is allowed to be on or off. Continuing with the musical analogy, it sets the rules for what notes can be played so that everything sounds good. We believe in giving an animator complete freedom when animating; however, that freedom should exist within barriers that they are unaware of, barriers that feel natural and unobtrusive. If you were to allow an actor's face to be like silly putty, whereby anyone could change it to however they saw fit, there would be no consistency between shots. Gollum is the perfect example, giving animators freedom to match the actor's performance within a set of boundaries that were realistic. That's the goal, and giving animators that kind of control requires an ironic level of precision.

For the face, we recommend basing your ideas on the Facial Action Coding System (FACS), which was developed in the laboratory of Paul Ekman and Wallace V. Friesen during the 1980s. The system breaks the muscular activity that produces momentary changes in facial appearance into Action Units (AUs). It looks for certain movements in the face and defines them as a numbered AU. Furthermore, these AUs can be combined to create emotion and have levels of intensity. The system has years of research behind it. For more information on FACS, check out www.face-and-emotion.com, where you can read more about it.

Basically, we want each combination of shapes to represent an AU properly and not to go outside of these boundaries. AU4, for example, is Brow Lowerer, which would be a Blend Shape with eyebrows down. AU5 is Upper Lid Raiser. According to FACS, a combination of AU4 and AU5 is acceptable and would result in an angry brow emotion. By understanding the combinations of the system, we could set up a custom attribute called "browsAngry" on a facial control that would drive AU4 and AU5 Blend Shapes together simultaneously without causing double transformation on the affected vertices. Unless you give the system a set of rules to work within, it will break.

What are the rules? Since each shape goes from 0 to 1, we know that there is a min and max. We also know that combining shapes causes double-transformations on the affected vertices.

Rule One states that all of the blendShapes that affect a certain part of the face must add up to 1.

If AU4 is set to .5, then the max for AU5 is .5. Each AU can only be combined with certain other action units, so priorities can be set up in Maya to help control how the Blend Shapes are added. This statement shows the algorithm that would need to be applied:

If $(AU4 > 0)$ AU5 ! > $(1 - AU4)$

If $(AU5 > 0)$ AU4 ! > $(1 - AU5)$

It's easy to see how this algorithm will get more complex as you add more shapes. Setting this algorithm up in Maya to work with the Blend Shape attributes requires extensive knowledge of utility nodes and MEL scripting.

Rule Two states that individual right and left shapes only count as half of a whole shape.

An important thing with a priority system is to never allow Blend Shapes to be combined in an unnatural way. All of the target poses should be sculpted at the most extreme they will be animated, allowing a little buffer room in case the animator needs to add in more. Whole shapes can be derived from combining right and left shapes together if necessary.

Rule Three states that emotions have priority over phonemes and individual shapes.

If you are trying to have a character look sad and talk at the same time, you have to apply the sadness before the phonemes, in order to keep from creating double transforms when the lips and lower cheeks are moving. Emotions can be represented as either a control driving individual shapes or as a whole shape that is blended before the individual controls get applied. In any case, the emotions should be applied first in the system. This should all happen behind the scenes automatically. The animator should never have to stop and think about the fact that the sad Blend Shape is getting applied before the lips moving up and down.

Gollum's face in *Lord Of The Rings* was set up at Weta Digital with a system that used over 900 target shapes. We relied on Blend Shapes at Tippett Studio for facial animation for creatures like Abe Sapien in *Hellboy* and the Scavengers in *Constantine*. These systems in production use simple controls for the animators that allow them to combine shapes without having to think about it. By understanding FACS and how each individual shape can be added to create emotions, you can then use the rules of a priority-based system to create a working Blend Shape solution.

We could write an entire book on facial animation, priority systems, and controls for Blend Shapes. If that's what you're after we recommend checking out Jason Osipa's book on facial animation, *Stop Staring*. It is Maya-centric and uses Blend Shapes and a very unique set of controls for facial animation. We believe that if you understand FACS and how priorities work that you will have a solid base to build from and can begin to navigate your own system.

Blend Shapes are one of the fastest deformers available to use in Maya and can be scripted for modularization and speed. Exploit this deformer as much as you possibly can in every aspect of your character setup pipeline (see Figure 16.16). From fixing problematic deformations to doing advanced facial systems, Blend Shapes are a reliable deformer that gets the job done quickly and efficiently while offering a superior level of control.

Figure 16.16
Posed character with shoulder fix Blend Shapes.

SECTION 5

Advanced Skinning

Steve Talkowski

chapter 17
CASE STUDY: BMW Angels Rig

Steve Talkowski, former Animation Director at Hornet Inc (http://www.hornetinc.com), discusses the creation of the BMW Angels spot for us.

This article will describe a typical process of dealing with character rigs for a commercial production, in this case the BMW Angels spot completed for Fallon Worldwide, MN (and shown here). On this job our team was fortunate to have quite a bit of up-front time devoted to character design, which allowed adequate experimentation during rig setup and testing before animation began.

Defining Character Requirements

When undertaking any project, it's important to look at the storyboard and determine how many shots a character will be in and what type of performance will be required of them. The BMW spot has four unique guardian angel cherubs that hover and fly alongside each tire. At no time did they need to make contact with the ground or car, which meant I didn't have to worry about setting up an IK structure for the legs. The main challenges were in figuring out how to deal with the stylized hair and toga flapping constantly from the force of wind.

Rigging Philosophy

I like to keep my rigs simple, light, and as efficient as possible, while at the same time giving the animator enough control to override and edit whichever attributes need to be keyed. I find that relying less on expressions and keeping constraints to a minimum will ensure faster rig feedback. I'm not a huge fan of full automation, though it is nice to have some procedural qualities to a rig—for instance, setting up "wobbly" deformers for jiggly parts or a follow-through tool for natural propagation of chain rotations. Maya 4.5 was used for this project. With the release of Maya 6.0 and its new dynamic curve simulation, I would have liked to implement this in both the character's hair and cloth rigs.

Another important factor in workflow is the use of referencing. A very simple cube character is used for quick layout (see Figure 17.1). A low-resolution poly cage, which will be up-rezed by poly smooth, will be what is rigged. In Figure 17.2, this resolution is acceptable for animation tests sent to the client. Finally, the hi-res version can be toggled on for final render (see Figure 17.3). All three resolutions exist in the final rig with visibility toggles included.

For the angel rig I wanted toggles to switch between the lo- and hi-rez versions of the head and body separately. The hi-rez models were in fact the lo-rez Polycagemodels with Poly Smoothed applied. A simple toggle allowed us to dial in how many "polySmooth Divisions" we needed at render time. In most cases, a value of 1 was sufficient. When creating 4K hi-rez stills for print, we upped the value to 2.

Figure 17.2
Base mesh pre-smooth.

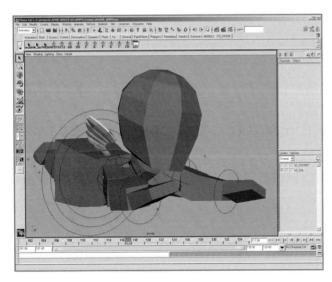

Figure 17.1
Low-resolution proxy version of the angel rig.

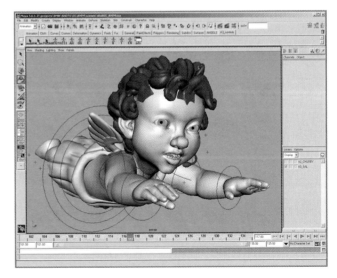

Figure 17.3
Render ready poly-smoothed version of the character.

17. CASE STUDY: BMW Angels Rig

Here's a simple example for creating your own controls using the Attribute Editor and the Connection Editor. We'll set up an attribute for toggling the visibility of layout geo.

1. Choose all of your layout geo and assign them to a unique layer named LAYOUT.

2. Next, pick your control object, open the Attribute Editor (Ctrl + A), create a new attribute (Attributes→Add Attributes), and name it LoRez, as shown in Figure 17.4.

3. Set the Data Type to Integer; then set a Minimum Value to 0, the Maximum Value to 1, and the Default to 0. Click Add.

4. Open the Connection Editor and load the control rig as the Output (left column), as in Figure 17.5. If you scroll down to the bottom of the list, you'll see the name of the newly created attribute, "LoRez." Now, right-click on the name of the layer, select Attributes, and then click Select in the window that pops up. This makes it active. You'll notice the visible attribute under the Drawing Override Options.

5. Return to the Connection Editor and click Reload Right. We can now connect the LoRez attribute of the control rig to the Visibility attribute of the LAYOUT layer. Using this technique, you can add as many extra attributes as you like to any given node.

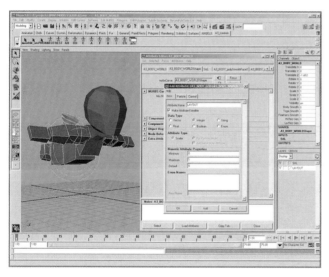

Figure 17.4
Custom attributes added to control visibility.

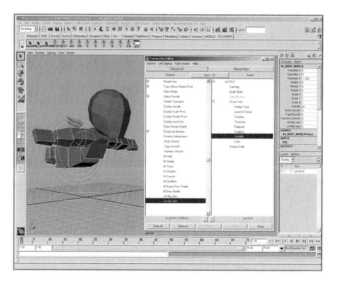

Figure 17.5
Making the connections to the attributes

The Head Rig

Considering that it would be very time-consuming to rig four separate characters, I instructed my modeler to use the exact same topology for each individual head shape. This way, I could rig and weight one head and export skin weight maps that could be imported and applied to the other three heads. Of course, the joint positions would have to be tweaked between the different head shapes, but by using an already meticulously weighted skin map, I saved myself a great deal of time when it came time to weighting the remainder of the characters. I also prefer to drive phoneme shapes with joints rather than with Blend Shapes, simply because relying solely on Blend Shapes results in a linear blend between the phonemes.

One very important MEL script was the pose2shelf MELscript by Erick Miller (downloadable from http://www.highend3d.com) This tool does two simple things really well—first, it allows you to save and label the setAttr(pose) commands for all keyable attributes of all selected nodes to your shelf, and second, save and label your current selection to the shelf. This tool was indispensable, as I used it to save different selected regions to the shelf for easy picking (rather than creating quick select sets) and for posing the mouth joints into individual phonemes and saving these poses to each character's individual shelf (see Figure 17.6).

My skeleton layout is pretty straightforward—12 joints point outward from the mouth to the lips, 2 joints for the wings of the nose, 7 joints for the eyebrows (3 per brow and one in-between), 1 joint for the upper eyelid, 1 joint for the lower eyelid, and 1 sculpt deformer per cheek (see Figures 17.7–17.9).

The stylized hair presented a unique challenge. It was decided early for practical as well as economical reasons that there would be only two hairstyles—one curly and one with straighter segments—and we would have four different hair shades: blonde, red, auburn, and brown.

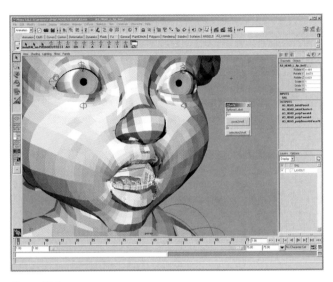

Figure 17.6
Quick pose tool for the face shapes.

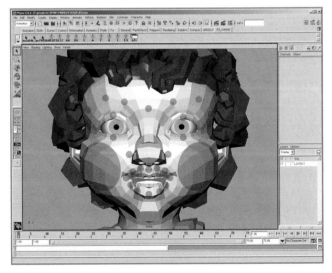

Figure 17.7
Main joint placement locations.

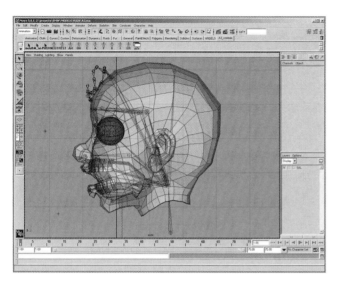

Figure 17.8
Joint placement detail.

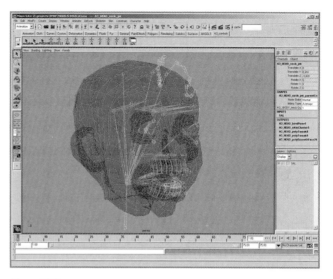

Figure 17.9
Joint placement detail continued.

I knew it was going to be impossible to stick joints inside every curl and came up with a pretty simple cheat. Why not run a non-linear wave deformer through the wig? The required action was constant flapping, and a wave with falloff achieved the desired results (see Figure 17.10). Two wave deformers were used—both point straight back with one orientated on the YZ axis (front/back wave) and the other on the XZ axis (side wave). Both deformers were point-constrained to the head so that the character could rotate and look around while the implied wind force always blew back in negative Z (see Figure 17.10). A lattice was added on top of this with selected clusters to offset the even wave. The Paint Cluster Weights tool was used to deselect points where the hair geo was supposed to be "attached" to the head, so only the outlying region would be affected by the deformers. This same technique was applied to the two pieces of cloth that comprised the toga, the top, and the skirt.

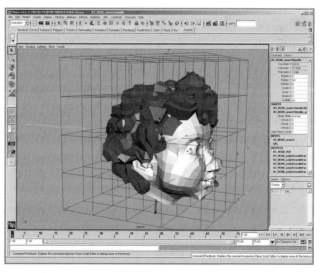

Figure 17.10
Wave deformers to simulate wind in the hair and clothing.

The Body Rig

Because our characters are in a constant "Superman" flying pose, special attention was paid to the shoulder rig. I used two joints for the shoulder so that I could weight accordingly for such an extreme pose, as shown in Figure 17.11. I also added two joints to help move the skin in the armpit and upper shoulder regions (see Figure17.12). The feathers of the wings had separate joints, but due to the quick motion they would have, any individual flapping motion was lost in the motion blur. The toga, in addition to wave deformers, had a Lattice with the bottom area clustered for added control with flapping and giving some weight to the cloth (see Figure 17.13).

An important factor in rigging the head and body separately is to be sure you have an extra joint where the two models will attach. This way, you can cross-weight knowing that the seam will be invisible. For example, the body skeleton has the neck joint included, and the upper region that will be affected gets the appropriate weights applied. The head skeleton already contains the neck joint that will be

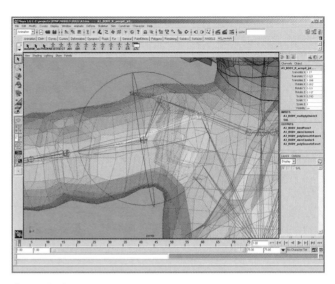

Figure 17.12
Helper joints for the armpit and upper shoulder.

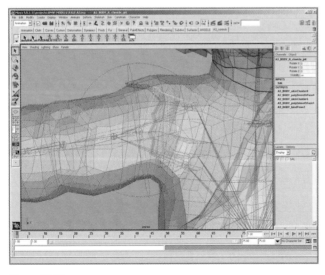

Figure 17.11
Extra shoulder joints help with extreme range of motion without collapsing the mesh.

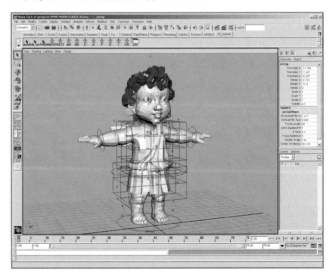

Figure 17.13
Deformation layers to control the toga using clusters, lattices, and wave deformers.

orient-constrained to the upper torso (see Figure 17.14). Mirror Skin Weights were used, but with much binding, testing, detaching, and rebinding, sometimes the symmetry would be lost—it still saved me time from having to weight both sides individually.

Overall, this was the most complex rig I've worked on since the alien creature for *Alien Resurrection*. Subsequent rigs have changed dramatically in the facial control setups, as I now favor having virtual sliders present in the camera workspace of a particular character. Shoulder rigs continue to be a challenge, and in this respect, I'm totally in support of automating the scapula/clavicle/shoulder relationships.

While the basics of rigging carry over from character to character, it's the unique qualities of a given creature and the animation requirements that challenge riggers to come up with new and better solutions to bring them to life.

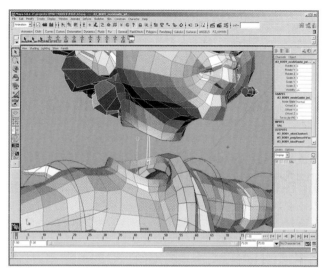

Figure 17.14
Extra joint helps with the weighting because the characters had separate heads and one body.

chapter 18
Cluster Deformer Applications

I nevitably, we get to the complex and typically frustrating world of clusters. Why are they so complicated? What makes them work? Are they really useful? These are questions you might be asking yourself. If you're totally unfamiliar with clusters, don't despair. We'll do a quick overview of the basics first, followed by a thorough explanation of their applications.

Clusters are mainly good for refining deformations, additional controls, added movements, fixes, and making small changes to the mesh (see Figure 18.1). Clusters are also used for deforming NURBS curves, such as a spline IK setup, by deforming the CVs of the curve, which controls the connecting joint chain.

The Basics

You might already be familiar with how to create a cluster, but you might not understand all of the options and how they operate to make the cluster work. The basics are important because the more complicated cluster topics that will be discussed require an understanding of all of these options and how they affect the cluster deformer.

In Maya, create a polygon sphere with at least 10 subdivisions. Select a group of the vertices and from the Animation menu go to Deformer→Create Cluster and open the options box. From this box, you can set all the options for the deformer before you create it. Create a cluster with the default settings (see Figure 18.2).

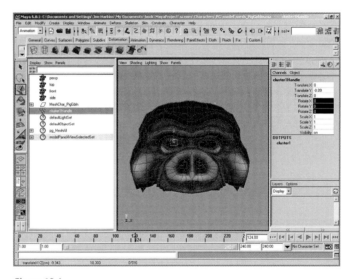

Figure 18.1
Cluster deformer on mesh.

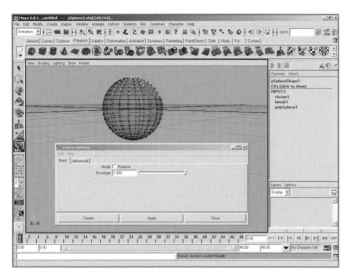

Figure 18.2
Sphere with cluster deformer applied.

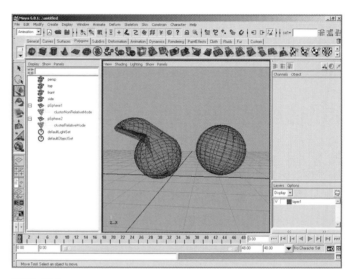

Figure 18.3
Cluster in non-relative mode has double transformation effects when parented to the mesh.

Relative Mode

Under the "basic" tab you should see the "relative" check box, which is generally referred to as the "mode" the cluster is in (see Figure 18.3). The mode specifies whether the cluster deformation will occur only when the cluster deformer handle itself is transformed or when the object it is parented to is transformed. With "relative" turned on, only transformations to the cluster deformer handle itself will cause deformation effects. With "relative" turned off, transformations to objects parented to the cluster deformer handle can cause deformation effects. If you create a cluster deformer with "relative" turned on and then parent the cluster deformer handle to a joint, you can rotate or translate the parent joints without causing cluster deformation effect. In "relative" mode, only when you move the cluster deformer handle itself will you cause cluster deformation effect.

Envelope

The envelope of a cluster is very similar to a skinCluster. It is a weighted grayscale map that determines on a point-by-point basis how much the deformer affects the points in the deformer set. You can set the global envelope during creation. By default, all points are weighted to 1, so the deformer has no falloff. To add or remove points into a cluster, use the Edit Membership Tool from the Deformer menu. Highlighted points are part of the membership "set," which means they will be deformed based on their weight to the cluster.

This can be changed, much like a skinCluster, by painting weights or through the Component Editor. To paint weights for a cluster, you have to open the Paint Cluster Weights tool options box from the Deformer menu and then select a cluster from the list that you want to weight (see Figure 18.4). Unlike a skinCluster, there is no normalization, which means that you can weight points with an influence of greater than one if you like.

18. Cluster Deformer Applications

Overlapping clusters that affect the same points in a mesh are transformed based on their weight to each cluster node, which means that you could have double transformations on some points. There is only one influence when weighting, so keep in mind that you are only affecting the way the loaded cluster affects the mesh, not how all the clusters affecting the mesh work together. This means there's no maximum influence and drop-off rate to worry about like a skinCluster. Those are the differences between the two when comparing how the envelopes work. The overlapping movements can be desirable if proper falloff weighting is done between clusters to keep the mesh looking smooth during deformations.

Weighted Node

This is an attribute you can set during the creation of the cluster or after. It is not included in the cluster creation GUI. The weighted node, by default, is the cluster handle that is created to transform the cluster in space. This is the "C" handle that gets created in Maya. You may specify this flag, if creating clusters from the command line or in a script. It is recommended to change the weighted node after the initial creation, not during (see Figure 18.5).

Deformation Order

Assuming the cluster is not the only deformer affecting your mesh, you'll need to specify its deformation order or how it gets applied to the history of the mesh (see Figure 18.6). In the order of deformers we've covered, we would want the skinCluster and Blend Shape deformer to get applied parallel and the cluster deformer to be applied on top of that, or after. The default is after, unless otherwise specified.

Exclusive Partitions

Partitions keep from having overlapping clusters affect the same points. You can essentially divide up the mesh into partitions during cluster creation, but this allows for no overlapping movement. Most people never bother with this; since the clusters can be weighted and controlled easily, there is no real benefit to creating individual partitions for the clusters.

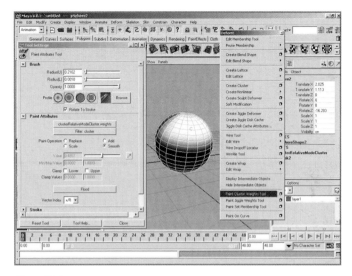

Figure 18.4
Cluster Paint Weights tool.

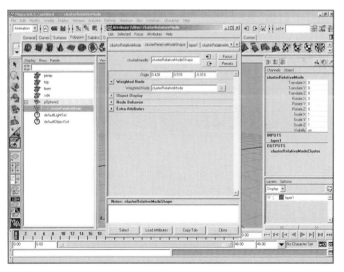

Figure 18.5
Cluster weighted node input in the Attribute Editor.

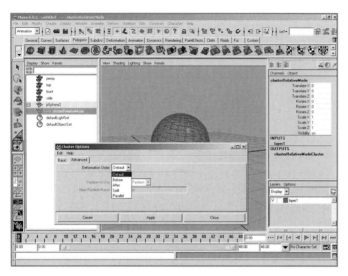

Figure 18.6
Cluster deformation order settings.

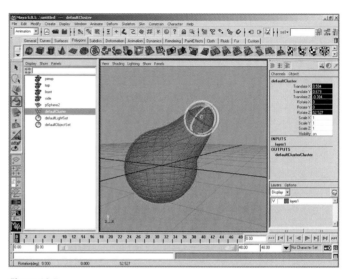

Figure 18.7
Cluster deformer transformed in space.

Investigating the Obvious

Let's go back to the sphere you created in Maya with the default cluster. Grab the "C" handle that Maya created for the cluster node and translate, rotate, and scale it in space. Notice how it affects the points on the mesh and how each point is moved according to the percentage by which it is weighted to the cluster (see Figure 18.7). Pretty simple, right?

Translate the sphere away from the origin. Notice how the cluster's "C" handle does not move with the sphere, but it stays at the original place of creation. Wait, but if you select it and translate it, it appears to move the points relative to the points on the sphere as opposed to moving them from the origin of the cluster handle! Try rotating and notice that the point of rotation is local to the center of the points in the cluster; it's not the cluster handle's rotation axis (see Figure 18.8).

The points are translating, rotating, and scaling based on their local space, not the cluster "C" handle's transformations. This is where it gets confusing,

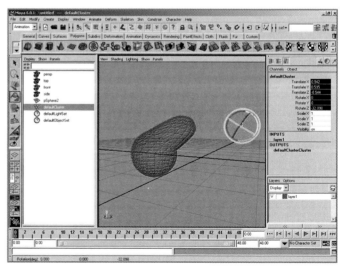

Figure 18.8
Cluster deformer and deformed object transformed.

because now you have a translated sphere with a cluster that appears to be working, but not quite how you intended.

Move the sphere back to its original position and open the Attribute Editor for the cluster. Check the "Relative" check box at the top and close the Attribute Editor (see Figure 18.9). Parent the cluster to the sphere and translate the sphere around in space.

Notice how the cluster's handle is now moving with the sphere, but the points are not? That's because it's ignoring the parent's translations and is now only looking at the transformations "relative" to the handle. This is all very annoying, isn't it? Now, making sure you're in local mode, translate the cluster around, rotate the sphere, and watch how everything magically works together. Now, it's time to throw a wrench in the wheel.

The Cluster Re-matrix

Herein lies the problem with clusters: Getting their control handles to move according to the points they are controlling without causing double transformations. There are several things to think about when solving this problem, so first, let's outline some rules.

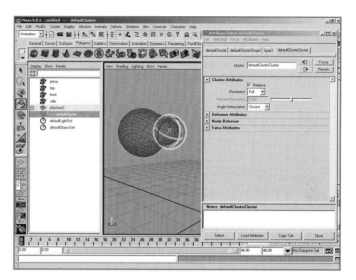

Figure 18.9
Cluster deformer in relative mode.

Rule one states that all clusters should have corresponding control objects that are frozen and selectable on the mesh.

Generally, you won't want to animate the cluster handles themselves directly. They are created at the center of the cluster's points by default, putting the default location in an awkward spot. It makes it harder to select the cluster, and the default "C" Maya creates is not exactly the prettiest control icon.

Rule two states that all clusters must rotate from the center of the cluster handle origin.

If you want to rotate a cluster from a pivot other than the default, then you begin to encounter problems with the rotation matrix of the cluster handle. Basically, if you try to rotate the cluster from any space other than its local rotation axis, it will cause cycle errors and other issues. Rotations and translations need to "appear" to happen from the cluster origin, even if the control object is not located at the same position.

Rule three states that clusters must be last in the deformation order on the mesh.

If the clusters are the last thing to be evaluated in the history, then they are a last resort refinement for deformations. Since they are so localized and used for final sculpting, this makes the most sense.

Rule four states that clusters should live outside of the standard character hierarchy.

With these rules in place, you can start creating controls and proper systems for the clusters. So back to that sphere in Maya with the cluster we created. Create a locator, scale it up a bit, and then snap it into position with the cluster handle. Finally, move it to a more desirable location outside the sphere and freeze its transformations (see Figure 18.10). This will be our cluster's control object.

For the sake of demonstration, create a joint in the middle of the sphere and smooth-bind the sphere to it. Make sure the deformation order is correct so that the skinCluster gets evaluated before the cluster node.

Open the Hypergraph and graph the upstream/downstream connections to the cluster. See how the cluster handle's world matrix is connected to the cluster's matrix? This is the connection between the handle (the "C" control object) and the actual cluster node. Select the pink line in the Hypergraph and delete the connection (see Figure 18.11).

With the cluster disconnected from its control object, we can now connect the locator to it. Open the Connection Editor. Load the locator into the left side and the actual cluster node into the right. Connect the world matrix of the locator to the matrix of the cluster. Graph the cluster's connections again in the Hypergraph and notice how the locator is now connected where the Cluster Handle node once was (see Figure 18.12).

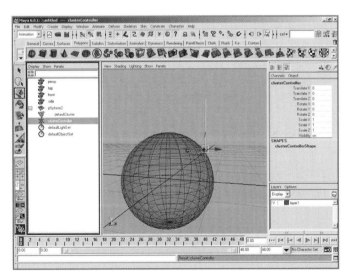

Figure 18.10
Cluster deformer and locator control object.

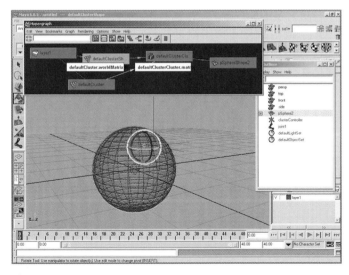

Figure 18.11
Delete control handle "C" connection.

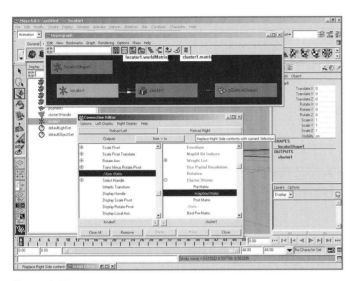

Figure 18.12
Connect the cluster matrix to the locator.

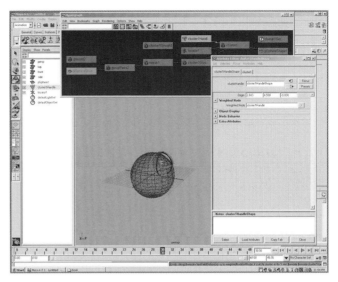

Figure 18.13
Weighted node attribute on a cluster.

The next step is to change the weighted node on the cluster to be the locator. To do this, select the cluster and open up the Attribute Editor. You should see a "weighted node" attribute that currently says "clusterHandle1." Change that to be "locator1" and then press Enter on the keyboard. Notice how the cluster is now parented to the locator automatically for you (see Figure 18.13).

The old clusterHandle will now be empty, like a null, so you can safely delete it. Open up the Attribute Editor for the cluster and check the "relative" check box.

Finally, create an empty group and point-, orient-, and scale-constrain it to the joint controlling the sphere. Parent the locator to this node. Move the joint in space and rotate it. Notice how the locator follows without a problem. Now select the locator and translate, rotate, and scale it. Make sure everything is working properly.

You have just re-matrixed a cluster into another object! What are the advantages? First, you have replaced the default "C" object with a better control object. Why not just point- and orient-constrain the "C" to another object, though, and have that be the control object? You can do that, but then the cluster cannot operate in relative mode. If you'd like to see the difference, try rotating the skinned joint before you parent the clusterHandle shape and turn on relative mode.

You also get the added benefit of the cluster not having to be parented to the joint to follow the rotation and scaling, and the control object can be any object you like. I recommend using NURBS circles or curves for your controls.

With this idea, you can go through each joint on your character and see how the deformations for that joint are looking. If you see any areas that need added refinements or additional controls, then you can add in a cluster, re-matrix it to a new control object, and have it follow the joint deformations. The hierarchy will be separated by a null object that is constrained to the joint so that everything is nice and neat.

Blend Shape and Cluster Relationships

With the clusters re-matrixed to fancy new control objects and hooked up to each joint in the mesh that you needed additional controls for, you might notice some conflicting problems with your Blend Shape setup. There are not any double transformations happening by default, but there is another problem—the control objects are not following the Blend Shapes, which means they are not following the mesh at all times. This can be awkward for an animator.

Say, for example, you are using Blend Shapes in combination with clusters on a facial setup. By default, the deformation order tells the mesh to follow the joint, add in the Blend Shape, and then add in any additional movement from the cluster. If you have a facial target such as a smile or frown, and you have clusters set up around the lips, you want those controls to follow the mesh for each Blend Shape. The problem is obvious when you turn on the Blend Shape and the controls are not following. So what can you do?

Blend Shapes Driving Clusters

For each cluster, you can create a group node that has the pivot centered in the same location as the handle. This group node can be used to move the cluster handle away from its position without affecting the deformations. Group the Locator Cluster from our sphere example and center its pivot. Now translate that group around in space. Notice how the locator is moving, but the cluster is not causing any deformations because the cluster is in relative mode (see Figure 18.14). If the cluster were not in relative mode, this would not work.

Next, duplicate the sphere and move some of the points around the same location as the cluster. Create a Blend Shape from the duplicated sphere; then delete it. Check your deformation order—the Blend Shape should come after the skinCluster, but before the cluster. Turn the Blend Shape on. The locator control handle will not move (see Figure 18.15). Try to picture if this was a face and you needed to refine the smile shape of the character and the cluster for the corner of the mouth was not following the corner of the mouth around, then you could see the problem.

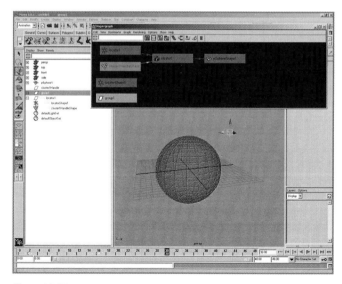

Figure 18.14
Manipulating the parent of a cluster in relative mode causes no deformations.

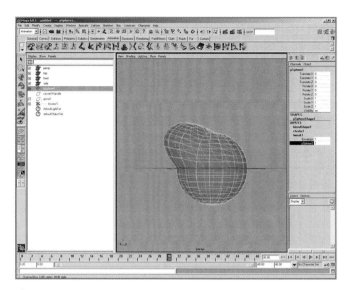

Figure 18.15
Blend Shape hiding cluster controls.

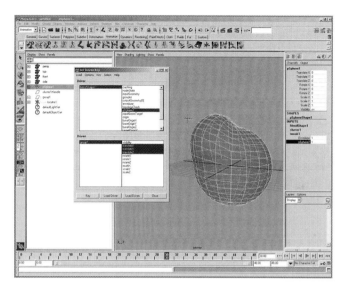

Figure 18.16
Set Driven Key on cluster handle.

We're going to use Set Driven Keyframes to work around this. Load the Blend Shape attribute as the driver and the locator group node translation attributes as the driven. Set a key for both at 0. Now, turn on the Blend Shape and move the group node so the locator moves with the Blend Shape. Set another key and close the Set Driven Key window. Test the cluster by moving it and turning the Blend Shape on and off (see Figure 18.16). You can see how this could be used in combination with many clusters on a face to follow extreme Blend Shapes. It will help avoid confusion during animation and keep the controls looking nice and clean.

Clusters Driving Blend Shapes

The flip side to having Blend Shapes drive cluster positioning is having cluster transformations drive Blend Shapes. This idea is good for cartoony style setups. A cartoony character in 3D needs to be like silly putty in an animator's hands. They need to be able to exaggerate natural movements and create wacky expressions. This is true especially in the face, which is where most refining movements will be needed on the character. Trying to keep the integrity of the model intact while giving animators complete freedom is not easy, so we're going to trick them. That's right; we're going to lie to the animators. Don't you love your job?

The trick is to make them think they are creating that wacky mess of a pose, but in reality they are turning on a Blend Shape that keeps the model topology in check. In Chapter 17, we talked about priority systems and how Blend Shapes can be applied in an intuitive way that will keep things clean. To add onto that, we need a new Blend Shape node that accounts for additional cluster deformers. Using the previously mentioned Blend Shapes driving cluster positions, you can step through all of the shapes that animators will encounter with your Blend Shape-based facial system, keying the position of the group nodes on the clusters so that the handles follow appropriately.

Logically, the next step for animators after they have done a pass of facial animation with key poses is to refine each pose by moving clusters around to exaggerate the shape and silhouette of the model. Animators like to break things, go too far, and really push the limits of what the model and character can do. It's their job to make your job hard, and it's your job to make their job easier. The result is that all TDs become disgruntled and angry, while all animators are happy and curious people who continually poke us around. And so we lie to them, and we feel good about it, too.

We tell them they created that really cool pose, but in reality, we knew it was coming all along. The joy of being predictable never gets old! So to accommodate their needs, we need to create additional Blend Shape targets that come on during cluster animation. Say, for example, a character needs this huge grin with the lips pulled all the way back for both corners. The animator can only take the "smile" Blend Shape so far, for example, so they need the clusters for additional posing. Predicting what they're going to do is the most important step in creating the Blend Shape target. Usually, I just ask. That seems to work pretty well. Just ask what they're planning, look at the character, the shot, and what it needs to do. Then go into Maya, turn on the default Blend Shapes, move the cluster to its extreme, and create a fixed shape for each side of the face. Smooth out the topology of the model where the cluster is stretching it, but make sure the pose is still looking good or the Blend Shape target will be pointless.

Using Set Driven Keys, load the cluster handle's translation as a driver and the Blend Shape target for that portion of the model as the driven. Translate the cluster about as far as you think the animator will go to get additional shaping, then key the Blend Shape to come on when it reaches that pose. The result will be a nice transition between the smile Blend Shape and the additional exaggeration. This will keep the model integrity intact, and the animators will think they've taken the default pose to a new level. If they try to take the pose further, it's OK, just watch over their shoulder to see how crazy they get. You can learn to predict the extremities of any character over time, and being able to accommodate for that will allow the animators to do their job more easily. If they catch you, and see that you predicted the pose, just laugh like a crazy person and walk away; works every time!

Cluster Weighting

Just like a skinCluster node, clusters can be weighted in Maya. They do not require normalization, and therefore can be weighted according to your personal preference. There are a few good painting tools that are available to you in Maya. Select the sphere in Maya that you have created a cluster on, and go to the Deformer→Paint Cluster Weights Tool→Options box (see Figure 18.17). From there, you'll see a list of clusters. Each cluster must be loaded and painted individually. Much like a skinCluster, you may add, remove, scale, replace, and smooth the weighting. The smoothing is the most important part, because

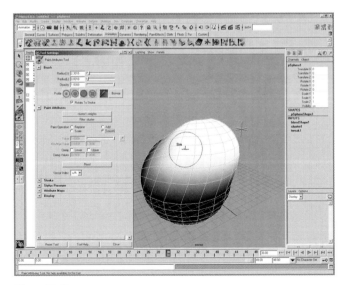

Figure 18.17
Cluster Paint Weights tools.

generally you're going to want your clusters to have nice falloff so the topology stays clean and evenly spaced. We recommend that you replace flooding the cluster with a value of one, and then do a couple of smooth flood passes, or paint scaling around the edges for a nice falloff.

Another paintable attribute is the Paint Set Membership tool, which gives you a nice UI with a list of all the clusters. When highlighted, the points in that cluster will be highlighted yellow, and the area will be brown. This makes adding and removing points easy. Between this and the Paint Cluster Weights tool, you should have everything you need to get a cluster looking good quickly. Painting, for most, feels natural, and once you get into the habit you'll never want to go back to doing it any other way!

Cluster Mirroring

Clusters are just like any other deformer in Maya in that you only want to do half the work to get the full result. With clusters, just like Blend Shapes, this is difficult because of point ID naming in Maya. Creating a cluster and then copying it over requires more than identifying opposite points, it also means copying any additional weighting changes you might have made from one side to another. It's messier than skinClusters because each cluster node is its own entity, and there's no default tool in Maya yet to help us out.

Mirroring can be done one of two ways—spatially based off of the closest point, or through Point IDs. The spatial need comes up when additional points are added to the model or the model needs to be changed slightly. Dramatic changes that affect the entire look of the model will likely result in having to start your work over. So, to avoid that, you can copy over by finding the nearest point on the new model and copying the clusters spatially.

Copying via Point IDs is much faster, and mirroring selections can be done relatively quickly; however, the amount of scripting required is quite the opposite. Here's a quick rundown of how it works. Basically, you have to get the world position for the points in the cluster. To do this, you need to find out first what points are in the cluster by listing the connections to the node:

```
String $set = `listConnections -type objectSet cluster1`;
```

This will return the name of a set that contains the points in the cluster node. Selecting this set will actually select all of its members at once:

```
select $set;
```

The next step is to list the selection, putting all of the points in an array:

```
string $verts[] = `ls -sl -fl`;
```

By parsing through the list, you can get the world space coordinates for each point in space:

```
for ($vert in $verts) float $worldPos[] = `xform -q -ws -t $vert`;
```

Using each point's world space coordinates, you can then find the polar opposite, assuming there is one, by changing the coordinate to have a negative value. This will only work if the model is symmetrical. You can define the axis through the array the xform command returns. The array has three parts, X, Y, and Z coordinates. So to get the negative of X:

```
float $mirrorX = (-($worldPos[0]));
```

This negative value in X will allow us to select the same point on the opposite side of the model. We know that $mirrorX is the new coordinate, but how do we select it? To go about this, you actually have to compare the world space of every point on the mesh with the point that you want to mirror to:

```
//$obj is the name of the object the cluster is deforming
String $obj = "sphere1";
select ($obj + ".vtx[*]");
string $allModelPoints[] = `ls -sl -fl`;
For ($point in $allModelPoints){
float $mdlPos[] = `xform -q -ws -t $point`;
If ($mdlPos[0] == $mirrorX)print "match found \n";}
```

When the script returns a matched point, add it to an array and at the end of the procedure, select the array. You can then list your new points, the polar opposite of the points in the cluster. From your original points, you can use the percent command to obtain their weight values and then copy them over symmetrically:

```
for ($vert in $verts) float $weight = `percent -q -v $vert`;
```

There are some scripts available on Highend3d.com that will select opposite vertices across a plane. Use them as a guide for creating your own script. To understand copying clusters, you need to understand xforms and working in world space. This is just the beginning of mirroring clusters, but it should point you in the right direction.

Clusters are great for refining controls on a mesh. The systems outlined here are just the beginning to a vast world of cluster applications and solutions. They are powerful and, as a result, sometimes frustrating, but an understanding of how they work will allow you to explore many options for controlling clusters and deforming objects.

There are also some scripts available on Highend3d.com that will help you with cluster weighting, mirroring, and creation. We recommend downloading as many as you can find and ripping them apart. To really exploit a deformer as powerful as a cluster, you need to be able to modularize its creation and common functions. This requires an in-depth understanding of the MEL scripting language and Maya. Once you see the results of your clusters being used on a character, you will appreciate all the hard work that went into creating them.

chapter 19
Muscle Systems and Skin Solvers

The basic idea of volume preservation has been around for a long time, but only recently has technology allowed us to apply the math at an artistic level. Today, we are able to simulate skin in 3D software using a variety of techniques that have been researched and developed over the years. Muscle systems allow us to come closer to cheating reality and matching the anatomy of characters (see Figures 19.1a and 19.1b). The closer we get, the more realistic something looks, and every little bit counts.

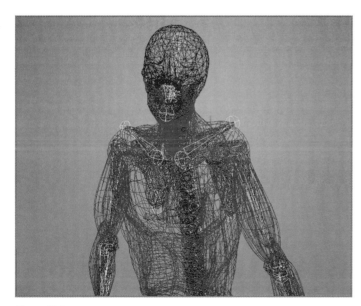

Figure 19.1a
Wireframe view of a muscle system.

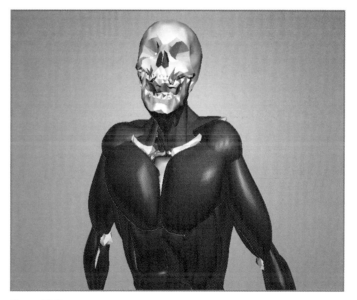

Figure 19.1b
Shaded view of a muscle system.

To clarify my intentions with this chapter, I'd like to let you know what you won't be learning about. Influence objects, jiggle deformers, soft body simulations, and cloth solvers are not muscle systems! You can get good results with each of these, and they are formidable solutions for deformations, but they are not true muscle systems. They can be added onto a muscle system after the fact to help aid in the deformation effects.

Geometrically influenced objects in a smooth bind are slow and require immense real-time computation requirements, so as a rule of practicality, they rule themselves out (see Figure 19.2). The same could be said for jiggle and soft body simulations, and while they are useful, they haven't the least bit to do with volume preservation. Only recently have cloth solvers been able to simulate faux volume representations, but the results are still questionable as to whether or not they could be applied to an entire character.

As a foundation, in order to understand muscles, you must first understand anatomy. The details of how our muscles work together to drive our bones and move our bodies through space is mind boggling, to say the least. The layers of fat, tendons, soft tissue, and muscles are so complex that it is almost impossible to focus on their underlying movements; instead, we will concern ourselves with how the skin looks. Understanding the anatomy of the character you're working on is essential when using muscle-based deformations.

The use of a muscle system is ideal on characters that are visually detailed to the extent that you are able to clearly see the underlying structures. In visual effects for film, most monsters and creatures have extremely exaggerated features and musculature, so simulating muscles is ideal in these situations. In the

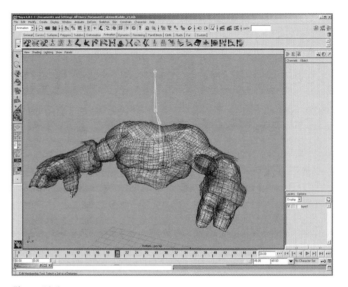

Figure 19.2
Influence object as a muscle.

case of a cartoon-style character, a muscle system is probably more limiting than it is helpful. The higher the resolution, the more it makes sense, and the more details that are incorporated into the mesh, the better chance you have of getting really great results. So before you go diving in headfirst, make sure that a muscle system is the right solution for your character or project.

What Is a Muscle System?

A true muscle system relies on a series of rules to keep it in check. Much like any other system, the rules are unique to its requirements, and as such, no other deformer can really act in its place. Following the rules will yield strong results, but remember that the end goal is to create a visually appealing mesh, and the rules are there to be broken if need be. First, you must decide what the goals for your system are and then evaluate the needs of the character, outline the parts the system might have, create a set of rules, and finally bring all of the pieces together to make a working skin. There is, of course, a long period of R&D that must be accounted for, and a working skin system could take you a very long time to develop (see Figure 19.3).

The goals for a working muscle system are as follows:

◆ Must be a layered system that accounts for bones, muscles, fat, tendons, soft tissue, and skin deformations.

◆ Must give real-time feedback for animation and must calculate mathematical skin solving quickly.

◆ Must keep volume, provide muscle tension, and allow for elasticity.

◆ Muscles should be affected by dynamic forces such as gravity and collisions.

◆ Muscles should appear to drive bones instead of bones driving muscles.

◆ Parts of the mesh must be able to be excluded from the muscle simulation.

◆ Must be modular and robust enough to be used on any character requiring muscles.

These are the parts we must address in our system:

◆ **Muscles**: A belly of tissue that contracts, preserves volume, and connects to bones or other muscles and tissue.

◆ **Fascia**: The inner connective tissue between muscles and tendons, and the binding constraints that will keep them glued together.

◆ **Tendons**: Tissue that connects muscles to bones to drive the skeleton movement.

◆ **Bones**: The innermost structure that kinematically drives the muscles.

◆ **Fat**: The area between the muscles, fascia, and the skin. This empty layer will be referred to as fat.

◆ **Skin**: The outermost dermal layer of the character, which will be simulated.

These are the rules for the system:

◆ In addition to an insertion and origin point, muscles must be able to attach to other geometry in multiple places. They must also be able to attach to other muscles as a means of creating fascia connective tissue.

◆ Muscle geometry must be light and robust and topologically flowing with the mesh.

◆ Layers of muscles should be built from the inside out, large to small.

◆ The volume of the character must be filled in entirely with muscles with only a thin layer of space between the muscle tissue and the actual skin.

◆ There should be no holes between the muscle layer and the bones and innards.

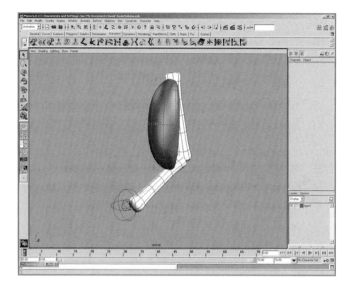

Figure 19.3
Basic bicep muscle volume.

- ◆ The first layer of muscles should attach directly to the bones.
- ◆ The second layer of muscles should attach between the first layer of muscles and should overlap any remaining bones.
- ◆ The third layer and any additional layers should offer refining details, including musculature and anatomical anomalies unique to the character.

We now have a distinct vision of our goals, the parts for our system, and the rules that will guide us during creation. The next step is to research our options in Maya. At Tippett Studio, you can find one of the most advanced muscle and skin solvers available. Paul Thuriot and Todd Stinson, who developed Tippett's proprietary skin tools, spent a great deal of time in research and development to come up with a similar set of rules and goals for their system. Some of the guidelines and rules are commonsense, others become obvious while researching anatomy, and some are a result of ideas that need to be expressed mathematically within the software.

Beginning with Bones

Once you have fleshed out all the ideas for the muscle system, you need to begin creating it. The first thing you're going to have to worry about is how the muscles are going to attach to your character's bones. Joints in Maya do not give us enough information to allow us to attach objects to them, and we are going to need geometry between joints that allows us to connect muscles in more than two places. To do this, we need an underlying skeleton for our character. Using NURBS geometry will allow you to connect muscles' origin and insertion points via pointOnSurfaceInfo nodes. You need one piece of geometry per joint, or point of articulation, in your character. The bones should be loosely connected together to resemble a skeleton (see Figure 19.4).

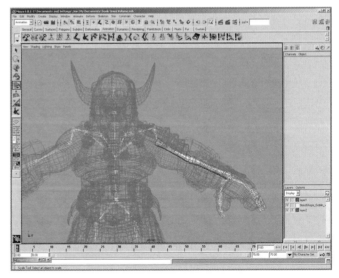

The bones are almost the most important part of the whole system, because once you start creating muscles, you are going to have a hard time going back and editing joint placement or adding more details to the bone geometry. Create closed caps for the top and bottom of the bones, and try to use at least three or four spans in-between to outline the details. The bones should be anatomical, so when you're trying to determine thickness, just use anatomy as a reference. Make sure you leave room between the bones at the joint hinges so they can rotate without intersecting too much. Also, remember that in some places like your ribs, there is only a small layer of tissue between your skin and the actual bones, so the bones will need to be able to connect to the skin safely as well, so the detail is more important in that area than say somewhere like the humerus.

You can either parent each bone to each joint in the hierarchy, or you can use constraints to keep them separated. Either way, they should follow a one-to-one relationship. If you have a stretchy back or a very complicated area, such as a tail or scapula, just try to get the general details into the bones. The important thing is that they are parented properly, move anatomically, and look accurate.

Figure 19.4
Arm bones for the Pig Goblin made from NURBS geometry.

A Basic Muscle Volume

The types of muscles we're going to be using are known as fusiform, which are made up of the volume of the surface and two points—the origin and the insertion points. The point that the muscle originates from (the origin point) is generally static and does not move. The insertion point is dynamic and connects to another bone via a tendon, generally following the kinematic hierarchy, and it will move during bone rotation. The surface geometry will change shape through isotonic contractions in which the muscle length changes as a result of the insertion point moving, or through isometric contractions in which the muscle expands without changing its overall length (see Figure 19.5).

To demonstrate how volume is calculated, we're going to break down the algorithm and apply it onto a NURBS sphere in Maya.

1. Create a default NURBS sphere in Maya and name it "muscle."

2. Add the following attributes (see Figure 19.6) to "muscle:"

   InitialVolume (no min/max/default)

   Tension (min .1 max 1 default 1)

   Length is represented in our case by the scale in Y. To derive this, we must find the distance between the two farthest points opposite the width. The easiest way is to plot the world space coordinates of two locators that will drive the muscle volume. We find the distance, and then divide the output by 2 to give us the actual scale in Y that would represent the length (see Figure 19.6).

   Length = distance between origin and insertion points / 2

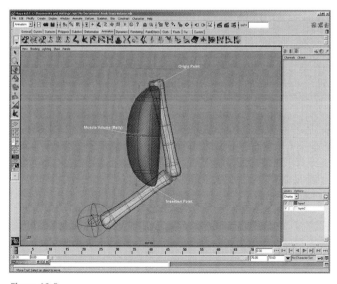

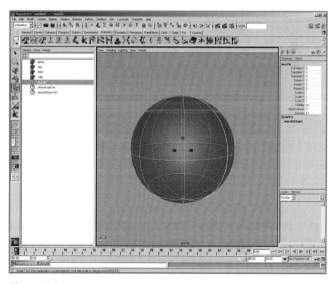

Figure 19.5
Muscle volume showing origin and insertion points.

Figure 19.6
NURBS sphere with added attributes for muscle volume.

3. Create a distanceDimension node in Maya and rename it "lengthCalc." The two locators that get created with it will be used as the origin and insertion points for our muscle node. Rename them "origin" and "insertion," respectively (see Figure 19.7).

InitialVolume is the result of the volume algorithm as it is applied during creation of the muscle. In our case, volume is not an initial mathematical equation because we are not taking into consideration the ratio of height to width, so initialVolume, in this case, represents the radius.

a = (((initialVolume-length)/ratio))+(tension*.1);

b = length;

c = (((initialVolume- length)/ratio))-(tension*.1);

volume = ((4*3.14*a*b*c)/3)

Ratio is the difference between the height and width. To find the difference, we must define the length and the width. The width is both the scale in X and Z, and the length is the scale in Y. A separate width in X and Z is represented by the addition of tension.

> A ratio is a comparison of two numbers. We generally separate the two numbers in the ratio with a colon (:). Suppose that we want to write the ratio of 4 and 6. We can write this as 4:6 or as a fraction ²/₃, and we say the ratio is *four to six*.

4. Create a chain of three joints in an L shape, almost representative of an arm chain. This will drive our muscle node and act as a means for demonstrating the muscle's purpose. Create a default IK chain between the root and end joint (see Figure 19.8).

5. Point-constrain the origin locator to the root IK joint. Point-constrain the insertion locator to the middle and end joints; then adjust the weights on the constraint so that the locator follows closer to the middle joint. Moving the IK handle should change the displayed lengthCalc node in real-time (see Figure 19.9).

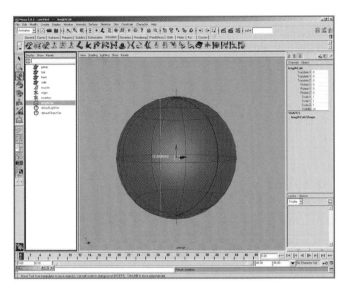

Figure 19.7
Distance dimension node as origin and insertion points.

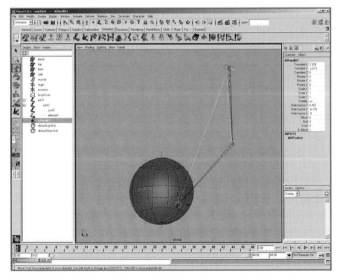

Figure 19.8
IK Chain to control muscle volume.

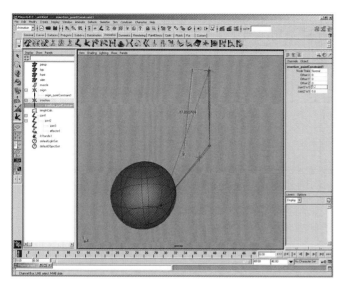

Figure 19.9
Length setup for proper calculations.

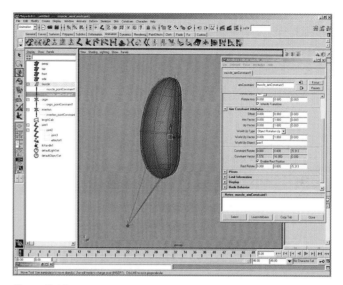

Figure 19.10
Shaped and constrained muscle volume.

6. With the locators in place, the muscle is now ready to be put into place and hooked up to the volume algorithm. First, shape the muscle so that it looks similar to a bicep, with the poles and surrounding points pulled back and parallel with the bone it will be attaching to. Next, move the pivot of the muscle to the bottom center CV on the muscle. This will act as a faux insertion point for our muscle.

7. Point-constrain the muscle to the insertion locator. Aim-constrain the muscle to the origin locator. Open up the attribute for the aim constraint after creation and change the "World Up Type" attribute to "World Object Up" and put the name of the root joint in the IK chain in the space provided. Finally, make sure the aim vectors and up vectors are 0,1,0 so that the muscle aims at the locator in Y with a Y up vector (see Figure 19.10).

8. We're going to create a system of utility nodes to calculate volume. This will be the result of the utility node connections in Maya, for those looking to experiment in other packages or for those who prefer the use of expressions:

```
muscle.scaleX = (((muscle.initialVolume - muscle.scaleY)/2))+(muscle.tension*.1);
muscle.scaleY = lengthCalcShape.distance/2;
muscle.scaleZ = (((muscle.initialVolume -muscle.scaleY)/2))-(muscle.tension*.1);
string $muscle = "muscle";
string $scales[] = {"scaleX","scaleY","scaleZ"};
for ($scale in $scales){
if ($scale != "scaleY"){
string $diff = `createNode plusMinusAverage`;
setAttr ($diff + ".operation") 2;
string $result = `createNode multiplyDivide`;
setAttr ($result+ ".operation") 2;
```

```
setAttr ($result + ".input2X") 2;
string $mult = `createNode multDoubleLinear`;
connectAttr ($muscle + ".initialVolume")($diff + ".input1D[0]");
connectAttr ($muscle + ".scaleY")($diff + ".input1D[1]");
connectAttr ($diff + ".output1D") ($result + ".input1X");
string $operation = `createNode plusMinusAverage`;
if ($scale == "scaleZ") setAttr ($operation + ".operation") 2;
connectAttr ($result + ".outputX") ($operation + ".input1D[0]");
connectAttr ($muscle + ".tension")($mult + ".input1");
setAttr ($mult + ".input2") .1;
connectAttr ($mult + ".output") ($operation + ".input1D[1]");
connectAttr ($operation + ".output1D")($muscle + "." + $scale);
}
else{
string $divide = `createNode multiplyDivide`;
setAttr ($divide + ".operation") 2;
setAttr ($divide + ".input2X") 2;
connectAttr "lengthCalcShape.distance"($divide + ".input1X");
connectAttr ($divide + ".outputX") ($muscle + ".scaleY");
}}
```

9. Move the IK Handle around and notice the muscle maintaining volume. Change the tension and initialVolume attributes on the node to see what happens. If everything was set up properly, you should have a working muscle node that will keep volume between the origin and insertion points.

    As you move the IK handle around in space, the belly of the muscle will change shape through isotonic contractions as a result of the insertion point moving. By adjusting the tension attribute, you are able to control the belly through isometric contractions in which the muscle expands without changing its overall length. Each type of contraction is important to have in order for the muscle system to work properly (see Figure 19.11).

The Need for a Plug-in

With bones in place, you can start creating muscles inside the mesh. For this, you could use the previous example to get started, or you could get a plug-in. The basic idea is to keep volume and have tension, and we are able to achieve those things in Maya without a plug-in, but for true volume calculation with the ability to connect muscles to each other, you will need something more. You also want to be able to change the default state of the muscle after creation, so attributes for default ratio and radius are helpful. In addition, you'll want to be

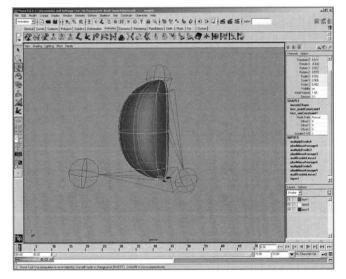

Figure 19.11
Muscle volume with proper contractions and faux volume.

able to stick the muscles to your actual bones, in which case a locator is not the best fit and a plug-in will have better ways of doing this (through the pointOnSurface node most likely), and a plug-in will probably offer a GUI to help you create the muscles themselves, leaving you to focus on the sculpting and placement instead of figuring out the algorithms.

Online, at cgmuscle.com, the community is developing its own public license muscle system. That means you can download their plug-ins and scripts for free. They're constantly being added to, and they have a good discussion board for the development of the tools they're implementing (see Figure 19.12). On the other hand, if you have the money, we highly recommend the Custom Character Toolkit DVD from Alias, taken from the 2003 Masterclass by Paul Thuriot and Erick Miller. On the DVD, they go over how to create a simple muscle plug-in for Maya, including rapid prototyping like we just demonstrated and how to create a skin deformer to connect the muscles to a mesh with paintable weights through use of the API.

Innerconnective Tissue

Innerconnective tissue, anatomically referred to as *fascia*, is what keeps the muscles from separating from each other. As you can see from the example in Maya previously, one muscle is pretty simple to create. You could have an entire setup of those muscles intersecting and the results would not be very accurate. The idea is to seal off the holes between the muscle bellies and create a smooth surface that the skin can interact with (see Figure 19.13).

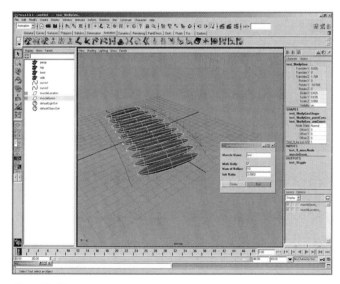

Figure 19.12
cgmuscle.com free plug-in and GUI muscle creator.

Figure 19.13
Layered muscle system with closed mesh design.

19. Muscle Systems and Skin Solvers

To create this smooth surface, we need muscles to be able to be connected to other muscles. As stated in the rules, the first layer of muscles should connect directly to the bones. The second layer could then create muscles that are connected by other muscles. As an example, to give you a basic idea of how you can stick one object to another, we'll walk through the pointOnSurfaceInfo node.

1. Create a NURBS sphere in Maya and call it "surfaceTest."

2. Right-click on surfaceTest and select "Surface Point;" then left mouse-drag to any point on the sphere. When you release the left mouse button, Maya will return the coordinates in U and V for the surface point you have selected. Note the point position as $u and $v float variables (in your mind for now).

3. Create a pointOnSurface node from the resulting $u and $v variables:
   ```
   string $infoNode = `pointOnSurface -ch on -u $u -v $v surfaceTest`
   ```

4. Insert the U and V coordinates from the surface point you selected into the command and then create the node. You should see a new output from surfaceTest in the Channel Box to the pointOnSurfaceInfo node. The node returns the position, in world space, of the U and V coordinates from the surface, regardless of direct deformations or hierarchical transformations on surfaceTest.

5. Create a locator in Maya and call it "connectTest." Run this from the command line:
   ```
   connectAttr ($infoNode + ".position") connectTest.translate;
   ```

   This will connect the position output of the pointOnSurfaceInfo node to the locator's translations. Rotate, translate, and scale "surfaceTest" in Maya and notice how the locator, "connectTest," always follows. Even if you deform the geometry, the locator will still follow. It is hooked into the position of U and V coordinates from the geometry.

   Just to be a little fancy, we'll add in attributes to change the U and V position of the pointOnSurfaceInfo node.

6. Add the following attributes to the "connectTest" locator: positionU, positionV

   To find out the initial position, we will first query it from the pointOnSurfaceInfo node and then set the "connectTest" position U and V accordingly. Finally, we'll connect the attributes. You can then change the U and V position of the locator along the surface by changing the positionU and positionV attributes on the "connectTest" locator. Use the following code to set up and make the connections:
   ```
   float $u = `getAttr ($infoNode + ".parameterU")`;
   float $v = `getAttr ($infoNode + ".parameterV")`;
   setAttr "connectTest.positionU" $u;
   setAttr "connectTest.positionV" $v;
   connectAttr "connectTest.positionU" ($infoNode + ".paramaterU");
   connectAttr "connectTest.positionU" ($infoNode + ".paramaterV");
   ```

   Applied in a muscle system, the pointOnSurfaceInfo node would allow you to create connections between deforming geometry. For example, you could create a muscle between two existing muscles that are keeping volume using pointOnSurfaceInfo nodes to derive the origin and insertion points. Ideally, you would want to be able to connect the muscle to more than two points for better sticking between surfaces (see Figure 19.14).

19. Muscle Systems and Skin Solvers

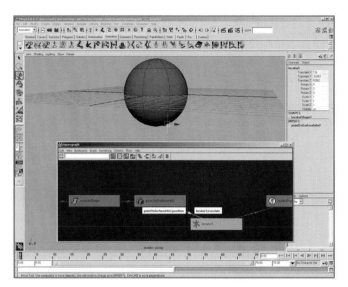

Figure 19.14
Locator connected to pointOnSurface node on a NURBS sphere.

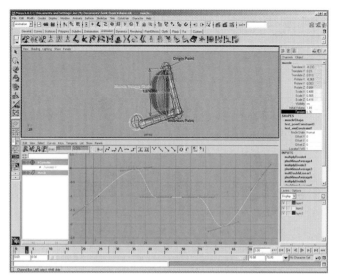

Figure 19.15
Animation curve on IK Handle used to determine muscle tension.

Keep in mind when creating muscles on top of each other that you don't need to concern yourself with the part of the muscle that won't affect the skin or other muscles. You can leave most muscles in an elliptical shape, allowing them to intersect during contractions, so long as the resulting contractions contact with the skin properly. Basically, it should look like a very nicely detailed muscle structure in shaded mode and should completely fill in the volume of the character.

Tendons

In a muscle system, tendons are realized as the connection between the muscle and the bone. This thin layer is represented by the locators that define the origin and insertion points of the muscle. Tendons cause the kinematic movements in our bones when connecting muscle bodies are contracted. It is these connections that force the bones to move. In 3D, tendons are not true to their anatomical relatives. Instead, they represent the start and end points of our muscles.

Tension is the added dynamic for animation that will help you achieve nice poses between key isotonic contractions and also help during times when you need additional movement within the mesh. Ideally, the tension attribute would be animated just before the kinematic joint that was driving it fired, in order to better simulate a real anatomical system (see Figure 19.15).

To reverse the process of kinematic rotations driving deformations in Maya, you can animate the tension attribute based on the speed of the driving joint rotation. Look at this simple algorithm to understand better how to reverse the operation of tendons and tension:

```
$a = jointA.rotation end value--start value
```

To find $a properly, you must look at an animation curve in Maya and evaluate when the curve changes in direction (positive and negative). The value that $a represents is the difference between the current rotational value and the end rotational value.

```
$b = tension attribute range (.1 to 1)
```

$b will represent tension and its range.

```
$time = range of $a
```

$time in this case refers to the number of frames it takes for $a to shift direction. If jointA.rotateY begins with a value of 45 and ends with a value of 90 before going back down, we know that $a = 45. If jointA.rotateY begins at frame 1 and reaches its goal value of 90 at frame 10, then $time = 9.

```
$speed = $a/$time
```

To determine the amount of tension, you must define how fast the joint is rotating. If $a = 45 and $time = 9, then $speed = 5. $speed could then be plugged into a scale of 1 to 10, 10 being the highest amount of tension that should be applied. You could then multiply the scale * .1 to give it the proper range for $b. The final output would look like this:

```
$b = (current value) + ($speed * .1)
```

For animation purposes, you could have the range of tension animated to be 1/10 the range of $a, in order to get a slight contraction. This means applying animation on the tension attribute one frame before $a starts rotating, and ending (1/10(+1)) frame of $time later.

For example, if $a starts at frame 1, $b starts at frame 0, if $a = 45 and $time = 20, then $speed = 2.5. $b = current value + .25 at frame 0 and $b reverts back to the start amount over the next 2 frames (2 frames is 10% of $time) ending animation frame 3.

Here's an analogy if you still don't quite get it. Imagine that you are running a relay race. When handed the baton, you take off running down the track. At the end of your journey is another runner who waits for the baton. As you get closer to him, he starts running for a short period of time until he's traveling the same speed as you. You hand off the baton and fade off slowly in the background while the runner continues to finish the race. Think of tension as the relay runner who passes the energy to the muscle during animation (see Figures 19.16 a, b, and c).

By animating tension to drive the kinematic rotations of joints in Maya, we are able to achieve a more realistic-looking skin simulation. In true anatomy, muscles drive bones, but in 3D, bones have always driven muscles. We still rely on joint rotation animation to drive the tension, but by applying the tension before the rotation, we are able to fake the muscles being driven by bones, and in effect, create realistic working tendons.

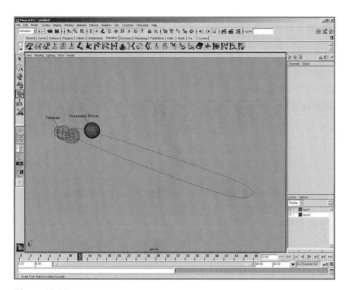

Figure 19.16a
Tension starts before kinematic driver.

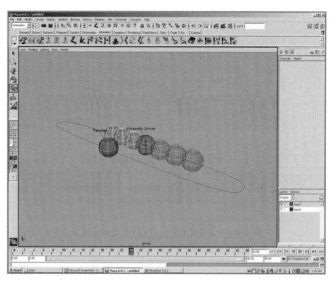

Figure 19.16c
Tension stops and kinematic driver continues.

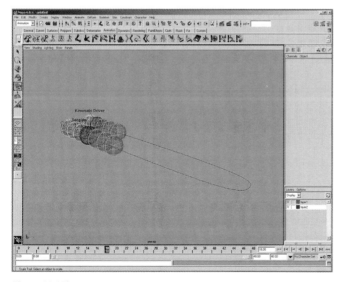

Figure 19.16b
Tension and kinematic driver catch up.

Fat Distance

The distance between the high-resolution mesh and the muscles is referred to as *fat*. Fatty tissue molds and jiggles in real life, but in our case, it is simply empty space between two points. Fat is useful for maintaining the volume of the character in its default rest state. If the muscles are connected directly to the skin with no offsets in place, then there is a chance that the skin will lose detail and be sucked toward the muscle bellies.

This distance can be calculated through ray-casting techniques in Maya. Ray casting is typically done during rendering. From the camera's point of view, a ray is cast from the first pixel in the scan line. Through a tiny window (the size of one pixel), it goes into the 3D world in search of a surface to bounce off and render. This happens on a pixel-by-pixel basis until the image is finished rendering.

A ray is a wave of light, so when it hits something, it has the ability to bounce off it. Raycasting with intersections in Maya requires the use of a plug-in because there is no way to cast rays from one vertex to another through the default tools. It is possible to create a plug-in that calculates fat using this idea.

Here's an example of what a Ray Intersection node would do in Maya (see Figure 19.17). This is only to be used as a visual reference. This is *not* an actual Ray Intersection!

1. Create a NURBS sphere and name it "muscle."

2. Create two locators, one called "castPoint" and one called "castGoal." Parent "castGoal" to "castPoint."

3. Create a pointOnSurfaceInfo node from any point on the sphere and then connect its position attribute to the translation of the "castPoint" locator.

4. Normal-constrain the "castPoint" locator to the sphere.

5. Create another sphere called "skin" and scale it up so that "cast" is inside it. Create a distanceBetween node in the scene. Point-constrain the start position locator to "castPoint" and the end position to "castGoal."

6. Now, you can safely translate "castGoal" along its local X axis, changing the distance between "castPoint" and "castGoal." If you were to translate "castGoal" so that it intersects with the skin, you could find the distance between "muscle" and "skin."

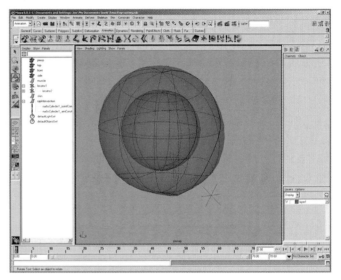

Figure 19.17
Faux ray intersection example; red circle represents intersection.

So each point on the muscle needs a fat distance initialized between itself and the skin. To do this, you would have to connect the skin to all of the muscles in one step. This connection would contain information about fat distances for each point. This could then get plugged into a skin solver and basically acts like a default offset between the muscles and the skin.

Skin Solvers

After you have created a complicated underlying structure of bones and muscles, you must figure out a way to connect it to the skin. The goal is for the skin to keep volume and slide around and look cool and stuff. Err, something to that effect. The basic idea is to connect each muscle to the skin in a way that looks natural and uniform.

The muscles keep volume, though exaggerated in some cases, and so keeping volume on the overlying surface should be relatively straightforward. If you can get the skin to slide on top of the muscles and fat properly, then it will keep volume naturally. The character should be a closed volume in order for the ray-casting theory to work properly. Calculating the fat distance for each point on the muscles is not going to be possible if there are holes in the mesh.

Fat is used to determine how far a point can be from the underlying muscle connecting point. This doesn't mean point A is stuck to point B in space. Point A could be any point on the mesh, but if it's connecting to point B, it must have a preset distance. This allows for sliding of skin without losing volume. The act of sliding the skin can be static, since the distance is baked into the muscle node.

You don't need an actual dynamic solve to figure the skin distances. In other words, it's not like a cloth solver, which has to solve for each frame, the shape of the mesh affecting each frame after it in a linear-stepped fashion. This idea states that the distance is figured for you, the only unknown attribute is which point the muscles will be connecting to on the mesh. We can still get affects like sliding and folding without having to dynamically solve each frame one after the other.

The skin is basically a massive spring system with editable tension between points. In this sense, it is almost cloth-like in its existence with underlying bodies that it collides with. The difference is that the collisions have offsets built in, and the amount of elasticity is far less than that of cloth. Ideally, a solver would step through each iteration of the simulation and solve the skin placement, leaving the topology evenly displaced and more natural looking.

Different mathematical algorithms can be applied to create a working skin solver. The one that is the most useful is the Euler Method, where each point is similar to a particle with differential equations being solved for distance between particles and time for every movement. The solver must also allow for dampening, dynamic forces, and elasticity. Finally, it must allow for non-solving points, like the hands and feet, where it is more practical to use a skinCluster node.

The only working muscle and skin solver we've seen was at Tippett Studio where they have developed a solver capable of all of the things we've specified, and more. Unfortunately, we can only tell you about the building blocks that helped create that system, and cannot go further into the proprietary nature of what's being done in the API. The ideas are here, though, and you can formulate a similar solution on your own as a result if given adequate time to research and develop.

> **The Euler Method:**
>
> A method for solving ordinary differential equations using the formula
>
> $$y_{n+1} = y_n + hf(x_n, y_n)$$
>
> This method step solves a solution through an interval h while using derivative information from only the beginning of the interval.

Faux Skin Solver Solutions

If you are seriously considering using a muscle system on your character, then you should consider investing in some higher-end plug-ins. If you buy the Character Custom Toolkit DVD from Alias, you will receive the muscleSkinDeformer plug-in that Erick Miller and Paul Thuriot wrote for the DVD. The muscleSkinDeformer node allows for a NURBS surface to be used as an influence on a polygon, connecting through a direct offset between the points, much like the fat distance example above. Developing your own plug-in requires programming knowledge, as well as a good understanding of the math involved. Another option is the slideBulge plug-in, which basically lets polygons act as sculpt deformers on other polygons. This plug-in can be downloaded for free from highend3d.com under the Maya→Plug-ins section. This application will require the use of polygonal shapes for muscle objects, which is fine, as long as you incorporate all of the rules into the system.

The latest option available to the Maya community is the MuscleTK plug-in, which has many of the features outlined in the rules previously listed. It includes a simple tool for creating muscles in a couple clicks, just like the ones described in this chapter. It also includes a tool to parent muscle insertion/origin points directly to other muscles, so you can easily have muscles drive other muscles. MuscleTK also offers its own skinning solution to solve skin, which is added on top of a normal smooth skin. You can also paint weights on this muscleSkin node to get sliding skin. You can currently download the plug-in from the Web site, CGToolkit.com, for $99. It includes full documentation and a full suite of muscle plug-ins.

Some of these alternatives are not true skin solvers, but they are good deformer alternatives for getting the muscles to interact with your skin. The most likely place that you would encounter a custom, high-end solver is at a high-end production facility at this point in time. If you're really looking to get out of using plug-ins altogether, you could just add the muscles as influence objects in a smooth skin and then paint their influence accordingly. This would be a slow and delicate process, but it could be done. We'd suggest you look around first, see what you can dig up for free, and then consider investing a little bit in someone else's hard work.

Muscle systems and skin solvers are complex and difficult to create and maintain. At this point in time, they are very new to us, and only recently have we been able to apply the algorithms required to get realistic skin and muscle simulations. Results have been good thus far, and many of the characters you see in 3D today are likely using some form of a muscle system. Sliding, realistic skin is still a hard task to accomplish, and developing a solver to accurately calculate the skin is a very complicated undertaking.

Remember that no matter what solution you go with, the final goal is to make the character you're working on look great. How you get from start to finish is almost irrelevant, as long as the final output is good. There are many different ways you can apply muscle systems into your existing deformation work-flows. Try to start small, only using muscles for adding in extra details and subtleties first before you consider using it as a primary deformation tool. At the end of the day, you'll end up using what works and looks good and is fast and reliable!

Index

Index

Index

Index

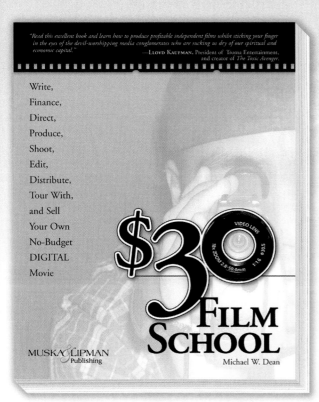

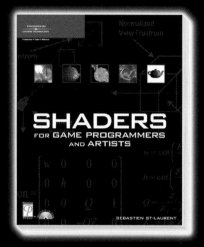
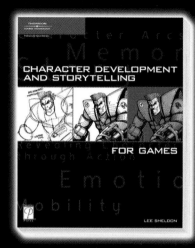